INFRINGEMENT NATION

Infringement Nation

COPYRIGHT 2.0 AND YOU

John Tehranian

OXFORD
UNIVERSITY PRESS

OXFORD
UNIVERSITY PRESS

*Oxford University Press, Inc., publishes works that further Oxford University's objective of excellence
in research, scholarship, and education.*

Oxford New York
Auckland   Cape Town   Dar es Salaam   Hong Kong   Karachi   Kuala Lumpur   Madrid   Melbourne
Mexico City   Nairobi   New Delhi   Shanghai   Taipei   Toronto

With offices in
Argentina   Austria   Brazil   Chile   Czech Republic   France   Greece   Guatemala   Hungary   Italy
Japan   Poland   Portugal   Singapore   South Korea   Switzerland   Thailand   Turkey   Ukraine
Vietnam

Published by Oxford University Press, Inc.
198 Madison Avenue, New York, New York 10016

Oxford is a registered trademark of Oxford University Press
Oxford University Press is a registered trademark of Oxford University Press, Inc.

Library of Congress Cataloging-in-Publication Data
Tehranian, John.
  Infringement nation : copyright 2.0 and you / John Tehranian.
    p. cm.
  Includes bibliographical references and index.
  ISBN 978-0-19-973317-0 (hardback : alk. paper)
  1. Copyright--United States. I. Title.
  KF2994.T44 2011
  346.7304'82--dc22
                                          2010044077

2 3 4 5 6 7 8 9
Printed in the United States of America on acid-free paper

Note to Readers
This publication is designed to provide accurate and authoritative information in regard to the subject matter covered.
It is based upon sources believed to be accurate and reliable and is intended to be current as of the time it was written.
It is sold with the understanding that the publisher is not engaged in rendering legal, accounting, or other professional
services. If legal advice or other expert assistance is required, the services of a competent professional person should be
sought. Also, to confirm that the information has not been affected or changed by recent developments, traditional
legal research techniques should be used, including checking primary sources where appropriate.

*(Based on the Declaration of Principles jointly adopted by a Committee of the
American Bar Association and a Committee of Publishers and Associations.)*

You may order this or any other Oxford University Press publication by
visiting the Oxford University Press website at www.oup.com

For Katie and Majid

Contents

Acknowledgments

I would like to thank Guy Chezrony, Ryan Connolly, Ian Gibson, Sanaz Jahangard, Chris Koras, Kelly Schwarm, Mona Shahabian, Dustin Simms, Joe Su, Pasha Tasvibi and Jeremy Wooden for their invaluable research assistance in writing this book. I would also like to express my gratitude to Peter Afrasiabi, Josh Agle, Safa Alamir, Chris Arledge, Mark Bartholomew, Tom Bell, Oren Bracha, Dan Burk, Dan Burn-Forti, Tim Canova, Anupam Chander, Hiram Chodosh, Chris Collins, Jay Daugherty, Zev Eigen, David Fagundes, Bill Gallagher, Shuba Ghosh, Eric Goldman, Wendy Gordon, Jed Gushman, Jonathan Handler, Mat Higbee, Justin Hughes, Peter Jaszi, Brett and Maryam Kia-Keating, Bobbi Kwall, Mark Lemley, David Levine, Jacqui Lipton, Ernesto Hernández-López, Mark Lemley, Francine Lipman, Eric Luna, Tom Lund, Brandy and Regis Navarre, David Nimmer, Tyler Ochoa, William Patry, Chad Pekron, Geoff Rapp, Tony Reese, Rita Reusch, Dan Rosenthal, Jennifer Rothman, Pam Samuelson, Ken Stahl, Madhavi Sunder, Katharine and Majid Tehranian, Rebecca Tushnet, Jeremy Williams, Todd Winter, Tim Wu, Peter Yu, and Jonathan Zittrain for the invaluable conversations that sparked portions of this book and for their encouragement, support, comments and suggestions.

Photo and Illustration Credits

Figure No.	Credit
Introduction 1	*Respect Copyrights Merit Badge,* Recording Industry Association of America and Boy Scouts of America
Introduction 2	*Captain Copyright Comic Strip,* Canadian Copyright Counsel and Access Copyright
1.1	*Guggenheim Bilbao,* Courtesy of Flicker User 'Kurtxio' via Creative Commons Attribution 2.0 License
1.2	*Puppies,* Art Rogers
1.3	*String of Puppies,* Jeff Koons
1.4	*Wives with Knives,* Courtesy of Josh Agle and John Agle, Inc.
2.1	*Justice Joseph Story,* George P.A. Healy
2.2	*Barney Oldfield's Race for a Life,* Mack Sennett (dir.)
2.3	*L.H.O.O.Q.,* Marcel Duchamp
2.4	*Barack Obama, National Press Club, April 2006,* Mannie Garcia and The Associated Press
2.5	*HOPE,* Shepard Fairey
2.6	*Moses Receives the Ten Commandments,* Domenico Beccafumi, Courtesy of Wikipedia Commons and The Yorck Project
2.7	*Thomas Pynchon,* United States Navy
3.1	*Newport Beach, California: Celebrating 4th of July . . . Sort of,* Courtesy of Will Denney via Creative Commons Attribution-NonCommercial-NoDerivs 2.0 Generic License
3.2	*The Great Library of Alexandria,* O. Von Corvin
3.3	*Bratz,* Courtesy of Dan Burn-Forti

(continued)

Photo and Illustration credits (Continued)

Figure No.	Credit
4.1	*The British Lion in America*, The Daily Joker (New York)
4.2	*Britney Spears, Paris Hilton and Lindsay Lohan in Car*, Courtesy of X17, Inc.
4.3	*El Guerrillero Heroica*, Alberto Korda
4.4	*Britney Spears Exposes Her Derriere*, Courtesy of X17, Inc.
4.5	*Photograph of Edmund Wilson in WWI Uniform*, General Collection, Beinecke Rare Book and Manuscript Library, Yale University
5.1	*The Constitution of the United States of America*, United States National Archives
5.2	*Silk Sandals*, Gucci Group N.V.
5.3	*Niagara*, Jeff Koons
5.4	*Slash-Shhh*, Courtesy of Scott Penner via Creative Commons Attribution-ShareAlike 2.0 Generic License
6.1	*Edison's Greatest Marvel the Vitascope*, Metropolitan Print of New York
6.2	*Stirk Family Design*, Courier Lithography Company

As a veteran listener at many lectures by
copyright specialists over the past decade,
I know it is almost obligatory for a speaker to
begin by invoking the communications revolution
of our time, [and] then to pronounce upon the
inadequacies of the present copyright act.
—Benjamin Kaplan, *An Unhurried View of*
Copyright (1966)

Introduction

The Copyright Wars

In which we contemplate Boy Scout merit badges, the bubble economy, Dr. Pangloss,
enclosing sheep, the Long Tail, Panopticons, the ecstasy of influence, and superheroes

IT WAS JUST OVER THREE CENTURIES ago that England enacted the world's first modern copyright law. Dubbed an "Act for the Encouragement of Learning," the Statute of Anne granted authors an exclusive right to print and reprint copies of their works for a term of fourteen years. The legislation proved influential and, just a few years later across the Atlantic, the Framers of the U.S. Constitution granted Congress the power to enact a federal copyright regime. Congress quickly obliged by providing a limited term of copyright protection starting in 1790 to authors of books and maps.

Yet for years, copyright law remained relegated to the judicial hinterlands. Generation after generation, developments in copyright law would receive scant attention. At best, the niceties of copyright legislation and jurisprudence remained the province of a small cadre of intellectual property attorneys and academics and the concern of a limited number of special interest groups representing the movie, music, and publishing industries. However, today that is no longer the case.

As it enters its fourth century of existence, copyright has begun to enjoy a much higher profile. Specifically, the advent of digital technology and the explosive growth of the Internet have forever changed copyright's place in our society. Copyright law has become vital to the hundreds of millions of individuals who download music and movies for their iPods, engage in time and place shifting with their TiVos or Slingboxes, own CD or DVD burners, operate their own websites, write blogs, or have personal pages on MySpace or Facebook. More broadly, copyright law mediates our relationship with cultural content, regulating our access to and use of any manner of written works, sound recordings and musical compositions, dramas and choreography, images and sculptures, motion pictures, computer software, and architecture.[1] In recent years, copyright litigation has impacted the types of books we can read, art we can see, games we can play, prayers we can say, information we can receive, homes we can build, movies we can watch, and songs we can hear and sing. This is particularly true because, in the words of Madhavi Sunder, we are in the midst of a "'Participation Age' of remix culture, blogs, podcasts, wikis, and peer-to-peer file-sharing."[2] For the new generation, "intellectual properties [constitute] the raw materials for its own creative acts, blurring the lines that have long separated producers from consumers."[3] In the digital age, we are all regular consumers and producers of copyrighted content.

Copyright law therefore plays a profound role in regulating our contemporary lives and shaping our very sense of self. Copyright's regulation, propertization, and monopolization of cultural content determine who can draw upon such content for the purposes of expression and identity formation. Thus, the contours of our intellectual property regime privilege certain individuals and groups over others and intricately affect notions of belonging, political and social organization, expressive rights, and semiotic structures. In short, copyright laws lie at the heart of "struggles over discursive power—the right to create, and control, cultural meanings."[4] IP (intellectual property) determines IP (identity politics).

Our increasing interaction with copyrighted content has also made acts of infringement both more possible and likely. As Tim Wu reminds us, "Once upon a time, even as recently as the 1960s, it was difficult to infringe the copyright law. One needed a printing press, a radio station, or a means of pressing records, and such facilities were not owned by many. Today every man, woman, corporation and child has the technological ability to copy and distribute, and therefore to potentially infringe copyright in ways both harmful and harmless."[5] With the personal computer in every home and workplace, the tools of copyright infringement are as ubiquitous as scissors and glue. Cut and paste applies not just to physical property: it is standard operating procedure in the digital age.

In the twenty-first century, copyright impacts us all. This book therefore focuses its attention on the relationship ordinary members of modern society share with our copyright regime. To that end, *Infringement Nation* is organized around the trope of the individual in five different copyright-related contexts. We consider the individual as an *infringer* of copyrighted works, as a *transformer* of copyrighted works, as a pure *consumer* of copyrighted works, as a *creator* of copyrighted works, and as a *reformer* of copyright law.

In beginning to think about the impact of copyright on ordinary individuals, three key trends bear close observation. First, copyright law is increasingly relevant to the daily life of the average American. Second, this growing pertinence has precipitated a heightened public consciousness over copyright issues. Finally, these two facts have magnified the vast disparity between copyright law and copyright norms, therefore highlighting the need for reform.

I. Copyright Relevance

Four decades have passed since Benjamin Kaplan delivered his wry admonition quoted at the beginning of this Introduction. Yet his epochal words ring just as true today. As the rapid pace of technological change continues to force a reconsideration of the vitality of our intellectual property regime, it is tempting indeed to cite the "communications revolution" of *our* time—the Internet—as disruptive to the delicate balance struck by pre-digital copyright laws between the rights of owners and users of creative works.

After all, it was no less than the Supreme Court who succumbed to this inexorable urge in its first encounter with cyberspace by famously proclaiming in 1997 that the Internet was "a unique and wholly new medium of worldwide human communication."[6] But the rush to tout the revolutionary potential of the Internet has subsided; the Panglossian cybernauts have faded like other findesiècle perpetrators of the "this time, it's different"[7] myth, including the dot-com boomers who embraced wild predictions of Dow 100,000[8] and the speculators who rode the real estate wave of the mid-2000s. A tide of skepticism[9] has followed the euphoria epitomized by John Perry Barlow's influential *Declaration of the Independence of Cyberspace.*[10] It turns out the Internet can be regulated even in the face of a fractured and anarchic international legal regime. Ironically, it is the Supreme Court itself that has retreated from its initial embrace of the medium's exceptionalism by finding the Internet is not sufficiently different to warrant reform of numerous long-standing legal doctrines.[11]

All the while, as Congress and the courts chart the course of regulation, a turf battle continues to rage over intellectual property rights in cyberspace. Copyright maximalists such as the Motion Picture Association of America (MPAA) and Recording Industry Association of America (RIAA) have bemoaned the Internet's potential to transform any teenager with a computer into a grand larcenist. They argue the ease of digital reproduction has enabled piracy on a scale never before witnessed in human history, and they have lobbied vigorously for statutory weapons with which to fight this scourge.[12] Meanwhile, skeptics such as Larry Lessig and Pamela Samuelson assert the digital revolution has radically enhanced the rights of owners rather than users.[13] They contend the development of digital rights management has enabled copyright owners to exercise unparalleled dominion over their property. By implementing access-control technologies, content creators can limit the rights consumers would otherwise have under certain circumstances to fair use (use without authorization or payment) of copyrighted works.[14] As a result, digital fences have begun to dot the online landscape, bringing a new enclosure movement to our cyber commons every bit as significant as the eighteenth-century edition.[15]

So what are we to make of this paradoxical gestalt in which the Supreme Court has simultaneously embraced and rebuffed the Internet's status as a unique medium, and educated observers recognize digital technology has simultaneously spurred unparalleled rates of piracy and granted unprecedented levels of control to copyright owners? And, what about Benjamin Kaplan's prescient admonition about the cavalier tendency to proclaim copyright law wholly inadequate to deal with each new "communications revolution," be it the player piano, radio, television, cable, videocassette recorder, or Internet?

Clearly, we are only beginning to grasp the massive changes afoot with the advent of our communications revolution—the mass dispersion of digital technology. Yet amidst the flux, one constant emerges: the 1976 Copyright Act. This last comprehensive revision to the federal statutes governing the protection of creative works always lies at the heart of these debates, inextricably mediating our relationship with cyberspace and new media. Three decades have passed since the current Copyright Act went into effect. Indisputably, tremendous economic, technological, and social changes have occurred in that time.

And although these changes do not necessarily warrant concomitant reform, we have reached an appropriate point to evaluate the efficacy of the extant Act and think holistically about the goals of our copyright regime and its continuing relevance in the digital age.

II. Copyright Consciousness

For centuries, the power of Guttenberg's invention rested in the hands of only an elite few. But as the personal computer continues to infiltrate every modern home and workplace, we all have the functional equivalent of a massive printing press at our disposal. And unlike Gutenberg's press, today's personal computer is networked, giving it access to incalculably large amounts of data from throughout the known universe. The power to create, manipulate, and widely disseminate copyrighted works therefore rests in the hands of an ever-increasing number of individuals. Yet with this technological change, a remarkable psychological change has taken place: copyright has begun to infiltrate the public consciousness like never before.

Take, for example, the growing awareness of copyright issues since the turn of the century. In 1998, Congress passed the Sonny Bono Copyright Term Extension Act (CTEA), which lengthened the copyright term of all subsisting and future creative works by an additional twenty years.[16] By altering the terms of the state-granted copyright monopoly for millions of creative works, the Act represented a multibillion-dollar allocation decision made by Congress and ensured over the following two decades that virtually no creative work would lose its copyright protection and enter the public domain. Yet the Act somehow slipped through both the House and Senate with little debate. Indeed, it passed via voice vote, thereby making it impossible to ascertain who voted yea or nay.[17]

Just a year later, however, the copyright maximalists were not so fortunate. In late 1999, at the behest of the RIAA, Congress amended the definition of "works made for hire"—works to which the copyright automatically belongs not to the author, but to a hiring party for whom the work is prepared—to explicitly include sound recordings.[18] In many industries, including the music business, the ambiguity over what types of works may qualify as works for hire has profound implications.[19] First, the designation affects copyright duration;[20] second and most importantly, it affects the exercise of section 203 rights. As a remarkably powerful provision buried in the 1976 Copyright Act, section 203 grants authors and their heirs the inalienable right to terminate after thirty-five years any copyright assignment or license made after January 1, 1978.[21] However, works made for hire are exempt from termination.[22] As most musicians assign their copyrights in their sound recordings to their record labels,[23] musicians can begin to terminate such assignments starting in 2013[24]—unless, of course, their sound recordings are deemed works made for hire.[25] Thus, the ambiguity surrounding works for hire has become a billion-dollar question for the music industry.

Once again, like the CTEA, this amendment to the Copyright Act sailed through Congress unblemished, and President Clinton quickly signed it into law. But this time, a grassroots effort immediately struck back. The CTEA's constriction of the public domain had rallied individuals and groups concerned about users' rights and the perceived excesses of industry lobbyists. The result was nothing short of extraordinary—as Mary LaFrance recounts, "When outraged musicians and scholars discovered that, virtually overnight, the substantive law of copyright had undergone this dramatic change, the reaction was swift, loud, and overwhelmingly disapproving. Reeling from the bad press, Congress held a brief hearing and retroactively repealed the amendment."[26] The issue of ownership and termination now remains unresolved and is likely to be litigated in the next few years as musicians begin to exercise their section 203 termination rights.

The repeal of the works-made-for-hire amendment epitomized the exceptional awakening of public consciousness over copyright issues. In recent years, mainstream publications such as *Harper's Magazine*, *The Atlantic Monthly*, and *The New Yorker* have regularly featured large spreads on copyright issues that would have previously seemed arcane and esoteric.[27] Groups such as the Electronic Frontier Foundation, the Creative Commons, and the Future of Music Coalition have emerged as powerful forces to offset the lobbying interests of the entertainment and publishing industries, and programs such as the Stanford Center for Internet and Society's Fair Use Project have begun public interest litigation to vindicate fair use rights against overly aggressive copyright holders.[28] Indeed, copyright activism has become commonplace. Witness the furor in 2007 over the Copyright Royalty Board's proposed increase in webcasting fees,[29] or efforts to increase the number of exemptions to the Digital Millennium Copyright Act (DMCA) granted by the Library of Congress.[30]

III. Copyright's Law/Norm Gap

The growth of copyright consciousness and activism has resulted in a more balanced struggle between copyright maximalists and skeptics, leading to a policy stalemate. During this impasse, the fundamental disconnect between our copyright laws and copyright norms has grown increasingly apparent with the march of technology, advent of more sophisticated anti-piracy enforcement methods, and increasing availability of draconian penalties against even de minimus infringers. On one hand, we have the ability to access, manipulate, and otherwise interact with intellectual property on an unprecedented scale. Simultaneously, however, copyright law has grown more broad in scope and longer in its duration.

A. THE DEFAULT RULE OF USE AS INFRINGEMENT

Our growing interaction with intellectual property in the Internet age has combined with seemingly minute changes in the law that radically alter the copyright landscape. Although in the past, use of a creative work was, as a default rule, noninfringing, the very opposite is now true. Before the passage of the 1976 Copyright Act, most creative works did not enjoy copyright protection. Quite simply, authors could only enforce exclusive rights to works if, among other things, they had promptly registered their copyright upon first publication,[31] timely renewed after twenty-eight years,[32] and properly observed certain notice formalities.[33] As a result, the vast majority of our society's creative output automatically belonged in the public domain—and use of this output did not raise any legal red flags.[34]

However, the passage of the 1976 Copyright Act and the Berne Convention Implementation Act of 1988 dramatically transformed our default regime from one of non-protection to one of automatic, instantaneous protection. Under the current Act, copyright subsists in authors the moment they fix a creative, original work in a tangible medium.[35] Moreover, the Berne Implementation eliminated any remaining notice formalities required for protection. Although formalities still affect the remedies available against infringers,[36] virtually the entire universe of creative works created over the past three decades is now subject to automatic copyright protection. Any use of a creative work is now, as a default matter, viewed as an infringement.[37] By making even more obscure works profitable, the "long tail"[38] has also exacerbated matters by extending what might be dubbed the "long copyright chastity belt." At the same time, the potential penalties facing copyright infringers have increased dramatically. Enforcement has therefore become increasingly worthwhile for a growing number of copyright holders, making copyright law relevant to any growing number of creators and, concomitantly, users. Increased legal protection for copyrighted works has matched increased use of copyrighted works, making infringement a commonplace occurrence. As a result, the average American unwittingly violates copyright law dozens of times per day.

B. TECHNOLOGICAL CHANGE AND THE LAW/NORM GAP

At the same time, technological changes have made individuals potentially subject to greater legal regulation of their copyright-related activities than ever before. Specifically, by facilitating superior tracking of the use of copyrighted works, technology is now forcing us to address the uncomfortable and ultimately untenable law/norm disparity. Although there may be a vast difference between what activities the Copyright Act proscribes and what the average American might consider fair or just, a lack of aggressive enforcement has long prevented this fundamental tension from coming to a head. As technology improves, however, and as privacy rights continue to erode, enforcement is becoming increasingly practicable.

Take the example of piracy. In the past, most piracy took place in the private realm, well beyond the Panopticonic gaze of copyright holders. For example, individuals would record songs from the radio, duplicate their friends' albums on cassettes, or swap mix tapes with there being few practical means for the record labels to monitor such activity and haul infringers into court. However, with the advent of peer-to-peer technology, individuals can share music not only with their best buddies, but with millions of their closest "friends" around the world. As we all know, peer-to-peer (P2P) networks have vastly expanded the scope of piracy to previously unknown levels. But peer-to-peer technology also did something else: it brought individual piracy into the light of day and made enforcement a viable option for copyright holders. Specifically, Internet Protocol addresses and log databases retained by Internet Service Providers made previously undetectable "sharing" both visible and traceable.

The expanded enforcement of copyright laws precipitated by the peer-to-peer revolution has forced us to reexamine the rationality of our reigning intellectual property regime. For example, the statutory damages provisions of the Copyright Act have enabled the RIAA to file multimillion-dollar infringement suits against thousands of individuals (including many children and grandparents)[39] on the basis of peer-to-peer activity. The cases rarely advance to an adjudication on the merits, as all but the bravest (or, perhaps, most foolhardy) defendants quickly settle instead of fighting the well-financed behemoth and the powerful threat of statutory damages (up to $150,000 per infringing act).[40] In one pro bono case I handled, the RIAA sued my client, a middle-aged, terminally ill Mexican immigrant on welfare who could not speak English, for the alleged file-sharing activities of his son. The copyright holders ultimately demanded he divert funds from his welfare checks to finance a settlement.

The P2P example is just one way in which technology has enabled expanded enforcement of copyright laws—a trend that is accelerating as technology improves. Imagine a world where every act currently deemed infringing under the law were actually prosecuted. Take, for instance, something we all do: sing along with our car stereo. Currently, such an activity (especially if the windows are rolled down) is potentially infringing,[41] but completely unenforceable. Yet as such acts become more legible, litigation over them is entirely plausible. The scenario, in fact, is not nearly as far-fetched as one may think. Recently, a performing rights society in the United Kingdom sued Kwik-Fit, a car repair chain, based on the allegedly infringing activities of its mechanics. The plaintiff claimed the mechanics were engaging in unauthorized public performances simply by playing their radios too loudly; it sought a licensing fee—approximated at £200,000—for the alleged infringement.[42] The suit survived an initial motion to dismiss. Although differences between American and British laws make a one-to-one comparison to the *Kwik-Fit* case inappropriate, the case underscores the very real threat of liability over unauthorized public performances. Consider that the idea of businesses paying licensing fees to ASCAP, BMI, and SESAC simply for the right to play music in the workplace seemed unusual only a few decades ago; yet today, it is de rigueur.

Indeed, the very technologies that enhance our media experiences are making greater enforcement of intellectual property rights viable. With the requisite advances in voice recognition software, every car stereo could be equipped with ears that monitor the noise in a car. Like a radio-frequency identification toll card, the mechanism could determine each song being hummed inside the car during the course of a month and then automatically bill the car's owner for the licensing rights to perform those copyrighted musical compositions or create such derivatives of the sound recordings. One can readily imagine a future dystopian world where the record labels, long since irrelevant to the development and distribution of new music, become nothing more than copyright trolls, drawing their revenue entirely from collections (or litigation) of this kind.[43] As surveillance technology grows more sophisticated, thereby allowing acts of infringement increasingly to come under the detection and enforcement power of copyright holders, we will be forced to confront this uncomfortable and widening law/norm gap.

C. THE MISADVENTURES OF CAPTAIN COPYRIGHT AND THE BATTLE TO SHAPE PUBLIC OPINION

Indeed, the law/norm gap has already begun to impact debate on the copyright issue, leading to policy stalemate. As a result, new theaters of operation for the copyright wars have debuted as skirmishes move outside of their traditional venues (Congress and the federal courthouses) into some basic American institutions previously removed from the fray. Elementary and high school classrooms along with key youth-oriented institutions such as the Boys Scouts have emerged as battlegrounds where interested parties have sought to mold the views of future generations toward copyright law.

Not long ago, the Motion Picture Association of America (MPAA) undertook a series of educational efforts to combat movie piracy by targeting children who, undeterred, might constitute the next generation of digital infringers. To fashion more favorable copyright norms for posterity, the MPAA worked with the Los Angeles Council of the Boy Scouts of America to create an anti-piracy "merit badge."[44] To earn their "Respect Copyrights" patch, Boy Scouts would complete a curriculum designed by the movie industry. Explained Dan Glickman, Chairman of the MPAA, "Working with the Boy Scouts of Los Angeles, we have a real opportunity to educate a new generation about how movies are made, why they are valuable, and hopefully change attitudes about intellectual property theft."[45] As the MPAA press release noted, "The curriculum is designed to teach participants about copyright theft and various forms of piracy, how to identify counterfeit CDs/DVDs, the consequences of film and music piracy, and why protecting copyrights is important to them and to the local economy."[46] The MPAA's version of the copyright law therefore threatened to make any unauthorized use of creative materials tantamount to an act of theft. In so doing, however, the MPAA entirely omitted notable mitigating features of the copyright regime, including the existence of fair use rights, the public domain, and the limited duration of copyright protection.[47]

A similar effort in Canada failed resoundingly, but not without a fight. The year 2006 marked the heralded birth of a new animated superhero dubbed Captain Copyright. Created by the Canadian Copyright Counsel at the behest of the content-creation industry and Access Copyright, a Canadian collecting society, Captain Copyright was supposed to be a consummate do-gooder who, in his own words, had dedicated his life "to protecting the rights of artists, writers, musicians, photographers, filmmakers."[48] Developed to appeal to youths and purportedly to educate them about copyright issues, Captain Copyright was not unlike many other superheroes—draped in a green cape and hood, square-jawed and muscular, and firmly devoted to a life of crime-fighting for the public weal. However, his definition of criminal activity went far beyond that of any other superhero, and oddly enough appeared to include (among other things) the unauthorized reproduction of any part of a written work for use as an example in an educational textbook.[49] The site provided teachers throughout Canada with lesson plans and sample activities for students ranging from first through eighth grade, and even included a segment that taught children how to write Op Ed pieces in newspapers to demonstrate their support for copyright law.[50]

Through the course of the lesson plans and activities, there was little to no mention of the public domain, the doctrine of fair dealing (the Canadian equivalent of fair use), or the existence of the Creative Commons, which allows creators to voluntarily relinquish certain rights to their works. The extreme legal positions of the initial forces behind the Captain Copyright project were perhaps best captured by the "Intellectual Property Disclaimer" section of the superhero's website, which stated

FIGURE 1 "Respect Copyrights" Merit Badge.

"permission to link [to the Captain Copyright website] is explicitly withheld from any website the contents of which may, in the opinion of the [sic] Access Copyright, be damaging or cause harm to the reputation of, Access Copyright."[51] Thus, according to the Canadian Copyright Counsel, sites that dared criticize Captain Copyright could be denied the right to link—one of the most fundamental features of the Internet. Apparently, Captain Copyright was publicity shy.

After a flurry of complaints about the imbalanced views of Captain Copyright, the website was suspended in August 2006.[52] Attempts were made to present a more even-handed approach to copyright, but those efforts ended in failure, and the site ultimately went blank. By early 2007, the Captain Copyright project had died. In the end, all that remained at www.captaincopyright.ca was a remarkable obituary that read in part:

> Despite the significant progress we made on addressing the concerns raised about the original Captain Copyright initiative, as well as the positive feedback and requests for literally hundreds of lesson kits from teachers and librarians, we have come to the conclusion that the current climate around copyright issues will not allow a project like this one to be successful. It is difficult for organizations to reach agreement on copyright issues at this time and we know that, in the face of continuing opposition, the materials will not be used in the classroom. Under these circumstances there is no point in our continuing to work on this project.
>
> We began this project because teachers told us that copyright had become too much a part of their students' daily lives for it not to be taught in the classroom, and they told us they needed a teaching tool to help them do it. We still believe that creating such a tool is important, but we also now believe that no single organization can take the lead on such an initiative. We truly hope that there will come a time when the copyright community—including educators, librarians and copyright collectives—can work together to provide a unbiased teaching tool that provides teachers and students with a balanced view of copyright.[53]

FIGURE 2 Captain Copyright to the Rescue.

One might think the controversy surrounded an edgy classroom program on sexual education named Captain *Condom*, not a seemingly innocuous educational effort about copyright law named Captain *Copyright*. At first blush, such a battle royale over an ostensibly harmless animated character appears perplexing. But the stakes in the copyright wars have risen dramatically in recent years, and the plight of Captain Copyright is emblematic of the resulting standoff between the maximalists (who equate any act of unauthorized reproduction with an act of unabashed theft) and the skeptics (who question the growing austerity of our copyright regime). By dictating control of and access to information, mediating our relationship with digital media, and regulating the use and abuse of expressive, intellectual, political, and cultural content, the results of this battle will determine how we live our lives in the twenty-first century and beyond. This book therefore examines the state of our copyright law, scrutinizes the historical impetus for arriving at the present system, and explores what a regime better aligned with the public policy goals of fostering innovation, creativity, and access might look like. As our analysis makes clear, these copyright wars are not just of esoteric significance to policy wonks, trade groups, and academics—they will have a profound impact on us all.

IV. Chapter and Verse

In assessing the impact of copyright law on ordinary members of twenty-first century societies, we consider the individual in five copyright-related roles: as an *infringer* of copyrighted works, *transformer* of copyrighted works, pure *consumer* of copyrighted works, *creator* of copyrighted works, and *reformer* of copyright law. In this process of contemplating the individual as *infringer*, *transformer*, *consumer*, *creator*, and *reformer*, we question some of the most fundamental assumptions about our copyright regime. Among other things, we tally the millions of dollars in infringement liability the average American rings up in an ordinary day (*Chapter 1*). We analyze the perverse role the fair use doctrine has played in expanding, rather than limiting, the copyright monopoly (*Chapter 2*). We highlight the expressive and developmental interests at play with the pure and even unauthorized copying and use of copyrighted content (*Chapter 3*). We challenge the myth of American copyright militancy by examining how our laws surprisingly provide creators of copyrighted content with far less protection than those of other countries (*Chapter 4*). Finally, we conclude by imagining what Copyright 2.0 might look like by considering the issue of reform holistically and advancing several concrete policy proposals (*Chapter 5*).

A. THE INDIVIDUAL AS INFRINGER

Chapter 1 focuses on the individual as infringer by examining copyright law's formal take on an average day in the life of an ordinary individual. In so doing, we build the case for rethinking our modern copyright regime. Drawing on the three trends we identified earlier—the increasing relevance of copyright law to the daily lives of the average American, the growing public consciousness over copyright issues, and the widening chasm between copyright law and copyright norms—we argue copyright law has grown increasingly restrictive, to the point that it simultaneously flouts our most fundamental tenets of reasonableness and undermines its goal of encouraging creativity and human development.

To illustrate the dangers of our modern copyright regime, we conduct a thought, or gedanken, experiment involving a hypothetical law professor named John. Illustrating the unwitting infringement that has become commonplace for any American, the narrative follows an otherwise ordinary day in John's life and finds that, in the course of his normal routine, John (like all of us) infringes the copyrights of dozens of protected works, racking up eighty-three acts of infringement. Though there is nothing extraordinary about John's activities, if copyright holders were inclined to enforce their rights against him to the maximum extent allowed by law (and barring last-minute salvation from the notoriously ambiguous fair use defense), he would face liability for a mind-boggling *$4.544 billion* in potential damages each year (to say nothing of potential criminal charges).[54] And, surprisingly, he has not even committed a single act of infringement through online file-sharing.

Such an outcome flies in the face of our basic sense of justice. Indeed, we must either irrationally conclude we are all criminal infringers—veritable grand larcenists—or blithely surmise copyright law must not mean what it appears to say. Something is clearly amiss, and the case for reform becomes manifest. Moreover, copyright enforcement is not just a problem for teenagers downloading music and movies on the latest file-sharing networks—it is a matter of concern for anyone living in a digital society.

B. THE INDIVIDUAL AS TRANSFORMER

Chapter 2 examines the role of the individual as transformer of copyrighted works and the relationship of this role to the key goals of our copyright regime: encouraging creative output and advancing progress in the arts. We therefore begin the book's analysis in earnest by exploring the history and purpose of copyright law and charting the evolution of its jurisprudence. Casting an eye toward the policy goals of the copyright system, the chapter examines the genesis of authorial protection, beginning with the source of all Anglo-American copyright law (England's Statute of Anne) and going through the early colonial copyright statutes, the Constitution's Copyright Clause, and the federal government's Copyright Act of 1790. As we see, the early debates over copyright law pitted two distinctly different visions of intellectual property rights against one another. On one hand, advocates of a natural-rights vision of copyright believed creators have an inherent property interest in the fruits of their intellectual efforts. By contrast, advocates of a utilitarian view reluctantly accepted the copyright monopoly to the extent it provided individuals with the necessary economic incentives to promote the production and dissemination of creative works. An analysis of the historical record indicates our copyright regime squarely rejected the notion of natural rights and embraced a utilitarian copyright law that balanced the interests of creators and users of works by limiting the property right in both scope and duration and focusing on the system's role in encouraging the dissemination of knowledge. This early vision is best understood through an exegesis of early decisions in the field, including cases involving the copyright to the Supreme Court's own opinions[55] and Harriet Beecher Stowe's classic *Uncle Tom's Cabin*.[56] Though these cases present recognizable fact patterns and works, their tenor is almost alien to a modern observer—and their outcomes surprising. The courts had no problem with the unauthorized translation of a best-selling novel, even if it destroyed the original author's market share. Similarly, they blessed unauthorized abridgements of unwieldy treatises and volumes. The reason was simple: if the use contributed to progress in the arts, the law permitted it. Although early copyright laws did prohibit slavish copying of a protected work, an unauthorized-yet-transformative use was per se noninfringing because it created something new and benefited the public.

However, copyright law has radically departed from these humble origins and forsaken its acute sensitivity to monopolization and the public good. In examining the reasons for the betrayal of copyright's utilitarian origins, we point to an unexpected culprit: the fair use doctrine. Since its advent in an 1841 case involving the collected works of George Washington,[57] the doctrine has been hailed as a powerful check on the copyright monopoly. Fair use, we are told, protects public access to the building blocks of creation and advances research and criticism. We directly challenge this conventional wisdom.

Specifically, far from protecting the public domain, the fair use doctrine has actually played a central role in the triumph of a natural-law vision of copyright that privileges the inherent property interests of authors in the fruits of their labor over the utilitarian goal of progress in the arts. Thus, the fair use doctrine has actually enabled the expansion of the copyright monopoly well beyond its original bounds and has undermined the goals of the copyright system as envisioned by the Founding Fathers. We document the seemingly benign genesis of the fair use doctrine and trace its impact on the copyright infringement calculus. With the advent of the fair use doctrine, transformative uses were no longer deemed noninfringing per se. Instead, the law considered any use of a copyrighted work—whether partial or complete, literal or nonliteral—to be infringing, excusable only after the *alleged infringer* proffers an effective fair use *defense*. The fair use elements, which include the amount and substantiality purloined from the copyrighted work, the nature of the copyrighted work, and the harm done to its economic value, focus more on what *was taken from* a copyrighted work than what *use was made of* the copyrighted work.

Drawing on a series of examples dealing with digital sampling in hip-hop music;[58] appropriationist techniques by postmodern artists such as Jeffrey Koons;[59] satires involving Mickey Mouse,[60] Dr. Seuss,[61] and *Star Trek*;[62] and the largely unknown, Pynchonian origins of Nirvana's smash hit "Smells Like Teen Spirit," we argue the fair use doctrine has reintroduced long-spurned natural-law elements into the infringement calculus—to the detriment of creativity and advancement in the arts. In recent years, courts have virtually eliminated any fair use of recorded music, eviscerated protections for satirical exploitations of copyrighted works, and generally restrained myriad transformative and educational uses. This trend is particularly troubling in the digital era. The artistic process is inevitably iterative and accretive, often remixing existing works to create new ones. When writer Donald Barthelme was once asked what he considered the most important tool of the genius today, he replied: "Rubber cement."[63] Technological developments have given us the potential to enjoy unparalleled access to the works of the past and the ability to manipulate them with remarkable ease. Yet copyright law prohibits our use of digital "rubber cement," thereby stifling ingenuity and transformative use in the process.

C. THE INDIVIDUAL AS CONSUMER

However, transformative uses of copyrighted works are not the only types of valuable interactions individuals enjoy with creative content. Chapter 3 turns our attention to the individual as a pure consumer by critiquing the underappreciated value of non-transformative use of copyrighted works. In so doing, we identify and illustrate the critical link between intellectual property and identity politics. We therefore expand on the tolls of the modern copyright regime, which cannot only repress many forms of artistic ingenuity but can impede identity formation, personal development, and the exercise of basic First Amendment rights by users of creative content.

As philosopher Ludwig Wittgenstein once posited, "The limits of my language mean the limits of my world."[64] Copyright law circumscribes our linguistic and artistic palettes by subjecting entire wings of Jorge Luis Borges' metaphoric "Library of Babel"[65] to monopolization and by restricting the reproduction and manipulation of cultural content. Using four case studies, we illustrate how intellectual property laws can mediate nationalistic, spiritual, sexual, racial, and gender-based identities by regulating core activities related to personal development and expression. We consider the power of copyright law to limit use and manipulation of the American flag, thereby granting the government the ability to control rights to one of our nation's most evocative symbols. We examine how authorship claims to the most famous prayer of the past century can have profound consequences as to the way in which individuals can conduct their spiritual lives, celebrate their religious convictions, and develop and express their theological identities. We link the struggle for gay rights with the battle over ownership of the term *Olympics* in infringement litigation brought by the U.S. Olympic Committee against organizers of the Gay Olympics.[66] And, with the copyright controversy involving the Australian folksong "Kookaburra", we contemplate the role of intellectual property in regulating the use of cultural and national heritage. As we demonstrate, intellectual property laws have the power to circumvent traditional First Amendment protections and patrol uses of cultural, patriotic, and religious symbols. Yet modern copyright law has paid insufficient attention to how such identity-based uses of cultural content can impact one's relationship with one's body, one's social community, one's country, and even one's God.

Meanwhile, technological and legal developments have increasingly allowed copyright to penetrate the private sphere, allowing putative rightsholders to regulate and control access to intellectual property and threaten personhood-related activities that have historically remained outside of copyright's gaze. Traditionally, the law has shielded the possession and private use of cultural content from liability, thereby enabling individuals to advance their personal development through the unauthorized use of copyright works in at least some capacities. However, as we argue, the days when such activities fell outside of the penumbra of copyright's liability regime are rapidly coming to an end. Specifically, the expansion of secondary liability theories, the nature of digital distribution, the enforcement of the anti-circumvention provisions of the DMCA, and fundamental policy changes being considered under the Anti-Counterfeiting Trade Agreement undermine the protection that individuals have enjoyed in the private use and possession of (even unauthorized copies of) copyrighted works, thereby squelching activities—from the sharing of photo albums by families and use of photocopied scholarly materials by students to the study of motion pictures by cinephiles—that ensure individual access to cultural content and promote identity formation and expression. All told, we advance a theory of copyright that recognizes the crucial link between identity development and the legal regime governing the monopolization and control of cultural symbols and creative works, and we demonstrate that, in the twenty-first century, control of IP (intellectual property) is central to the understanding of IP (identity politics).

D. THE INDIVIDUAL AS CREATOR

With the first few chapters of the book, we examine the individual as a user of copyrighted content and challenge the expanding scope of intellectual property laws that make infringers of us all, suppress transformative uses that are accretive to progress in the arts, and impede critical expressive and First Amendment activities by consumers. In Chapter 4, however, we turn our attention from the individual as *infringer, transformer,* and *consumer* to the individual as *creator* of intellectual property. In so doing, we examine where American copyright law may actually do too little to vindicate the rights of creators. In the process, we question one of the most steadfast and widely held assumptions about our country's copyright laws: that we vigorously protect the rights of creators with one of the most protective copyright regimes in the world.

Specifically, Chapter 4 performs a socio-legal deconstruction of our copyright regime, assessing the epistemological, philological, and hegemonic consequences of copyright law's technicalities and formalities, especially the timely registration requirement. In the process of the analysis, we subvert the myth of American copyright militancy and provide a more nuanced view of our protection and enforcement regime. Copyrighted works, it turns out, are effectively placed into a hierarchy of care that, in many ways, safeguards creators less vigorously than regimes in other countries. Through its ostensibly neutral formalities, the current system privileges the interests of repeat, sophisticated rightsholders—typically corporations in the content-creation industries. It does so at the expense of smaller, less sophisticated individual creators. Moreover, existing law practically encourages certain kinds of infringement. Sophisticated players therefore enjoy strong rights when seeking to enforce their copyrights, often wielding the threat of disproportional penalties against accused infringers. In sharp contrast, when they function as users of intellectual property (something all creators do), these same players often face only the most parsimonious of penalties, even when they infringe willfully.

The result is a cultural hierarchy. By creating a two-tiered system of protection, seemingly neutral formalities have allowed the construction of a hierarchy of works defined by their violability. Works by sophisticated creators have the opportunity to become part of the commercial canon. Their aura is secured through artificial scarcity perpetuated by copyright law and the dramatic penalties facing infringers for unauthorized exploitation of such works. Other works—generally those by unsophisticated creators such as individual artists—are fodder for remix, reinterpretation, transformation, and unauthorized use. These works lack any aura, their violability is not patrolled, and they may be infringed, in some cases with impunity. We focus on two case studies to illustrate this selective sacralization process in action: the development of the modern music industry and Hollywood's above-the-line hierarchy.

In the end, Chapter 4's analysis is not meant to buttress calls for even greater copyright protection for all creators. Rather, it is meant to deconstruct the beneficiaries of the existing regime and highlight the need for holistic reform that seeks to equalize protection among different classes of authors and rightsholders while protecting the interests of copyright transformers and consumers identified in Chapters 2 and 3.

E. THE INDIVIDUAL AS REFORMER

After we have charted the ways in which the modern copyright regime impacts the individual as transformer, consumer, and creator of copyrighted works, and how it regulates individual conduct as a broader hegemonic project, Chapter 5 turns our attention to the issue of copyright reform. Although the matter of recasting a Copyright 2.0 for the digital age is wrought with challenges, we offer a few modest suggestions to address some of the concerns regarding artistic progress, expressive rights, information access, and technological development raised in the course of our analysis. The proposals we present are not meant to be comprehensive; rather, they are intended to serve as a starting point for a broader dialogue about what Copyright 2.0 might look like.

Our reforms focus on three particular goals: (1) restoring the balance between users of and rightsholders to copyrighted content; (2) tempering the disparity between copyright law's treatment of sophisticated and unsophisticated parties; and (3) recalibrating the relationship between transformative users and original creators of copyrighted content. In particular, we bolster pure consumer rights by proposing a series of reforms that ameliorate the harsh results of copyright's strict liability regime while discouraging the kind of overreaching copyright claims that have grown all too common in recent years. Such claims threaten both to chill legitimate activities by users of copyright content and to advance "copyright creep"—the accretion of sui generis legal protections for rightsholders that often begins with seemingly small changes in norms and expectations. We also attempt to remedy the vast disparity between sophisticated and unsophisticated actors by expanding the availability of important infringement remedies to all creators while simultaneously limiting statutory damages awards so as to reduce the in terrorem effect of modern copyright litigation and limit its more inequitable results.

Finally, in perhaps our most fundamental and far-reaching proposal, we address the growing tension between transformative users and creators and, more broadly, between First Amendment rights and copyright protection. We propose an intermediate liability scheme that would encourage progress in the arts and vindicate free speech rights while still preserving the rights of creators to benefit financially from the use of their works. When confronting a question over the permissibility of a potentially transformative use, the statutory scheme of the present copyright regime forces courts to choose between two extreme options: fair use or infringement. If courts find infringement, hefty statutory damages often result. However, if courts rule fair use, an unauthorized user of a copyrighted work is able to exploit (without permission or payment) the work of another with impunity, thereby free riding on the creative success of the original author. We support the creation of an intermediate liability option that undermines the harsh binary that precludes courts from effectively balancing First Amendment and intellectual property considerations. Under the intermediate liability scheme, transformative uses of copyrighted works would be deemed noninfringing. However, commercial exploitation of transformative works would be subject to an accounting of profits—profits that would, as a default rule, be evenly split between the author of the original work and the transformative user. This intermediate liability option serves key First Amendment interests and advances the original utilitarian vision of the federal copyright system: the maximization of dissemination of creative works to the public so as to advance progress in the arts. Meanwhile, it ensures copyright owners will continue to receive reasonable payments for the commercial exploitation of their works. Moreover, certain types of uses would be deemed per se transformative by law so as to undermine one of the most pernicious aspects of the modern copyright regime—the lack of ex ante guidance as to what constitutes infringement or fair use.

All told, *Infringement Nation* argues that our modern copyright regime, which was first enacted to encourage creativity, is now standing in the way of artistic progress and important expressive rights. This book consequently calls for a fundamental reexamination of our existing copyright laws. In the process, we make the case for holistic reform that recalibrates the balance between users and creators of copyrighted content in the digital world and addresses the needs of ordinary individuals in the twenty-first century.

1

THE INDIVIDUAL AS INFRINGER

In which we contemplate the Eighth Commandment, Captain Caveman, nuclear weapons and Hindu aphorisms, birthday celebrations, presidential memoirs, reclusive authors, Dr. Seuss, O.J. Simpson, the dangers of doodling, a famous Olaf, celebrity tattoos, and the civil rights movement

COPYRIGHT LAW IS omnipresent in the modern world. With personal computers at our homes and offices, smartphones in our pockets, digital video recorders attached to our televisions, and widespread broadband Internet access, we have greater access to the world's creative content than ever before. But digital technology is not a one-way road: it also places at our fingertips the tools to reproduce, manipulate, and disseminate this creative content around the globe in a split second to billions of other content consumers. Copyright law mediates our relationship with all of this content. In the process, it also manages to regulate some of our most basic (and often expressive) behaviors: speaking, singing, hearing, dancing, watching, drawing, writing, and painting. Copyright law determines the words we can and cannot use and the melodies we can and cannot sing. In short, copyright law constrains our freedoms. Sometimes it does so with good purpose, but, increasingly, our copyright regime has lost its bearings in the delicate balancing of authorial rewards with user rights and of property interests with expressive values.

Copyright's growing ubiquity, when combined with the particular way in which our legal regulations have been written and interpreted, has put us in constant danger of running afoul of the law. In the twenty-first century, we have become, technically speaking, a nation of constant infringers. On any given day, even the most law-abiding American engages in thousands of actions that likely constitute copyright infringement. The widespread use of peer-to-peer (P2P) file-sharing technology, which has enabled ordinary Americans to become mass copyright infringers with spectacular ease, has brought to light the wide chasm separating our norms (which guide our daily activities) and our laws (which subject all sorts of conduct to civil and criminal liability). However, the problem extends far beyond P2P activities to encompass far less illicit conduct.

To illustrate the unwitting infringement that has become a recurring event for the average American, we begin by presenting an ordinary day in the life of a hypothetical law professor named John. We trace his activities through the course of twenty-four hours and ask one simple question: what would happen if everyone who could sue him for copyright infringement did so and sought the maximum penalties allowed by law? As we shall see, there is nothing particularly extraordinary about John's activities. Yet, at the end of the day, he will have accumulated millions of dollars in civil liability (not to mention potential criminal sanctions) for actions that, at first blush, appear relatively innocuous. In the end, John's potential fate highlights the troubling disconnect between our laws and norms—a disconnect that will only grow more disconcerting as the diffusion of digital technology continues to advance. This gedanken experiment therefore highlights the need to reassess the vitality of our existing copyright regime before it threatens to make criminals of us all.

I. Infringement Nation: A Gedanken Experiment

For the purposes of this gedanken experiment, we make three basic assumptions:

(1) a worst-case scenario of full enforcement of rights by copyright holders;
(2) an uncharitable, though perfectly plausible, reading of existing case law and the fair use doctrine (which, as we shall see, is a notoriously fickle defense that offers little ex ante refuge to users of copyrighted works); and
(3) the availability and assessment of maximum statutory damages in the amount of $150,000 for each act of infringement.[1]

John's day begins with the most elementary of acts for any American living in the twenty-first century: checking his e-mail. In the process he begins to accumulate infringement liability. Following common practice, he has set his mail browser to automatically reproduce the text to which he is responding in any message he drafts. Each unauthorized reproduction of someone else's copyrighted text (including e-mail) represents a separate act of brazen infringement, as does each instance of e-mail forwarding.[2] Within an hour, the twenty reply and forward messages sent by John have unwittingly exposed him to $3 million in statutory damages.[3]

After spending some time catching up on the latest news, Professor John goes to his Constitutional Law class, where he distributes copies of three just-published Internet articles presenting analyses of a Supreme Court decision handed down only hours before. Unfortunately, despite his concern for his students' edification, John has just engaged in the unauthorized reproduction of three literary works in violation of the Copyright Act.[4]

John then attends a faculty meeting that fails to capture his full attention. Doodling on his notepad provides an ideal escape. A fan of post-modern architecture, he finds himself thinking of Frank Gehry's early sketches for the Bilbao Guggenheim as he draws

FIGURE 1.1 The Swirling curves of Gehry's Bilbao Guggenheim.

a series of swirling lines that roughly approximate the design of the building. He has created an unauthorized derivative of a copyrighted architectural rendering.[5]

Later that afternoon, John teaches his Law and Literature class, where the focus of the day is on the potential tensions among law, morality, and duty. He has assigned e.e. cumming's 1931 poem "i sing of Olaf glad and big" to the students. As a prelude to class discussion, he reads the poem in its entirety, thereby engaging in an unauthorized public performance of the copyrighted literary work.[6]

Before leaving work, he remembers to post on Facebook five photographs from a college football game he attended the previous Saturday. His friend had taken the photographs, and although she had given him the prints, ownership of the physical work and its underlying intellectual property are not tied together;[7] quite simply, the copyright to the photograph subsists in and remains with its author, John's friend. As such, by copying, distributing, and publicly displaying the copyrighted photographs, John is once again piling up infringements.[8]

In the late afternoon, John enjoys his daily swim at the university pool. Before he jumps into the water, he discards his T-shirt, revealing a Captain Caveman tattoo on his right shoulder. Not only did he violate Hanna-Barbera's copyright when he got the tattoo (after all, it is an unauthorized reproduction of a copyrighted work),[9] he has now engaged in an unauthorized public display of the animated character.[10] More ominously, the Copyright Act allows for the "impounding"[11] and "destruction or other reasonable disposition"[12] of any infringing work. Paraphrasing J. Robert Oppenheimer's haunting words upon the first successful test of the atomic bomb, John is become tattoo, the infringer of works.[13] At best, he will have to undergo court-mandated laser tattoo removal; at worst, he faces imminent "destruction."[14]

That evening, John attends a restaurant dinner celebrating a friend's birthday. At the end of the evening, he joins the other guests and waiters in singing "Happy Birthday."[15] The moment is captured on his iPhone's camera. He has consequently infringed on the copyrighted musical composition by reproducing the song in the recording without authorization.[16] Additionally, his video footage captures not only his friends, but also clearly documents the artwork hanging on the wall behind them—*Wives with Knives*, a print by renowned retro-themed painter Shag. John's incidental and even accidental use of *Wives with Knives* in the video nevertheless constitutes an unauthorized reproduction of Shag's work.[17]

At the end of the day, John checks his mailbox, where he finds the latest issue of an artsy hipster rag to which he subscribes. The zine, named *Found*, is a nationally distributed quarterly that collects and catalogues the curious notes, drawings, and other items of interest its readers find lying in city streets, on public transportation, and in other random places. In short, John has purchased a magazine containing the unauthorized reproduction, distribution, and public display of fifty copyrighted notes and drawings.[18] His knowing, material contribution to *Found*'s fifty acts of infringement alone subjects John to potential secondary liability[19] in the amount of $7.5 million.[20]

All told, by the end of the day, John has infringed the copyrights of twenty e-mails, three legal articles, an architectural rendering, a poem, five photographs, an animated character, a musical composition, a painting, and fifty notes and drawings. In sum, he has committed at least eighty-three acts of infringement and faces liability in the amount of $12.45 million (to say nothing of potential criminal charges).[21]

There is nothing especially unusual about John's activities. Yet if those copyright holders were inclined to enforce their rights to the maximum extent allowed by law, barring last-minute salvation from the notoriously ambiguous fair use defense, he would be liable for a mind-boggling *$4.544 billion* in potential damages each year.[22] And, surprisingly, he has not even committed a single act of infringement through P2P file-sharing. Such an outcome flies in the face of our basic sense of justice. Indeed, we must either irrationally conclude that John is a criminal infringer—a veritable grand larcenist—or blithely surmise that copyright law must not mean what it appears to say. Something is clearly amiss. In the next chapters, we will examine how we arrived at such a state of affairs, and we will ask what we can do to create a more balanced, vigorous copyright system that protects authors, publishers, consumers, and the public alike while averting the types of absurd results that threaten to undermine the system's efficacy and legitimacy in the long run.

II. The Gedanken Experiment Deconstructed

At first blush, one might be tempted to critique the hypothetical presented in this chaper by arguing that its implications seem almost too fantastic. In some ways, that is true—many of the examples (and their attendant facts) are delivered with tongue firmly planted in cheek. But the point of the hypothetical is to present a worst-case scenario using the actual text of the Copyright Act and relevant precedent from the federal courts. Indeed, as a careful examination of the strictures of the 1976 Copyright Act and the jurisprudence interpreting them reveals, the liability risks posed by Professor John's pedestrian activities are all-too real.

At the outset, several global observations bear mentioning. First, one might be tempted to argue that many, if not all, of John's activities are excused by the fair use doctrine. This is certainly a reasonable point: indeed, many, if not all, of John's activities *should* be protected by the fair use doctrine. However, as we shall see, that is not necessarily the state of the law. Moreover, fair use is an affirmative defense. Although this fact makes little difference to theorists speaking about fair use in a vacuum, it makes a profound difference to copyright defendants facing the specter of multiple millions in liability in federal court as the doctrine places the burden squarely on the defendant to prove fair use.

Second, the analysis provides an uncharitable (albeit entirely plausible) reading of existing jurisprudence on the notoriously fickle fair use defense. It does not intend to present a predicative analysis of what *would* happen, but rather a cautionary tale about what reasonably *could*. There is still a substantive basis for the conclusions drawn from the hypothetical, as there are entire lines of case law that raise the specter—no matter how absurd—of liability. To that effect, much of the precedent cited below is still good case law, and much of it even comes from the Supreme Court or the U.S. Courts of Appeals for the Second Circuit and the Ninth Circuit. The latter rulings govern the copyright hubs of New York and Los Angeles, respectively, and therefore control the law where the publishing and entertainment industries reside. Thus, these cases supporting the threat of liability are not merely outlier or rogue copyright decisions from the judicial hinterlands.

As we draw on the available jurisprudence and statutes, here is the gedanken experiment deconstructed in more technical terms:

Example 1. *When replying and forwarding e-mails, John automatically reproduces the original text.*

Under federal law, copyright ownership generally vests in the author of a creative work.[23] There is little doubt a typical e-mail message meets the "minimal" creativity requirement for copyright protection dictated by the Supreme Court.[24] Moreover, unauthorized reproduction (such as forwarding an e-mail) of a copyrighted work is a violation of the exclusive rights of a copyright owner,[25] and thus is actionable as infringement.[26]

One could dispute liability by arguing fair use or an implied license would exonerate John from charges of infringement. However, under existing jurisprudence such defenses are far from certain. First, any private e-mail directed to another person is an unpublished work, as it is not meant for mass distribution. Courts have repeatedly deemed fair use rights to a previously unpublished work (such as a piece of correspondence) to be exceedingly limited. In *Harper & Row v. Nation Enterprises*, the Supreme Court rejected a fair use defense to the leaking of excerpts from Gerald Ford's forthcoming memoirs by noting a *strong* presumption against unauthorized use of any unpublished work.[27] Other courts have gone even further. The Second Circuit forbade extensive quotation of the unpublished works of L. Ron Hubbard—the copyrights to which he had bequeathed to the Church of Scientology—in a biography about him, noting that reciting "a small, but more than negligible, body of unpublished material *cannot pass* the fair use test."[28] The Second Circuit similarly rejected a fair use defense by a publisher seeking to paraphrase closely and quote directly from a series of unpublished letters written by novelist J.D. Salinger to Ernest Hemingway and Judge Learned Hand, among others.[29]

In all three of these cases, there was a strong public-interest argument favoring the unauthorized use of the unpublished works. Ford's work gave a direct window into the mind of a U.S. president, Hubbard's a unique perspective on the founder of a controversial but rapidly growing religion, and Salinger's a rare insight into a towering literary figure and famous recluse. Yet in all three instances, the courts rejected the fair use defense. If these uses do not constitute fair use, it is certainly arguable John's unauthorized reproduction of pedestrian e-mails also does not pass muster.

An implied-license defense may be similarly unavailing. One of the most fundamental tenets of copyright law holds that *owning a copy* is not the same as *owning the copyright*. Buying a physical object does not make you the owner of the copyright to that physical object. For example, when you buy the latest U2 album, all you have is title to the actual CD that embodies U2's sound recording; you do not own the copyright to the album. Thus, even if you own a CD, you may not violate any of the exclusive rights held by the CD's copyright owner (such as the right to reproduce the sound recording on the Internet). Section 202 of the Copyright Act enshrines this principle in explicit language: "Ownership of a copyright, or of any of the exclusive rights under a copyright, is distinct from ownership of any material object in which the work is embodied. Transfer of ownership of any material object, including the copy or phonorecord in which the work is first fixed, does not of itself convey any rights in the copyrighted work embodied in the object."[30] As a result, we cannot conclude the mere act of e-mailing someone necessarily constitutes an implied license to allow the recipient to engage in wholesale reproduction of the contents of the e-mail to anyone, anywhere.

Consider the *Salinger* case. Quoting *Nimmer on Copyright*, the leading treatise on copyright law, the Second Circuit stated: "The copyright owner owns the literary property rights, including the right to complain of infringing copying, while the recipient of the letter retains ownership of 'the tangible physical property of the letter itself.'"[31] Thus, the court held J.D. Salinger owned the copyrights to letters he had mailed, even though he no longer physically owned the missives themselves. We could make the same argument about the e-mails in the hypothetical. Indeed, imputing a license from the mere transfer of a copy of a work would defeat the basic public policy enshrined in section 202 distinguishing between transfer of a copy and transfer of the copyright. At the very best, therefore, the implied-license defense in this example is a viable, though uncertain, option. At worst, the defense is DOA.

One other point about this scenario bears mentioning: it not only creates the potential for liability for any user of e-mail, it raises the specter of liability for the author and distributor of any mail browser (such as Microsoft Outlook) that provides automatic copying with use of the reply and forward commands. Existing secondary liability principles in copyright law—the theories of contributory and vicarious infringement—allow recovery against certain individuals or entities who enable infringement, even if they do not directly infringe themselves. Specifically, anyone who has knowledge of an infringement and materially aids it can be liable under a theory of contributory infringement; anyone who possesses the right and ability to control the activities of an infringer and gains a direct financial benefit from these activities can be held liable under a theory of vicarious infringement.[32] Indeed, in recent years courts have read both of these secondary liability doctrines with increasing liberality.[33]

Thus, if Professor John has infringed a copyright through the unauthorized reproduction of an e-mail through the forwarding feature, one could certainly argue Microsoft materially contributed to the infringement and had full knowledge of the infringing activity enabled by its program. After all, the reproduction of e-mails is a specifically designed feature of Outlook (and many other mail browsers).

Of course, one might argue Microsoft could enjoy the safe harbor the Supreme Court has given to distributors of staples of commerce that are capable of substantial noninfringing uses. Although famously used to shield Sony from contributory infringement claims by the major studios over its Betamax product,[34] this safe harbor has narrowed significantly with the Supreme Court's decision in *Grokster*.[35] In that case, the Court found distributors of staples of commerce with substantial noninfringing uses can, in fact, be found liable for contributory infringement "when an actual purpose to cause infringing use is shown by evidence independent of design and distribution of the product."[36] As a result, Microsoft and other mail browser creators could theoretically face contributory liability for the infringing activities made possible by their products. Moreover, the *Sony* safe harbor does not necessarily immunize against vicarious liability.[37] One could make a case that the creators of mail browsers possess the right and ability to control user activity through design parameters and choices and that they certainly profit from the distribution of mail browser software. Thus, a perfectly plausible reading of the Copyright Act might precipitate not only dire consequences for all users of e-mail, but for the companies who make e-mail usage possible.

Example 2. John distributes copies to his Constitutional Law class of three just-published articles analyzing a Supreme Court decision handed down only hours ago.

In Example Two, John has reproduced three articles without the permission of the copyright holder and has therefore violated the holder's exclusive rights secured under the Copyright Act.[38] Consequently, John's actions have made him vulnerable to a potential infringement action.[39]

Upon cursory review of the Copyright Act, such a conclusion may appear strange. After all, the text of the 1976 Act explicitly states "the fair use of a copyrighted work, . . . for purposes such as . . . teaching (including multiple copies for classroom use), scholarship, or research, *is not an infringement of copyright*."[40] Yet despite this language, courts have repeatedly imposed liability for the unauthorized use of a copyrighted work for teaching, research, or scholarship.[41] Take, for instance, a line of infringement actions against providers of university course materials. In one such case, Princeton University Press prevailed against Michigan Document Services, Inc., a company providing coursepacks to students at the University of Michigan.[42] Ubiquitous on college campuses, coursepacks combine excerpts from journals and books to create reading materials for specific use in courses. By the court's own admission in that case, coursepacks provided enormous scholastic benefits: by enabling professors to "select[] readings from a variety of sources, the professor can create what amounts to an anthology perfectly tailored to the course the professor wants to present."[43] Nevertheless, and in spite of the explicit refrain in section 106 regarding photocopying for use in classrooms, liability resulted. And, although the photocopying cases have usually dealt with course material providers, the reason is simple: professors do not have deep pockets, but universities and photo-copying companies often do. There is certainly reason to think a court would have no com-punction under such a scenario with finding a professor liable for infringement as well.

Of course, the results of photocopying cases have not been without their vocal critics, even within the judiciary. As Chief Judge Boyce F. Martin Jr. wrote in his dissenting opin-ion in the *Michigan Document Services* case:

> This case presents for me one of the more obvious examples of how laudable soci-etal objectives, recognized by both the Constitution and statute, have been thwarted by a decided lack of judicial prudence. Copyright protection as embodied in the Copyright Act of 1976 is intended as a public service to both the creator and the consumer of published works. Although the Act grants to individuals limited control over their original works, it was drafted to stimulate the production of those original works for the benefit of the whole nation. The fair use doctrine, which requires unlimited public access to published works in educational settings, is one of the essential checks on the otherwise exclusive property rights given to copyright holders under the Copyright Act.[44]

As it turns out, the judicial legerdemain that has enabled courts to ignore the Copyright Act's apparent grant of fair use protection to academic photocopying resides in the courts' particular interpretation of the fourth—and often most important—fair use factor: market harm. Indeed, in Example Two, one might attempt to dismiss liability by arguing that an absence of market harm stemming from John's actions warrants a find-ing of fair use. However, in many notable copyright infringement cases, the courts have found liability under the most attenuated circumstances of market harm. Market harm is not just determined by whether *actual* sales were taken away from a copyright holder—rather, the judicial calculus can include the loss of *potential* sales in even *hypothetical* markets. As the courts have held, to assess market harm in a fair use defense, the analysis "must extend to the *potential market* for as yet *nonexistent* derivative works."[45]

Three high-profile copyright infringement suits make this point clear. In *Rogers v. Koons*,[46] contemporary artist Jeff Koons appropriated an image of a couple with some puppies that he had seen featured on a cheap postcard in a tourist shop. He transformed the image into a kitschy, ghastly statue that mocked the Rockwellian image of the American family. Unfortunately, Art Rogers, the photographer in whose work Koons found inspiration, did not take kindly to the unauthorized and uncompensated use: he sued for copyright infringement and ultimately prevailed, despite Koons's claim of fair use. The court's analysis in the case is particularly instructive. As the court noted, "The owner of a copyright with respect to this market-factor need only demonstrate that if the unauthorized use becomes 'widespread' it would prejudice his potential market for his work."[47] On this basis, the court found market harm in that Koons's unauthorized use of the *Puppies* photograph deprived Rogers of potential revenue should Rogers ever license the right to make derivative works based on his photograph.

In another significant ruling, the holding company for Dr. Seuss's intellectual property rights sued Penguin Books for publishing a satire entitled *The Cat NOT in the Hat!* that viewed the O.J. Simpson murder trial through the lens of Dr. Seuss's beloved *Cat in the Hat*.[48] Despite Penguin's claim of fair use, a federal appeals court found in favor of the plaintiff. A key portion of the court's ruling lay in its analysis of the issue of market harm.

FIGURE 1.2 *Puppies* By Art Rogers.

FIGURE 1.3 *String of Puppies* by Jeff Koons.

Specifically, the court found the Simpson satire caused economic damage to the market for Dr. Seuss's copyrights.[49] As the court explained, "We consider both the extent of market harm caused by the publication and distribution of *The Cat NOT in the Hat!* and whether unrestricted and widespread dissemination would hurt the potential market for the original and derivatives of *The Cat in the Hat*."[50] Although it is difficult to imagine Dr. Seuss Enterprises would ever contemplate entering the market for send-ups of the O.J. Simpson trial, the court noted that, as an affirmative defense, the burden was on the defendants to demonstrate an absence of market harm—something they had failed to do. The court then affirmed the preliminary injunction against publication of the book.[51]

Finally, in *Castle Rock Entertainment v. Carol Publishing*,[52] a federal court in New York acknowledged a book of trivia about the *Seinfeld* television series was a transformative use for the purposes of the fair use test. Nevertheless, the court still held no fair use had occurred. The imputed market harm found by the court was central to this decision. As the court reasoned, the allegedly infringing book harmed the market for derivative works such as trivia books that the copyright owners of *Seinfeld* might want to publish. The conclusions of *Koons*, *Dr. Seuss*, and *Castle Rock* are particularly troubling given the expansive definition of derivative works adopted by the Copyright Act and the courts.

By focusing on potential derivative markets and assuming cumulative effects, the courts have often embraced a remarkably expansive view of market harm. Given the holdings in *Dr. Seuss*, *Koons*, and *Castle Rock*, combined with John's failure to attempt to obtain reproduction licenses before he engaged in whole reproduction of the copyrighted work, it is entirely conceivable a court might find market harm and reject his fair use defense.

Example 3. John does a rendition of Frank Gehry's Bilbao Guggenheim while doodling to pass the time away during a faculty meeting.

If John circulated his doodles too widely and Gehry were feeling extraordinarily litigious, John could find himself in court. There is no reason this example should not constitute fair use. However, given the market harm analysis discussion in Example Two, a finding of fair use is by no means assured. Specifically, a derivative market need not exist for a finding of market harm. Instead, courts can impute market harm from a hypothetical postulation about what a potential market for derivatives might look like.

Example 4. John reads e.e. cummings's "i sing of Olaf glad and big" to his Law & Literature class.

Courts have often noted that even minimal unauthorized use of a poem can constitute infringement. For example, in *BMG Music v. Gonzalez*, the Seventh Circuit found that for poetry, "copying of more than a couplet or two is deemed excessive" and thus not fair use.[53] To encourage educational uses of literary texts, section 110(1) of the Copyright Act does exempt certain unauthorized performances from infringement liability.[54] However, this exemption only applies to nonprofit educational institutions, not to for-profit schools (of which there are many). One could even argue the conspicuous absence of for-profit schools from the exemption implies a public performance at such an institution is necessarily infringing and not fair use.

Example 5. On Facebook, John posts five photographs of himself that were taken by a friend.

As the discussion in Example One details, the unpublished nature of the photographs and the uncertainty of an implied license creates a real specter of liability in this scenario, no matter how absurd or troublesome.

Example 6. John reveals his Captain Caveman tattoo while swimming at a public pool.

Once again, by drawing on the attenuated concept of market harm in existing jurisprudence, it would hardly be a stretch for a court to argue that donning a Captain Caveman tattoo is a commercial use creating market harm by depriving Hanna-Barbera of the licensing revenue it might gain for selling tattoos of animated characters, should it chose to enter that market. In fact, the growing tattoo industry raises a minefield of ink-related intellectual property issues (and potential marketing opportunities).[55] After all, one could argue that Megan Fox is free riding on the glamour, sex appeal, and mystery of Marilyn Monroe by donning a large, visible tattoo of Norma Jean on her right arm—a mark that enhances her implicit claims to Monroe's legacy as Hollywood's leading sex symbol. Similarly, Shaquille O'Neal famously bears the Superman insignia on his left bicep, thereby solidifying his image as the NBA's Man of Steel—unflappable, strong and steady on the court, and Good Samaritan off the court.[56] On one hand, Fox and O'Neal's tattoos represent free advertising for the Monroe and Superman brands. But on the other, they could constitute infringement of Monroe's right to publicity, dilution of Superman's trademark (especially during Shaq's decline-phase years), and even copyright infringement.

As to the tattoo example, two caveats bear mentioning. First, lest someone take the hypothetical's language too seriously, the idea a court might order removal of a tattoo is somewhat whimsical. But, an all-too literal reading of the Copyright Act suggests judges might possess such authority. Section 503(b) of the Copyright Act explicitly provides that "[a]s part of a final judgment or decree, the court may order the destruction or other reasonable disposition of all copies or phonorecords found to have been made or used in violation of the copyright owner's exclusive rights."[57]

Second, should some imaginative (albeit misguided) reader somehow equate Professor John with the author of this book, a critical fact should be clarified for the sake of posterity: after careful investigation, I can confirm the author of this book does *not* have a Captain Caveman tattoo in real life.

Example 7. John (a) reproduces a rendition of "Happy Birthday" at a public restaurant on his iPhone camera; and (b) incidentally records an image of Shag's Wives with Knives painting, which happens to be hanging in the background.

In a surprise to many, the song "Happy Birthday to You" remains under copyright and requires licensing and payment for each reproduction and non-exempt public performance—at least according to its purported rightsholder, Warner Music Group, which is a part of the Time Warner media conglomerate. Specifically, Warner claims ownership over the lyrics to "Happy Birthday to You" and vigorously enforces its purported

FIGURE 1.4 *Wives with Knives* by Shag.

exclusive rights based thereon. As such, a seemingly harmless rendition of the song for a friend could lead to substantial infringement liability.[58]

Ironically, there is strong reason to believe "Happy Birthday to You" has actually fallen into the public domain and should be free for anyone to use. The music to the song has long been in the public domain—it was first written and published in the late nineteenth century by Mildred J. Hill and Patty Smith Hill, two sisters from Kentucky, to accompany the lyrics for "Good Morning to All." However, Warner dates the creation and publication of the combination of the melody with the famous lyrics to a songbook published and registered in 1935, thereby narrowly qualifying it for potential protection until 2030.[59] But, in what is perhaps the most extensively researched analysis of the subject to date, Professor Robert Brauneis concludes "[i]t is doubtful that 'Happy Birthday to You'. . . is really still under copyright."[60] At least three facts render the copyright's survival less than likely. First, its melody and lyrics appeared together in many published songbooks during the 1910s and 1920s, and there is no evidence to suggest either of the Hill sisters actually wrote the lyrics to the song, thereby frustrating a claim based on a publication and regis- tration date of 1935. Second, the 1962 renewal application upon which the validity of the copyright rests laid claim only to the particular arrangements made by the song publisher's employees, not the underlying song itself. Third, the 1935 publication likely bore an improper copyright notice, which, under the clear precedent of the time, would lead to a forfeiture of copyright. Yet despite these significant problems with Warner's position, to date no one has possessed the necessary financial resources and will to challenge the rights it claims.[61]

The consequences of the resulting situation are not insubstantial. It is estimated that Warner continues to collect millions of dollars in revenue from its claimed rights to "Happy Birthday to You." To avoid paying a license, many restaurants have developed their own (typically cacophonic) renditions of a birthday song.[62] Another consequence is that the award-winning documentary *Eyes on the Prize*—perhaps the greatest movie ever made about the American civil rights movement—can no longer be shown without risk- ing substantial infringement liability, as the licenses for the music and footage contained in the movie have expired. Among other things, the producers have been unable to afford renewal of clearances for such works as "Happy Birthday to You" since the movie features a scene where a group of friends and supporters sing it to Martin Luther King, Jr.[63] In a similar vein, the makers of the documentary *The Corporation* (winner of Sundance's audience award in 2003) have a minute of silence in their movie during a birthday party scene. Rather than pay thousands of dollars, they elected not to license the rights to the song.[64]

With respect to the unauthorized reproduction of *Wives with Knives*, the use appears to be both accidental and minimal. But such facts can be unavailing as a defense. First, copyright law is a strict liability regime with no mens rea requirement for liability.[65] Infringement occurs whether an individual acts with bad faith or complete innocence.[66] Awareness of the infringement is similarly unimportant: it is absolutely irrelevant whether a defendant had knowledge of his or her infringing actions for liability to be imposed for direct infringement.[67] Courts have not hesitated to find liability for even unconscious acts of infringement, as George Harrison famously found out when he was on the receiving end of a multimillion-dollar judgment for infringing The Chiffons' pop hit "He's So Fine" with his pensive and brooding "My Sweet Lord."[68] Second, one might claim that here (as well as in the other examples above), only a technical (de minimus) infringement has occurred, which is hardly worthy of action by the courts. After all, according to the common-law maxim *de minimis non curat lex*, the law will not entertain mere trivialities. But whatever the continued weight of the maxim may be in other bodies of law, a de minimus-use defense is typically ignored by courts in copyright cases. Nimmer notes, "The overwhelming thrust of authority upholds liability even under circumstances in which the use of the copyrighted work is of minimal consequence."[69]

For example, in the related area of sound recordings, the slightest unauthorized sample can result in a multimillion-dollar judgment, even if a significant and expressive new musical work is created through use of the sample. Generally, any unauthorized sample of a sound recording, no matter how small, constitutes infringement, and the available precedent is in accord. The first court to consider the legality of sampling set the tone for the judiciary's rigid response to the issue by invoking the ultimate black letter law: the Eighth Commandment—"Thou shall not steal," the court admonished in resoundingly rejecting any fair use defense.[70] Defendants have not fared well since. As one appellate court sternly warned all prospective DJs, "Get a license or do not sample."[71]

As for the incidental background recording of a copyrighted work, the Second Circuit's decision in *Ringgold v. Black Entertainment Television, Inc.*[72] should bring pause to those who would rely on a de minimus defense to avoid liability.[73] In *Ringgold*, the court reversed summary judgment for defendants on a fair use defense and allowed the suit to proceed to trial on a claim of infringement for the unauthorized use of a poster, which was part of the set decoration in the background of a five-minute scene in a single episode of a television sitcom.[74]

One could try to distinguish *Ringgold* by arguing there is no commercial use in Example Seven. However, courts have frequently adopted broad readings of what constitutes commercial use. For example, in *A & M Records, Inc. v. Napster, Inc.*,[75] the Ninth Circuit held that P2P trading (a quintessential sharing activity with no quid pro quo attached)[76] constituted commercial use of copyrighted materials simply because users were not paying the "customary price" for the copyrighted works they received.[77] Whether trading music on Napster or any similar P2P network is illegal, it is certainly not commercial activity in any meaningful sense. Specifically, this definition of commercial use conflates infringement with the fair use defense. As an affirmative defense to infringement, fair use grants individuals the right not to pay the customary price for a work even if their activity constitutes infringement. Yet *Napster* is no outlier.

For example, in *Worldwide Church of God v. Philadelphia Church of God, Inc.*,[78] the Ninth Circuit held that *giving away* thirty thousand free copies of a religious work constituted a commercial activity because the defendant "profited" from the use of the work by attracting new members who ultimately tithed.[79] Based on these cases, one could argue that virtually all use is commercial in nature because, at some level, any unpaid use of a copyrighted work causes someone to lose potential revenue. Moreover, almost any use has some conceivable commercial motivation. Although the courts have not consistently adopted such untenable definitions,[80] the *Napster* and *Worldwide Church of God* decisions certainly highlight the dangers inherent to a nebulous notion of commercial use. All told, therefore, even a de minimus reproduction of a painting caught on a videotape could give rise to infringement liability under existing precedent.

> **Example 8.** *John subscribes to* Found, *a magazine that collects and catalogs curious notes, drawings, and other items of interest its readers find lying in city streets, on public transportation, and in other random places.*

There is little doubt that, under existing law, *Found* would be considered a work of mass infringement. After all, the magazine consists entirely of wholesale unauthorized reproductions of the copyrighted works of others. The unpublished nature of these works severely jeopardizes the viability of any potential fair use defense to *Found*'s activities.

John's potential legal responsibility for *Found*'s acts of infringement stems from secondary liability principles. Specifically, courts impose contributory liability where an individual has knowledge of an infringement and materially contributes to it.[81] John indisputably has knowledge of what he is buying: a magazine that accumulates unpublished works without authorization from copyright holders and publishes them for the first time. Moreover, he arguably directly contributes to the infringement by serving as a regular subscriber to the magazine—thereby making the magazine's acts of infringement profitable.

III. The Making of the Infringement Nation

Copyright law did not exist in earnest until the eighteenth century. During the course of the nineteenth century, the United States was regarded as the world's leading pirate nation, a charge fueled by (among other things) its steadfast refusal to grant copyright protection to foreign authors. And, for most of the twentieth century, we consistently declined to join the world's leading copyright protection treaty. Yet for all of this history, at the dawn of the twenty-first century, we find ourselves operating under a legal regime that threatens to make criminal infringers of us all. The next chapter charts this radical change in American copyright doctrine over the centuries and assesses its impact on the ultimate goal of our copyright regime: progress in the arts. We focus, in particular, on one key aspect of artistic advancement—the individual as a transformer of copyrighted works.

Q: What do you consider the most important
tool of the genius of today?
A: Rubber cement
—Donald Barthelme, *The Genius* (1971)

2

THE INDIVIDUAL AS TRANSFORMER

In which we contemplate rubber cement, activist judging in the nineteenth century, the power of earthy moralisms, the backward-bending labor supply curve, bloated rock stars, damsels in distress tied to railroad tracks, Bill Shakespeare as a man of the people, Italian porn stars, the walls above urinals, defenestration, and "Smells Like Teen Spirit"

I. Revaluing Rubber Cement

ON ONE HAND, the results of the infringement-nation hypothetical in the previous chapter are resoundingly absurd. The idea that the average American could face annual liability in the amount of $4.544 billion for engaging in seemingly harmless and innocuous activities that happen to involve copyrighted materials undermines the faith we might have in the rationality of the legal system. On the other hand, the results are the perfectly logical and cumulative product of almost two centuries of gradual, ostensibly reasonable changes to the copyright regime. Thus, to understand how we arrived at a regime that threatens to make criminals of us all, it is first necessary to trace the origins and development of our copyright system.

As we shall see, the first American Copyright Act, which planted its roots in English law, differed dramatically from the present regime. Despite copyright being at its core a state-granted *monopoly*, our regime of copyright protection originally stemmed from profoundly *anti-monopolistic* impulses.[1] To the Framers, copyright represented a form of compensation—a quid pro quo for a benefit granted to society—not a natural right to which authors were inherently entitled for their creative efforts. Specifically, the

Copyright Clause of the Constitution, the 1790 Copyright Act, and the early jurisprudence of the Republic envisioned copyright as a property right limited in both scope and duration that had the particular goal of encouraging the dissemination of knowledge. With its relatively short life and narrow breadth, copyright was therefore grounded in utilitarian concerns and driven by a policy goal to maximize "progress in . . . the useful arts." Thus, while early copyright laws prohibited slavish copying of a protected work, no interdiction precluded transformative uses of a protected work because such uses were considered accretive to progress in the arts. This original understanding of copyright law was best epitomized by early cases that refused to forbid the unauthorized translation or abridgement of a copyrighted work. In these cases, courts rejected theories of liability by emphasizing the accretive use being made of the copyrighted works at issue. If the results advanced progress in the arts, the action was considered per se noninfringing. This view would not last, however, as copyright law would ultimately undergo a radical transformation. As we contend, a central basis for this remarkable shift comes from an unlikely source: fair use.

Since its advent in 1841, the fair use doctrine has been hailed as the most powerful and important check on the copyright monopoly. Fair use, we are told, protects public access to the building blocks of creation and advances research and criticism. However, this chapter challenges the conventional wisdom about fair use. In fact, far from protecting the public domain, the fair use doctrine has played a central role in the triumph of a natural-law vision of copyright that privileges the inherent property interests of authors in the fruits of their labor over the utilitarian goal of progress in the arts. Thus, the fair use doctrine has actually enabled the expansion of the copyright monopoly well beyond its original bounds and undermined the goals of the copyright system as envisioned by the Framers of the Constitution.

As it turns out, the fair use doctrine, first announced by Justice Joseph Story in his 1841 decision in *Folson v. Marsh*,[2] set into motion a striking departure from the original copyright heuristic by reintroducing long-spurned natural-law elements into the liability calculus and thus rendering transformative uses no longer per se noninfringing.[3] Instead, the law considered any use of a copyrighted work—whether partial or complete, literal or nonliteral—to be potentially infringing, excusable only if the alleged infringers met their burden of proof in proffering an effective fair use defense. The fair use elements (which included the amount and substantiality purloined from the copyrighted work, the nature of the copyrighted work, and the harm done to its economic value) focused more on what *was taken from* a copyrighted work than what *use was made of* the copyrighted work.

Transformative use lay at the heart of the Framers' understanding of the copyright infringement calculus. The fair use test betrayed this understanding by shifting copyright toward a natural-law, rather than utilitarian, vision. Thus, fair use privileged the inherent property rights of authors in the fruits of their intellectual labor above all else, including an alleged infringing user's potential contribution to the ultimate purpose of federal copyright protection: promotion of progress in the arts. Despite some limited rhetorical nods to the importance of transformative uses, the natural-rights view has come to dominate modern copyright jurisprudence, resulting in the extension of the copyright monopoly well beyond its original bounds. The ballooning girth of protection extended to rightsholders has threatened to overshadow the original goals of the copyright regime, a trend best epitomized by several cases involving the permissibility of unauthorized digital sampling and the rights of satirists.

A careful exegesis of these cases reveals their significant and troubling implications in an era where the widespread distribution of digital rubber cement (in the form of networked computers and malleable digital content) has enabled new forms of artistic and postmodern experimentation and expression. In short, the natural-law vision of copyright has threatened to take the rubber cement away from the creativity community—the producers of pastiche, the builders of bricolage, and the composers of collage—in defiance of the overarching goals of the federal copyright regime. This chapter traces the origins of this shifting theoretical framework for copyright protection and its significant practical implications for the individual as a transformer of copyrighted works.

II. The Triumph of Instrumentalism: A History of Copyright's Early Years

A. THE ENGLISH ORIGINS OF AMERICAN COPYRIGHT LAW

To the surprise of many, our federal copyright system finds its direct genesis in the U.S. Constitution. Though not nearly as well known as the celebrated First Amendment or the infamous Three-Fifths Clause, the Copyright Clause drafted in 1787 resides in Article I, Section I, Clause 8 and grants Congress the power "[t]o promote the Progress of Science and useful Arts, by securing for limited Times to Authors and Inventors the exclusive Right to their respective Writings and Discoveries."[4] It is pursuant to this constitutional authority that Congress passed the first federal Copyright Act in 1790. However, the context in which the Framers drafted the Copyright Clause and enacted the first Copyright Act is vital to understanding the philosophical underpinnings of federal copyright law.

Not surprisingly, as with much of our law, the background story begins in England, which had passed the world's first "modern" copyright act, the Statute of Anne, in 1710—just three centuries ago. Copyright existed in England prior to 1710, but not in the modern sense. Rather, copyright functioned as a means to effectuate censorship by the British crown by limiting the kinds of works that could be published and distributed in the country. Since 1557, the British crown had issued a royal letters patent that granted the Stationers' Company, a guild of booksellers and printers, a virtual monopoly to publish works in England. Under the letters patent system, the members of the Stationers' Company—not the author—would possess a copyright in published works that lasted in perpetuity. In addition, as the sole guild licensed to publish in England, the Stationers' Company also acted as a royal censor. Dependent on the crown for its specially granted monopoly, it would deny publication to any controversial writings.

Unsatisfied with the publishers' reliance on the crown and the censorious state of affairs that resulted, Parliament sought to break up the publishing monopoly with the passage of the Statute of Anne. First, the Statute granted authors, rather than publishers, the copyright to their works and with it, the exclusive right to publish their intellectual creations.[5] Second, the Statute severely curtailed the duration of copyright, decreasing it from perpetuity to a mere fourteen years[6] for all new works, with the possibility of a single renewal if the author was still alive at the end of the fourteen-year term.[7] Meanwhile, existing works received twenty-one years of copyright protection.[8] Finally, by breaking the copyright monopoly from the Stationers Company, Parliament undermined the power of the crown to suppress works it deemed inappropriate.

The Statute therefore represented a radical theoretical shift from the prior regime of perpetual copyright. The Statute of Anne's anti-monopolistic origins were inextricably tied to the utilitarian philosophy underlying the Statute. The perpetual copyright formerly enjoyed by publishers at common law and through the crown's letters patent had been legitimated through an appeal to the natural rights of authors in their labor, regardless of the impact on progress in the arts. Consistent with the popular theories of philosopher John Locke, this view held that property rights emerged sua sponte in that with which one's labor was mixed. As Locke posited:

> Though the Earth, and all inferior Creatures be common to all Men, yet every Man has a *Property* in his own *Person*. This no Body has any Right to but himself. The *Labour* of his Body, and the *Work* of his Hands, we may say, are properly his. Whatsoever then he removes out of the State that Nature hath provided, and left it in, he hath mixed his *Labour* with, and joyned to it something that is his own, and thereby makes it his *Property*.[9]

The seemingly irrepressible Lockean logic therefore held that, by putting labor into their intellectual creations, authors automatically earned a natural property right in their works. This right was perpetual, just like the right to real property or chattel, and it passed undiminished to publishers when they purchased works from authors.[10]

However, the Statute of Anne explicitly rejected this notion. The title of the Statute reflected its different purpose: "An act for the encouragement of learning, by vesting the copies of printed books in the authors or purchasers of such copies, during the times therein mentioned."[11] Therefore, the Statute sought to maximize the encouragement of learning, not to protect the inherent property rights that authors (or publishers) possessed in their works. In fact, a preamble declaring copyright as "the undoubted property" of authors was removed prior to the Statute's passage.[12] Thus, to the extent property rights were granted in intellectual creations, they were endured by legislative fiat, not natural law, and were tolerated for instrumental purposes.

Despite passage of the Statute of Anne, the Stationers' Company would not go without a fight. For the next half century, the guild of publishers continued to insist upon the continuing validity of its perpetual copyrights. As it argued, authors had a natural-law property right in the fruits of their intellectual labors—a right that should last forever and that could not be supplanted by statute. To close the loop in accord with its self-interest, the guild held this right was naturally transferred to publishers upon publication. The position of the Stationers' Company had much support. William Blackstone, the famous English jurist renowned for his influential commentaries on the law, was an ardent and influential proponent of this vision, arguing for the absolute and interminable dominion of authors over their intellectual property. To Blackstone, natural law entitled authors to the right to deny any authorized use of their literal words and even styles and sentiments: an author "has clearly a right to dispose of [his work] as he pleases, and any attempt to take it from him, or vary the disposition he has made of it, is an invasion of his right to property."[13] Thus, as the guild and Blackstone maintained, the Statute of Anne merely appended a statutory copyright system to the existing natural and perpetual right to one's creations.

It was not until 1774 that the death knell for the natural-law vision of copyright ultimately rang with the decision in *Donaldson v. Becket*.[14] In the suit, the House of Lords was asked to determine whether the copyright granted by the Statute of Anne merely coexisted with the prior common-law copyright scheme for creative works or supplanted it. As the House of Lords ruled, copyright was a mere statutory construct developed for instrumental reasons by the legislature, not a natural and perpetual right; or, in the parlance of French legalese, copyright was deemed *privilège* rather than *propriété*.[15] Copyright was a pragmatic creature of public policy, limited in duration and scope, granted to the extent it advanced the "encouragement of learning"; it was not an inherent property right to which all authors were entitled. Thus, the task first undertaken with the Statute of Anne appeared complete: utilitarian copyright had trumped its natural-law predecessor.

B. THE CREATION OF AMERICAN COPYRIGHT

It is within this context that the Framers drafted the U.S. Constitution's Copyright Clause in 1787. There was little recorded debate or controversy.[16] Indeed, the only mention of the Copyright Clause in the *Federalist Papers* is a brief reference in *The Federalist No. 43* noting, without further comment, the obvious need for federal protection.[17] To understand the intent behind the Clause, we are therefore left with the plain text, historical context, and relevant statements made by its drafters.

To this end, the Copyright Clause of the Constitution is clearly grounded in an instrumentalist discourse, granting Congress the power to "promote the progress of Science and useful Arts, by securing for limited Times to Authors and Inventors the exclusive Right to their respective Writings and Discoveries."[18] Reflecting a utilitarian, rather than a natural-law, impulse, the language of the Copyright Clause was borrowed directly from the Statute of Anne. Beyond this expressly utilitarian rationale, the Clause advances no notion of the inviolability of intellectual property rights and explicitly limits copyright and patent protection to a finite duration, not perpetuity. Thus, the Copyright Clause carefully eschews any embrace of a natural-law or labor theory of intellectual property—a fact made all the more remarkable by the rather heavy influence of Lockean hermeneutics on the Framers.[19] In addition, the Copyright Clause is the only part of the Constitution (save the Second Amendment) that contains language explaining the grant of power. The First Amendment does not indicate why Congress shall make no law abridging the freedom of speech, and the Commerce Clause does not explain why Congress shall have the authority to regulate interstate commerce, but the Copyright Clause rationalizes copyright's limited monopoly as serving to promote progress of the useful arts.

The Copyright Clause further revealed its utilitarian intent through the various niceties of the first Copyright Act, passed in 1790 pursuant to the authority of the Copyright Clause. The title of the Act is instrumentalist in bent, emphasizing the ends of the law and the temporary nature of the monopoly granted therein: "An Act *for the encouragement of learning,* by securing the copies of maps, charts and books, to the authors and proprietors of such copies, *during the times therein mentioned.*"[20] Moreover, the federal copyright scheme Congress adopted only conferred protection upon publication, or when a work was first made available to the public. The instrumental quid pro quo was, therefore, explicit: in return for publishing a work and disseminating it to the public, a writer would receive a limited monopoly for exclusive exploitation of the publication. Additionally, by making the benefits of copyright protection available only to American citizens and residents, Congress eschewed a natural-law vision of copyright as an inherent property right.[21]

All told, "[t]he limited monopoly granted to authors by [the Copyright Act] was justified by the need to maximize the production of new works for public consumption, and its scope was measured by that justification."[22] Thus, contrary to the views of some scholars,[23] it was copyright's ability to serve the public needs that made its monopoly defensible, not the moral claims of the author.[24] Loathe to tolerate monopoly in any form, both James Madison and Thomas Jefferson reflected this view in their writings. As Thomas Jefferson once poignantly noted:

> If nature has made any one thing less susceptible than all others of exclusive property, it is the action of the thinking power called an idea, which an individual may exclusively possess as long as he keeps it to himself; but the moment it is divulged, it forces itself into the possession of everyone. . . . He who receives an idea from me receives instruction himself without lessening mine. . . . That ideas should freely spread from one to another over the globe, for the moral and mutual instruction of man. . . seems to have been peculiarly and benevolently designed by nature.[25]

To Jefferson, the fundamental differences between material and intellectual property dictate different legal and business regimes for their exploitation, protection, and regulation. Although property rights in tangible goods may legitimately require the exclusion of others from their use, this is not necessarily the case with intellectual property. Intellectual property is a non-rival property form with expensive creation and cheap duplication costs. For example, the discovery of a vaccine for a terminal illness may take billions of dollars in research and development, but once it is discovered, duplication of that vaccine is comparatively inexpensive. Moreover, the peculiar characteristic of intellectual property—which Jefferson eloquently notes—is that no one possesses the less, because every other possesses the whole of it. If I allow you to use my car, I am necessarily deprived of its use. But although someone's unauthorized use of my words or musical notes may damage me in some way (whether economic or moral), it does not deprive me of the continued use of those words or musical notes. As such, the natural-law theories that rationalize the protection of physical property may not entirely translate to the realm of intellectual property. This is particularly so when progress, or "moral and mutual instruction," is at stake.

James Madison agreed. In a manuscript published posthumously, Madison balanced his distaste for monopoly with the need for copyright protection to encourage dissemination. "Monopolies though in certain cases useful ought to be granted with caution, and guarded with strictness against abuse," he warned:

> The Constitution of the U.S. has limited [monopolies] to two cases, the authors of books, and of useful inventions, in both which they are considered as a compensation for a benefit actually gained to the community as a purchase of property which the owner otherwise might withhold from public use. There can be no just objection to a temporary monopoly in these cases; but it ought to be temporary, because under that limitation a sufficient recompense and encouragement may be given.[26]

Madison's statement on the nature of the copyright monopoly is both revealing and instructive. First, his thoughts are grounded in an instrumentalist discourse that envisions copyright as a form of compensation—a quid pro quo for a benefit granted to society—not as a natural right to which authors are entitled for their creative efforts. Moreover, Madison emphasizes the temporary nature of the monopoly and its key role in providing encouragement for the sharing of knowledge. Thus, the Constitution would tolerate intellectual property monopolies only to the extent they served a clear, instrumental purpose that benefited society. And, conversely, intellectual property rights would be curtailed when they failed to serve the public good.

C. *WHEATON*: THE APPARENT END OF NATURAL-LAW COPYRIGHT

Any lingering doubts about the viability of a natural-law vision of copyright in the United States ostensibly vanished with *Wheaton v. Peters*.[27] In that case, the U.S. Supreme Court followed the lead of the House of Lords in *Donaldson* and rejected the natural-rights view that held all published creative works imbued in their authors a perpetual, common-law monopoly right. The Court was readily familiar with the facts of *Wheaton*, in which Peters had succeeded Wheaton as the Supreme Court reporter. Because Wheaton had not undertaken the proper procedures to obtain copyright protection under federal law,[28] Peters argued that he owned a copyright in his reports by virtue of the common-law right (justified under natural-law theory) that predated the establishment of the statutory copyright. But Wheaton maintained, "The import of the act of congress of 1790 is that, before its enactment, there were legal rights of authorship existing; it provides for existing property, not for property created by the statute. . . . That law is not one of grant or bounty; it recognizes existing rights, which it secures."[29] The Court rejected his argument and held that, with respect to published works, there was only one copyright: federal statutory copyright.[30] After all, if copyright were a common-law right, the statutory grant would be thoroughly superfluous.[31]

The upshot of the Court's ruling was its rejection of a strong, natural-law, property-based vision of copyright. Under the natural-law view "[t]he right of an author to the production of his mind is acknowledged every where. It is a prevailing feeling, and none can doubt that a man's book is his book—is his property."[32] By contrast, the Court held copyright was an instrumental construction of the state that granted strictly delimited rights to authors; published works fell under the exclusive jurisdiction of federal statutory copyright protection. This protection aimed to reward authors via a limited monopoly term in their creative works that would encourage the works' dissemination to the public and advance progress in the arts. The Court thereby confirmed the Framers' intention for a limited-duration copyright that served the public interest.[33]

It is critical to note the *Wheaton* Court did acknowledge one exception to this framework: at common law, authors continued to retain rights in unpublished manuscripts because unpublished works remained outside of the purview of the Copyright Act.[34] This common-law protection for authors' unpublished writings continued until 1978.[35] Significantly, it was not rationalized on strict property or natural-law grounds; instead, it represented the enforcement of the more general right of the individual "to be let alone."[36] As Samuel D. Warren and Louis D. Brandeis famously noted in *The Right of Privacy*, "The principle which protects personal writings and all other personal productions, not against theft and physical appropriation, but against publication in any form, is in reality not the principle of *private property*, but that of an *inviolate personality*,"[37] or, put another way, the right of privacy. The very act of publication changes the nature of authorial rights in a work—publication constitutes a waiver of the right to privacy and subjects the work to the limited intellectual property rights dictated by the Copyright Act.

All told, by the mid-nineteenth century, "the constitutional principle of copyright was that one is entitled to only a limited monopoly of material taken from the public domain and then only if its use benefits society."[38] With *Wheaton*, it appeared the utilitarian vision of copyright had triumphed. The infringement test the courts developed consequently reflected this instrumentalist interpretation of the Copyright Clause and the Copyright Act by embracing the principle of a *limited* monopoly in two different senses. First, as we have already discussed, there was a temporal limitation to the monopoly. Second, even during a copyright's term, a stringent notion of infringement limited the monopoly. The nature of this latter constraint, which was radically different from that of our modern regime, bears closer analysis.

D. EARLY COPYRIGHT JURISPRUDENCE: ABRIDGEMENT, TRANSLATION, AND THE PRIMACY OF TRANSFORMATIVE USE

A series of Anglo-American rulings on the right to translation and abridgement epitomizes the utilitarian understanding of copyright embraced by the Founders and enforced in the United States until the early part of the last century.[39] Operating from the premise that copyright was a statutory construct with an instrumentalist bent (rather than a natural-law property right), courts viewed the act of infringement in a light largely unfamiliar to contemporary standards. Consequently, these cases focused on the transformative use made of the original work by the defendant rather than on the value of the material wrested from the original author.

The English courts' early judicial interpretations of the Statute of Anne, the antecedent for the Constitution's Copyright Clause, are the starting point of this examination. The first substantial question addressed under the Statute was whether a complete word-for-word translation of a copyrighted book automatically constituted a form of infringement. The English courts ultimately held in the negative. In the seminal case of *Burnett v. Chetwood*, Lord Mansfield reasoned "a translation might not be the same with the reprinting [of] the original, on account that the translator has bestowed his care and pains upon it."[40] Ultimately, this observation prevailed and became the law.[41] Proceeding from the premise that translations were formidable intellectual enterprises, English courts held their transformative quality transcended the original work and granted a tremendous benefit to the public. As a result, translations were not copyright infringements.

The translation rule is significant for what it reflects about the nature of infringement and the power granted by copyright: there is no infringement so long as an accused infringer creates a substantial work of authorship with the use of the original work.[42] The focus of infringement was, therefore, not on the inherent property rights held by an original work's creator but on the transformative application undertaken by subsequent users.

The English view of translation carried across the Atlantic, with the case of *Stowe v. Thomas*[43] best illustrating this westward migration in jurisprudence. In 1853 when Harriet

Beecher Stowe sued the author of a German translation of her celebrated work, *Uncle Tom's Cabin*, for copyright infringement, American courts were apparently faced with the translation question for the first time.[44] Drawing from the available English jurisprudence, Justice Grier found no infringement. His reasoning, particularly in light of the facts of the case, is significant.

Stowe had urged the court to adopt a distinctly natural-rights vision of copyright, arguing "[t]he right is original, inherent; a right founded on nature, acknowledged, we think, at common-law; a right which stands on better ground and is more deeply rooted than the right to any other property whatever. . . . What a man earns by thought, study, and care, is as much his own, as what he obtains by his hands."[45] Based on her vision that copyright should grant absolute property rights to its owner, Stowe argued the transformative value of the translation to society should be irrelevant to the court's infringement analysis. Instead, the court should acknowledge the defendant's German translation was free riding on Stowe's intellectual efforts and trampling upon her natural property rights stemming from those efforts. Thus, translation inherently constituted infringement of the natural right to one's intellectual property, as

> [t]he translator aims to convey to the mind of his reader the ideas and thoughts of the author; nay, the very shades of his ideas and thoughts; his exact manner and form of expression, and even his words, so far as represented by similarly constructed expressions in the new language.[46]

As the causal chain of Stowe's argument reveals, the philosophical underpinnings of a court's view of copyright would ultimately determine the result. If the court conceptualized copyright as a natural-law property right, translation would constitute infringement. By contrast, if the court viewed copyright as utilitarian in nature, the transformative nature of the translation process would lead to a finding of no infringement.

Besides the natural-rights appeal of her argument and the popularity of her work, the circumstances surrounding the case were particularly favorable to Ms. Stowe. When a translator renders an author's work into a foreign language, the translation effectively introduces a new audience to the work and perhaps even stimulates the market for the original work. Thus, barring plaintiff's intention to enter the translation market, the original work suffers little to no harm. This certainly was not the case in *Stowe*, however. Prior to defendant's translation of *Uncle Tom's Cabin*, Stowe had commissioned a German translation so that her book could be purchased and read by the Pennsylvania Dutch and other constituents of the large German-speaking population in the United States at that time. In fact, her husband helped put together the translation.[47] Stowe had every intention of profiting in the translation market for her book, and defendant's translation caused her direct market harm: as a result of its superior readability, the German translation by Thomas virtually killed the market for the one authorized by Stowe. In a remarkable concession, the defendants happily acknowledged this fact: "The sale of [Stowe's] translation, indeed, was impaired [by defendants' work]."[48]

However, rather than using this fact as a basis for *finding infringement* (due to the market harm to Stowe's work and her right to reap the just rewards for her intellectual labor), the court drew upon this fact as a reason for *finding no infringement*. The court squarely rejected Stowe's philosophical position regarding her natural, exclusive right to use and exploit her creation. Casting the copyright bargain in a light largely unfamiliar to any modern judge, the court noted:

> By the publication of Mrs. Stowe's book, the creations of the genius and imagination of the author have become as much public property as those of Homer or Cervantes. (Uncle Tom and Topsy are as much publici juris as Don Quixote and Sancho Panza.) All her conceptions and inventions may be used and abused by imitators, play-rights and poetasters. (They are no longer her own—those who have purchased her book, may clothe them in English doggerel, in German or Chinese prose. Her absolute dominion and property in the creations of her genius and imagination have been voluntarily relinquished.)[49]

The fact that Thomas's German translation caused market harm to Stowe garnered no sympathy from the court, thereby reflecting just how strongly the infringement test embraced a utilitarian analysis that assessed the intellectual use made of a work. As the defendants argued, the injury to Stowe's translation was the simple result of the competitive forces of the marketplace. As they observed, "the reason why [her authorized translation] is injured, is that her translation has less genius than ours."[50] The court seized upon this observation when it performed its utilitarian calculus on the infringement claim. Justice Grier noted:

> To make a good translation of a work often requires more learning, talent and judgment, than was required to write the original. Many can transfer from one language to another, but few can translate. To call the translations of an author's ideas and conceptions into another language, a copy of his book, would be an abuse of terms, and arbitrary judicial legislation.[51]

Although the court suggested a word-for-word mechanical translation *might* constitute infringement, it held that a learned rendition, such as Thomas's work, clearly did not run afoul of copyright law.[52] The reason was plain to the court: at the core, copyright was not about protection of an authorial monopoly based on a natural-rights theory of property. Instead, it was about striking a utilitarian balance that enables authors to reap economic rewards for publishing and disseminating their creations while also enabling others to make progressive uses of these disseminated works for the public benefit. Thus, the intellectual craft undertaken in the creation of the translation was central to the court's decision. Instead of looking at what was taken from the plaintiff, the court examined what *use* the defendant made of that work and how it impacted the promotion of the arts. Because the availability of a superior translation advanced progress in the arts, Stowe lost her infringement claim.

The abridgement jurisprudence announced during copyright's early years is similarly revealing. The English courts first addressed the issue of abridgement in *Gyles v. Wilcox*.[53] In that case, the publisher who owned the copyright for Sir Matthew Hale's *Pleas of the Crown* pursued an infringement suit against the publishers of *Modern Crown Law*, accusing them of abridging Hale's work. The language of the opinion is highly instructive. According to presiding Lord Chancellor Hardwicke, a work only "colourably shortened" constituted piracy.[54] However, as he cautioned, this principle must not be carried so far as to restrain persons from making a real and fair abridgement, for abridgements may with great propriety be called a new book, because not only the paper and print, but the invention, learning, and judgment of the author is shown in them, and in many cases are extremely useful, though in some cases prejudicial, by mistaking and curtailing the sense of an author.[55]

Hardwicke, therefore, expounded on the notion that an abridgement could constitute a new work of authorship, imbued with invention, learning, and judgment, despite how heavily an abridger borrows from a copyrighted work.

Although he did not fully adjudicate the instant case,[56] Hardwicke did provide guidance for an infringement test that would focus less on what was taken from the copyrighted work and more on the nature and extent of the defendant's use of it. Under Hardwicke's view, courts should eschew any recognition of a plaintiff's inherent, natural-law-based property right in his or her work and instead look to an instrumentalist calculation of how that work was being used by the allegedly infringing party. If the use was transformative and helped to promote progress in the arts, a court should find no infringement. This fundamentally utilitarian analysis would still allow for authors and publishers to obtain just rewards for their intellectual labors—the exclusive right of plaintiffs to have their work, as it existed, published in the marketplace.

Drawing on Hardwicke's opinion in *Gyles*, the court in *Newbery's Case* found the act of abridgement did not infringe an author's copyright.[57] Newbery had condensed and abstracted Hawkesworth's novel, *Voyages*.[58] Just as Chancellor Hardwicke had done, Lord Chancellor Apsley, the presiding judge in *Newbery*, argued an abridgement preserving "the whole" of a work constituted "an act of understanding . . . in the nature of a new and meritorious work."[59] As a consequence, Newbery escaped liability for infringement. Remarkably, as Benjamin Kaplan points out, "Newbery was not only exculpated but congratulated for reducing Hawkesworth and preserving the substance in different language perhaps better than the original."[60]

As with translation, courts considered abridgement an intellectual exercise, which, when performed with superior competence, only improved an original work. As a consequence, it advanced the central jurisprudential concern in an infringement suit—progress in the arts. Thus, the act of abridgement could escape infringement liability. As with the British tolerance of unauthorized translations, the United States adopted the abridgement rule.[61] In *Wheaton*, the plaintiff even acknowledged the right of an individual to create an abridgment.[62] Similarly, Justice Story's decision in *Folsom v. Marsh*—an opinion that, as we shall see, launched the strong break from utilitarian copyright—actually affirmed the vitality of the abridgement rule.[63]

E. THE LAW IN CULTURAL CONTEXT: NORMS IN THE REPUBLIC'S EARLY YEARS

The cultural context of the early American copyright jurisprudence on abridgement and translation further demonstrates the profoundly different attitudes that existed in the late eighteenth and early nineteenth centuries toward the use of creative works. Abridgement and translation were viewed as per se noninfringing activities because they constituted a transformative use of preexisting works that was accretive to progress in the arts and benefited the public. Undergirding this widespread acceptance of transformative use were critical social norms that supported such recasting. Specifically, society at large did not view creative output—especially the "great works"—as the immutable and consecrated products of authorial genius with which no one could tamper. Indeed, the very notion of "great works" or elite culture did not exist as we know it. An examination of the historical record reveals the very works that lie at the pinnacle of our cultural hierarchy today (for example, William Shakespeare, opera, and symphonic music) were popular among the masses in the nineteenth century, and prevailing norms supported their reinterpretation, mutilation, and transformation. In short, modernity's notion of the elite and hallowed work did not exist, and remix was the province of all.

Consider Shakespeare—a man whose works never enjoyed copyright protection, but whose oeuvre is firmly entrenched at the pinnacle of our cultural hierarchy. Although his works have long been part of the firmament of a sacred Western canon, this was not always the case. As much as it may surprise contemporary observers, the Bard's works had a radically different cultural standing during the nineteenth century, when his plays were widely disseminated and enjoyed across a wide swath of American society.

In his book *Highbrow/Lowbrow*, Lawrence Levine documents the ubiquity of Shakespeare in the early popular culture of the Republic and charts the changing position of Shakespeare in American life over the course of the past century. As it turns out, during the nineteenth century, the Bard's works were the very definition of popular (not elite) entertainment. Shakespeare's plays were not only performed in venues throughout our country, but his characters and plotlines were frequently the subject of minstrel parodies, abridgements, and reinterpretations—intermingled with popular songs, farces, novelty acts, and dances. In the absence of any consecrating ethos,[64] his works were free to be manipulated and altered so they might appeal to audiences of all stripes. From working-class burlesque and vaudeville shows along the frontier to the Brahman's East Coast theater, Shakespeare played a central role in entertaining the American masses. As a German observer from the era put it, one could always count on Shakespeare taking his rightful place alongside the Bible in the American home: "There is, assuredly, no other country on earth in which Shakespeare and the Bible are held in such general high esteem as in America, the very country so much decried for its lust for money. If you were to enter an isolated log cabin in the Far West and even if its inhabitant were to exhibit many of the traces of backwoods living, he will most likely have one small room nicely furnished in which to spend his few leisure hours and in which you will certainly find the Bible and in most cases also some cheap edition of the works of the poet Shakespeare."[65]

Other creative works that now enjoy elite status had similarly popular appeal and were subject to endless transformative use. As Katherine Preston's research on nineteenth-century opera reveals, troupes performed extensively in both English and Italian to large audiences throughout antebellum America.[66] Explains Levine, "Opera in America, like Shakespeare in America, was not presented as a sacred text; it was performed by artists who felt free to embellish and alter, add and subtract."[67] The limited nature of the copyright monopoly enabled the types of activities that characterized the early and mid-nineteenth-century American cultural scene: the frequent reinterpretation, remixing, transformation, parody, embellishment, abridgement, adaptation, and alteration of a panoply of works that now form the inviolable canon.

In short, the sacred text—outside of religion, where norms demanded it—did not exist as we know it. Celebrated works remained dynamic, ever-changing, and responsive to the particular needs of diverse audiences. In the nineteenth century, the elite culture of modern times—Shakespeare, opera, fine art, and symphonic music, to name a few examples—was equally as popular with the proletariat and the patriciate. Law and norms functioned together to encourage transformative use and minimize the bifurcation of cultural content into elite and lowbrow categories.

As epitomized by the translation and abridgement cases, an examination of eighteenth- and nineteenth-century copyright jurisprudence demonstrates the notion of transformation lay at the heart of any infringement analysis. Whether appropriation of someone's work resulted in a finding of infringement depended largely upon the benefit of the use to society. As a consequence, the value of an expropriated copyrighted work was often irrelevant to a court's infringement calculus. This is not to say that all natural-law supporters of authors' rights (both in the law and in society at large) had been silenced. However, the infringement test was largely utilitarian in bent, as the Constitution and Copyright Act intended. Moreover, such a regime was buoyed by prevailing norms at the time, which resisted the urge to consecrate "great works" as immutable and eschewed creative hierarchies. But all of that would change over the next century and a half. The morphing of copyright law began, most centrally, with Justice Joseph Story's 1841 decision in *Folsom v. Marsh*,[68] which gave us the modern fair use doctrine. The betrayal of the Framer's conception of copyright protection, as realized through the widespread implementation of the fair use doctrine, is the subject of our next examination.

III. Et Tu, Fair Use? Natural Law Redux

The radical change in the theoretical underpinnings of our federal copyright system began with Justice Story's decision in *Folsom v. Marsh* in 1841. With *Folsom*, the traditional emphasis on transformative use withered as courts began to focus on natural-law factors that had long been rejected by the Framers and in the courts' early applications of copyright law. This sharp change in the underlying rationale for copyright protection continues to have a profound and unappreciated influence to this day.

A. *FOLSON V. MARSH*: JUSTICE STORY AND THE BETRAYAL OF UTILITARIAN COPYRIGHT

The *Folsom v. Marsh*[69] decision of course marks the origin of the fair use test. Although the author of the decision did not specifically bandy about the term, the opinion is the first to set out the modern balancing test for fair use analysis.[70] Celebrated by many observers as a triumphant victory for the public domain,[71] *Folsom* achieves nothing of the sort. Quite to the contrary, *Folsom* represents a fundamental betrayal of almost a century and a half of copyright law and a re-embracing of the monopolistic, natural-rights-based vision of copyright rejected by the Constitution, the Framers, and the jurisprudence of the time. For this reason, at least one scholar has hailed *Folsom* as the worst intellectual property decision ever.[72] Unfortunately, it is also the most-cited case in copyright law and the foundation of modern copyright jurisprudence.

As L. Ray Patterson notes, two prevalent myths surround the *Folsom* decision. First, commentators claim *Folsom* created fair use. Instead, it merely redefined what constituted infringement.[73] Second, *Folsom* is viewed as having diminished the rights of copyright holders. Rather, Patterson argues "the case enlarged those rights beyond what arguably Congress could do in light of the limitations on its copyright power and, indeed, fair use today continues to be an engine for expanding the copyright monopoly."[74] Far from creating fair use and carving a hole into the copyright monopoly, Justice Story's decision in *Folsom* transformed copyright law and expanded its monopoly. As Patterson argues, Story accomplished this coup by categorizing copyright as a subset of property law grounded in natural rights instead of a subset of public domain law characterized by a limited statutory monopoly:

> Since the law of which copyright is a subset is the source of copyright rules, the choice has important consequences. Whether copyright is a statutory monopoly or a proprietary right is significant for both copyright owners and users of copyrighted material. The former concept provides greater, the latter less, leeway for use by others.[75]

The tenor and logic, rather than the actual (and probably rightful) outcome, of *Folsom* is most salient. In the case, plaintiffs argued the Reverend Charles Upham's 866-page, two-volume *The Life of Washington*, which lifted 255 pages directly from Jared Sparks's former work, infringed Sparks's 6763-page, twelve-volume *The Writings of George Washington*, a collection of Washington's official and private papers with additional narrative and editorial notes.[76] Justice Story of the U.S. Supreme Court, acting in his capacity as a Circuit Court Judge, heard the case.

Story's bent is clear from the outset of the opinion, when he immediately emphasized Sparks's work "has been accomplished at great expense and labor, and after great intellectual efforts, and the very patient and comprehensive researches, both at home and abroad."[77] Therefore, only a few lines into the decision, the court begins to appeal to a sweat-of-the-brow logic that would award the plaintiff strong property rights for his efforts in creating the work at issue. This emphasis comes at the expense of considering what value the defendant's use of the work might reap for society. Indeed, such a focus represents a radical departure from prior jurisprudence, especially as reflected in the translation and abridgement cases discussed earlier.

Story's legal analysis shows little regard for the potential benefit dissemination of the allegedly infringing work may have for society. In fact, he readily admitted the value of the defendant's work to society: with his "very meritorious labors"[78] in this "great undertaking,"[79] Story conceded the defendant had "produced an exceedingly valuable book."[80] However, the admitted value of the defendant's work had little bearing on his analysis or decision. Rather, Story likened the act of borrowing to an act of stealing—a clear violation of property rights. To any potential borrower or "free rider," Story sternly warned, "None are entitled to save themselves trouble and expense, by availing themselves, for their own profit, of other men's works, still entitled to the protection of copyright."[81]

In many ways, Story's natural-law vision of copyright, which harkened back to the view of the Stationers' Company and William Blackstone, was not entirely surprising. After all, Story was known to be a disciple of Blackstone. Indeed, his three-volume series of *Commentaries on the Constitution and the United States* quoted so many passages from Blackstone's own *Commentaries* that, as Hannibal Travis has quipped, "he may have been liable for infringement."[82] With a Blackstonian theory of copyright guiding his opinion, both the potentially transformative use by the defendant and the benefit to public were of little import—a stark contrast to and departure from the translation and abridgement jurisprudence of the time.

Story's property-based analysis became more pronounced further along in the decision. Adopting strong natural-rights language, Story maintained "the entirety of the copyright is the property of the author; and it is no defense, that another person has appropriated a part, and not the whole, of any property."[83] With these words, Story explicitly expanded copyright protection to prevent filching of parts of a work rather than just the

FIGURE 2.1 The Honorable Joseph Story, Judicial Activist?

slavish duplication of an entire work. However, this alone is not necessarily a dangerous, or even inappropriate, position: it is the next step in Story's logic that is particularly pernicious. With a quick stroke of his pen, Justice Story presumed that an act of borrowing, either in whole or in part (to the tiniest bit), constituted an act of infringement. After all, to Story, the borrowing party usurped control of someone else's property. Borrowing could still be excused, but only if it did not amount to conversion—if, in fact, the borrowing was de minimis and did not affect the value of the property taken. Thus, under *Folsom*, a court might *excuse* the act of borrowing if the defendant effectively proffers a defense of fair use.

In numerous respects, this is a striking reversal of prior copyright jurisprudence. Previously, courts viewed acts of borrowing (if they were sufficiently transformative) as simply *noninfringing* uses. In other words, the burden of persuasion lay with the copyright holder to demonstrate the work was both infringing and *not transformative*. Under *Folsom* and its progeny, once the copyright holder made a prima facie showing the alleged infringer had borrowed the protected work, the burden shifted to the alleged infringer to demonstrate the use was excusable.

Second, a showing of transformative use no longer constituted a legitimate defense to an infringement claim. Instead, the transformative use of a copyrighted work would become, at best, one of several criteria used in determining whether a defendant proffered a proper fair use defense. According to Story, to determine fair use, courts should look "to the nature and objects of the selections made, the quantity and value of the materials used, and the degree in which the use may prejudice the sale, or diminish the profits, or supersede the objects, of the original work."[84] The factors enumerated by

Justice Story are now enshrined in section 107 of the Copyright Act, which calls on courts to use a four-part balancing test to resolve fair use issues. In the words of the Copyright Act, the (nonexclusive) factors include:

(1) the purpose and character of the use, including whether such use is of a commercial nature or is for nonprofit educational purposes;
(2) the nature of the copyrighted work;
(3) the amount and substantiality of the portion used in relation to the copyrighted work as a whole; and
(4) the effect of the use upon the potential market for and value of the copyrighted work. [85]

Grounded in a natural-rights vision of copyright, Justice Story's fair use test advances a Lockean imperative, seeking to protect an original work's value by emphasizing what an alleged infringer took from it. It does so at the expense of a more utilitarian calculus that would consider, above all, the output generated from the act of borrowing.

Thus, the paramount purpose of an infringement action became the assurance of the rights of authors in the commercial value of their intellectual labors, not the balancing of a fair return on intellectual creations with the public's right to make transformative uses of them and to advance the arts. Indeed, three of the four fair use factors now codified in the Copyright Act—factors two ("The nature of the copyrighted work"),[86] three ("the amount and substantiality of the portion used in relation to the copyrighted work as a whole"),[87] and four ("the effect of the use upon the potential market for and value of the copyrighted work")[88]—focus on what a potential infringer is taking from a copyright owner rather than on the use made with the copyrighted work. All told, fair use introduced natural-rights-based protections explicitly into the judicial calculus on infringement. As I discuss later, these considerations were vital to the outcome of copyright disputes because they altered the fundamental nature of the infringement equation.

Moreover, a disingenuous air permeates Justice Story's opinion. Justice Story was on the Supreme Court at the time of the *Wheaton* decision; yet, *Folsom* utterly ignores *Wheaton* and chooses instead to rewrite the law of copyright. Patterson observes:

> Since the two theories—natural law and statutory monopoly—were fully argued and considered in *Wheaton* when Story was a member of the Court, he must have been familiar with them and conscious of the fact that the Court had rejected the natural-law theory in favor of the statutory monopoly theory. Against this background, one is justified in concluding that Story's use of natural-law copyright ideas in deciding *Folsom* is a classic case of intellectual dishonesty, and that the *Wheaton* case was one of his targets.[89]

However, Patterson may slightly overstate his case here. After all, Story's shifts in the infringement calculus were subtle. Moreover, after 1841, courts were totally free to ignore *Folsom* and follow *Wheaton* as well as the previous translation and abridgement cases. But, significantly, subsequent courts *did not ignore Folsom*, and *Folsom* laid the groundwork for a fundamental change in infringement analysis. With its embrace of a natural-law, property-rights vision of intellectual property and its development of a fair use test based thereon, *Folsom* marked a basic reversal in copyright jurisprudence through its reinterpretation of the infringement test. In fact, instead of limiting the scope of the copyright monopoly, the fair use test expanded the property rights of copyright holders, thereby frustrating copyright's utilitarian goals.

Significantly, Justice Story's revised formulation of the infringement test and his fair use criteria in *Folsom* did not emerge from thin air. Rather, Story's prior jurisprudence in the copyright arena reflected a recurring interest in providing strong property protection to authors under a natural-law framework. For example, in *Gray v. Russell*,[90] a case involving infringement claims over the abridgement of a Latin grammar book, Story took the key step of announcing the prior rule excusing abridgements as noninfringement "must be received with many qualifications."[91] Story "clarified" that, in determining whether an abridgement constitutes a bona fide use of an existing work rather than an infringement, one must examine the value of the selections made and the probable effect on the market for the original work.[92] In so doing, Story focused the infringement calculus on what a defendant had taken from the original work, not on the defendant's use of that work— thereby demonstrating not only his lack of discomfort with unilaterally overturning existing precedent but foreshadowing the fair use test he would announce in *Folsom*. It was on the basis of these criteria that, in the end, he found the contested grammar book—which another court may well have characterized as a protected abridgement— to be infringing.

Similarly, in *Emerson v. Davies*,[93] his first major infringement opinion following *Folsom*, Story further developed his natural-law vision of copyright. In *Emerson*, Story resolved a dispute over the alleged infringement of a map. Acknowledging the existing state of law, Story conceded that he "who by his own skill, judgment and labor, writes a new work, and does not merely copy that of another, is entitled to a copy-right therein; if the variations are not merely formal and shadowy, from existing works."[94] However, just as he did in *Folsom* and *Gray*, he acknowledged the existing law with one hand while altering it with the other. By broadly defining which variations were merely "formal and shadowy," Story was able to find the defendant's work to be infringing despite the rhetoric of his previous proclamation. In the end, his decision profoundly strengthened the rights of copyright owners in largely factual works (such as maps)—and did so on Lockean grounds: "A man has a right to the copy-right of a map of a state or country, which he has surveyed or caused to be compiled from existing materials, at his own expense, or skill, or labor, or money."[95] With his rulings in *Folsom*, *Gray*, and *Emerson*, Justice Story paved the way for a radical alteration in the modern copyright infringement inquiry.

B. THE HEGEMONY OF NATURAL-LAW COPYRIGHT: *FOLSOM* AND ITS PROGENY

All told, the rulings of Justice Story unleashed a steady morphing of copyright law that would fully take shape in the twentieth century. According to Hannibal Travis, copyright law has transformed along two axes during the past 150 years.[96] First, the definition of copyright infringement expanded from merely proscribing unauthorized duplication of a copyrighted work to forbidding literal copying of small fragments of a work. This trend began with *Folsom v. Marsh*, which found infringement in the borrowing of only a portion of a work and, according to Travis, perhaps reached its apex in *Harper & Row*.[97]

Second, copyright protection expanded from protecting the literal language of a work to nonliteral elements such as characters and scenes.[98] As did Justice Story in *Folsom*, judges have rationalized each step of the expansion by appealing to the need to safeguard authors' natural rights to the fruit of their intellectual labors.

The two axes Travis identified can really be characterized as one significant mutation in copyright law: the focus in the infringement test has shifted from the product created by the allegedly infringing use to the original copyrighted work itself. This shift in focus eventually led to the reversal of both the abridgement and translation rules. As our previous discussion revealed, abridgement and translation were noninfringing acts precisely because of their transformative quality. However, with the diminished importance of transformative use and the development of a fair use test largely based on natural-law criteria, abridgement and translation activities became infringing actions not excused by fair use. First, such uses inherently drew too greatly (both in terms of quantity and value) on original copyrighted works. Second, such uses had the ability to destroy the market for the original work and, more importantly, its derivatives.

Consequently, in 1870 Congress overturned the *Stowe* decision by statute,[99] explicitly adding the right to translate one's work to the list of exclusive rights guaranteed to a copyright owner.[100] In addition, the protection afforded to abridgement and commentary has shrunk markedly over the past century, particularly in recent years, despite the enunciation of an explicit fair use test in the 1976 Copyright Act.[101] In short, abridgement is no longer considered a noninfringing act—or even fair use.[102]

Besides the overturning of the abridgement and translation rules, the unwitting hegemony of the property rights vision of copyright has been reflected in numerous other trends. Historically, the courts and Congress have grounded the rationale for the Copyright Clause in the discourse of use/access, not production rights. However, with the notable exception of the rejection of the Lockean sweat-of-the-brow theory by the U.S. Supreme Court in *Feist*,[103] natural rights continue to taint the copyright equation and increasingly dominate the direction of intellectual property laws.

First, in recent decades, the rhetoric of copyright law has changed. For example, in both academia and practice, we now talk about the field of *intellectual property*. The use of the term (clearly grounded in a discourse of *property*) is a recent phenomenon;[104] in fact, use of the term in its current meaning can only be traced to 1967.[105] Moreover, as Mark Lemley has persuasively demonstrated, courts are increasingly foregoing detailed analyses of intellectual property cases. Instead, courts decide copyright disputes based on "earthy moralisms"[106] grounded in a natural-rights discourse that inevitably favors plaintiffs.[107] The knee-jerk equating of any unauthorized use of a copyrighted work with an act of theft is a prime example.

In recent years, copyright doctrine has also expanded well beyond the point at which enhanced protection provides authors with greater incentives to create or publish their works.[108] For example, it is far from clear how retroactive expansion of copyright terms under the Copyright Term Extension Act (CTEA)[109] encourages more creativity from artists and benefits the public.[110] However, the CTEA and the endless string of copyright term extensions that preceded it are entirely consistent with a natural-law vision of copyright that grants authors an inherent property right in the fruits of their intellectual labors.

Similarly, through the years Congress has expanded derivative rights significantly. Under the 1831 Copyright Act (as with the 1790 Copyright Act and the Statute of Anne before it), a copyright holder only possessed "the sole right and liberty of printing, reprinting, publishing, and vending" a work.[111] In 1870, Congress added the right to dramatize or translate one's work to the list of exclusive rights of copyright holders.[112] The 1909 Act went even further, securing such derivative rights as novelization and musicalization for copyright holders.[113] Finally, the 1976 Act gave authors the exclusive right to prepare all derivatives of their copyrighted works[114] and provided an expansive definition of what constituted a derivative work.[115]

Derivative rights appear much more justifiable on natural-law rather than utilitarian grounds.[116] As Stewart Sterk notes, the argument that derivative rights are necessary to help authors recover their costs is a weak one,[117] as such situations are exceedingly rare.[118] As a consequence, it is not surprising that even derivative-rights advocates such as William Landes and Richard Posner reject this justification.[119] Moreover, two other justifications Landes and Posner offer—that derivative rights prevent delays in production while authors simultaneously produce derivative works, and that derivative rights reduce transaction costs by placing the copyright of the original work and any derivative rights in one person—are similarly untenable. As Sterk points out, the first justification can work both ways: derivative protections may actually result in delayed production of the derivative works by an author in order to increase sales of the original.[120] The second justification is also specious as the legal unavailability of derivative rights reduces transaction costs just as effectively.[121]

Moreover, as applied to individual authors, the existence of derivative rights may actually serve to stifle artistic progress. Given that people at the upper echelons of wealth often face backward-bending labor supply curves, it could be argued that copyright itself harms the rate of output by those creators of content deemed most valuable by society.[122] On utilitarian grounds, therefore, we may not want to reward the biggest sellers in the content-creation community quite so much, lest they become lazy, bloated rockers. For example, in the 1950s and 1960s, top music acts such as Elvis Presley and the Beatles routinely released at least one album per year. In those days, creators of copyrighted content received far lower rates of return on their creative output. With the advent of greater intellectual property enforcement, improved opportunities for licensing of derivative and original rights, and superior contract negotiations by content creators, artists such as Bruce Springsteen and U2 release a new album only once every few years, if that often.

However, derivative rights are entirely consistent with a natural-law vision of copyright, which maintains authors should have exclusive control over any works derived from their intellectual creations. Indeed, as derivative rights expanded, courts no longer gave great weight to the transformative value of the alleged infringing works in copyright cases.[123] Instead, so long as a plaintiff demonstrated the defendant appropriated the work, the courts' infringement inquiries emphasized protection of the commercial value of original works.

The jurisprudential basis for derivative rights is particularly revealing. In *Daly v. Palmer*,[124] the first derivative rights case in American jurisprudence, a New York court found Dion Boucicault's play, *After Dark*, infringed Augustin Daly's play, *Under the Gaslight*. Specifically, Daly claimed a copyright in the now all-too familiar "Railroad Scene," wherein an evil character ties someone to a railroad track, thereby putting that person at risk of imminent death. However, just before a train appears and disaster strikes, a hero leaps onto the scene to conduct a valiant recue.[125] Extensively citing Justice Story's rulings in *Folsom*, *Gray*, and *Emerson*, the *Daly* court issued an injunction preventing defendants from publicly performing any version of the Railroad Scene. The justification for such equitable relief was particularly significant. As the court rationalized, a dramatic work based on a copyrighted play constitutes a piracy

> if the appropriated series of events, when represented on the stage, although performed by new and different characters, using different language, is recognized by the spectator, through any of the senses to which the representation is addressed, as conveying substantially the same impressions to, and exciting the same emotions in, the mind, in the same sequence or order.[126]

With these words, *Daly* conferred copyright in nonliteral elements. Thus, mere copying of a part or the whole of a work no longer would be the sole acts constituting infringement. Rather, an infringement finding could result from a transformative use of a copyrighted work where the underlying nonliteral elements of the work were still recognizable. Therefore, derivative rights were not so much about encouraging progress in the arts as they were about protecting the natural property rights authors had in both the literal and nonliteral elements ascribed to their creation.

FIGURE 2.2 The Famous Damsel-in-Distress Twist on *Daly*'s "Railroad Scene"—"Mabel, Sweet & Lovely" and the "Villainous Rival" in *Barney Oldfield's Race for a Life* (1913).

With the derivative rights doctrine in place, the ability to make transformative use of copyrighted works was significantly curtailed. At the same time, changing norms matched the changing state of the law. The works of Shakespeare—veritably a celebrated part of popular culture—became a consecrated element of elite culture, celebrated only in their single "authentic" form that could not be modified or reinterpreted. Notes Levin, "By the turn of the century Shakespeare has been converted from a popular playwright whose dramas were the property of those who flocked to see them, into a sacred author who had to be protected from ignorant audiences and overbearing actors threatening the integrity of his creations."[127] For example, unlike the days of yore when transformations, abridgements, and adaptations of Shakespeare were encouraged, "actors were admonished not to take liberties with the text of a Shakespearean play."[128] The malleable, populist Shakespeare gave way to an embalmed, sacred version characterized by inviolability.

The transformation in Shakespeare during the late eighteenth century was not unique. Similar changes occurred in opera, symphonic music, and the fine arts as they joined the ranks of elite culture.[129] The remixing of Shakespeare, opera, and symphonic music—accepted practice in the nineteenth century—had become verboten. Copyright law had ushered in the notion of sacred texts. While norms depressed efforts to bastardize the "authentic" language, plots, characters, and themes of Shakespeare's works, copyright law emerged as a leading force in protecting works from rampant popular manipulation and reinterpretation.[130] The aura of works was patrolled and protected, in large part, by making derivative works the sole province of a copyright holder. The appeal of this sacralizing impulse stemmed from natural-law rationales. The fetishized quest for authenticity served to protect authors' inherent interest in the integrity of their artistic vision, no matter what the consequences to progress in the arts. Ultimately, the modern infringement calculus and the fair use doctrine help make this triumph of natural-law copyright possible.

IV. Transformative Use and Progress in the Arts

Despite rhetoric to the contrary, modern courts have largely eviscerated transformative use and progress in the arts from the infringement calculus. An examination of contemporary jurisprudence in two particular arenas—digital sampling and satire—demonstrates the degree to which courts have come to embrace an unadulterated, natural-law vision of copyright at the expense of the utilitarian rationale. In particular, Justice Story's fair use doctrine continues to drive this sharp disjuncture from the original basis for copyright protection.

A. THE IMPORTANCE OF TRANSFORMATIVE USE

As Marcel Duchamp pointed out at the beginning of the last century, and as postmodern artists such as Negativland have argued at the beginning of this century, "the act of selection can be a form of inspiration as original and significant as any other."[131] Consider dadism and surrealism—two of the leading art movements of the past hundred years. Although the dadaists and surrealists rarely discussed copyright per se, their core ideas were imbued with their relationship to the concept of intellectual property. Specifically, they rejected notions of originality and authorial genius and challenged the rights of exclusion that might go with such constructs. As the enigmatic and self-styled Comte de Lautréamont, a leading influence on the surrealists, argued, "Plagiarism is necessary. It is implied in the idea of progress. It clasps the author's sentence tight, uses his expressions, eliminates a false idea, replaces it with the right idea."[132] On this basis, Lautréamont freely "borrowed" from the works of Pascal, Kant, La Fontaine, and others in making his own. As Anna Nimus observes, Lautréamont's view "subverted the myth of individual creativity, which was used to justify property relations in the name of progress when it actually impeded progress by privatizing culture. The natural response was to reappropriate culture as a sphere of collective production without acknowledging artificial enclosures of authorship."[133] Thus, Lautréamont's mantra "became a benchmark for the 20th century avant-gardes. Dada rejected originality and portrayed all artistic production as recycling and reassembling—from Duchamp's ready-mades, to Tzara's rule for making poems from cut-up newspapers, to the photomontages of Hoech, Hausmann and Heartfield."[134]

With their ready-mades, collages, photomontages, assemblages, and automatic drawings, the dadaists, surrealists, and others members of the avant-garde fervently challenged the sanctity of sacred texts, freely creating unauthorized derivative works in defiance of social norms. For example, Marcel Duchamp's infamous *L.H.O.O.Q.* performed the ultimate sacrilege by mutilating Leonardo da Vinci's hallowed *Mona Lisa* by giving her a moustache, goatee, and tawdry new title.[135] Duchamp's own masterpiece, the ready-made *Fountain*, utterly annihilated the distinction between highbrow and lowbrow by bringing the urinal to the museum.[136] More recently, pop artists such as Andy Warhol and appropriationist artists such as Barbara Kruger have carried on the tradition of making transformative use of protected preexisting materials and sacred personalities and images.

The impact of these appropriationist works often resonates far beyond just artistic circles. Consider the remarkable influence of artist Shepard Fairey's *HOPE* poster, which framed the popular view of Barack Obama in the public imagination and served as perhaps the most critical and enduring image of the 2008 presidential campaign. Dubbed by *New Yorker* art critical Peter Schjeldalhl as "the most efficacious American political illustration since 'Uncle Sam Wants You,'"[137] the poster was a stylized reconstruction and reinterpretation of a snapshot taken of Barack Obama at the National Press Club in 2006 by Associated Press photographer Mannie Garcia. After the AP claimed Fairley had created an unauthorized

FIGURE 2.3 *L.H.O.O.Q.*, Marcel Duchamp's Tribute to the *Mona Lisa*.

derivative work based on its copyrighted photograph, the parties ended up in infringement litigation in federal court just shortly after the election.[138] As we shall see, based on
the available precedent, the AP has good reason to think it could win the suit. And with
the rise of digital technology and potential for new forms of appropriation (and new
forms of art based upon the act of appropriation), the dangers of modern infringement
jurisprudence are even more significant. Digital technology has enabled a world of new
transformative uses in the arts likely to remain unexploited due to copyright's limitations on derivative works.

In its current guise, copyright law threatens public dissemination of these transformative, progressive, instructive, and enlightening uses. The infringement and fair use tests
(delineated in *Folsom* and adopted by the courts and Congress over the past 150 years)
come dangerously close to an unadulterated embrace of a natural right in intellectual creation—and they do so at the expense of the utilitarian rationale for copyright. The modern notion of copyright infringement operates from the premise that substantial
similarity and illicit copying form a prima facie case for infringement, which can then be
refuted by a defendant, who (bearing the burden of persuasion) offers a successful fair
use defense. But such a gestalt ignores the origin[139] of copyright as a privilege that is
bestowed through legislative act and that serves utilitarian purposes. Indeed, in the
modern copyright calculus, little room remains for considering transformative use and
progress in the arts.

Consider, for example, the issue of music sampling. In 1991, a federal court in
New York confronted the novel legal questions raised by the practice when Raymond
"Gilbert" O'Sullivan sued rapper Biz Markie and his label, Warner Brothers, for unlaw-
fully sampling "Alone Again (Naturally)," a song written and recorded by O'Sullivan.[140]

FIGURE 2.4 Mannie Garcia's
Photograph of Barack Obama.

FIGURE 2.5 *HOPE*, Shepard Fairley's
Rendering of Barack Obama.

In issuing the first reported decision on the legality of sampling, the court demonstrated how the modern infringement test (with its embrace of a property-based view of copyright) largely ignores the question of progress in the arts.

In its rather brief opinion in *Grand Upright Music, Ltd. v. Warner Brothers Records, Inc.*, the court resolved the matter by quoting Exodus and sophistically equating the eighth commandment with the law of copyright. "Thou shalt not steal,"[141] the court tersely warned, thereby completing its simplistic, property-based analysis. The matter to the court was apparently quite straightforward: Biz Markie had taken something from O'Sullivan without authorization. As such, he was a thief and liable for damages. Yet the court's reductionist logic leaped over a fundamental and far-from-settled threshold question: whether the actions of the defendants were really akin to stealing. After all, the law censures the act of stealing precisely because it makes plaintiffs worse off while making defendants better off by depriving plaintiffs of the use of their property. By contrast, the act of digital sampling does no such thing—copyright owners can still use their work in any way they choose even after someone else has digitally sampled it.[142] Yet the court's decision in *Grand Upright Music* laid the framework for legal resolution of the sampling conundrum. More recently, a federal circuit court addressing the same question left God out of the equation but remained equally blunt when it cautioned "get a license or do not sample."[143] In the process, the court held that any unauthorized sample of a sound recording, no matter how small, constituted copyright infringement.[144]

Thus, courts have made it clear that the practice of digital sampling, used frequently in hip-hop and increasingly in other modern genres, requires the permission of a sound recording's copyright owner in just about any instance. Depending on the quantity of the material copied, a sampler may also need to request permission from the musical work's copyright owner.[145] However, in denying fair use to digital samplers, courts have not considered the impact of their decisions on progress in the arts, despite its comtemplation in the Constitution. Moreover, the digital sampling cases have epitomized how hegemonic the natural-rights vision of copyright has become. Sampling helps to create a new work—one that possibly advances the arts. In most digital sampling cases, the allegedly infringing use actually makes a plaintiff better off economically by generating increased exposure for commercially (though not critically) passé artists such as P-Funk/Parliament/Funkadelic, Rick James, the Isley Brothers, and James Brown.

Yet despite this fact, sampling without a license almost invariably constitutes an act of infringement. When viewed in both comparative and historical contexts, this is a striking result. One certainly possesses some level of fair use rights to quote poetry and prose without authorization in the process of writing one's own literary work. By the same token, one could argue music sampling is nothing more than "quoting" portions of the music of others—making reference, if you will—in the process of creating one's own compositions and sound recordings. Yet the rulings on digital sampling effectively have foreclosed the ability to quote music at all. Meanwhile, the rulings in the digital sampling cases stand in sharp contrast to the copyright jurisprudence of the nineteenth century. In *Stowe v. Thomas*, for example, a court found no infringement from the act of translation, even where the defendants happily conceded their allegedly infringing work had obliterated the plaintiff's market for her translated work.[146] A century and a half later, in the *MP3.com* case a court held that even if the MP3.com website had improved the market for a copyright owner's work, there could be no fair use.[147] As modern fair use cases

FIGURE 2.6 Thou Shalt Not Infringe.

demonstrate, copyright is increasingly protected like real property and viewed as so inviolable a plaintiff need not even show real damages to recover on a theory of trespass.[148]

B. FAIR USE'S FAILURE TO PROMOTE PROGRESS IN THE ARTS

The fair use doctrine has played a central role in the move toward a natural-law-based protection of copyright. As the preceding analysis of *Folsom* revealed, fair use is a resoundingly natural-rights-based doctrine that subverts the utilitarian logic of copyright protection under the U.S. Constitution. Ray Patterson notes:

If copyright is a statutory monopoly, fair use should be viewed as a limitation on the monopoly in the public interest, which means that it is an affirmative right, not excused infringement. The paradox is that while U.S. copyright is a statutory monopoly copyright, fair use is treated as a natural law right to protect that monopoly.[149]

As an examination of relevant jurisprudence reveals, a multitude of transformative uses that advance progress in the arts cannot survive the modern fair use test.

To begin with, transformative quality constitutes only a meager fraction of the fair use test, playing a role in only one of the section 107 factors—"the purpose and character of the use."[150] Admittedly, on a rhetorical level transformative use has grown increasingly important in the fair use calculus. In *Campbell v. Acuff-Rose*,[151] the Supreme Court extensively cited and adopted the reasoning in Judge Pierre Leval's influential article, *Toward a Fair Use Standard*,[152] wherein Leval advocated making transformative use the focus of the first factor of the fair use test.[153] As the Court held, the "central purpose" of its inquiry into the character and purpose of an allegedly infringing work should be to determine whether the work is "transformative."[154] However, such findings have not been sufficient to meaningfully reestablish transformative use as part of the infringement calculus.

To the extent transformation has infiltrated infringement jurisprudence in recent years, it has done so under a limited definition of transformation. As Rebecca Tushnet notes, fair use has consistently favored criticism and parody over other transformative uses.[155] Thus, with the exception of parody, cases have repeatedly demonstrated that the slightest appropriation of a copyrighted work will result in a finding of infringement, even when the use is transformative and the result receives critical acclaim.[156]

On this point, *Rogers v. Koons*[157] is instructive. Celebrated artist Jeff Koons[158] found inspiration in a cheap postcard he saw in a tourist shop. The postcard, *Puppies* by Art Rogers, featured a photograph of a couple and some puppies, posing in Rockwellian tranquility, embodying the quintessence of the American ideal. Koons appropriated the kitschy depiction of the couple and the puppies and accentuated various elements of the photography in order to create a work that served as a satire of suburban American aesthetic sensibilities. As Koons's attorney, Martin Garbus, eloquently explained:

[Koons] saw sentimentality, inanity and kitsch. When he blew up the image to larger than life size, stuck daisies in the hair of the sickly sweet smiling couple (the flowers were not in the photograph) and painted the finished ceramic, the sculpture acquired a horrific quality quite distinct from the original.[159]

This explanation of Koons's transformative use of the work was no ex post facto rationalization. Indeed, it was utterly consistent with Koons's artistic and philosophical leanings, as illustrated by his body of work. However, despite Koons's critical use of the *Puppies* photo to satirize suburban American aesthetic sensibilities, the court found no fair use and no transformative use. As the *Koons* court reasoned:

It is the rule in this Circuit that though the satire need not be only of the copied work and may . . . also be a parody of modern society, the copied work must be, at least in part, an object of the parody, otherwise there would be no need to conjure up the original work.[160]

The rulings of the Second and Ninth Circuits govern the copyright creation meccas of New York and Los Angeles respectively. So, it is particularly significant the Ninth Circuit has concurred with the logic of *Koons*.[161]

Such a limited view of what constitutes transformative use is not surprising given the Supreme Court's guidance in *Campbell v. Acuff-Rose*.[162] In *Campbell*, the Court offered a broad definition that allegedly categorized works as transformative if they did not "merely 'supersede the objects' of the original creation" but "instead add[] something new, with a further purpose or different character, altering the first with new expression, meaning, or message."[163] Observers have either hailed[164] or criticized[165] this move as a dramatic reinvigoration of transformative use in the infringement calculus. However, *Campbell* achieved no such thing. Significantly, the Court retreated as to its own definition of transformation by restricting fair use to parodies (i.e., by not allowing it for other transformative uses).[166] As the Court rationalized:

> For the purposes of copyright law, the nub of definitions, and the heart of any parodist's claim to quote from existing material, is the use of some elements of a prior author's composition to create a new one that, at least in part, comments on that author's works. If, on the contrary, the commentary has no critical bearing on the substance or style of the original composition, which the alleged infringer merely uses to get attention to avoid the drudgery in working up something fresh, the claim to fairness in borrowing from another's work diminishes accordingly (if it does not vanish). . . . Parody needs to mimic an original to make its point . . . whereas satire can stand on its own two feet.[167]

Thus, to the extent an appropriationist's work does not directly criticize the original, the "claim to fairness in borrowing from another's work diminishes accordingly."[168]

The Supreme Court's distinction between satire and parody in the application of the fair use test is ultimately unsatisfying. Such a formulation reduces fair use to a test about *necessity*. Thus, where use is necessary to produce a form of speech (parody), it will be reluctantly tolerated as fair. But, where use is unnecessary to produce a form of speech (satire), it will not be tolerated.[169] Such a conceptualization of fair use is highly propertized, allowing borrowing only when conditions *require* it. Such a view casts fair use as a privilege, not a right—a stark contrast to the former view of copyright itself as a privilege rather than a natural right. Under a utilitarian vision of copyright, progress in the arts rather than a necessity calculus should drive the fair use doctrine. As a consequence, there is no inherent reason why satire should be subject to different fair use rights than parody.

In fact, if one subscribed to Ernest Hemingway's views on the matter, parody should receive no special protection (and certainly no more than satire). Hemingway vehemently denied the transformative or productive value of parody. "The parody is the last refuge of the frustrated writer," he decreed. "Parodies are what you write when you are associate editor of the Harvard Lampoon. The greater the work of literature, the easier the parody. The step up from writing parodies is writing on the walls above the urinal."[170]

Whatever one's feeling about parody, it is important to note an individual need not address the original work itself (as in parody) to make "transformative" use of it. As many appropriationist artists have demonstrated, something new, expressive, and meaningful can emerge from the combination or alteration of copyrighted works of the past.[171] However, under the modern copyright infringement test and its fair use provisions, absent licensing, those engaged in appropriationist art and transformative uses of existing copyrighted works will risk sizeable liability.[172] An examination of the most salient jurisprudence following *Campbell* is illustrative.

In *Paramount Pictures Corp. v. Carol Publishing Group*,[173] the owners of the *Star Trek* copyright sued the publishers of *The Joy of Trek* (a guide to all things *Star Trek*), which included brief descriptions of plots, major characters, technologies, and alien races in the series, famous lines from the series, and accounts of the Trekkie movement. In holding the book infringed on the *Star Trek* copyright, the court found no transformative use, noting the book was not a parody:[174] "Asides such as [various quips] do not sufficiently transform a summary that the book's own cover admits is 'everything a Star Trek novice needs to know.'"[175] But such a statement reveals confusion about the notion of transformation. As Michael Bunker argues:

> [*The Joy of Trek*] borrowed certain factual elements from the *Star Trek* story line and cosmology and combined those with humor, commentary, comic sociological analysis and other transformative elements. It seems fairly clear that a work dealing with, among other things, the idiosyncrasies of *Star Trek* fans and humorous interpretations of the television show's plots and cosmology adds at least some new message and meaning to the original story, [and, therefore, constitutes transformative use.][176]

However, the fact *The Joy of Trek* did not constitute parody doomed its creators to losing the first factor of the fair use test[177]—and ultimately the case.

Such a restrictive notion of transformative use also determined the decision in another key copyright decision. In the *Dr. Seuss* case,[178] a satire of the O.J. Simpson murder trial based on Dr. Seuss's *Cat in the Hat* failed the fair use test. In considering the issue, the court found the use was non-transformative and that there was market harm.[179] On the first factor of the fair use inquiry, the court virtually equated transformative use with parody; as the court reasoned, because the book did not meet the definition of parody, it could not constitute transformative use.[180] As noted earlier, this syllogistic logic is specious, because it ignores the fact that satirical works can be highly transformative, advance progress in the arts, and implicate free expression rights.[181] On the fourth factor, the court inferred market damage from its conclusion that the work was non-transformative,[182] therefore compounding its error. Such a finding, even absent evidence on this point,[183] is patently silly. The notion that the *Cat in the Hat* copyright owners were contemplating entering the market for satires of the O.J. Simpson trial does not survive the laughter test. Nevertheless, the appeals court affirmed a preliminary injunction against publication of the book.[184]

Additionally, even where courts have heralded the importance of transformative use and adopted a broad definition of transformation that includes nonparodic uses, the other elements of the fair use test have limited the ability of transformative users to escape liability for copyright infringement. Consequently, the rhetoric supporting transformative use in the infringement calculus is frequently mere lip service. For example, a federal court in New York acknowledged that a book of trivia about the *Seinfeld* television series was a transformative use for the purposes of the fair use test.[185] As the court noted, the *Seinfeld Aptitude Test* (*SAT*) met the Supreme Court's transformation test as enunciated in *Campbell*: "By testing *Seinfeld* devotees on their facility at recalling seemingly random plot elements from various of the show's episodes, defendants have 'added something new' to *Seinfeld,* and have created a work of a 'different character' from the program."[186] In so holding, the court repeatedly emphasized the importance of transformative use in the fair use balancing equation.[187] However, the court's palaver regarding the importance of transformative use, which the court later called "generous,"[188] ultimately rang hollow. The court noted the expansive and exclusive right to create derivative works granted under the Copyright Act, then rejected the defendant's fair use test and found infringement.[189]

Two points in the court's analysis are particularly salient. First, the court found that "without *Seinfeld*, there can be no SAT" and, as such, determined the third element of the fair use test (amount of borrowing) strongly favored the plaintiff.[190] However, such reasoning renders the purported importance of transformative use utterly null. After all, *no transformative use can ever exist without the original work.* Secondly, the court found the fourth element of the fair use test, market harm,[191] also strongly favored the plaintiff. As the court reasoned, although the transformative *SAT* did not hurt the demand for the *Seinfeld* television program, it harmed the market for derivative works such as trivia books the copyright owners of *Seinfeld* might want to publish.

Once again, such logic crushes any hope for transformative users to receive the protection of the fair use doctrine. Because the inquiry for market harm "must extend to the potential market for as yet nonexistent derivative works,"[192] virtually any transformative use will harm the potential market for as yet nonexistent derivative works, particularly under the expansive definition of derivative works adopted by the Copyright Act and the courts. The *SAT* may or may not have constituted a transformative work; however, the court's approach to and analysis of that question presupposed an answer in the negative. Thus, even where transformative use is considered and its prominence in the first factor is acknowledged, courts' typical readings of the other fair use factors (as illustrated by *Castle Rock*) render the importance of transformative use null.[193]

The logic of *Castle Rock* has continued to resonate with courts. When J.K. Rowling and Warner Brothers sued the publisher of *The Lexicon*—an encyclopedic guide to all things relevant to the *Harry Potter* universe—for creating an unauthorized derivative work, a New York district court rejected the publisher's fair use defense.[194] Although the court acknowledged that *The Lexicon* was transformative (though not consistently so), by "occasionally" offering "'new information, new aesthetics, new insights and understandings'. . . as to the themes and characters in the *Harry Potter* works,"[195] the critical reference source failed to qualify as fair use because it took "too much original expression"[196] from the plaintiff's works. It also caused market harm, not just to the two existing companion works Rowling already had on the market but future works because it "would impair the market for derivative works that Rowling is entitled or likely to license."[197]

At the same time, the other portion of the first part of the fair use test (which determines whether a use is commercial)[198] also undermines the impact that transformation has in the fair use calculus. Courts repeatedly bog themselves down in determining whether a use is commercial or noncommercial. Finding a meaningful and consistent definition of commercial use has proved an elusive goal. For example, as we saw in Chapter One, courts have deemed unauthorized activities to be commercial so long as users are not paying the "customary price" for the copyrighted works they receive.[199] But such a definition of commercial use is entirely tautological. After all, if an unauthorized, uncompensated exploitation of work is excused by the fair use doctrine, the "customary price" being paid is not one that is required. The notion of the "customary price" is also problematic because it is typically interpreted as the price being imposed by the plaintiffs in the suit on the defendants. In short, fair use always causes some loss in potential revenue to someone. To the extent market harm is an appropriate consideration, it is already covered by the fourth factor in the fair use test and need not be redundantly considered in the first factor as well. Similarly, courts have found the free distribution of infringing copies of a work is commercial if, in some way, the distributor ultimately "profits" from its actions.[200] Ultimately, such a definition of commercial threatens to render all unpaid exploitations of copyrighted works "commercial" in nature.

All told, most transformative-use defenses stand little chance of success under the current infringement test, despite the influence of Judge Leval and the Supreme Court's rhetoric in *Campbell*. As a natural-rights vision has firmly taken hold of modern copyright law, this result is not surprising. The dominant role of fair use in the protection of authors' natural rights is best illustrated by the Supreme Court's declaration in recent years that the fourth factor of the fair use test—"the effect of the use upon the potential market for or value of the copyrighted work"[201]—is the most important.[202] This assertion is somewhat curious when one considers the explicit congressional guidance given in 1976 that the fair use factors be balanced together.[203] Presumably, if Congress had intended to make one factor in the fair use test more important than any other, it would have said so. Nevertheless, the Court has deemed the economic harm caused by a potentially infringing use of a copyrighted work to be paramount in ascertaining whether use of a copyrighted work is fair.[204] However, such a reading of fair use, especially under the expansive notions of market harm espoused by modern courts, is anathema to the utilitarian origins of copyright.

After all, before considering a fair use defense, a court has to make a finding of infringement. It accomplishes this by determining substantial similarity between the original copyrighted work and the use. Unfortunately, substantial similarity itself becomes a proxy for the fourth factor. The more similar the two works, the more likely it is the secondary use will subvert the commercial market for the copyrighted work. Thus, by considering the issue of market harm in the fair use test (and particularly by elevating market harm to the highest level in that test), a court is largely duplicating a task already accomplished when it considers the threshold requirement of substantial similarity. However, the placement of the fourth factor at the forefront of fair use is entirely consistent with the natural-law vision of copyright, which seeks to protect authors' property rights in their works even if this clashes with the advancement of the arts. The increasing natural-law bent of copyright certainly has strengthened the ability of copyright owners to profit from their creations. But under the current fair use test, modern copyright law has proscribed most transformative uses at a great price to progress in the arts.

Simply consider how far we have come from the *Stowe* case. A century and a half ago, courts heralded the unauthorized translation of a work as a valuable transformative act that spread knowledge and learning to new audiences and indubitably promoted progress in the arts. Today, by sharp contrast, unauthorized translations can land you in prison. For example, in 2009 Professor Horacio Potel of the Universidad Nacional de Lanús in Argentina faced criminal charges for engaging in the unauthorized translation of several works by renowned postmodern theorist Jacques Derrida. Potel had posted the translations on his website so that his students could read the works—most of which were out of print or had never been translated.[205] The translations were the results of decades of work by Potel, who offered them free of charge to visitors of his nonprofit site. Yet none of this stopped Argentinian authorities from pressing forward with a criminal case against him, and he subsequently faced a prison term ranging from one month to six years.[206]

C. BORROWING AND PROGRESS IN THE ARTS: "SMELLS LIKE TEEN SPIRIT"

Critics of the modern copyright system frequently point to the fact that many of Shakespeare's greatest works would never have been written if Elizabethan England had embraced our stringent notion of authorial protection. Shakespeare, they argue, could not have existed under the modern copyright regime.[207] The point is a fair one: the modern notion of plagiarism did not exist in Elizabethan times,[208] when imitation (though not mere "servile imitation") was truly considered the greatest form of flattery. However, the analysis does not need to be confined to the Elizabethan era to demonstrate the negative impact a strict notion of copyright protection has on progress in the arts. A more current example poignantly highlights just how much creativity and development in the arts we may be missing as a consequence of the expansive ambit of our modern copyright paradigm. Take, for example, the band Nirvana and their 1991 hit song, "Smells Like Teen Spirit,"[209] arguably the most important and critically lauded musical work of the past few decades.

With its syncopated rhythm and charged lyrics that constituted a scathing indictment of pop culture, the mass media, and cliquish society, the song played a critical role in altering the landscape of modern music. The work was nothing short of "progress in the arts," as deserving as any song of copyright protection and widespread dissemination. Yet, for all of its lyrical and musical originality, the song may never have been released to the public had it not been for a peculiar series of circumstances that allowed Nirvana to eschew copyright infringement litigation. A little background to the inspiration of the song sheds light on this point. The lyrics to "Smells Like Teen Spirit" are, depending on one's perspective, either inspired by or plagiarized from Thomas Pynchon's acclaimed novel, *Gravity's Rainbow*.[210] Indeed, the similarities are eerie.

In a section of *Gravity's Rainbow*, one of Pynchon's characters hums a whimsical ditty, inspired by the spirits of teenage woman: "Ah, they do bother him, these free women in their teens/their spirits are so contagious."[211] From these words by Pynchon (and, it should be noted, the name of a deodorant noxiously marketed by Mennon and often advertised on MTV to teens of the era), the title of Nirvana's "Smells Like Teen Spirit" was born. Moreover, the actual lyrics found in *Gravity's Rainbow* are strikingly similar to those of "Smells Like Teen Spirit."

The chorus to Pynchon's song, replete with textualized intonations adopted by Nirvana, reads:

> I'll tell you it's just -out, -ray, -juss
> Spirit is so -con, -tay, -juss
> Nobody knows their a-ges [212]

With a similar rhyme scheme, phrasing, and syncopation, the chorus to "Smells Like Teen Spirit" reads:

> With the lights out it's less dangerous
> Here we are now
> Entertain us
> I feel stupid and contagious
> Here we are now
> Entertain us [213]

The rejoinder to Pynchon's song utters the phrase *nevermind* repeatedly, reading:

> Nev –ver, –mind, watcha hear from your car
> Take a lookit just –how –keen –they are,
> Nev –ver, –mind, –what, your calendar say,
> Ev-rybody's nine months old today! Hey [214]

Meanwhile, the album on which "Smells Like Teen Spirit" resides is entitled *Nevermind*, and that phrase is mentioned in the song as Kurt Cobain repeatedly sings "well, whatever, nevermind. . . ." Moreover, the rejoinder to "Smells Like Teen Spirit" invokes a similar intonation and pattern:

> A mulatto
> An albino
> A mosquito
> My libido
> Yeah, hey, yay [215]

Thus, in appropriating and transforming Pynchon's lyrics, Nirvana took a course of action that could have subjected the group to a cognizable copyright infringement suit. The unique and unusual phrasing in the *Gravity's Rainbow* lyrics as well as their intonations certainly would be enough to raise an inference of remarkable similarity and borrowing. This is particularly true in light of recent decisions that have upheld the viability of an infringement action based entirely on a theory of subconscious filching—the precise result when a federal court found George Harrison liable for plagiarizing The Chiffons' perky hit "He's So Fine" with his somber and reflective ballad "My Sweet Lord."[216] Moreover, a court would likely find no fair use under the modern balancing test. As a commercial and non-parodic use, "Smells Like Teen Spirit" would decidedly lose the first factor. Because Pynchon's song was a creative and original work, the second factor would also go against Nirvana. The lifting of significant lyrics and the unusual and unique syncopated rhythm of Pynchon's song would weigh the third factor against Nirvana. Finally, a court would likely infer economic harm as Nirvana would be occupying the market for setting Pynchon's copyrighted song to music. All told, Nirvana would, at the very least, face a serious infringement suit for creating an unauthorized derivative work.

However, a unique series of circumstances enabled Nirvana to appropriate Pynchon's lyrics with little regard for the legal consequences. Pynchon is an infamous recluse and as unlikely as anyone to pursue an infringement suit.[217] Such an action would be far too public for a man who assiduously has averted efforts by the media to track him down. In fact, until some recent stalking of Pynchon,[218] no picture of him had been published since his high school yearbook photo from a half-century ago.[219] Just to avoid a brush with publicity, Pynchon once defenestrated from an apartment when a reporter tracked him down in Mexico City.[220] His desire to avoid publicity is so great that, instead of personally accepting the prestigious National Book Award in 1974, he sent a stand-up comic. In fact, in his entire career (which has spanned over four decades), Pynchon has never granted an interview.

Thus, the idea of Pynchon testifying in court, appearing for depositions, or engaging in any kind of public appearance is unthinkable. Nirvana could consequently borrow without threat of a suit, which, if waged, might have prevented Nirvana from ever writing and releasing "Smells Like Teen Spirit." At the very least, the threat of a plausible suit would have discouraged a garage band from Seattle, Washington, and its record label from taking a chance at bankrupting litigation.

The Nirvana example illustrates the social benefits from the reiterative process of works building upon one another. However, under the modern infringement regime, such a reiterative process cannot occur. Because most copyright owners are not Thomas Pynchon, transformative works will not enter the public sphere without permission from and payment to rightsholders. Such a system ultimately deprives the public of progress in the arts.

D. THE PERMISSION PROBLEM: THE ENDOWMENT AND ENTITLEMENT EFFECTS

Requiring copyright holders to approve transformative uses is particularly problematic when one considers some of the exacerbating effects

FIGURE 2.7 One of the Few Known Photographs of Thomas Pynchon (Age 18 at the Navy's Bainbridge, Maryland Training Center).

that result from the unilateral right to exclusion that our copyright regime grants. In recent years, psychologists and economists have observed that the subjective valuation an individual will give a particular object increases significantly when the individual possesses that object, even for a limited time.[221] As a consequence of this "endowment" effect, individuals will "demand much more to give up an object than they are willing to spend to acquire it."[222] Although not without its critics,[223] this result appears to subvert neoclassical economic theory, which assumes an individual's willingness to pay (WTP) for a good should equal the willingness to accept (WTA) compensation for the loss of the good. In a now-classic experiment, Kahneman, Knetsch, and Thaler found randomly assigned buyers valued a particular mug at $3 on average.[224] By sharp contrast, randomly assigned owners of the very same mug required substantially more money ($7 on average) to part with it.[225] In short, the owners' loss in divesting themselves of the mug was valued at more than twice the buyers' gain in acquiring the exact same mug. Thus, under the endowment effect, most people appear to require a much higher price to part with a product to which they hold a legal entitlement (i.e., through possession or ownership) than they would pay to purchase the very same product.

In copyright, the endowment effect is especially pronounced and dangerous. First, the tendency toward overvaluing endowed goods is amplified when measurements of value are more subjective. Second, holdout problems are especially likely due to the lack of fungibility that characterizes most valuable creative works. Third, the steady accretion of rights granted to copyright holders over time has buttressed the *endowment* effect with a veritable *entitlement* effect.

In categories of goods characterized by notoriously subjective valuation metrics, the endowment effect can wreak particular havoc. As a result, there is strong reason to believe the endowment effect may be particularly pronounced with intangible property such as copyrights. Valuation of copyrighted content is significantly more difficult than that of ordinary goods. Each copyrighted work is inherently unique—a fact courts readily concede when they assume inherent irreparable harm for the infringement of any copyright.[226] Because a particular copyrighted work has no perfect economic substitute, it is non-fungible, unlike many physical goods. While oil, D-RAM chips, and oranges all have clear going-market rates, the value of the copyright to a painting by a celebrated avant-garde artist is much more difficult to peg.

Additionally, where permission of a copyright holder may be required for a project to reach fruition, the endowment effect can create a holdout problem of severe magnitude. Psychologist Sven Vanneste and legal academic Ben Depoorter have conducted experimental work suggesting rightsholders to a property necessary for the success of a venture—no matter how small that property's contribution—will tend to demand the entire value of the venture as a permission fee. This leads to what James Surowiecki and others have billed as the permission problem.[227] And the impact is not merely the stifling of creative rights of scholars, critics, satirists, and others: as the endowment effect raises the price otherwise demanded for access to a copyrighted work, "members of society do not enjoy the increased access to art that the copyright law is designed to provide."[228]

Finally, as we have recounted, the duration and scope of rights granted to copyright holders has steadily increased over the past century. For example, the repeated enactment of term extensions has left rightsholders unable to envision a day when their works will actually fall out of copyright. A work created in 1923 had an initial copyright term lasting until 1951; with proper renewal, the work would receive protection until 1979 at best. However, as a result of amendments to the Copyright Act, the same work will not fall into the public domain until 2019 at the earliest. And, a new round of lobbying efforts for a term extension will no doubt begin shortly. Meanwhile, norms on use and permission have grown increasingly restrictive. Such solicitude to the interests of rightsholders has only served to generate a sense of entitlement (i.e., an entitlement effect) that bolsters the endowment effect.

For example, in recent years, the heirs to numerous copyright-rich estates have illustrated the depths of these holdout problems. In the 2000s, James Joyce scholarship began to disappear from academia as a result of the aggressive tactics of Stephen Joyce, the author's grandson.[229] This Joyce heir, who controls the literary giant's copyrights, has taken the position that virtually any use of his grandfather's works (including quotation for academic works) constitutes an infringement requiring permission and payment. As *The New Yorker* has noted, Stephen's view is absolute: "If you want to write about James Joyce and plan to quote more than a few short passages, you need Stephen's consent."[230] In turning down a use request from a Purdue scholar, Joyce exclaimed that he found the name of the school's sports teams—the Boilermakers—to be vulgar.[231] Another scholar, Michael Groden of University of Western Ontario, spent seven years developing a multimedia version of *Ulysses* only to be blocked by Stephen, who was upset with him for showering praise on an edition of *Ulysses* Stephen disdained. In response, Stephen simply gave Groden the following advice: "You should consider a new career as a garbage collector in New York City, because you'll never quote a Joyce text again."[232] And Stephen Joyce is not alone, as many scholars have bemoaned.[233]

As a result, there is strong reason to believe the endowment effect can frustrate many economically desirable licensing transactions in the copyright arena.[234] Holdout problems can stifle creative activity, thereby harming the public good and inhibiting the advancement of the arts. As the principal defense to the unauthorized use of copyrighted works, the contours of the fair use doctrine therefore take on heightened importance when both the endowment and entitlement effects threaten to undermine the economic efficiency of licensing markets for copyrighted works.

V. From Fair Use to Fared Use

All told, our examination of fair use in a historical context reveals that, far from championing the right of the public to access creative works, the fair use doctrine has played a key role in the problematic expansion of the copyright monopoly. As a means to incorporate First Amendment and public-access concerns into copyright law, the fair use test has failed. And, as our analysis has shown, the doctrine's origins help explain why. Quite simply, the fair use doctrine has transformed the federal copyright regime from a utilitarian system of compensation—a carefully delimited quid pro quo for a benefit granted to society—into a natural-law right to which authors are entitled for their creative efforts. Such a vision of copyright not only betrays the intentions of the Framers, it comes at a great price to expressive rights and progress in the arts—thereby undermining the important role of the individual as a transformer of copyrighted works. At the same time, the increasingly natural-law bent of copyright has also had a profound impact on basic issues of identity formation and expression. This latter issue, explored through the prism of the individual as user, is the subject of the next chapter.

3

THE INDIVIDUAL AS CONSUMER

In which we contemplate hot rods, the meaning of jeans, the neurological imprints of music, crowd-sourcing prayer, the poisonous tomato, Bono's car, the ancient Library of Alexandria, innumeracy in the Amazon, flag burning as copyright infringement, a long-lost silent cinematic masterpiece, Alcoholics Anonymous, and the smell of rotting film

IN THE LAST CHAPTER, we explored the fundamental alteration of our copyright regime over the past two centuries and the resulting impact of these changes on the original goal of the system: progress in the arts. Specifically, we highlighted how the increasingly radical shift toward a natural-law conception of copyright, especially as achieved through the creation and development of the fair use doctrine, has resulted in a significant narrowing of the right to make transformative uses of creative works. These uses—coming in such guises as commentary, criticism, satire, and parody—are themselves accretive to progress in the arts. With such uses suppressed, the public good suffers. In emphasizing the importance of protecting transformative uses, however, one risks overlooking the critical value of other ways in which copyrighted works can be utilized. Thus, in this chapter, we turn our attention from the individual as a transformer of copyrighted works to the individual as a pure consumer of copyrighted works.

As philosopher Ludwig Wittgenstein once posited, "the limits of my language mean the limits of my world."[2] Copyright law circumscribes our linguistic and artistic palettes by subjecting entire wings of Jorge Luis Borges' metaphoric *Library of Babel*[3] to monopolization and by restricting the reproduction and manipulation of cultural content. In the following pages, we highlight the critical role that copyrighted works play in personal development by tracing how our relationship with intellectual property impacts both the formation and expression of our identities. In the process, we critique the insufficient weight traditionally given to the personhood interests of copyright consumers and assess the growing threat to these interests posed by both technical and legal changes.

As Liu has argued, although copyright law has a rather developed theory of the author, it lacks a coherent theory of the consumer.[4] To date, copyright law has typically viewed the consumer[5] either as a passive receiver of copyrighted content or an active creator of new content from old.[6] However, in recent years, scholarship has begun to move beyond this narrow binary. Liu, for example, has challenged this bifurcation by emphasizing the important interests consumers possess in the use of copyrighted works for advancement of autonomy (e.g., customizing the order in which you may play a CD or what scenes you might view in a movie),[7] communication (e.g., being able to talk about the latest episode of *The Office* or the new *Harry Potter* movie at the watercooler),[8] and self-expression (e.g., engaging in such acts of "mini-authorship" as creating a mix tape).[9] Meanwhile, Rebecca Tushnet asserts the right to engage in non-transformative copying is an important part of vindicating First Amendment values.[10] The ability (or inability) to reproduce a copyrighted work, even without authorization, can affect the right of individuals to participate in our culture and the body politic;[11] it can regulate access to certain forms of knowledge;[12] and it can impact the ability to ground one's expressive activities in a particular cultural context or meaning.[13] As the scholarship of Tushnet and Liu makes clear, it would be a mistake to fetishize transformative use while failing to recognize the social benefits of noncritical copying of creative works. Nevertheless, traditional copyright theory has long underappreciated the role intellectual property possession, use, and consumption—even of the non-transformative variety—play in mediating personal development and advancing identity interests.

The importance of fully accounting for consumer interests is especially warranted at this juncture given the growing complexity of the relationship between intellectual property and consumers. First, intellectual property has become increasingly decoupled from its physical moorings.[14] Second, mass consumption of intellectual property has increased.[15] Finally, and most importantly, technology has provided consumers with greater means of manipulating intellectual property and of customizing one's experiences with it.[16] These three conditions, in turn, have precipitated new techniques and mechanisms for the formation of identity, many of which are mediated (for better or worse) by intellectual property rights. After all, both the meaning and value of intellectual property occurs at the interface of production and consumption.

We begin by examining the place of the user in the intellectual underpinnings of our copyright regime and conducting an exegesis of the jurisprudence on copyright term extensions. In the process, we identify the utilitarian, labor-desert, and personhood theories at play in copyright policy. These theories of copyright protection have traditionally focused on the repercussions of intellectual property rules on creators while eschewing almost any analysis of the law's impact on its other significant subject: *consumers*. Seeking to remedy this critical oversight, we scrutinize the increasing use of personhood interests to call for expanded protection of authorial rights in copyrighted works and propose instead a Hegelian refutation of intellectual property maximalism.

Toward this end, we then examine how personhood interests develop through the interaction of individual users with property. After first discussing the role of consumption and customization of tangible goods in the development and actualization of personal identities—specifically, though the *formation* and *expression* of identity interests—we then assess the analogous process with the consumption and customization of intangible property and observe how the structure of our intellectual property laws regulate and restrict such interaction with cultural content. Thus, although a purchased pair of jeans can be ripped, dyed, bleached, acid-washed, or disfigured, the equivalent piece of intellectual property cannot be altered without violating intellectual property protections. As a consequence, intellectual property rights play a significant role in shaping the contours and processes of identity formation and expression, especially in a digital society.

The implications of this regime are significant; intellectual property laws can and do control access to some of our most important symbolic signifiers. They regulate the semiotic devices[17] fostering cultural reproduction and patrol the relationship between individuals and society. In that spirit, we present four case studies illustrating the impact of several specific doctrinal features of our intellectual property regime: the treatment of government works under copyright law; the notion of "authorship" that undergirds the copyright monopoly; the growing adoption of sui generis intellectual property rights beyond traditional boundaries; and the expanding duration of copyright protection. These case studies demonstrate how our intellectual property laws enable putative rightsholders to control individual use and invocation of national and international symbols, spiritual homilies, cultural heritage, and even basic language. Thus, specific features of our intellectual property regime regulate relationships between insiders and outsiders, mediate the development of cultural networks, and demarcate social strata, thereby playing a critical and underappreciated role in the formation and expression of identity.

Of course, features of our intellectual property regime do provide some implicit—if not explicit—protection for the personhood interests of users. Along with certain statutory exemptions from infringement and the application of the fair use doctrine, one of the most significant sources of this protection stems from the large measure of immunization the unauthorized possession and private use of copyrighted works have enjoyed historically. In this way, the law has supported the rights of users to obtain access to cultural content—a vital predicate for the vindication of identity interests. But, as we detail in the final portion of the chapter, technological and legal developments are posing a radical threat to the right to private use and possession of both authorized and unauthorized copies of copyrighted works. Specifically, the expansion of secondary liability theories, the nature of digital distribution, the enforcement of the anti-circumvention provisions of the Digital Millennium Copyright Act, and fundamental policy changes being considered as part of the multilateral Anti-Counterfeiting Trade Agreement have allowed government and putative rightsholders to invade the private sphere to regulate such previously protected activities as the sharing of family photo albums, the use of photocopied scholarly articles by students, and the enjoyment and study of motion pictures by cinephiles. In the process, we are squelching personal development and identity formation in contexts traditionally invisible to the gaze of the law. Thus, it is not simply traditional features of copyright—rationalized through theories of utilitarianism, labor-desert, and personhood that have typically focused on the relationship between copyright law and the author—that have given short shrift to user identity interests. Rather, technological and legal changes are increasingly undermining the access and use rights that consumers of copyrighted works have long enjoyed.

All told, we take a modest step toward identifying the personhood interests consumers possess in the use of creative content, examining the ways in which the law has failed to account fully for these interests, and providing a theoretical framework for their future consideration. Greater and more explicit consideration and protection of these consumer interests are particularly warranted in the copyright calculus since, in the twenty-first century, control of IP (intellectual property) has become essential to the control of IP (identity politics).

I. Locating Users in the Copyright Skein

A. UTILITARIAN, LABOR-DESERT, AND PERSONHOOD JUSTIFICATIONS FOR COPYRIGHT

To understand the place of the consumer in modern copyright jurisprudence, we must first examine the theoretical underpinnings of our copyright regime. To this end, we begin by identifying three dominant conceptions of copyright: utilitarian, labor-desert, and personhood. We then exemplify the application of these concepts in the debate over copyright term extensions. This analysis identifies how user interests—especially the complex and personal relationship consumers enjoy with copyrighted subject matter—have received insufficient consideration in the law.

As we saw in Chapter 2, the historical battle over copyright protection pitted adherents of two different theoretical frameworks against one another: utilitarianism and natural law.[18] The utilitarians emphasized copyright's role in providing individuals with the necessary economic incentives to encourage the production and dissemination of creative works. Generally speaking, utilitarians reluctantly tolerated the monopolistic nature of copyright to the extent it served the goal of promoting progress in the arts, and no further.[19] The utilitarians found the best expression for their vision of copyright in the instrumentalist language of the Copyright Clause of the Constitution and the original system of copyright established by the Founding Fathers with the Copyright Act of 1790.[20]

However, over the past century and a half, utilitarianism has gradually given way to a natural-law vision of copyright heavily influenced by the theories of John Locke[21] and William Blackstone.[22] Borne less of welfare maximization than labor-desert factors, this vision is grounded in the inherent rights of authors in the fruits of their labor and the Lockean premise that as every man has a property right in his body, "[t]he Labour of his Body, and the Work of his hands . . . are properly his."[23] As intellectual property is the labor of the mind, the labor-desert theory seeks to protect the natural-law right of authors to exert absolute Blackstonian dominion over creative works.[24] As documented in Chapter 2, this theory of copyright has played a profound role in shaping the development of our modern copyright regime, sometimes to the detriment of utilitarian concerns.

At the same time, a different type of natural-law theory—one based less on labor-desert than on the inherent personhood interests artists have in their work—has grown increasingly influential in recent years. Built on Hegelian insights[25] and epitomized by the work of Margaret Jane Radin,[26] the personhood framework focuses on the relationship between objects and identity interests. Starting with the premise "human individuality is inseparable from object relations of some kind,"[27] personhood theory promotes the strongest property rights where individuals have interwoven their identity with a good, almost metaphysically imbuing it with a part of themselves. While the Lockean theory of natural-law copyright emphasizes the need for strong property rights in creative works based on the intellectual labor put into those works, adherents to personhood theory believe in protecting authorial property rights on the grounds that the creative works of artists are an indissoluble and inseparable part of their soul, spirit, and vision. Over the years, this view has found its greatest expression in the laws of several European countries where so-called "moral rights" have protected (among other things) the rights of attribution and integrity.[28] Under this theory, artists possess an inalienable right to be associated (or not associated) with their artwork in accordance with their wishes. Further, creators possess the inalienable right to preserve the integrity of their artistic vision. As a result, owners of the physical piece of art cannot compromise the vision of the original artist through the unauthorized modification or mutilation of the work in question.[29]

B. COPYRIGHT THEORY AND THE DEBATE OVER TERM EXTENSIONS

One can identify the presence of all three theoretical strands—utilitarian, labor-desert, and personhood—in leading debates over copyright doctrine. Consider, for example, the controversy over copyright term extensions. In *Eldred v. Ashcroft*,[30] the Supreme Court heard and rejected a constitutional challenge to Congress's ability to extend all subsisting copyrights by a term of twenty years through the Sonny Bono Copyright Term Extension Act of 1998 (CTEA).[31] The different opinions issued by the Justices capture the theoretical undercurrents at play.

The majority opinion, crafted by Justice Ginsberg, draws upon labor-desert theory to reject the constitutional challenge.[32] In the appeal, plaintiff Eldred argued the CTEA violated the First Amendment because, among other things, it constituted a regulation of speech properly subject to heightened judicial scrutiny—scrutiny it could not withstand.[33] Following its lower court predecessors, the Court squarely rejected this proposition.[34] In a key passage from the majority decision, Justice Ginsberg posits "[t]he First Amendment securely protects the freedom to make—or decline to make— one's own speech; it bears less heavily when speakers assert the right to make *other people's speeches*."[35] With these words, Ginsberg denotes a bright-line between the constitutionally guaranteed right to make our "own speech" and the far more attenuated ability to borrow "other people's speeches." The notion one can separate speech into these two categories is readily in accord with a labor-desert vision of copyright, which implicitly recognizes this bifurcation. After all, proponents of labor-desert theory assume creative works emerge from an author's independent genius and are therefore rightfully granted strong copyright protection. In so doing, however, they either overlook or downplay the fact that many (if not all) creators borrow from the public domain or preexisting works and inevitably stand on the shoulders of giants.[36] Thus, Ginsberg relies upon a facile and problematic differentiation between one's own speech and the speech of others. She assumes authors create ex nihilo, drawing solely upon their own labors (and not the previous efforts of others) to produce their copyrighted works. In the view of the majority, therefore, authors are properly entitled to the fruits of their creative endeavors as those efforts are the product of their minds—and theirs alone.

In stark contrast, Justice Breyer's dissenting opinion in *Eldred* draws upon the utilitarian theory of copyright that ultimately leads him a very different conclusion.[37] To Breyer, the central query on the constitutionality of the CTEA is whether it meaningfully incentivizes increased creation and dissemination of copyrighted works. "[M]ost importantly," he writes, the CTEA's "practical effect is not to promote, but to inhibit, the progress of 'Science'—by which word the Framers meant learning or knowledge,"[38] a factor glossed over in Ginsberg's analysis. While Ginsberg focuses on the right of individuals to the just fruits of their labor, Breyer looks at the ability of copyright law to confer public benefits by advancing learning and the dissemination of knowledge.[39] At best, Breyer argues, the CTEA only fractionally increases the average author's incentive to create.[40] Moreover, it stifles the interests of "historians, scholars, teachers, writers, artists, database operators, and researchers of all kinds—those who want to make the past accessible for their own use or for that of others."[41] Overall, the CTEA imposes a high cost on the public by impeding the propagation of vast tracts of knowledge while providing little benefit to the public in the way of incentivizing the creation of new works. Thus, on utilitarian grounds, Breyer finds the CTEA constitutionally infirm.

Similarly, in *Eldred*'s other dissenting opinion, Justice Stevens questions the validity of the CTEA by drawing upon a utilitarian vision of intellectual property rights.[42] As he writes, "Neither the purpose of encouraging new inventions nor the overriding interest in advancing progress by adding knowledge to the public domain is served by retroactively increasing the inventor's compensation for a completed invention and frustrating the legitimate expectations of members of the public who want to make use of it in a free market. We have recognized that these twin purposes of encouraging new works and adding to the public domain apply to copyrights as well as patents."[43] To Stevens, the copyright calculus should eschew any singular desire to reward a creator's labor simply on the grounds of just desert.

Finally, strains of the personhood theory have also permeated the debate on copyright duration. Advocates of personhood interests ask whether a copyrighted work constitutes an extension of an author's own identity and, therefore, the extent to which control of the work is tantamount to control over one's own person.[44] This personhood trope is perhaps best epitomized by the changing contours of copyright terms. Prior to 1976, copyright duration was both finite and fixed, governed by absolute terms. Between the first Copyright Act in 1790 and the most recent revisions to the Copyright Act in 1976, the maximum copyright duration (i.e., the original term plus the renewal term) gradually expanded from twenty-eight to forty-two, and then to fifty-six years.[45] Since 1976, however, copyright terms have been pegged to an exogenous variable: the lifetime of the author plus fifty years under the 1976 Act, and lifetime of the author plus seventy years with the passage of the CTEA.[46] The underlying concept is simple: there is a link between the author's life, or physical existence, and the property right the author possesses in his or her creative output. Under the modern "lifetime-plus" heuristic, the intellectual property right is inextricably tied to an author's mortality. The duration of the author's life therefore determines the duration of the author's intellectual property rights.

Perhaps above all, personhood interests have played an especially strong role in guiding the public discourse over copyright. In particular, rightsholders and authors have appealed to such interests to rationalize the expansion and strengthening of protection and enforcement mechanisms by drawing upon a romanticized vision of authorship. Under this heuristic, authors are conceptualized as solitary geniuses whose mythic individual efforts result in the ex nihilo creation of original works—works that contain essential parts of the artists' personhood and being.[47] In recent years, this notion has fueled the expansion of moral rights in the United States through the broader reading of such existing laws as the Lanham Act[48] and the enactment of such new statutory protections as the Visual Artists Rights Act.[49] In recognizing these authorial identity interests, legislators and courts have legitimated copyright protectionism by elevating the mental labors of the author to "a privileged category of human enterprise."[50] In testimony before Congress and in advertisements pleading with the public not to engage in piracy, the face of copyright—the sympathetic artist or creator—breeds the perception among consumers that copyright infringement is a personally violative act—a veritable usurpation and mutilation of the author's identity.[51]

C. CONSIDERING USER INTERESTS AND RIGHTS

As the debate surrounding copyright term extensions reveals, intellectual property minimalists have typically seized upon the utilitarian theory to resist expansions in protection. As Jamie Boyle has noted, "Minimalists are used to fighting off covert sweat of the brow claims, concealed appeals to natural right and Hegelian notions of personality made manifest in expression—all deployed to argue that rights holders should have their legally protected interests expanded yet again. Against these rhetorics, they insist on both constitutional and economic grounds that the reason to extend intellectual property rights can only be the promotion of innovation."[52] Meanwhile, intellectual property maximalists have seized upon labor-desert and personhood theories to advocate greater protections. For example, Madhavi Sunder has observed a profound transformation in the underlying discourse legitimating intellectual property protections: where once they were rationalized as incentivizing production by providing exclusive control over intellectual creations, they are increasingly viewed as necessary to protect the identity interests of property owners.[53] Indeed, it is almost impossible to legitimize most recent intellectual property legislation on incentivization grounds alone.[54] As a result, the modern intellectual property regime is increasingly tethered to a theoretical framework bent on labor-desert and personhood protection—a framework that has been used to rationalize the increasing scope of intellectual property protections.

However, the debate between minimalists and maximalists is incomplete. The existing polemic, which typically pits labor-desert and personhood interests against utilitarian interests, does not and should not fully define the metes and bounds of the public policy discourse. Specifically, proponents of all three theories of copyright—utilitarian, labor-desert, and personhood—have typically emphasized the relationship of the intellectual property regime to the creator or owner of the intellectual property. By focusing on the impact of copyright on creators, however, the theories have given short shrift to the critical impact of our legal regime on consumers and users of intellectual property. For example, the utilitarian line emphasizes the impact of copyright law on *encouraging creation by artists,*[55] the labor-desert line focuses on properly *rewarding the independent genius of authors,*[56] and the personhood line recognizes the degree to which *authors imbue their works with a part of themselves.*[57] Yet consumers of intellectual property have strong, often underappreciated, identity interests in the intellectual property with which they interact.

In so arguing, we add to a nascent body of literature that focuses on developing copyright's theory of the consumer/user. Julie Cohen, who builds on the work of Tushnet and Liu, argues copyright law would benefit from greater consideration of the situated user—a user whose "patterns of consumption and the extent and direction of her own authorship will be shaped and continually reshaped by the artifacts, conventions, and institutions that make up her cultural environment."[58] To Cohen, the situated user, who is neither a passive consumer nor active transformer of existing copyrighted content, "engages cultural goods and artifacts found within the context of her culture through a variety of activities, ranging from consumption to creative play. The cumulative effect of these activities, and the unexpected cultural juxtapositions and interconnections that they both exploit and produce, yield what the copyright system names, and prizes, as 'progress.'"[59] Thus, as Cohen posits, consumption of copyrighted works can do as much to advance the ultimate goal of our copyright regime—progress—as does their creation. In a sense, therefore, Cohen provides a utilitarian justification for a greater emphasis on user rights in order to spark "intellectual and creative progress."[60] But consideration of users' rights does more than simply advance the traditional utilitarian goals of the copyright regime.

In the spirit of Wittgenstein's observation at the outset of this chapter, the scope of one's available semiotic palette inextricably impacts the process of self-definition. Copyright (and even trademark and patent laws) shape identity development through their regulation, propertization, and monopolization of cultural content. Specifically, the contours of our intellectual property regime privilege certain individuals and groups over others and intricately affect notions of belonging, political and social organization, expressive rights, and semiotic structures. In short, intellectual property laws lie at the heart of what Madhavi Sunder has observed as the "struggles over discursive power— the right to create, and control, cultural meanings."[61]

Drawing on the groundbreaking work of Sunder and others,[62] this chapter of the book advances a theory of intellectual property that recognizes the crucial link between identity formation/actualization and the legal regime governing the monopolization and control of cultural symbols and creative works. Specifically, the analysis builds on prior scholarship in identifying the interests that users possess in the consumption of intellectual property by casting these interests (and their suppression) against the comparatively wider breadth of rights that putative consumers of tangible property enjoy. In the process, the argument focuses on both the internal and external components of personhood actualization: the formation and expression of identity. These personhood interests serve as a powerful countervailing force against the prevailing narrative on personhood, which has typically focused on the identity interests of authors in their creative works. Thus, the analysis evokes the personhood trope as a means not to justify the strengthening of intellectual property rights but, rather, to at least question it.[63]

II. A Theory of Consumption and Communication: Comparing the Treatment of Identity Interests for Tangible and Intellectual Property

A. PROPERTY RIGHTS AND PERSONHOOD

Our analysis begins by considering the interplay between property rights and personhood, and the way in which intellectual property rules control and even restrict such relationships, often with underappreciated socio-structural consequences. In a modern capitalistic society, consumption—both private and conspicuous—represents an instrumental component in the process of identity development. The institution in which we have the closest semblance of universal democratic participation is not the franchise, but the marketplace. The majority of Americans may not exercise their political rights to vote at the polls biennially on election day, but we exercise our economic rights at the store (or cybershop) on a daily basis. And, through these myriad quotidian decisions, we cast our monetary votes by spending our dollars. These economic votes—cast as consumption decisions—are a central part of our individual definition.

As Hegel once observed, "The person has for its substantive end the right of placing its will in any and every thing, which thing is thereby mine; [and] because that thing has no such end in itself, its destiny and soul take on my will. [This constitutes] mankind's absolute right of appropriation over all things."[64] It is through this exercise of the individual will over material objects in the external world that personhood or identity—previously a nebulous, inchoate, and malleable concept—actualizes. To Hegel, individual definition comes into being from simultaneously differentiating oneself from one's physical environment, while maintaining relationships with parts of that environment.[65]

Thus, the actualization of personhood comes about through acts of consumption—our interaction with objects in the external world—and personhood interests manifest themselves through consumption in at least two ways: in the *formation* of personhood and in the *expression* of personhood. Formation of personhood takes place internally as an individual's identity is shaped through interaction with objects in the external world. Meanwhile, the expression of personhood occurs when the individual communicates some aspect of her (already formed) identity to others as a way of contextualizing herself, through her relationship with objects, within the broader community.

Individual consumption of property serves as a powerful tool for both identity formation and expression. This relationship becomes clear when one considers the interaction of individuals with their property. With respect to the formation and development of identity interests, Erving Goffman famously documented the critical role that the mere private possession of objects played as a mechanism for asylum patients to maintain a sense of self.[66] Indeed, property interests can arguably even advance the survival of individual identity. An empirical study on the lives of nursing home residents by psychologists Ellen Langer and Judith Rodin demonstrates the powerful impact that the exertion of control over property can have on individuals.[67] In the experiment, half of the studied residents were invited to select a plant and charged fully with both the right to the plant and the responsibility for its care.[68] As such, they exercised complete dominion over the plant.[69] The other half of the residents were "given" a plant, selected by others for them, and were limited in what they could do with that plant—responsibility for its care, for example, was left exclusively to the nursing staff and not the resident.[70] As such, they possessed only the weakest of property rights in "their" plant.[71] Among other things, the study and its follow-up research found that those residents who were given rights to and responsibility for the plants ultimately enjoyed significant health benefits and possessed one-half the mortality rate of those without such strong rights and responsibilities.[72]

With respect to the expression of identity interests, consider the ways in which individuals customize tangible goods to suit their particular "needs" and then consume these goods publicly. People customize their cars, tricking them out as hot rods or using them as vehicles for political expression, and astute car marketers have increasingly drawn upon the relational interface between a car and its driver to push product. Witness the success of Scion, Toyota's junior vehicle line. A lifestyle brand aimed at a young male demographic, Scions are sold as customizable cars with a plethora of options, all aimed toward enabling an owner to individualize the brand to match his lifestyle, values, and identity.[73] Scion has even encouraged interaction with the brand in such experimental events as "Scion Dashboard," a series of rave-like events in major American cities where cutting-edge artists and DJs interact with bystanders and render their own interpretations of the Scion brand with multimedia tools provided by the company.[74]

Similarly, people customize their clothing in multiple ways, to the point where a pair of pants communicates a wholly different message when it is merely hanging, uncustomized, in a store window than when it is worn, and customized, by an individual. Think of the myriad alterations of jeans—rolled, torn, frayed, faded, acid-washed, and bejeweled. Both the "look" and the symbolic meaning of the jeans transform radically when placed in a particular context or when worn in a particular way. For example, let them ride low and baggy for a "hip-hop" look that challenges dominant middle-class aesthetics.[75] Or don a pair of women's jeans, preferably skinny, for the male "indie-rock" look that challenges traditional gender divisions.[76]

In his landmark analysis of popular culture, John Fiske discusses the cultural semiotics of denim.[77] As a hallmark of the American West (and, as Fiske notes, "perhaps America's only contribution to the international fashion industry"),[78] jeans evoke the mythology of the frontier in our collective imagination, thereby embodying "not only the familiar [themes] of freedom, naturalness, toughness, and hard work (and hard leisure), but also progress and development and, above all, Americanness."[79] Worn by locals in more traditional societies, jeans can also connote resistance to authoritarianism and repression or embrace of Western decadence and youthful rebellion. Therefore, jeans and their various styles are laden with meaning.

One's "customization" of jeans is of particular salience. The contemporary trend of wearing "disfigured" jeans (i.e., jeans that are irregularly bleached, dyed, or torn) can be read as a distancing of oneself from, but not a complete rejection of, dominant American values. As Fiske reminds us, "The wearer of torn jeans is, after all, wearing jeans and not, for instance, . . . Buddhist-derived robes."[80] Thus, the "disfigured" jeans reveal a complex and contradictory relationship with mainstream mores. And such a tack is not surprising, as popular culture is frequently imbued with paradoxical tensions. Writes Fiske,

"Popular culture bears within it signs of power relations, traces of the forces of domination and subordination that are central to our social system and therefore to our social experience. Equally, it shows signs of resisting or evading these forces: popular culture contradicts itself . . . . So jeans can bear meanings of both community and individualism, of unisexuality and masculinity and femininity. This semiotic richness of jeans means that they cannot have a single defined meaning, but they are a resource bank of potential meanings."[81] On one hand, the universality of jeans in American life serves an important purpose: it allows us, in relevant social situations, to blend together and present the image of the mythic America without class differentiation. Dressed in jeans, we are all members of the working class sharing a core set of basic values. On the other hand, the customization of jeans supports notions of individuality. For example, the genteel mutilation of their traditional form subtly challenges and subverts some of our society's core values—including those related to gender divisions, notions of propriety and formality, racial and class lines, and aesthetic judgments.

All told, individuals negotiate their relationship with physical property in numerous ways each and every day as a basic mechanism of identity actualization, both in forming one's identity internally and in defining and expressing oneself to the outside world. And, they are given room to do so without running afoul of the law. After all, if you purchase a pair of jeans, it becomes a tangible piece of property that you own, and you can modify it to suit your tastes or cater to your expressive impulses. But with intellectual property, the acts of consumption, customization, and communication are fraught with potential legal liability, and they are directly restrained by the features of the copyright and trademark monopolies. As we shall see, the contours of our intellectual property regime therefore play a significant role in mediating the formation and expression of identities.

B. REGULATING CONSUMPTION, CUSTOMIZATION, AND CONTEXTUALIZATION: INTELLECTUAL PROPERTY LAW AND THE MEDIATION OF IDENTITY INTERESTS

Intellectual property laws directly mediate the vindication of formative and expressive identity interests. The modern copyright and trademark regimes do not allow individuals to manipulate and utilize intellectual property in the same way they can customize and contextualize their experience with physical property. Simply put, most customizations or contextualizations of intellectual property are considered potential violations of a copyright owner's exclusive rights under the Copyright Act[82] or a trademark owner's rights under the Lanham Act.[83] So, for example, by performing the equivalent of ripping holes in one's jeans (e.g., remixing a song or altering a brand name), a consumer of intellectual property runs afoul of a copyright holder's exclusive right to create derivative works or a trademark holder's right to prevent dilution. One can contextualize and communicate one's relationship with one's jeans by wearing them in public, but the equivalent act of publicly utilizing a copyrighted work would impinge on an author's exclusive right to control public displays and performances.[84] In twenty-first-century America, our relationship with intellectual property is an essential part of defining ourselves. And in an increasingly digital and virtual world, the semiotic value of intellectual property is just as significant as physical property, if not more so.

Our identity interests therefore can become intermingled with and wrapped up in a form of property to which we technically, and legally, possess no ownership rights.[85] As intellectual property laws control access to and manipulation of cultural content—books, art, architecture, photographic images, and music—this sacralization has profound epistemological consequences.

Although we develop relationships with our personal property, we do not do so with the remote physical property of others. The exclusive and rival nature of private physical property means that fans do not enjoy a relationship with Bono's car, house, or personal jet. But they do have a relationship with his melodies and lyrics, his persona and look—his intellectual property, which digital technology can readily disseminate to the four corners of the earth. We mix and interact with intellectual property precisely because of its nonexclusive nature and because ownership of it can be separated from ownership of the physical vessel through which it might be delivered. In fact, owners of intellectual property often encourage such mingling as it can serve to increase the market value of their intellectual property.[86] In the liner notes to R.E.M.'s greatest hits collection, *In Time*, guitarist Peter Buck echoes the sentiments of Michael Stipe and his other bandmates when he discusses the group's relationship to its hit song "Everybody Hurts": "This song doesn't really belong to us anymore; it belongs to everybody who has ever gotten solace from it."[87] Buck's statement is not just metaphoric, as music embeds itself in our neurological circuits. As philosopher Colin McGuinn writes, "Musical memory connects with our sense of self, since musical taste and experience are closely linked to personality and emotion. The music we remember is, without exaggeration, part of who we are."[88]

Intellectual property laws impact both the formation and expression of personhood. First, our intellectual property regime shapes identify formation by regulating access to and use of cultural content, thereby determining which creative works individuals can interact with and how they can interact with them. Without the ability to access and consume works, an individual's identity cannot be shaped by those works. To illustrate the effect that exposure to certain pieces of intellectual property can have on the development of the self, consider *The Lives of Others*—Florian Henckel von Donnersmarck's Academy Award-winning drama about life under the police state in East Germany.[89] In the film, Captain Gerd Wiesler, a stern Stasi bureaucrat living a Spartan, monastic existence and exhibiting an unwavering, joyless commitment to his work, is charged with spying on playwright Georg Dreyman, a suspected subversive.[90] Although he initially takes upon the assignment with his usual solemn sense of duty, Wiesler undergoes a fundamental and poignant transformation and begins to question, for the first time, his unsavory mission after coming upon Dreyman's volume of Bertolt Brecht's works and reading the poem *Remembrances of Marie A.*[91] His interaction with the poem reignites his sense of humanity and causes him to forgo his customary interrogation when a neighborhood child recounts a critical comment that his father had made about Stasi.[92] Wiesler's new found perspective then leads him to make a series of choices to protect Dreyman and his artist friends from Stasi—decisions that ultimately cost Wiesler his career.[93] The potential impact of art on one's character is not merely fodder for fiction. As it turns out, the auteur of *The Lives of Others* found thematic inspiration from the real world: one of the twentieth century's most significant political figure's relationship with art. In a famous anecdote, Maxim Gorky recounted Lenin's sentiments toward Beethoven's *Appassionata*:

> I know of nothing better than the *Appassionata* and could listen to it every day.... But I can't listen to music very often. It affects my nerves. I want to say sweet, silly things and pat the heads of people who, living in a filthy hell, can create such beauty.[94]

Intellectual property's role in developing the personhood of consumers is not limited to the internal formation of identity. By controlling the ability of individuals to exhibit or display publicly their use of cultural content, our intellectual property regime also impacts the way in which individuals can express personhood interests to the external world. As Kurt Vonnegut famously observed: "We are what we pretend to be . . . ."[95] Thus, the expressive use of cultural content before the public does not merely represent one interpretation of our identity, as framed for the outside world; rather, it arguably represents the reflection of our identity's very essence. Visible consumption of intellectual property also serves a vital semiotic purpose by communicating one's complex web of entanglements with social, cultural, political, and economic networks and by facilitating one's interaction with in the broader community. Without the ability to exhibit or display one's uses of certain works to the public, one cannot effectively communicate such contextualized relationships.

Indeed, as Jean Baudrillard posits, the primary function of products no longer lies in their use, but rather in their communicative status.[96] Although one may quibble with this assertion when considering products that provide basic sustenance (to the hungry, the primary function of a loaf of bread is still very much in its use as food), Baudrillard's point is particularly salient in richer societies and in the context of intellectual property. With trademarks, the process of branding and the act of conspicuous consumption communicates social status, exclusivity, and affiliation.[97] Meanwhile, users merge their own sense of self with the creative works that enjoy copyright protection and draw upon these works for expressive purposes, especially when seeking to couch their interests or activities within a particular cultural context. "All consumption is cultural," because, as sociologist Don Slater has argued, "in order to 'have a need' and act on it we must be able to interpret sensations, experiences, and situations and we must be able to make sense of (as well as transform) various objects, actions, resources in relation to those needs."[98] This act of making sense is necessarily grounded in a cultural context of shared meanings, for "when we meaningfully formulate our needs in relation to available resources, we draw on languages, values, rituals, habitats and so on that are social in nature, even when we individually contest, reject or reinterpret them."[99] Individuals define their relationship with and status in their social milieu—be it oppositional, harmonious, insider, or outsider—through their consumptive actions.

To illustrate the expressive personhood interests implicated with the use of intellectual property in the digital environment, witness the communication of identity on social networking sites such as MySpace.[100] Along with rival Facebook,[101] the site is one of the most popular destinations on the Internet, especially for the teenage and twenty-something crowd. The site allows individuals to create their own home web page on the MySpace system, then link their page to those of their other friends. By allowing individuals to customize their own web pages within the confines of the general parameters of the site's format, MySpace is a laboratory of identity formation and expression—an ideal place to contemplate the intersection of intellectual property and identity politics.

A typical MySpace user web page organizes itself along three different axes. First, individuals define themselves through their *physical property*—their resources—by noting their incomes—and their body—by providing information such as their body's size (height and weight), where it resides (geographical location), and what it ingests (drinking and smoking habits). Second, individuals define themselves through their *relationships* to other individuals and institutions (friends, schools, and social groups). Finally, individuals define themselves through *intellectual property* in several ways. Users describe their likes and dislikes (specifically, their favorite books, movies, television shows, and music). In other words, individuals define themselves through the *intellectual property they consume*. A taste for *The Daily Show* might signal liberalism, keen political awareness, fondness for irreverent humor, or a blue-state alignment. Meanwhile, an appreciation for *The O'Reilly Factor* might communicate conservatism, a strong interest in the culture wars, or a red-state alignment. Meanwhile, the profiles do not merely reference intellectual property; they often make active (and unauthorized) use of it. Users will frequently decorate their pages with wallpaper that reproduces (usually without permission) copyrighted works or trademarked logos, including celebrity photographs, works of art, and stylized band names. Users can also customize their site to stream a particular song when visitors arrive. The emo teen can play Death Cab for Cutie's "I Will Possess Your Heart," the audacious prom queen can blast Beyoncé's "Single Ladies (Put a Ring on It)," and the gangsta-wannabe can crank the latest rhymes from Flo Rida, all to the effect of creating a strong implied nexus between the song and the individual. They also decorate their pages with the trademarks of certain bands and brands in order to communicate social identity.[102] The Veblenian[103] references to and uses of intellectual property (i.e., its *conspicuous consumption*) on a MySpace page communicate important details about users' perceived relationships with the world, their self-image or desired portrait, and their links to certain social, cultural, or political identifiers, networks, and groups.

Finally, the divide between formative and expressive uses of intellectual property is by no means rigid or absolute. Interacting with cultural content can sometimes advance both types of identity interests. Consider basketball superstar LeBron James rapping loudly to Eminem's verse in Drake's *Forever*—a brash celebration of the self, indulgence, and conquest—during a timeout in an NBA game in early 2010.[104] James's team at the time, the Cleveland Cavaliers, held a slim 89–87 lead over the Los Angeles Lakers with a mere 23.4 seconds left in the fourth quarter. First, based on the timing of the use and its fervor, James's rapping of the song's lyrics may well have an internal impact on James by igniting his sense of competition and ego, filling him with confidence and pumping him up to join his team on the floor and lead them to victory—something he ultimately accomplished when the Cavaliers held on for the 93–87 win. Thus, the use of the song affected James, ultimately actualizing a part of his personality. Second, the song was expressive—it was done in public and communicated to the arena audience and millions who saw the game on television—thereby contextualizing LeBron within the global community of Eminem fans and those who relate to the particular messages of his songs.

All told, as these examples indicate, identity is a pastiche of the tangible, intangible, and relational that is frequently mediated by intellectual property. We construct our narrative plots by incorporating cultural signifiers, many of which constitute copyrighted content. In the process, we inevitably mingle elements of ourselves with the copyrighted works of others to create the mélange that represents self-definition in the twenty-first century. Yet, increasingly, the law regards our identities as unauthorized derivative works.

C. INTELLECTUAL PROPERTY AND IDENTITY POLITICS: FOUR CASE STUDIES

As we have seen, intellectual property laws negotiate identity formation by regulating the consumption of cultural content for personal development purposes. They also impact identity expression by controlling the public display or exhibition of cultural content for semiotic purposes. And, it is through the exertion of ownership rights that user interests in both identity formation and expression can be curtailed.

To illustrate this process, we turn to four case studies relating to four different doctrinal aspects of our intellectual property regime: the limited exemption of some federal, but not state or local, government works from copyright protection, the notion of "authorship" that triggers copyright protection, the expansion of *sui generis* protections beyond their traditional bounds (e.g., trademark infringement actionable without showings of consumer confusion), and the sizeable (and growing) duration of the copyright term. As our examples—which involve Old Glory and the Lone Star flag, "The Serenity Prayer," the term "Olympics," and the song "Kookaburra"—illustrate, such features of our intellectual property regime enable potential rightsholders to patrol uses of patriotic symbols, important religious works, our very language, and key aspects of our heritage. The exertion of such exclusive rights granted to putative authors of copyrightable subject matter can undermine the rights that individual users of these works have in the formation and expression of national, spiritual, sexual, and cultural identities. The regulation and control of access to intellectual property can impact one's relationship with one's community, one's country, and even one's God. IP (intellectual property) directly mediates IP (identity politics).

1. Patriotism, Cultural Patrimony, and Propertization of the American Flag

In our first example, we examine how features of our copyright regime enable the potential beatification of certain key cultural and political symbols, thereby protecting them from unwanted use and manipulation. This, in turn, impacts the rights that individuals have in identity expression.

Under federal law, some government works—but not all—are exempt from copyright protection. Specifically, section 105 of the Copyright Act dedicates the creative output of the *federal* government—but not that of the state or local governments—to the public domain.[105] Moreover, nothing prevents the federal government from holding copyright interests.[106] Specifically, the federal government can hold the rights in works that it did not author, but which are assigned to it.[107] Based on these features of the Copyright Act, it would be entirely possible for government entities to claim copyright protection in such works imbued with patriotic and symbolic meaning as flags. After all, assuming the apocryphal tale that Betsy Ross created Old Glory is true, she could have assigned her copyright to the government, which the Feds could then enforce for the duration of its term. In addition, each new version of the flag could potentially receive a new copyright.[108] For example, the newest version of the American flag, which features fifty stars for the fifty states, only came into being with the admission of Hawai'i to the

Union in 1959. As such, the current American flag could continue to enjoy copyright protection. Just as importantly, there is nothing preventing states or municipalities from protecting their flags or seals under federal copyright law.[109]

If either the federal government or the states began to enforce copyrights in flags, the consequences for individual rights, especially identity expression interests, could be dramatic. Pursuant to section 106(5) of the Copyright Act, the holder of the copyright to the flag could enjoy the exclusive right to control (among other things) its public display, especially if the government characterized all physical exchanges of the flag as licenses.[110] To fly the flag, one would need the express permission of the government. Disfavored displays of the flag or uses on clothing could trigger cease-and-desist letters that, unheeded, would lead to suits for injunctions and damages. The mere reproduction of the flag in association with unpopular causes could result in sizeable liability.[111] In sum, friends of the government would enjoy the right to raise the flag and honor our country at their whim while foes would do so at their legal peril. The ability to align oneself or one's organization with patriotic values would be determined by the rights-holder to Old Glory, the Lone Star flag, or Ka Hae Hawai'i. Thus, the exertion of copyright over the flag would lead to a means of controlling access to what is perhaps our most important national symbol.

Even if one gets past the public display issue by arguing fair use[112] or waiver by virtue of the government having designated a particular design as the national or state flag, the problematic relationship between intellectual property and our national symbol does not end. Under section 106(2) of the Copyright Act, copyright holders alone enjoy the privilege of creating derivative versions of their works.[113] As such, not only do the famous artistic interpretations of the American flag by Jasper Johns and others risk liability and interdiction, but something more unusual might occur: flag burning could even be banned.

Efforts to outlaw flag burning by direct statute have famously failed. In 1989, the Supreme Court deemed a Texas statute criminalizing the conflagration of the American flag as unconstitutional on First Amendment grounds.[114] A federal statute that operated similarly was struck down in 1992.[115] However, courts have shown little compunction about enforcing intellectual property laws, especially copyright, in the face of potential First Amendment problems. As the Supreme Court has argued, you may have a right to *your own* free speech, but not to make or use the speech (i.e., the copyrighted works) *of others*.[116] Indeed, one could argue the burning of a flag is the production of an unauthorized derivative work. The argument has had traction in other contexts. Several appellate courts have found taking a copyrighted work and permanently mounting it without the permission of a copyright holder can constitute the creation of an unauthorized derivative work in violation of 17 U.S.C. § 106(2).[117] Courts have similarly suggested the mutilation of a copyrighted work can constitute an act of infringement.[118] After all, the Copyright Act specifically excludes architectural works from this potential consequence of the derivative rights doctrine.[119] The existence of such an exemption for architectural works suggests that, for copyrightable subject matter outside of architecture, alteration, mutilation, or destruction might in fact give rise to the creation of a derivative work in violation of section 106(2). Given the tenor of recent intellectual property decisions,[120] it is not unfathomable a court might dismiss any free-speech implications by arguing

© 2007 Will Denney

FIGURE 3.1 Putting an End
to Such Regrettable Fashion
Choices: the Best Argument
for Enforcing Copyright in the
American Flag.

copyright law, as a neutral law of general application, does not target speech for content, and that, if one wants to destroy a flag, one is free to create and destroy one's own flag with a different design. As such, it is not too far afield to inquire whether the scenario recounted above might arise upon the burning of the Lone Star flag, for example. The state of Texas could very well copyright its flag and proceed to regulate the use of the flag in the manner in which any intellectual property rightsholder restricts use of its creative output.

The control copyright law might provide over such symbols as a flag illustrates its ability to mediate meaning, identity, and relationships. Indeed, command of important patriotic, humanistic, and cultural symbols is regularly achieved through intellectual property law, thereby impacting notions of Americanness, patrolling insider–outsider boundaries within mainstream society, and limiting expressive activities that are central to the development of one's identity. Just as subtle differences in the way individuals wear their jeans can situate their complex relationship with American ideals and mainstream mores, communal-versus-individualistic values, and gender, racial and class divides, so too does one's uses and manipulations of the American flag. In regulating, and even forbidding, certain forms of consumption and customization, intellectual property law inevitably impacts processes of identity expression. And the fact that only certain government works—those actually authored by the federal government and not assigned to it—are dedicated to the public domain creates a direct conflict between individual rights of identity expression in critical symbols of collective heritage and our intellectual property regime as currently constituted. After all, it is precisely government works—content that speaks for and represents the collective state or nation producing them—that are the types of creative output most likely to be imbued with powerful ontological meanings for a state's or nation's citizens.

2. Propertizing Prayer: Creation Stories and Copyright

As a default rule, the author of any creative work fixed in a tangible medium owns the copyright to the work,[121] and therefore receives the exclusive right to reproduce, derivatize, distribute, publicly perform, and publicly display that work[122] for a period of the lifetime of the author plus seventy years.[123] Thus, an author receives dramatic rights of exclusion vis-à-vis the rest of the world. However, the issue of authorship is not always easy to determine. This is especially so when a work is the result of numerous efforts by multiple individuals—collective efforts that make a grant of exclusive rights to a single putative author potentially inequitable.

Copyright law fosters a myth of purity by advancing an image of creation as a deific act solely traceable to the inspiration and genius of the author.[124] With this genesis narrative in place, copyright law grants authors exclusive property rights to their creative output. For example, according to the labor-desert theory of copyright, authors receive monopoly-like control over certain forms of expression as a reward for their putative originality and intellectual efforts. However, a closer examination suggests the notion of authorship is fraught with complexity, as the creative process usually involves more than just a single author acting ex nihilo to bring great art to life. In many cases, the process is irretrievably iterative,[125] and the placing of exclusive control of a given work in the hands of a putative "author," rather than dedicating it to public use, can impact both identity formation and expression.

To begin with, the idea of purity and the tracing of any innovation to a single source are concepts dangerously susceptible to oversimplification. Consider the world of food. Tomato sauce and pasta are inextricably associated with Italian cuisine, and we typically view both products as integral to any "authentic" old-fashioned Italian meal. But that view is largely misguided. The tomato is indigenous to the New World, and did not make its way to Europe until it was brought back by the Spanish in the sixteenth century.[126] In the United States and in many parts of Europe, the fruit was grown only for ornamental purposes. For many centuries, tomatoes were actually considered poisonous.[127] This popular view persisted until the late eighteenth century, when fears receded after such prominent individuals as Thomas Jefferson vouched for the fruit's safety.[128]

Meanwhile, pasta was not even known to the city-states that later became Italy until the Renaissance.[129] According to legend, Marco Polo brought noodles to Europe from China.[130] In short, an "authentic" traditional Italian meal might feature neither pasta nor tomato sauce.

The same observation extends to other purportedly "authentic" ethnic cuisines. Although noodles actually came from China, the chili peppers often associated with spicy Szechuan cuisine are not indigenous to East Asia. In fact, it was not until European expansion into the New World that chili peppers made their way from their native lands in Central and South America across the Pacific.[131] Meanwhile, the plantains that now form a staple of Central and Latin American cuisine actually came from South Asia.[132] Potatoes, a quintessential feature of Germanic cuisine, are of course a New World discovery and did not make their way across the Atlantic until the 1500s.[133] The same is true of corn, a typical product in "traditional" African cuisines.[134] In short, many of the quintessential ingredients of national cuisines are relatively modern additions. And an "authentic" ethnic meal rarely is so.

By the same token, the creation myths we assign to the origins of copyrighted works can be similarly suspect. Just as tomato sauce and pasta are not "authentic" to Italian cuisine, we oversimplify matters when we assign authorship of certain expressions to a single individual. In his seminal work *The Death of the Author*, published in 1968, Roland Barthes challenged the notion of authorship, positing "the text is a tissue of quotations drawn from the innumerable centres of culture."[135] In the words of Christian Stallberg, "It is a common occurrence that intellectual works never originate exclusively from the person authorship is attributed to. Instead, every author is integrated into the manifold social and cultural contexts from which he steadily borrows. Thus, creating intellectual works always means the appropriation of preceding ideas."[136] A generation after Barthes, digital media is allowing us to quantify just how far astray the mythology of authorial creation may have led us.

To illustrate this point, consider the radical reconstruction of originality being posed with the advent of Google's book-scan feature. In recent years, Google has begun to make all of the world's published works text-searchable. Despite legal resistance and a major lawsuit from book publishers,[137] the effort—billed Google Books—continues.[138] The ability to text-search digital books is, of course, invaluable to research in a variety of ways. But, for our purposes, the most notable consequence of making humanity's literary output text-searchable is how it has begun to undermine the creation myths of copyrighted works. Librarians, historians, and bibliophiles have already used the feature to make some surprising findings about the origins of numerous works.

For example, while using Google Books as well as several other digital archives, Yale Law School librarian Fred Shapiro discovered that the most famous piece of liturgy in the twentieth century, "The Serenity Prayer" ("the Prayer"),[139] may not have been authored by theologian Reinhold Niebuhr—the man who has historically received credit for the text.[140] As Shapiro uncovered, various versions of the Prayer's text had been published and in use as early as 1936—seven years before Niebuhr apparently claimed its creation.[141] As Shapiro speculates, Niebuhr may have subconsciously[142] adopted the Prayer as his own after having come into contact with prior incarnations.[143] It is entirely possible the work was collective in nature, crowd-sourced in voluntary, educational, and religious circles for a number of years before being popularly attributed to Niebuhr.[144]

If this is the case, arguably no single person or entity should possess strong property rights in the *Prayer*.

Indeed, consider the intellectual property consequences of this creation myth—especially if Niebuhr had been inclined to enforce his potential intellectual property rights to the maximum extent allowable under the law. Niebuhr, as ostensible author of the Prayer, would have been granted a copyright in it, and that copyright could still be in effect.[145] Besides the fair use doctrine, there would of course be certain limits on Niebuhr's control over the use of the Prayer. In particular, section 110(3) of the Copyright Act exempts from infringement liability a "performance of a nondramatic literary or musical work or of a dramatico-musical work of a religious nature, or display of a work, in the course of services at a place of worship or other religious assembly."[146] However, this provision has never been cited in a reported decision,[147] so there is little guidance on its use as a shield against claims of infringement. There is also a question as to whether a prayer is, in fact, a *nondramatic* literary work.[148] Moreover, there are arguments the exemption under section 110(3) is actually unconstitutional. One might legitimately argue the exemption "confers a special benefit upon religion in violation of the Establishment Clause"[149] or that the exemption contravenes the Free Exercise Clause,[150] if one posits that the use of an author's prayer by a religious group of whom the author does not approve diminishes the author's free exercise rights. Finally, the exemption only permits public performance in the course of religious services and does not apply to reproduction of such works.[151]

Thus, Niebuhr and his heirs could potentially control use of the Prayer, deciding which favored religious institutions might be allowed to use it and which might not be. After all, invocation of the Prayer at a religious service without permission of the rightsholder may very well constitute an unauthorized public performance of the work in violation of the exclusive rights secured for copyright owners.[152] Alcoholics Anonymous—which has adopted the Prayer for its twelve-step program[153]—would be beholden to the rightsholders for permission to use the Prayer at its meetings under all but the most generous readings of section 110(3). Millions who have found solace in the comforting words of the Prayer might have been denied its use (or would have had to pay a licensing fee). In short, both formative and expressive identity interests would be impacted. The palliative use of the Prayer, and the internal comfort it has given to millions, could be significantly tempered. Meanwhile, its expressive use—its power as a collective benediction that forms a unifying bond, sense of community, and shared purpose among the friends of Bill W.—would be compromised.

The control of religious works through copyright law can allow a third party to dictate aspects of a fundamental and intimate area of personal development—both in the formation of spiritual identity and its expression.[154] In the case of "The Serenity Prayer," what is likely to have been a work of many individuals (rather than one), has become reified as a work of one individual who, under copyright law, is then given the ability to control use by the many. Concepts of authorship and labor-desert are thereby elevated above user interests, with profound consequences to the way in which individuals can conduct their spiritual lives, celebrate their religious convictions, and develop their theological identities. This scenario is not merely relegated to the realm of the theoretical. In a panoply of cases, religious organizations have (often successfully) sought to enjoin the unauthorized use of their scriptures through claims of copyright infringement.[155] As a result, religious groups have silenced criticism of their doctrines and also effectively quashed the worship activities of splinter groups. With the assistance of the modern copyright regime, religious texts have become sacred—both spiritually and legally.

3. Owning the Word: Intellectual Property, Linguistics, and Identity

Language is a universal aspect of human communication. But although we generally think of words as free for all to use, intellectual property laws actually regulate language in a variety of ways, granting exclusive ownership rights to words in certain contexts. Trademark law can proscribe the use of a single word as a designation of the source or origin of a product in a way that is likely to cause consumer confusion or dilution (through either blurring or tarnishment).[156] Copyright law can prohibit the use of a string of words when it bears substantial similarity to a preexisting string of words.[157] As we shall see, intellectual property's regulation of words can have a significant impact on both expressive and formative identity interests. First, the expression of identity is mediated by the use of language as a tool of cultural semiotics and political discourse. Second, the regulation of language impacts identity formation by literally determining the range of our informational and conceptual palettes for personal development.

The impact of intellectual property protections on identity interests can be particularly pernicious when doctrines step out of their carefully balanced, historical bounds. This problem has emerged in recent years with the passage of *sui generis* statutory protections that grant strong private property rights to constituent parts of our language. To illustrate this dynamic, consider the word *Olympic*; it belongs not to the public, but to the U.S. Olympic Committee (USOC). Under federal law—specifically, section 110 of the Amateur Sports Act of 1978[158]—the USOC possesses the exclusive right to promotional and commercial uses of the word *Olympic* and the related Olympic symbol. As such, the statute grants the USOC the power to enjoin and receive damages from any person who "uses for the purposes of trade, to induce the sale of any goods or services, or to promote any theatrical exhibition, athletic performance, or competition" the word *Olympic* or *Olympiad*.[159] Thus, more than two millennia after the invention of the word *Olympic* and the inception of the inaugural games in ancient Greece, the federal government propertized the word and put its use in the hands of a single organization.

The USOC has vigorously enforced its state-granted monopoly in the term *Olympic*, most prominently against a nonprofit organization's attempt to hold the "Gay Olympic Games" in San Francisco.[160] The resulting dispute, which included a lengthy court battle, illustrates the relationship between intellectual property and power, culture, and identity, and highlights the importance of considering user interests. In 1987, the Supreme Court upheld the validity of section 110 of the Amateur Sports Act and affirmed the ability of the USOC to enjoin San Francisco Arts & Athletics, Inc. from holding an event known as the "Gay Olympic Games."[161] As the Court reasoned, the value of the term *Olympic* "was the product of the USOC's 'own talents and energy, the end result of much time, effort, and expense,'"[162] and, as such, it was within Congress's Commerce Clause powers to create a form of "super" trademark protection through special legislation that granted the USOC exclusive rights to the word that no ordinary trademark holder would enjoy. Specifically, the protection extended to even noncommercial uses of the word and applied regardless of whether there was a likelihood of consumer confusion—the usual threshold inquiry in trademark analysis.[163] By upholding this extraordinary grant of rights to the USOC, the High Court's ruling consecrated Congress's decision to extend to the USOC powers far beyond the traditional ambit of trademark law.[164] In short, the decision marked a fundamental expansion in the gamut of intellectual property rights despite the potential impact on the expressive rights of those wishing to use the term *Olympic* in noncommercial contexts.[165]

By creating a private property right in the word *Olympic*, the Court blessed a system of differential access to key terms in the English language. While athletes in the "official" Olympics and other events such as the Special Olympics, Police Olympics, Canine Olympics, and Junior Olympics (which had not been on the receiving end of a suit seeking to enjoin their use of the moniker)[166] could associate themselves with the ultimate emblem of honorable competition, restrained patriotism, and virility, participants in the Gay Games could not. With its ruling, therefore, the Court effectively gave constitutional approval to a heuristic structure that withheld from unpopular or marginalized social groups access to the very words that constitute our language and make up our history. Of course, SFAA was still free to hold an athletic competition featuring gay athletes, but they could not refer to it as an *Olympic*. The consequences of this injunction are significant: *Olympic*, after all, is more than just a word—it is a semiotic device imbued with powerful meaning. Simply consider the connotations that such appellations as "the San Francisco Athletic Competition," "the Gay Games," or "Outheltics Fest 1987" generate and compare those connotations to the singular and distinctive strength of the name "Gay Olympics." Indeed, to this day, there is a stunning absence of openly gay athletes at the Olympics—a particularly surprising fact considering the role of the Games in bringing together individuals of all races, nationalities, creeds, and walks of life. Of the 10,708 athletes at the 2008 Olympics in Beijing, only ten were openly gay—and only one was male.[167]

Moreover, the Supreme Court has recognized the right to use certain words, rather than their synonyms, as fundamental to the exercise of First Amendment rights. In *Cohen v. California*, the Court overturned the conviction of Paul Robert Cohen for disturbing the peace when he entered a Los Angeles courtroom wearing a jacket bearing the words "Fuck the draft."[168] Writing for a 5–4 majority, Justice Harlan found Cohen's actions immunized from liability under the First Amendment.[169] Against arguments that Cohen could have expressed his message using less offensive language, the Court noted "much linguistic expression serves a dual communicative function: it conveys not only ideas capable of relatively precise, detached explication, but otherwise inexpressible emotions as well. In fact, words are often chosen as much for their emotive as their cognitive force. We cannot sanction the view that the Constitution, while solicitous of the cognitive content of individual speech, has little or no regard for that emotive function which, practically speaking, may often be the more important element of the overall message sought to be communicated."[170] With this reasoning, the Court implicitly recognized uttering "I hate the draft" or "Selective Service sucks" is simply not the communicative equivalent of declaring "Fuck the draft."

Quite simply, word choice matters. A politically charged exclamation with profanity and its genteel, synonymous analogue may have similar literal translations, but their expressive value differs radically. By forcing Cohen to state his opinion in a particular manner, the verdict—if upheld—would have effectively suppressed content. As the Court concluded, "We cannot indulge the facile assumption that one can forbid particular words without also running a substantial risk of suppressing ideas in the process. Indeed, governments might soon seize upon the censorship of particular words as a convenient guise for banning the expression of unpopular views."[171] By the same token, one cannot pretend the appellations "Outhletics Fest 1987" or "Gay Games" carry the same weight, cultural context, or historical meaning as "Gay Olympics," and, as such, they are not equivalent expressions.

More broadly speaking, the struggle to gain access to the term *Olympic* becomes part and parcel of the gay community's struggle for civil rights and the gaining of acceptance in mainstream American society. The gay community's efforts to use the word *Olympic* could be viewed as a precursor to the community's battle to use the word *marriage* to describe the union of same-sex couples.[172] In both instances, another term is available, be it "Gay Games" or "domestic partnership," but the semiotic and political impact of the alternate designation is not the same. If separate is truly seen as inherently unequal,[173] the dangerous role of intellectual property law in creating differential access to basic social codifiers such as *Olympic* must not be overlooked. In sum, the *SFAA* case provides a salient example of how our intellectual property regime can become a powerful means to regulate and control access to our most enduring cultural symbols, and thereby impact the process of identity expression.

At the same time, use of the word "Gay" in conjunction with the word *Olympic* can also impact identity formation. Besides its semiotic and ritualistic value, control of the language can even affect the content of knowledge and thought. In recent decades, the theories of Noam Chomsky and Steven Pinker have dominated academic discourse on linguistics, thereby leading most scholars to support the existence of a universal grammar and language instinct.[174] According to prevailing views, human beings all share an innate linguistic palate.[175] However, growing awareness about a group of people known as the Pirahã has forced a reconsideration of the size of this inherent palate and brought Whorf's work to the forefront of contemporary discourse. Whorf posited people are only capable of constructing thoughts for which they possess actual words.[176] Specifically, language inextricably affects the nature and content of thought, and a language's lack of words for a concept can preclude the very understanding of that concept by native speakers. As Wittgenstein later elaborated, one only knows that for which one has words.[177]

Residing deep within the Amazon rain forest in central Brazil, the Pirahã are hunter-gatherers who apparently possess in their language no notion of time, no descriptive words, no subordinate clauses, no fixed terms for color, and no numbers in their language.[178] Given the research conducted by linguist Dan Everett and anthropologist Peter Gordon, the very existence of the Pirahã appears to call into question the universalism of such human faculties as the qualification of time and material objects.[179]

The Pirahã have a word that roughly means "about one" (*hoi* said with a falling tone) and another word that roughly means "about two" (*hoi* said with a rising tone).[180] After that, however, their language stops them from counting and they only use a word referring to "many."[181] The limitations in the Pirahã language, it turns out, appear to reflect a limitation in thought. Although perfectly intelligent in any other respect, the Pirahã seem to be unable to learn numeracy. For example, while they showed no difficulty matching groups of one, two, or even three objects, their ability to differentiate between quantities greater than three falls off dramatically. Efforts to improve their counting skills have failed.[182] Thus, they can differentiate quantities for which they have linguistic code (one, two, and many), but not quantities for which they lack a term. In short, Gordon concludes they are incapable of learning numeracy. The limits of their language, as Wittgenstein posited, literally determine the limits of their world.

Of course, this analysis does not reference the revitalization of Whorfian theory to suggest depriving a group of the use of the word *Olympic* may lead to its utter inability to conceptualize the notion of a quadrennial international sports competition imbued with the spirit of honor and fair play. But, when intellectual property laws begin to control the use of our language (especially outside of the realm of commerce), we risk creating a class of linguistic haves and have-nots. Symbolic modifiers such as words, after all, mediate one's identity and perceived relationship with broader society. After all, seeing and using the word *Olympic* in association with a gay event helps attenuate residual prejudices about sport and sexual preference. It can imbue individuals with the sense that one's sexual orientation is immaterial to one's ability to attain athletic excellence, thereby impacting identity formation. At the same time, the ability to use the word *Olympic* in association with a gay event sends a powerful expressive message about a particular community's relationship with a broader international tradition. By restricting the use of linguistic tools such as basic words imbued with cultural meaning, we ultimately limit self-definition and expression, the very hallmarks of personhood development. Intellectual property laws therefore patrol insider-outsider boundaries within mainstream society and perpetuate social hierarchy by artificially limiting the use of language by non-preferred groups.

4. Controlling Culture: Copyright Terms and the Propertization of National Heritage

It is well known that, over the past two centuries, copyright terms have expanded dramatically.[183] Currently, of course, copyright subsists in individual authors for the duration of their lifetime plus seventy years.[184] As the earlier referenced discussion of the *Eldred v. Ashcroft* case made clear, there are many arguments both for and against this expansion.[185] However, the growing length of copyright terms has exacerbated the potential clash between copyright protection and the identity interests that individual users might possess in works representing their cultural or national heritage. After all, it can take decades for works to transcend their original narrow purposes and take upon broader meanings to society at large. For example, in an era where copyright protections lasted only fourteen years—as they did under the Copyright Act of 1790[186]— a work would typically have long since passed into the public domain before it could make a legitimate claim to representing cultural or national heritage. Admittedly, copyright law has always granted limited monopoly rights over creative content. But with protections for works now lasting more than a century, we increasingly face the dilemma that our cultural and national heritage may be under copyright protection.

Consider the recent lawsuit against the pop group Men at Work for the infringement of a music composition that was written more than three-quarters of a century ago. In February 2010, an Australian court found that the band and their former record label, EMI, had infringed the copyright to one of Australia's most famous and beloved songs, "Kookaburra Sits in the Old Gum Tree".[187] Written in 1934 by teacher Marion Sinclair for use by the Aussie Girl Scouts (known as the Girl Guides), "Kookaburra" quickly rose to prominence as a classic folk melody sung by generations of children huddled by camp fires around the world.[188] With its sound and references to the Antipodean bush, the work has become indelibly associated with Australian national identity.[189] In the suit, the court found that Men at Work had improperly lifted a distinctive sixteen-note sequence from "Kookaburra" as a part of the flute riff in their international hit "Down Under", which was first released in 1981.[190] Men at Work songwriter Colin Hay readily admitted that he had not received a license for the use of the "Kookaburra" sequence and acknowledged that the riff was an "unconscious" reference to the folk song.[191] After all, the use—whether intentional or unconscious—of the sequence made imminent thematic sense for *Down Under*, which was a comical, lyrical mediation on being "from the land down under."[192] In short, as a contemporary song about Australian national identity, "Down Under" made reference and paid homage to an earlier work about Australian national identity.

Ultimately, the court awarded Sinclair's successor-in-interest, Larrikin Music Publishing, a relatively meager five percent royalty for all revenue generated from the song since 2002, a fraction of the forty to sixty percent royalty that it had initially sought.[193] Nevertheless, the case cost the defendants a judgment estimated to reach well into the six figures,[194] providing another powerful monetary disincentive against the unauthorized use of "Kookaburra". In addition, consider how the case may have come out, especially under American law. First, the plaintiff could have elected to receive statutory damages, thereby allowing it to collect a sizeable judgment against defendants using the work but making no profit at all from it.[195] Secondly, an injunction could have issued, thereby interdicting use of the work altogether by anyone unwilling to pay the sampling-license rate unilaterally determined by the plaintiff (if the plaintiff chose to license at all).[196] Either of these results could make the use of a key part of Australia's national heritage either prohibitively expensive or outright impermissible, thereby suppressing expressive, identity-driven uses of "Kookaburra" in the process. As Men at Work member Greg Ham stated, the flute line was added to "Down Under" to "try to inject some Australian flavour into the song."[197] The exertion of restrictive exclusive rights to the "Kookaburra" sound would fundamentally impact the ability of individuals and groups to express cultural and national identity interests.

The consequences of propertizing and sacralizing a musical composition synonymous with Antipodean identity—one likely better known abroad than even Australia's own national anthem—are particularly troubling when one considers the likely origins of the "Kookaburra" riff itself. To some observers, the famous sequence is actually onomatopoeic and simply captures the famously good-natured, mirthful sound of the kookaburra— a bird indigenous to Australia and a veritable national symbol.[198] In a sense, therefore, the "Kookaburra" riff reflects nothing more than the sound of nature—specifically, that of the Australian bush. That sound is arguably a part of the country's natural heritage and not properly subject to propertization.

All told, our four case studies have illustrated how intellectual property laws regulate the individual consumption and customization of cultural, religious, and political symbols, thereby impacting the formation, and expression of nationalistic, spiritual, and sexual identities. This is especially the case in a world where consumption is driven increasingly by wants rather than needs, and product value is driven less by bare utility than communicative status.[199] This observation contradicts the general thrust of personhood theories of copyright, which have historically rationalized the extension of moral rights for artists and justified the expansion of authorial control over creative works. As such, the personhood interests of copyright users are an important factor that should be weighed in any framework for assigning and evaluating copyright interests.

Take the example of "Kookaburra". The song's continued protection is a direct result of term extensions that applied retroactively to existing works.[200] Such extensions are difficult to rationalize on utilitarian grounds since, after all, the works are already created.[201] There is also little in the way of an author's personhood interests to protect. As Justice Breyer points out, for works created in the 1920s and 1930s, it is likely that "the copyright holder making the decision is not the work's creator, but, say, a corporation or a great-grandchild whom the work's creator never knew."[202] This is precisely the case with "Kookaburra", whose author is long dead and whose rights reside in a corporation dedicated to litigation as a means of generating revenue. Whatever labor-desert justifications remain for the continued protection of "Kookaburra" some three-quarters of a century after its publication, they must be balanced against the weighty personhood interests that users possess in the work.

As our examples have shown, personhood interests may be served just as well through *consumption*, rather than creation, of protected works, in the form of spiritual exploration through the invocation of religious homilies, expressive perfection through referential, reverential, disrespectful uses of one's national flag or works of cultural heritage, and symbolic defiance of traditional notions of virility and masculinity through the convocation of nontraditional athletic games. By dictating the scope of allowable uses of our leading semiotic signposts and by determining which groups possess such use rights, intellectual property plays a profound role in mediating identity politics. And, outside of the existence of limited statutory exemptions and last-minute salvation from the notoriously ambiguous fair use doctrine,[203] present law provides insufficient recognition or protection of such user-based interests.

III. Parchment, Pixels, and Personhood: The Unauthorized Possession and Private Use of Copyrighted Works

As we have seen, intellectual property laws impact the formation of identity interests and their ultimate expression. However, in order to realize these identity interests, users require access to cultural content. Indeed, access is the *sina qua non* of the manifestation of such identity interests. Without it, neither formative nor expressive uses of intellectual property are possible. Historically, one vehicle to safeguard such access has stemmed from the relatively wide breadth of immunity that even the unauthorized possession and private use of copyrighted works enjoyed from liability. In this way, our copyright regime tacitly protected the personhood interests of users by supporting the dissemination and preservation of knowledge and access to creative content imbued with ontological meaning. Yet, as we shall see, both legal and technological changes now threaten the ambit of this access as more activities have come under the scope of civil, and even criminal, liability.

A. ACCESS TO KNOWLEDGE AND INFORMATION AND THE IMPORTANCE OF PRIVATE USE RIGHTS

To illustrate the role of possession and private use of unauthorized copies of creative work in fostering identity formation and personhood development, we look to examples from both antiquity and the twenty-first century. Consider the Royal Library, which helped make the ancient city of Alexandria the epicenter of learning and scholarship in the pre-modern world.[204] At the height of its glory, the Library housed almost half a million books.[205] As it turns out, the law combined with a thorough disrespect for any notion of copyright to make the very existence of the Library possible.[206] Alexandria was a key hub for commerce that brought to its shores merchants from around the world. When those people came to the metropolis, they carried with them reading materials: literature, philosophical tracts, maps, and scientific treatises. The Library quickly grew in size to achieve its legendary status.[207] Interestingly enough, the fabled Alexandria collection may well have been gathered through outright piracy. According to legend, by decree of Ptolemy III of Egypt, all individuals visiting Alexandria were required to deposit their reading materials with the Library so that copies could be made.[208] It was this act of infringement[209]—the wholesale reproduction of a work without permission of the author or publisher, which was sanctioned (and even dictated) by law—that allowed the creation of one of the great meccas of education in the ancient world.[210] The private use of these unauthorized copies fostered learning and the dissemination of knowledge so

FIGURE 3.2 *The Great Library of Alexandria* by O. Von Corvin.

critical to both personal development and artistic and scientific progress. Indeed, without the extensive collection of learning housed at the Library, the scholarship that emerged from the institution would not have been possible.[211]

Although the tale of Ptolemy's decree may be apocryphal, housing repositories of knowledge culled without the blessing of rightsholders remains a valuable and even lofty goal in the modern world. In the first instance, modern libraries (and used bookstores) only exist legally because of the exception to copyright liability stemming from the first sale doctrine, which allows purchasers of books and others copyrighted works to dispose of those copies at they see fit (and without permission of a copyright holder)—whether that means reselling them, giving them away, or lending them out.[212] Otherwise, a library could implicate a copyright holder's exclusive right to "to distribute copies . . . of the copyrighted work to the public by sale or other transfer of ownership, or by rental, lease, or lending."[213]

Unfortunately for consumers, the first sale doctrine is increasingly coming under threat as content creators have attempted to circumvent its application by characterizing distribution of their product to purchasers as licenses rather than outright sales.[214] Accordingly, creators argue that purchasers are never "the owner of a particular copy . . . lawfully made"[215] who would have any rights under the first sale doctrine.[216] As a consequence, purchasers are subject to restrictive terms-of-use that waive rights previously secured under the first sale doctrine, including the ability to dispose of their copy of a protected work as they please. Courts have frequently upheld such terms despite arguments that they are properly preempted by the federal Copyright Act and the Constitution's Copyright and Supremacy Clauses.[217]

Additionally, even in an era of relative wealth, many communities and even countries simply cannot afford the high costs of acquiring initial copies of copyrighted content to sustain a library. In fact, to the surprise of modern observers, early American copyright law even acknowledged this problem directly. During the Articles of Confederation era, there was no federal copyright protection;[218] instead, states passed their own copyright laws.[219] And although these statutes generally resembled the eventual protection regime adopted under the Constitution and the federal Copyright Act of 1790, many differed in at least one significant way. Several states—including New York, North Carolina, South Carolina, and Georgia—had statutes that explicitly recognized the rights consumers had to "sufficient" quantities of books offered at "reasonable" prices—a far cry from public policy today.[220]

Public access to copyrighted works, including their possession and private use, is a paramount value, especially when it can have lifesaving consequences. Indeed, access to copyrighted works not only can advance personal *development* but also personal *preservation*. Consider the example of copyrighted medical literature. In a study published by the Commission on Intellectual Property Rights, Alan Story found the required payment of copyright royalties has significantly inhibited the distribution in South Africa of copyrighted materials about HIV and AIDS to students and patients.[221] As a result, educational efforts aimed at stemming the spread of infection and assisting affected individuals with care have faltered, costing lives in the process.[222] Meanwhile, the expense of acquiring translation rights has meant many books that could advance the dissemination of knowledge in developing countries remain available only in major Western languages.[223] As Story notes, this problem is particularly serious in many African countries characterized by linguistic heterogeneity.[224] In these particular instances, unauthorized copying can even save lives.

Unauthorized copying can also help preserve knowledge for future generations, even in the digital age. Admittedly, one might speculate that with easy digital reproduction and mass dissemination, we enjoy a surfeit of copies of important works in the Internet era. However, this is not necessarily the case, as long-term preservation of digital copies of works presents a number of challenges. Indeed, the archiving challenges that plague digital content have received scant attention. Each time a new digital version of a work supplants an old one, the old version is gone forever unless an independent copy of it is made before the revision. And although rightsholders may archive works themselves, they are less-than-reliable forces for doing so. For example, if the original version of a document reveals something embarrassing or information against rights-holders' interests, they have a strong incentive to avoid archiving. As a result, there is a strong need for independent archiving of digital works[225]—something that cannot always be accomplished without potentially running afoul of copyright laws. Indeed, archiving of digital content can play a critical role in historical preservation and knowledge dissemination.

In addition, archiving has grown increasingly (rather than less) necessary in the digital age. Surprisingly, digital media is not as durable as traditional media for a variety of reasons. First, the vessels that house digital media are often more corruptible than their analog equivalents. Although a book may survive several thousand years, one could hardly say the same about a CD, which can be ruined with a simple scratch. Second, even if its packaging remains viable, digital media usually relies upon a particular machine to grant access to it. For example, during the brief transition point between old 3.5-inch floppy disks (which held up to 1.44 megabytes) and rewritable CDs and DVDs (which could hold several gigabytes), zip drives emerged during the late 1990s as the storage platform of choice.[226] However, to read one, the zip disk must not only be in good shape, but also the user has to find a working zip-drive reader to access it. Only a decade after their heyday, zip-drive readers are quickly fading to obscurity. Moreover, unlike traditional media, the degradation of digital media is not visibly evident. Paper deteriorates before our eyes, and film emits a vinegar smell when it begins to rot, but the integrity of digital media is more difficult to ascertain. Thus, copyright provisions that prevent the effective preservation of creative works in digital form can impede access to knowledge and creative content for future generations.

B. THE HISTORICAL PROTECTION OF UNAUTHORIZED POSSESSION AND PRIVATE USE

Historically, our copyright jurisprudence has provided both implicit and explicit acknowledgement of user interests in the unauthorized possession and private use of copyrighted works. But these protections are coming under fire as they lose their immunity from copyright liability. To illustrate this point, we begin by examining the statutory and juridical framework that has traditionally guarded user rights in the unauthorized possession and private use of copyrighted works. In particular, we locate strong tacit support for such rights in the historical treatment of publication under the Copyright Act, the specific absence of certain exclusive rights from section 106 of the Act, and the surprisingly relevant First Amendment jurisprudence in the area of obscenity.

We then examine the ways in which both technological and legal changes are undermining these former protections.

1. User Rights and the Act of Publication

The historical role publication has played in determining the scope of an author's monopoly speaks to the implicit user interests acknowledged in our copyright regime. Prior to publication, the personhood interests in a work of intellectual property lay chiefly with the author. After all, the work is an extension of the author, who has decided not to disseminate the work (yet). At this point, the personhood interests of the author are at their apex while the personhood interests of users are at their nadir. However, this balance changes upon publication, which especially in the digital age can be tantamount to mass dissemination. Now, the author is not the only person to interact with the work; indeed, millions of individuals can as well (for the right price). As consumers of the intellectual property mingle with the work, they also begin to acquire identity interests in it, especially as it takes on semiotic value. In a sense, these user interests are tacitly acknowledged by the law when it actually reduces the monopolistic control creators have on their intellectual output upon publication.

It is often stated that federal copyright protection serves to encourage dissemination of creative works: in exchange for the publication of a work, an author receives federal copyright protection—a government-granted monopoly entitling an author to a bundle of exclusive exploitation rights.[227] Upon cursory examination, it would appear such a system would incentivize mass distribution by enhancing an author's intellectual property rights upon the act of publication. After all, for most of American history (i.e., until the passage of the 1976 Copyright Act), unpublished works were generally not protected under federal law.[228]

However, in exchange for the right to profit through mass dissemination of their work, authors typically *lose* certain rights upon the act of publication. Among other things, a work becomes subject to greater fair use rights[229] and to certain compulsory licenses.[230] And, until the passage of the 1976 Copyright Act, publication actually *reduced* the duration of copyright protection an author enjoyed. Although unpublished works did not receive *federal* copyright protection, they did enjoy another form of protection under the aegis of state law. Colloquially referred to as "common law" copyrights, these state laws typically granted authors exclusive rights to their unpublished works.[231] However, unlike federal protections, "common law" copyright lasted forever. Take an author who created a work in 1975. So long as she did not publish the work, she enjoyed a "common law" copyright through which she exercised the exclusive right of reproduction in perpetuity.[232] However, if she published the work, her "common law" copyright morphed into a federal copyright (so long as certain formalities were observed), and she secured the exclusive right of reproduction for fifty-six years, after which the work would fall into the public domain.[233] Thus, the act of publication diminished the level of effective property protection a work received. Of course, this small disincentive against publication did not override the overwhelming incentive for it: the ability to profit through mass reproduction and distribution.

Thus, for most of American history, the act of publication has resulted in an effective shortening of a work's copyright duration from perpetuity to a fixed term. After all, by deciding to profit from a copyrighted work, the creator is giving some part of that work to the world. Consequently, although the Framers chose to draft a constitutional clause empowering Congress to grant copyrights for "a limited time," this federal copyright regime existed compatibly with a common law system of perpetual copyrights for unpublished works that endured for more than two centuries.

As a result, our copyright regime has tacitly recognized the non-authorial interests triggered upon a work's publication in at least three ways: through the reduced term of protection given published works vis-à-vis unpublished works (at least prior to 2003), the greater fair use rights enjoyed for published works, and the wider availability of certain compulsory licenses to works upon their publication. Admittedly, the nature of these non-authorial interests is ambiguous. On one hand, we could argue that limiting the scope of protection given to published works serves primarily to bolster user rights to transform existing works so that they might advance progress in the arts—the chief goal of the copyright regime. On the other hand, these non-authorial rights also encompass the right to simply use and reproduce works to serve First Amendment interests, disseminate knowledge, facilitate learning, and advance identity formation. Indeed, when considered in combination with other limitations in the copyright regime, the implicit recognition given to non-transformative user interests becomes clear.

2. What Copyright Does Not Protect: Learning from the Limits on Exclusive Rights

Consider section 106,[234] arguably the most important section of the Copyright Act, which defines the specific exclusive rights to which copyright holders are entitled. Section 106's list of exclusive rights is revealing, not just for what it protects, but for what it does not protect. In other words, the negative space of the Copyright Act provides a basis for greater recognition of user interests. Specifically, the law tacitly acknowledges the importance of both transformative manipulations of copyrighted works and noncritical uses. It does so through one of its more significant (albeit less appreciated) limitations: the absence of penalties against possession or private use of infringing works.

As the Supreme Court has noted, "The Copyright Act does not give a copyright holder control over all uses of his copyrighted work. Instead, . . . the Act enumerates several 'rights' that are made 'exclusive' to the holder of the copyright. If a person, without authorization from the copyright holder, puts a copyrighted work to a use within the scope of one of these 'exclusive rights,' he infringes the copyright. If he puts the work to a use not enumerated . . . , he does not infringe."[235] For example, the Act only grants owners the exclusive right to perform a protected work publicly.[236] As such, performing a copyrighted musical composition in the privacy of one's shower does not constitute an act of infringement.[237] Section 106 proscribes unauthorized reproduction, adaptation, distribution, public performance, or public display of a copyrighted work.[238] However, unauthorized possession and private use are conspicuously missing from this list.[239] As a result, by possessing an illegal copy of a copyrighted work, one does not violate any rights secured under federal law for the copyright holder. Bootleggers (of the recording variety) may therefore face legal sanctions for recording and distributing unauthorized concert recordings, but a mere possessor, private user, or even a purchaser[240] incurs no such liability risk.

This tack differs significantly from the law of black-market goods or of property in general, where wrongful possession is not just sanctionable, but criminal. Knowingly housing a stolen automobile is a felony.[241] Meanwhile, it is not merely a crime to sell illicit narcotics: it is also a crime (though a lesser one) to purchase or possess them.[242] As a result, it is fair to wonder why we have such copyright exceptionalism in the regulation of possession. One might find the answer in an unusual place: First Amendment jurisprudence on the law of obscenity.

3. Constitutionalizing Rights to Authorized and *Unauthorized* Possession and Private Use: Copyright, Obscenity, and the First Amendment

Although the Supreme Court has allowed the criminalization of sexually explicit materials deemed obscene under the reigning *Miller* standard,[243] it has carved a notable safe harbor for those who simply possess, but do not produce or distribute, such materials. In *Stanley v. Georgia*, the Supreme Court unanimously held government cannot punish the private possession of obscenity in the home.[244] In part, this result was justified by substantive due process norms protecting the right of privacy, especially in one's home.[245] On another level, however, such a result also reflects a hesitation to interfere with the right of individuals to possess expressive works, as protected by the First Amendment, no matter how base and repulsive they might be according to local community standards.[246]

As with obscenity jurisprudence, the law of copyright is considered an exception to the First Amendment and its general interdiction against government abridgement of speech. Despite its literal status as speech, obscenity can be banned outright because of its purported lack of socially redeeming value.[247] And, despite its literal status as speech, copyrighted works can be protected from unauthorized use because they are reified as a species of property; according to the Supreme Court, although one may have a right to make one's own speech, one does not necessarily have the right to make the speech of others.[248] Yet if the government cannot outlaw the private possession of obscenity without running afoul of the constitutional right to freedom of speech and expression, one could surmise a similar constitutional limitation would prevent punishment of the private possession of infringing works. Indeed, the closing words of Justice Marshall's opinion in *Stanley* could well apply to copyrighted works as well as obscene works: "If the First Amendment means anything, it means that a State has no business telling a man, sitting alone in his own house, what books he may read or what films he may watch."[249]

The Court's holding is particularly noteworthy when one considers the materials at issue have been deemed legally obscene and, therefore, judged to lack "serious literary, artistic, political or scientific value."[250] Nevertheless, the Court goes out of its way in the *Stanley* decision to protect the affirmative right of individuals to access such materials—not just to limit the power of government to enter the home, but to also allow for the personal development of individuals, no matter how at odds that development may seem with societal values. As the Court explained, legalizing the private possession of obscene materials that could neither be produced nor distributed under the law was necessary to protect "the right [of an individual] to read or observe what he pleases—the right to satisfy his intellectual and emotional needs in the privacy of his own home."[251] By the same token, the possession and private use of copyrighted works—whether authorized or infringing—advances expressive interests and personal development. This is particularly true as the universe of copyrighted materials (contrary, apparently, to the universe of obscenity) includes many works of serious literary, artistic, political, or scientific value.

C. THE GROWING THREAT TO POSSESSION AND PRIVATE USE RIGHTS

All told, the right to unauthorized possession and use of copyrighted works is not simply limited to such specific statutory exemptions as the fair use and first sale doctrines. Rather, the Copyright Act's treatment of publication, the delimited nature of its exclusive rights grant, and the development of First Amendment jurisprudence also provide firm bases for greater recognition of such possession and usage rights. However, in recent years, technological and legal developments have enabled the penumbra of copyright liability to cast a shadow on previously immunized activities. With the conception of the author as authority growing more powerful, copyright law has increasingly invaded the private sphere, extending into our living rooms to mediate how we interact with intellectual property in myriad ways. In particular, the development of ancillary copyright doctrines and the nature of digital distribution have combined to make unauthorized possession and private use of copyrighted works the subject of liability, despite their specific exclusion from section 106's enumeration of exclusive rights. In the process, we threaten the noncritical utilization of copyrighted works for the advancement of personal development.

1. Secondary Liability Doctrine Unbound

First, the expansion of secondary liability doctrine (especially the contributory variety) has created a backdoor mechanism for rendering the purchase and possession of infringing goods potentially actionable. Secondary liability doctrines, of course, allow a plaintiff to pursue infringement claims under certain circumstances against parties who facilitate the violation of a copyright holder's exclusive rights, even though those parties do not directly infringe those rights themselves. Such secondary liability theories are a powerful tool for the vindication of copyright holders' interests, especially because direct infringers can be difficult to track, immune from personal jurisdiction or impractical to pursue since they may be judgment-proof.

Over the past few decades, the scope of secondary liability theories has increased markedly.[252] Oddly enough, there is no explicit provision for secondary liability in the Copyright Act. In fact, there is almost no legislative acknowledgment of such causes of action,[253] save a fleeting comment in the Digital Millennium Copyright Act[254] and an oblique reference to "authorizing" infringement in a House Report for the 1976 Copyright Act.[255] Nevertheless, courts have recognized the availability of both common law theories of secondary liability—contributory and vicarious—in assisting content creators in their legal battles against facilitators of intellectual property infringement.[256] Both secondary liability theories require an underlying act of direct infringement.[257] Contributory liability then attaches where there also exists (1) the defendant's knowledge of the infringement and (2) the defendant's material contribution to the infringement.[258] Vicarious liability, as an outgrowth of the respondeat superior doctrine, requires (1) the right and ability of the defendant to control the actions of the infringer and (2) a direct financial benefit to the defendant from the infringement.[259]

As these doctrines have expanded, they have threatened to bring the possession and private use of infringing works within the scope of civil liability. Courts have read the material-contribution element of contributory liability increasingly broadly.[260] Indeed, a person's or entity's role in establishing the situs for an infringing activity may suffice as a cognizable material contribution for which liability can attach.[261] For example, a commercial operator of sound recording or video duplication facilities may be held liable for the infringing acts of its customers even if the customers bring in the copyrighted materials they improperly copy.[262] Similarly, a swap-meet landlord can be held liable for contributory infringement based on the actions of vendors on its property.[263] As the Ninth Circuit has explicitly held, the mere provision of "the site and facilities for known infringing activity is sufficient to establish contributory liability."[264] Or, in a more technologically advanced setting, an operator of a computer bulletin board service that automatically distributed all bulletin board postings (infringing or not) to service subscribers faced contributory liability for a subscriber's posting of infringing work,[265] a ruling that precipitated congressional adoption of the Digital Millennium Copyright Act's safe harbor provisions that protect Internet Service Providers from contributory liability in such situations.[266] Indeed, the Supreme Court's most recent consideration of secondary liability explicitly held "intentionally inducing or encouraging direct infringement," regardless of one's actual knowledge of specific infringing acts, could be a sufficient basis for liability.[267] Based on these holdings, it is not much of a stretch to argue that providing infringers with a profit motivation for their activities could constitute a material contribution toward their acts of infringement. For example, in 2007, in a case of first impression, the Ninth Circuit narrowly rejected an attempt by a content owner to hold Visa and other payment services secondarily liable for processing credit card payments for websites that infringed the content owner's copyrights.[268] However, the court did so by only a single vote, and the opinion featured a vigorous dissent by Judge Alex Kozinski,[269] who asserted that Visa could be found liable both for contributory liability—for knowingly processing financial payments that substantially assist users in accessing and downloading infringing content[270]—and for vicarious liability—for undoubtedly profiting from the infringing activities of websites delivering stolen content by taking a cut of virtually every economic transaction on those websites, and by failing to exercise their right and ability to limit the infringing activity.[271] Admittedly, the *Visa* majority found that the automated processing of payments meant the defendants do not "affirmatively promote each product that their cards are used to purchase."[272] But, the same may not be true for the direct act of purchasing an infringing good (be it a copy of the unauthorized sequel to *Catcher in the Rye* successfully interdicted by J.D. Salinger,[273] a Bratz children's doll from MGA Entertainment famously put out to legal pasture by Barbie-doll-making rival Mattel,[274] or a bootleg recording of one's favorite band), which could very well incur contributory, if not vicarious, liability.

Currently, for example, the major publishers are systematically pursuing litigation against copy shops around the country that photocopy coursepacks for use in college classes.[275] According to the publishers, the preparation of these coursepacks constitutes a willful act

FIGURE 3.3 Barbie and the Bratz Do Battle.

of infringement for which there is no fair use defense.[276] The publishers have even enjoyed some success in their fight, including the high-profile decision in *Michigan Document Services*, where an en banc panel of the Sixth Circuit reversed a prior finding of fair use and held a copy shop preparing coursepacks at the University of Michigan liable for infringement.[277] To date, the publishers have not pursued litigation against those who use these allegedly infringing coursepacks: students. However, under the increasingly generous reading of the contributory liability doctrine, all of that could change. After all, by paying for them, the students are making the creation of the packets profitable and inducing the allegedly infringing activity. Accordingly, they quite arguably provide material aide to the infringement and could face contributory liability. In addition, students might face vicarious liability under the Supreme Court's most recent characterization of the doctrine, which asserted that "[o]ne . . . infringes vicariously by profiting from direct infringement while declining to exercise a right to stop or limit it."[278] Students arguably derive a financial benefit from the creation of unauthorized course packets because they are able to use these packets in lieu of much costlier, full, authorized versions of texts. In addition, students arguably decline to exercise their right to stop or limit this infringement by refusing to purchase the allegedly infringing course packets.

All told, by bringing the unauthorized possession and private use of educational materials—even for purely academic and non-profit purposes—under the scope of infringement liability, such a result threatens to stifle the dissemination of knowledge and hamstring a critical way in which use of copyrighted works advances personal development. Doing one's homework could become very costly indeed.

2. Digital Distribution and the Violation of the Reproduction Right

The nature of digital distribution also makes it increasingly possible to render actionable the possession and private use of an infringing work. The process of obtaining an infringing work in digital form almost inevitably involves an act of reproduction directly triggered, at some level, by the user/possessor.[279] This contrasts sharply with the process of obtaining an infringing good in the pre-digital world, where user/possessors cannot be held directly liable for the reproduction of the works themselves. For example, if I purchase an unauthorized recording of a live concert from a bootlegger, I have not committed a direct act of infringement because I have not reproduced, distributed, displayed, or performed the work in a way that violates any exclusive right secured under section 106. This is true even though the bootleg represents an unauthorized fixation of a musical composition without permission of the appropriate rightsholder. And if a friend makes me a mix tape and hands it to me, section 106 is not invoked even though the mix tape represents an unauthorized reproduction of several sound recordings without permission of the appropriate rightsholders. But, if I obtain the bootleg online, I have made a reproduction of a copyrighted work without authorization in direct violation of section 106(1). And if a friend e-mails me a mix "tape" in the form of a digital file, the reproduction of that work based on the nature of digital distribution also triggers a section 106(1) violation. As some courts have recently held, the act of "requesting" a digital version of a protected work—which causes the work to be transmitted to one's computer as a copy—constitutes a direct infringement of the exclusive right to reproduction.[280] Subject to fair use or another affirmative defense, this act of reproduction is infringing whether or not it is strictly for private purposes.[281] Indeed, unlike unauthorized distribution, performance, and display (which must be public to implicate section 106), violation of the reproduction right (and accompanying right to prepare derivatives) requires no publicly related act to constitute infringement.[282]

The nature of digital distribution not only triggers section 106 rights that pre-digital distribution did not, it also renders such activities more detectable and, therefore, susceptible to legal action. With logged IP addresses, digital fingerprints surround any infringing act, making tracking possible. For example, the previous sharing of music that flew under the radar in the pre-digital era is now made visible—a fact the unfortunate targets of the RIAA's litigation campaign against peer-to-peer file-sharing have learned the hard way.[283]

The implications on identity formation and personal development issues become clear when we consider one of the most powerful ways in which we connect with our distant and deceased family members and with our ancestors: via photographs. Since the invention of the daguerreotype in the mid-nineteenth century,[284] familial identity and kinship bonds have been both generated and intensified through the act of sharing family photo albums. In prior years, this act rarely implicated copyright issues. For example, if you had a trove of family photographs in your possession, you could freely share those photographs with your relatives when they came to your house. After all, the act of sharing family photographs in the pre-digital era did not implicate any section 106 rights—no reproduction, derivation, public distribution, public performance, or public display had taken place. Thus, it did not matter that you were not the owner of the copyright to many of the photographs in your possession. After all, the copyright to photographs is typically held by the individual who positions the shot and hits the shutter button, whether it is a professional photographer doing a family portrait, a random stranger kind enough to take a family shot at a tourist spot, or your cousin Belinda's boyfriend who, because he has not yet earned his stripes as a bona fide family member, dutifully volunteers to snap a shot and forgo being memorialized on celluloid as one of the clan. Moreover, it did not matter if the photographs in your possession were themselves a work of infringement: a reproduction of a photograph without authorization of the rightsholder. Thus, the traditional sharing of family photographs did not infringe any exclusive right enjoyed by the works' copyright holders. In other words, possession and private use of an image without permission of the copyright holder created no specter of liability.

However, this analysis changes radically in the digital environment. On one hand, the Internet allows the family photo album to be shared more easily with relatives. Websites such as myheritage.com have cropped up allowing family members to create pages dedicated to the assemblage of family trees and repository of family photographs. But the sharing of the photo album necessarily implicates at least one section 106 right: the right to reproduce.[285] To put the albums on myheritage.com, we must make copies of the photographs. To do so, copyright law requires we obtain permission of the copyright holder[286] or seek refuge in an affirmative defense such as fair use. Thus, a form of non-transformative use involving substantial identity issues that was previously immunized from infringement liability now poses substantial liability questions.

3. The DMCA and the Criminalization of Private Use of Copyrighted Works

Additionally, critics have long bemoaned the dangers of the anti-circumvention provisions of the DMCA for their ability to retard fair use rights, especially as more copyrighted works become available only or primarily in digital form.[287] But it is not just "fair uses" of copyrighted works (i.e., violations of section 106 rights excused under the fair use doctrine) that the DMCA anti-circumvention provisions implicate. By keeping copyrighted works under a digital lock that limits their uses specifically to those for which the rightsholder provide approval, the DMCA anti-circumvention provisions also create liability for certain acts of possession and private use that do not run afoul of section 106 in the first place.[288] So long as there is no reproduction or derivation involved, private use of a creative work cannot constitute an act of infringement even when the use occurs in a manner not authorized by a copyright holder.[289] Don Henley and Danny Kortchmar cannot step into your bedroom and prevent you from making "All She Wants to Do Is Dance" the theme song for your self-actualizing naked-shaving ritual each morning, as repulsive as it might be to them, even if you possess an unauthorized copy of the song. But, this could result in liability under the DMCA, which provides "[n]o person shall circumvent a technological measure that effectively controls access" to a copyrighted work.[290]

Under the DMCA, unauthorized private performances—acts that were previously non-infringing per se—can become potential felonies.[291]

The consequences of this legal transformation can be significant. Consider the impact on knowledge dissemination and study, for example. Imagine that, in an abandoned farmhouse in rural South Island, someone locates a complete print of *Salomé*, the long-lost epic silent masterpiece by legendary New Zealand auteur Colin McKenzie—a film-maker who has never received his rightful due as one of the towering figures of silent cinema.[292] The movie, which was completed and released in the early part of the twentieth century, has long fallen into the public domain and lost any copyright protection it may have had. No one has seen the movie for decades, so to reintroduce the motion picture to the world, a DVD is released. As the work will likely not enjoy a widespread audience but rather just the small group of devoted film aficionados who are desperate to view it, the DVD will also sell for a premium retail price. Using digital rights management, the DVD also limits purchasers to a single play.

Although a film studies professor may want to view the movie for purposes of study to appreciate McKenzie's pioneering shooting techniques, unique narrative structures, and innovative contributions to New Zealand cinema, he will be limited in his ability and right to experience this important piece of cultural heritage and motion picture history. Although the professor's private performance of the movie at his own home would not implicate any section 106 rights—even if the film were still in copyright—he could face serious liability under the DMCA. He cannot borrow the film from a library—the DVD's one-play-only feature curtails the ability of libraries to loan out the movie—and he cannot borrow the movie from a friend. He can purchase a copy, if he can afford to do so, but he can only watch the movie once, something no serious student of film would find sufficient. And should he successfully view it more than once—say, by circumventing the DVD's protection measures—he will be in violation of the DMCA's anti-circumvention provisions.[293] Thus, the private viewing of a public domain work—something that would involve no liability whatsoever in the pre-DMCA world—would now give rise to tremendous legal risk. By criminalizing the use of circumvention tools, the DMCA therefore makes copies of digital works significantly less available for private use and can adversely impact both the dissemination of knowledge and the study of important cultural works.

4. The Anti-Counterfeiting Trade Agreement and the Future of Copyright Liability

Finally, pending international treaties and proposed legislation threaten to bring unauthorized possession and private use of copyrighted works under the scope of liability. In particular, the infamous Anti-Counterfeiting Trade Agreement (ACTA) could pose a radical threat to previously protected user rights if its leaked early versions provide an accurate indication of things to come. Although its particulars are still shrouded in secrecy,[294] ACTA purportedly seeks to enact a series of copyright enforcement mechanisms that could undermine user rights worldwide.[295] Among other things, ACTA reportedly advances a three-strikes policy to which Internet Service Providers must adhere to retain their safe harbor from liability for the infringing activities that might occur on their networks.[296] Specifically, the three-strikes policy would potentially require Internet Service Providers to terminate the broadband Internet connection of any customer who is three times accused of infringement.[297] Early critics of the proposals have questioned the types of procedural safeguards ACTA provides prior to termination to ensure the banishment conforms with due process norms and provides for reasonable adjudication of disputed infringement claims.[298] Indeed, these critics raise concerns that unsubstantiated accusations of infringement, or the invocation of one's fair use rights, may lead to complete loss of Internet access.[299] Whatever the actual procedures, it is only slight hyperbole to suggest that, in the twenty-first century, this is the legal equivalent of being banished from civilization—the strongest punishment (aside from death) traditional societies inflicted upon their members.

Consider the example of Cathi Paradiso, a grandmother from Pueblo, Colorado. Responding to pressure from the content-creation industries, her Internet Service Provider, Qwest, had instituted a policy to suspend (if not terminate) the accounts of those accused by copyright holders of online infringement.[300] One day, without notification, Paradiso found herself unable to connect any longer to the Internet at home. When Paradiso investigated the matter, Qwest informed her she had illegally downloaded eighteen television shows and movies, including *South Park* and *Zombieland*. Grandmothers do not usually fall into the *South Park* and *Zombieland* demographic, and Paradiso was no different in this regard. In fact, she had never used the Internet to download any movies of any kind. "Take me off your hit list," Paradiso pleaded, "I have never downloaded a movie. Period."[301] But Paradiso's protests fell on deaf ears until the media caught wind of the story and rallied to her aid. However, had she not received support from the Fourth Estate, she would have had no independent third party to hear her complaint and would have received no due process to challenge the allegations against her: Qwest would have simply terminated her connection at their sole discretion. And, to make matters worse, her name would have been made available to other Internet Service Providers, thereby creating a veritable "infringer blacklist" that would have hampered her ability to purchase broadband from an alternative source.[302] The consequences of such a move would have been particularly damaging for Paradiso, who is an artist working from home on her computer. "My computer is not a toy," she told Qwest. "My livelihood depends on my ISP's reliability."[303]

Meanwhile, ACTA also empowers customs officers at border crossings to search laptops, smartphones, and other devices with hard drives—not for detonation devices that might threaten national security, but for content that infringes copyright law. Besides raising substantial privacy concerns, the viability of charging customs officers with the interpretation and application of copyright law—a complex field that has few hard-and-fast rules and creates exegetical disagreements among even experts—in the span of seconds at a border crossing strains credulity. With the strong support ACTA is receiving from lobbying interests acting on behalf of the content-creation industries, the proposal also raises serious concerns that hard-drive searches will create an in terrorem effect to stifle any manner of unauthorized possession or use of copyrighted content, whether or not legitimately excused by law.

ACTA also threatens to authorize the imposition of criminal sanctions against those who willfully infringe, regardless of any absence of motivation for financial gain—a dramatic expansion of criminal liability without parallel in copyright history. The consequences of this radical change in law would be significant, criminalizing many more acts of infringement (including private ones) than ever before. Combined with the reality that the nature of digital distribution has enabled unauthorized acts of possession and private use to come under the scope of the Copyright Act and be subjected to track-ing, adoption of ACTA could easily transform our infringement nation into a criminal nation.

ACTA is driven by a popular narrative about how the creative industries have ceded control of their production to the seemingly irreversible tides of online infringement. To be sure, piracy is a serious concern, but it does not represent the entire story of the digi-tal revolution. Although the diffusion of duplication technologies has enabled individu-als to infringe the copyrights of rightsholders on a scale never before witnessed, recent technological and legal developments have done something else altogether: they have paradoxically enabled copyright holders to exercise greater control over how individuals can consume works than at any other point in human history. The vital personhood inter-ests identified here offer yet another key reason to scrutinize that trend closely.

IV. Conclusion

As we have seen, it is not just transformative uses of copyrighted works that vindicate key developmental and expressive values. Rather, the non-critical, pure consumption of copyrighted works plays a vital role in advancing consumption personhood interests in at least two ways: through the formation of identity and the expression of identity. The existence of these formative and expressive processes provides a strong Hegelian basis to question the unfettered expansion of copyright protection for authors and owners. Yet, although extant theories of copyright support the rights of putative creators to control use of their intellectual property on utilitarian, labor-desert, and personhood grounds, the interests of the user in the definitional and semiotic values of these properties has received short shrift.

Indeed, as we have seen in our case studies involving Old Glory and the Lone Star flag, "The Serenity Prayer," the term *Olympic*, and the song "Kookaburra", doctrinal features of our intellectual property regime—the limited dedication of certain government works to the public domain, the notion of authorship upon which copyright protection is depen-dent, the growth of trademark law beyond guarding against consumer confusion, and the expanding duration of the copyright term—have resulted in a failure to account fully for the identity interests that users possess in intellectual property. As such, we enable our intellectual property regime to patrol the development and expression of nationalistic, religious, cultural, and sexual identities with insufficient scrutiny of the broader conse-quences of this regulation.

Meanwhile, even where our regime has traditionally granted implicit recognition of user identity interests—through the relative immunization granted to the private use and possession of unauthorized copies of copyrighted works—such protections are growing increasingly fragile. The nature of digital distribution along with legal develop-ments such as the implementation of the DMCA's anti-circumvention provisions, the growing scope of secondary liability doctrine, and the proposed reforms in ACTA threaten to make possession and private use of copyrighted works punishable. Activities that form identities, shape familial bonds, and advance personal development (e.g., the private sharing of family photo albums, the private use of photocopied scholarly articles by students, and the private enjoyment and study of film by cinephiles) now risk generating liability exposure for the first time in history.

This chapter has taken a modest, but important, first step in identifying the personhood interests at stake for users of copyrighted works, in providing a theoretical framework for consideration of these interests, and in highlighting the ways in which the law insufficiently accounts for them. Thus, our analysis provides a template for both resistance and reform. On one hand, a personhood theory of user interests warrants skepticism over attempts to expand the scope of infringement liability to include the private possession and use of unauthorized editions of copyrighted works, a heretofore protected zone of activity that supported individual access to cultural works and advanced the use of creative content for personal development. Indeed, the invasion of copyright law into the private sphere is afoot. Without counteractive measures, policy proposals in ACTA suggest we may soon witness the mass criminalization of unauthorized uses within the home and the transformation of our border patrols into veritable Keystone Kopyright Kops, charged with searching private laptops and hard drives for unauthorized materials.

On the other hand, a personhood theory of user interests also causes us to re-examine extant features of our intellectual property regime. As protection terms have grown longer, we have seen aspects of our cultural and national heritage become owned and regulated by copyright holders, thereby impacting the formation and expression of cultural and nationalistic identities. As crowd-sourcing and interactive acts of authorship continue to occur more frequently, especially with the rise of digital technology that enables strangers from around the world to collaborate in the creation of collective works, copyright's problematic notion of authorship increasingly threatens to place exclusive rights in the hands of a single entity that can then inequitably limit uses of those works by all others. As trademark law has expanded beyond consumer confusion, and sui generis protections are passed for such terms as *Olympic*, we have witnessed the very components of our language—words—placed in the hands of private entities who, in turn, can constrict our imaginative palettes and patrol insider-outsider divides and social fault lines.

All the while, however, the predominant discourse of intellectual property maximalists continues to appeal to personhood interests—of authors, not users—as a basis for the further ratcheting up of protection. Ironically, current efforts by copyright maximalists to prosecute their vision of copyright law—efforts that center on convincing, either by economic muscle or legal reform, Internet Service Providers to terminate the Internet connections of accused infringers—betray their denial of the very real personhood interests that users possess in intellectual property. After all, the ultimate punishment in the digital age is the loss of one's digital lifeline. Termination of one's broadband Internet is akin to digital execution: the death of one's person in the twenty-first century. Perhaps more than anything else, the very weight of this threat (upon which the content creation industries now rely for enforcement) speaks to the identity politics of intellectual property and to the inherent personhood interests users have in the copyrighted works with which they interact. After all, Internet access secures intellectual property access, and, without such access, individuals are cut off from modern digital society. In the end, therefore, the threatened punishment for infringement proves the existence and value of the very personhood interests for users that copyright maximalists have for so long downplayed.

4

THE INDIVIDUAL AS CREATOR

In which we contemplate parochial nations, auras, Charles Dickens as lobbyist, Che Guevara as salesman, Britney Spears in flagrante commando, the names of photographs, the meaning of "fringe" benefits, the impact of steroids, movies without writers, Hollywood as an intractable magnetic mountain, and Newton's Third Law

SO FAR IN OUR ANALYSIS, we have focused on the individual's role in consuming copyrighted content—be it as a transformer or as a pure copier. In the process, we have criticized the expanding scope of copyright protection for its suppression of transformative uses that advance progress in the arts; its limitation of critical expressive, identity formation, and First Amendment activities; and its role in making veritable grand larcenists of us all. We now turn our attention to the individual not as *consumer*, but as *creator*. In so doing, we find that, although copyright may go too far in vindicating the rights of some creators, it actually does too little for others. Formalities lie at the heart of this hierarchy of protection, and, as we demonstrate, they provide insight into the particular interests the modern copyright regime serves. This deconstruction of copyright code is both revealing and instructive. Most prominently, it shatters the myth of American copyright militancy by demonstrating how our copyright system is far less protective of creator interests than those of other countries. But just as importantly, it suggests it is not necessarily greater or lesser copyright that we need, but rather a regime that more fully considers the interests of ordinary individuals acting as both users and creators of creative content.

I. Art, Aura, and Authenticity

In his seminal meditation on art and technology, Walter Benjamin contemplated the transformative role of mechanical reproduction on society's relationship with creative works.[1]

Specifically, he postulated the increasing ease of replication would destroy art's *aura*—its perceived authenticity and ritualistic value. "For the first time in world history," argued Benjamin, "mechanical reproduction emancipates the work of art from its parasitical dependence on ritual."[2] To Benjamin, mass mechanical reproduction would result in the demystification of art by liberating it from its erstwhile settings. He concluded "the technique of reproduction detaches the reproduced object from the domain of tradition. . . . [I]n permitting the reproduction to meet the beholder or listener in his own particular situation, it reactivates the object reproduced."[3]

Benjamin's prescient views on art in the postmodern and digital eras have been widely appreciated.[4] But just as nature cannot escape Newton's Third Law of Motion,[5] there have been forces pushing against the inexorable march of technology. Benjamin underestimated the way in which law could emerge as a powerful countervailing force against the demystification of art. Indeed, as mechanical reproduction has flourished (thereby subverting art's *aura*), copyright law has concomitantly grown more robust (thereby policing authenticity and reaffirming the *aura*). In short, copyright law has served as a powerful bulwark against the demystifying tide of mechanical reproduction.

Copyright law, where it is most strictly applied, prohibits any kind of reproduction, whether manual or mechanical.[6] It controls exhibition of works through public performance and display rights.[7] And it carefully patrols a creative work's cultural value through the derivative-works doctrine.[8] Moreover, the decoupling of a copyright from ownership of a physical object enables the exertion of control over a creative work to be distant and omnipresent. As Christian Stallberg points out, "If intellectual works can be used everywhere, then the exclusive protection of those works restricts people everywhere."[9] After all, in the age of mechanical (and digital) reproduction, creative works can be disseminated universally. Yet copyright law imposes an artificial scarcity. It may do so with very good reason, but the consequences of this regulatory power bear careful scrutiny.

To understand the role of copyright law in enforcing artificial scarcity, this chapter closely examines the practicalities of infringement litigation, specifically the issue of copyright registration and damages. Perhaps due to its banal technicalities, our registration regime has received little attention from academics, who have eschewed analysis of its various niceties in favor of more substantive aspects of copyright law. However, the registration system is deeply relevant to anyone attempting to enforce his or her copyright and, as such, plays a key role in understanding how copyright law functions in practice. As we shall see, the remedies afforded under the Copyright Act, and the prerequisites for their availability, inextricably affect infringement behavior. Moreover, they determine the types of works that are entitled, in the age of mechanical reproduction, to resurrect the Benjaminian aura, and the types of works that are not. As theory begets praxis, these seemingly procedural rules have a profound and substantive impact on the fundamental nature of our copyright regime. Specifically, the registration system reifies the divide between highbrow and lowbrow works, sustaining the aura of art according to a cultural hierarchy policed by legal formalities.

The implications of this gestalt are significant, contradicting one of the most oft-repeated axioms about our intellectual property laws: that we take copyright seriously and enforce it vigorously with one of the most protective regimes in the world. Academics, politicians, trade representatives, and the content-creation industries alike have reiterated this apparent truism time and time again.[10] But it is not entirely accurate. In a sense, the Emperor has been sold a suit of copyright that leaves unsophisticated creators naked—that is, without sufficiently meaningful remedies for infringements of their creative works. Copyrighted works are effectively placed into a hierarchy of care that in many ways safeguards creators less vigorously than regimes in other countries. At its core, the current system privileges the interests of repeat, sophisticated, and monied rightsholders—rightsholders who are invariably also users of content. And it does so at the expense of smaller, less sophisticated creators and authors.[11] Moreover, existing law practically encourages certain kinds of infringement.

Unlike any of its intellectual property allies, the United States demands timely registration of a copyright in order for rightsholders to qualify for the recovery of statutory damages and attorneys' fees. Through the use of this ostensibly neutral formality, a vast disparity has emerged between sophisticated and unsophisticated creators of copyrightable content—a divide enforced through a single technical feature of our copyright regime: the registration requirement. For the sophisticated creators who timely register their copyrighted content, the inviolable aura of their works is virtually assured. For unsophisticated creators who fail to timely register their copyrighted content, their works enjoy only low-tier protection and remain vulnerable to unauthorized manipulation and appropriation.

By unfurling the unique importance of timely registration in shaping remedies, this chapter punctures the myth of American copyright militancy. We begin by examining how judicial interpretations of the Copyright Act have narrowed the availability of enhanced damages for continuing infringements, created a one-way risk of attorneys' fees assessments for unsophisticated plaintiffs, foreclosed availability of punitive and reputational damages, and, in short, left most authors at a comparative disadvantage in protecting their intellectual property rights in the United States vis-à-vis the rest of the world. As a result, the registration system has failed to achieve its basic notice function and has potentially shirked our international treaty obligations—a particularly salient problem in light of our efforts to combat lax copyright enforcement in many developing countries.

We next deconstruct the failure of prior efforts to amend the harsh results of the timely registration requirement. This analysis suggests that certain sophisticated, repeat players in the content industries derive the best of both worlds from the timely registration requirement. On one hand, they enjoy strong rights when seeking to enforce their copyrights, often wielding the threat of disproportional penalties against accused infringers. On the other, when they function as users of intellectual property (something all creators do), these same players often face only the most paltry of penalties, even when they infringe willfully. By drawing on a wide range of examples—from Hollywood screenplays to the formative blues riffs upon which rock music is built, paparazzi shots of Britney Spears to the iconic portrait of Che Guevara qua revolutionary, and congressional testimony from Scott Turow to publisher battles against university copy shops—we deconstruct the beneficiaries of the existing regime.

Finally, we assess possible avenues for change and offer some caveats regarding outright repeal of the timely registration requirement. Specifically, upon consideration of the consequences of copyright law's remaining technicalities, this chapter advances the case for holistic reforms that place creators—both sophisticated and unsophisticated alike—on a relatively equal footing while balancing the rights of copyright holders with copyright users.

II. The Emperor Has No Copyright: Reexamining Copyright's Registration Requirement

A. CHALLENGING THE CONVENTIONAL WISDOM ON AMERICAN COPYRIGHT PROTECTION: CONTENT HIERARCHY AND THE REGISTRATION REQUIREMENT

Conventional wisdom maintains that we enjoy one of the world's most robust intellectual property regimes through our arduous protection of the exclusive right of creators to control the reproduction, distribution, and exploitation of their works. Indeed, we pride ourselves on our respect for creations of the mind, often analogizing the piracy of copyrighted works to the outright theft of tangible property.[12] This view is further buoyed by our reputation on the international scene and the heated rhetoric of federal officials and entertainment industry players in chastising some countries for their more lax intellectual property regimes. Our demands for stronger copyright enforcement abroad have led to high profile clashes with officials in such countries as China[13] and Russia,[14] where loose enforcement and rampant piracy have drawn our ire.

There are two limited exceptions, however, to this general proposition. First, as many observers have noted, our legal regime is less protective of the moral rights of creators than regimes in some other countries, especially those in Western Europe.[15] But, our resistance to moral rights has not been explained as a product of hostility toward copyright protection or even the rights of authors. Instead, it has been rationalized as a product of American capitalism and its desire to maximize the alienability of property rights and to preserve a marketplace for copyrighted works.[16] Moral rights, we are told, may unduly interfere with the disposition of tangible property that incorporates copyrighted content.

Second, observers have pointed out that the hard line the United States has taken on copyright issues is of relatively recent vintage. Specifically, these critics have questioned the moral undertones of the international North–South discourse on copyright protection by calling attention to the selective historical consciousness at play.[17] Despite efforts by the United States and its copyright allies to pressure some developing countries to increase their enforcement efforts in combating piracy and protecting copyright, it is important to recognize that, at a similar point in our nation's development, we adamantly refused to recognize the copyrights of foreign authors. In short, until the early twentieth century, the United States was the most prominent rogue nation on the international copyright scene.

As law professor Harry G. Henn wrote in 1953, "The United States has been among the most parochial of nations so far as copyright protection for published works is concerned. For over a hundred years, this nation not only denied copyright protection to published works by foreigners . . . but appeared to encourage the piracy of such works."[18] Our nation's first Copyright Act, passed in 1790, explicitly denied protection to any creative work "written, printed or published by any person not a citizen of the United States, in foreign parts or places without the jurisdiction of the United States."[19] Indeed, between 1800 and 1860, nearly fifty percent of the bestsellers in the United States were pirated English novels.[20] It was not until the end of the nineteenth century that things changed, after heavy lobbying by prominent British and American writers. Authors across the pond, such as Charles Dickens, were being deprived of royalties for sales in the States.

Domestic authors, such as Mark Twain,[21] were being denied foreign royalties as other countries were reciprocally declining to grant copyright to American authors.[22] Not until the passage of the International Copyright Act of 1891, also known as the Chase Act, would foreign authors finally enjoy copyright protection in the United States.[23]

According to the popular narrative, such unabashedly piratical lapses are merely vestiges of a bygone era.[24] As a result, we continue to view our modern copyright regime as muscular and highly protective of creators. Indeed, many observers—myself included—have critiqued the growing magnitude of our copyright monopoly and how it has often come at the expense of the public interest and the rights of users of expressive materials.[25] However, broadly speaking, the copyright regime is not nearly as uniformly protective of copyright holders

FIGURE 4.1 A Caricature of Charles Dickens Published During His American Reading Tour in 1867–68.

and creators as we often think. On the surface, we appear to advance the interests of copyright holders with vigor—perhaps too much so. But, the formalities of copyright protection and enforcement reveal a more complex system in operation.

Through formalities, the 1976 Copyright Act actually created two distinct tiers of effective protection for copyrighted works. Sophisticated, routine creators—generally corporations in content-creation industries—timely register their works and therefore enjoy generous remedies against infringers. These remedies include the recovery of reasonable attorneys' fees and the assessment of statutory damages—which can rise to the draconian level of up to $150,000 per willful act of infringement. Absent any proof of actual damages, such plaintiffs can elect statutory damages that quickly create the possibility of a multimillion-dollar judgment in their favor. By sharp contrast, unsophisticated creators (such as individual artists) typically do not timely register their works and are often left with little except moral force and the uncertain threat of injunctive relief to enforce their intellectual property rights. The dichotomy between sophisticated and unsophisticated creators thereby determines the relative sanctity of copyrighted works.

B. REGISTRATION AND THE PIVOTAL ROLE OF STATUTORY DAMAGES AND ATTORNEYS' FEES

The registration requirement is a critical aspect of the governing 1976 Copyright Act. Oddly enough, however, the abandonment of key formalities required for copyright protection was a purported hallmark of the Act.[26] Most notably, the Act vested an automatic federal copyright with authors from the moment they fix an original work in a tangible medium, without the need for registration or any other procedural step.[27] Nevertheless, upon closer examination, the 1976 Act's general reputation for eschewing formalism appears vastly exaggerated.

Although formalities for subsistence may have been eliminated under the 1976 Act, formalities for effective enforcement of a copyright actually *increased*. First, the 1976 Act retained its predecessor's requirement of registration prior to the filing of an infringement action.[28] Even more significantly, the 1976 Act dramatically expanded formalities in a key regard. Under the 1909 Act, a prevailing plaintiff could recover statutory damages and attorneys' fees without timely registration.[29] All of that changed with the 1976 Act. What the 1976 Act gave to creators of copyrighted works through its purported reduction of vesting formalities, it more than took away through the imposition of timely registration as a precondition for recovery of statutory damages and attorneys' fees—two of the most powerful weapons in a copyright holder's arsenal.[30] Thus, although creative works are now "protected" under federal law from the moment of creation, litigation rarely makes sense without proper and timely registration. In an ordinary case of copyright infringement—where an infringed work is not registered before the infringement begins—a plaintiff can only recover actual damages that directly result from the defendant's action. As we shall see, such a remedy is rarely adequate to enable a copyright holder to vindicate his or her interests in even the most clear-cut and brazen case of infringement.

Moreover, rather than further harmonizing our copyright regime with those of other countries, through its timely registration requirement, the 1976 Act has ironically enhanced the exceptionalism of the American copyright system. Specifically, the United States is the only major country in the world with a timely registration prerequisite for the recovery of certain forms of damages and attorneys' fees.[31] In other countries, full legal vindication of one's exclusive rights does not require the added procedure of registration, let alone timely registration.[32]

The registration requirement plays an instrumental role in the enforcement of copyright in the United States. As Nimmer reminds us, "statutory damages may often constitute the only meaningful remedy available to a copyright owner for infringement of his work."[33] Yet not all copyright holders can qualify for statutory damages in an infringement suit—far from it, in fact. Under the reigning 1976 Copyright Act, statutory damages are only available to a certain class of copyright holders: those who register their works with the U.S. Copyright Office in a timely manner in relation to the infringement. The absence of timely registration also precludes an award of attorneys' fees to a prevailing plaintiff. As 17 U.S.C. § 412 provides,

> no award of statutory damages or of attorney's fees . . . shall be made for . . . any infringement of copyright commenced after first publication of the work and before the effective date of its registration, unless such registration is made within three months after the first publication of the work.[34]

Thus, to qualify for statutory damages and the potential recovery of attorneys' fees, a copyright plaintiff must register before a defendant's act of infringement or within ninety days of publication. Registration, especially timely registration, therefore represents a pivotal feature on the copyright landscape. Without it, a plaintiff's remedies are dramatically constrained.

Assume, for example, that a pharmaceutical company usurps five of an artist's illustrations for use on the packaging of its new male enhancement drug. With proper and timely registration, the artist can immediately force the pharmaceutical company to pay attention to her infringement claims and to cease the infringing conduct. Even without a demonstration of actual damages or profit from the infringement, a suit would expose the defendant to potential liability for statutory damages in the amount of $750,000 ($150,000 for each of five acts of infringement), reimbursement of the artist's reasonable attorneys' fees, and expenditure of its own attorneys' fees.

Without proper and timely registration, however, the situation is radically different. The artist can generally recover only actual economic damages from the company—lost sales, or disgorgement of profits. Not surprisingly, the amount of these damages is often riddled with ambiguity. Moreover, unless the artist is world renowned, her damages claim will rarely amount to more than a few thousand dollars, while pursuing an infringement suit will cost her several hundred thousand dollars in attorneys' fees. And although the artist might receive an injunction to prevent further infringement, it will be costly to obtain as the significant fees she would have to incur in its pursuit are not recoupable. Thus, even under the most optimistic scenario, legal action will not be worth pursuing, unless she has a desire to fight for principle and end up bankrupt. In short, the artist may ultimately recover $5000 from the defendant, but such a victory would be Pyrrhic at best, especially after accounting for the $250,000 invoice from her attorney.[35]

To make matters worse, a quarter of a million dollars is a conservative estimate for the cost of copyright litigation. According to the 2009 Report of the Economic Survey conducted by the American Intellectual Property Law Association, the mean cost of taking a relatively small instance of copyright infringement (one involving less than $1 million in potential liability) to trial in United States is $310,000.[36] For a middle-of-the-road infringement case (one involving $1 million to $25 million in potential liability), that figure rises to a mean of $749,000.[37]

As such, it frequently makes no economic sense to pursue litigation. The cost of filing a complaint in federal court will likely exceed the total amount of damages recoverable under even the most sanguine scenario. And this is true even though a defendant has undoubtedly infringed the work and done so with gusto. In short, the law fails to provide an effective remedy from the wrongdoing the artist has suffered at the hands of the pharmaceutical company, even though we think of our laws as protecting the sanctity and inviolability of intellectual property rights, especially when they are indisputably infringed.

This all-too common situation allows large, sophisticated corporations to enforce their copyright with a vast array of tools, including statutory damages and attorneys' fees, while simultaneously enabling them to laugh in the face of less sophisticated players who lodge infringement claims against them. If you infringe the copyrights of the major motion picture studios or the major record labels, the specter of statutory damages and fees will squarely put you on the defensive. Witness the onslaught of suits against ordinary Americans filed by the Recording Industry Association of American (RIAA) for unauthorized peer-to-peer file-sharing.[38] By contrast, if a large corporation violates your copyright, it can often thumb its nose at claims of infringement. In many cases, there is little you can do as most copyright holders are unlikely to register their copyright on a timely basis. As such, you are left with an appeal not to law but to morality. Thus, the dynamics of the existing registration regime—put into place on January 1, 1978 and largely unchanged by the implementation of the Berne Convention and other subsequent amendments to the Copyright Act—elevate procedural steps into outcome-determinative hurdles. The impact is both dramatic and underappreciated.

Consider, for example, the hypothetical situation presented in Chapter 1, where we followed a day in the life of an imaginary law professor named John. Through the course of an ordinary twenty-four hours, Professor John managed to engage in at least eighty-three acts of infringement. However, when one considers the implications of the registration regime, it becomes clear that, in all likelihood, not all of his infringements are valued similarly. In the hypothetical, John arguably infringed twenty e-mail messages, three law-related articles, Frank Gehry's Bilbao Guggenheim, e.e. cummings' "I sing of Olaf glad and big," Hanna-Barbera's Captain Caveman, Time Warner's "Happy Birthday," Shag's *Wives with Knives*, and fifty anonymous notes and drawings. Of these eighty-three works, the five works by sophisticated creators/owners—those by Gehry, cummings, Hanna-Barbera, Time Warner and Shag—are almost certainly registered. Additionally, the three law-related articles are possibly registered. But the remaining seventy-five works—the e-mails, photographs, and notes by unsophisticated creators—are unlikely to be registered. Although works by Gehry, cummings, Hanna-Barbera, Time Warner, and Shag may have high general economic value, and registration may serve as a (highly imperfect) proxy of such, the harm stemming from their unauthorized use in this scenario is no greater than the actual harm suffered by the owners of the non-registered works. Yet for infringing the eight registered works, should litigation be pursued against him, Professor John faces liability in the amount of $1.2 million in statutory damages plus responsibility for attorneys' fees. For infringing the seventy-five unregistered works, however, Professor John likely faces liability only in the amount of a few pennies.

C. HIERARCHY AND THE UNSOPHISTICATED CONTENT CREATOR

A closer examination of the language and extant interpretation of the Copyright Act reveals the particular difficulties facing unsophisticated creators in seeking to vindicate their rights in the United States, especially in comparison to their peers in foreign countries. First, courts have found that section 412 precludes recovery of statutory damages and attorneys' fees when an infringement continues after registration. As a result, an infringer has veritable carte blanche to continue its wrongful activity with impunity if a work is not timely registered at the moment of first infringement. Second, unsophisticated creators face a dangerous one-way risk of attorneys' fees. Plaintiffs who fail to register their copyright on a timely basis are *never* eligible to recover their fees if they prevail in a suit, no matter how wanton the infringement at issue. By contrast, defendants are *always* eligible to recover their fees if they prevail. This unbalanced fees matrix dampens any enthusiasm unsophisticated creators might have about seeking redress through the judicial system. Third, unsophisticated creators have no ability to seek punitive or reputational damages; the actual damages they can receive are insufficient to make them whole and provide no deterrent effect against infringers. All told, these factors combine to create a rather bleak enforcement regime for the rights of creators who do not register in a timely manner.

1. Interpreting Section 412's Timeliness Requirement: The Unavailability of Partial Eligibility for Statutory Damages or Attorneys' Fees

First, the challenges facing unsophisticated creators seeking to be made whole for unauthorized exploitation of their copyrighted works have grown more pronounced with the courts' reading of section 412's timely registration requirement. Specifically, even in cases of egregious and continuing infringement after registration, courts have denied plaintiffs access to statutory damages and attorneys' fees. On one hand, courts may have had no other alternative but to do this: there is little doubt section 412 is perfectly clear in proscribing the imposition of statutory damages and attorneys' fees when all acts of infringement by a defendant occur before registration. On the other hand, the issue is more ambiguous when an infringement occurs, the copyright holder then registers the work, and the infringement continues. Nevertheless, courts have almost uniformly resolved this issue in favor of defendants, holding that in such an instance statutory damages and attorneys' fees may not be awarded for any act of infringement either before or after registration.

Courts have adopted this narrow view of the scope of plaintiff eligibility for statutory damages and attorneys' fees through their interpretation of the term "any infringement." Indeed, the reported cases considering the issue have determined "infringement 'commences' for the purposes of § 412 when the first act in a series of acts constituting continuing infringement occurs."[39] Thus, "*the first act of infringement* in a series of ongoing infringements of the same kind marks the commencement of one continuing infringement under [§] 412."[40] As a result, if an artist discovers a company is infringing her work and then registers that work and sues for infringement, the artist cannot seek any recompense in the way of statutory damages or attorneys' fees, even for those acts of infringement that occur *after* the registration. Moreover, the narrow construction of "any infringement" under section 412 has led courts to insulate from statutory damages and attorneys' fees defendants who infringed prior to registration of the operative work, even if they conduct new acts of infringement after registration occurs.[41] The results of this rule are dramatic and perverse. As one disgruntled copyright claimant put it, this judicial interpretation grants infringers a "license to steal."[42]

Consider a scenario where officials at a major clothing manufacturer decide to use the work of an artist for their new autumn line. Assume they contemplate approaching the artist for a license but ultimately decide to use the work without authorization. Maybe they cannot be bothered to track down the artist, they are concerned about the extra costs a license would add to product development, they think the chance of getting caught is remote, or their attempts to obtain a license are frustrated as talks with the artist break down when the parties cannot agree on a rate of compensation. Regardless of the particular context and motivations at play, the officials are aware of the need to license under federal law, but they decide to bring the product to market without a license. Several months later, the artist discovers the wholesale infringement. He immediately registers his work with the Copyright Office and then files suit against the company.

Because of the courts' narrow interpretation of section 412, the best the artist can hope for is to receive actual damages for the company's willful infringement. As a result, there is little incentive for the company to stop infringing. After all, whether the company ceases and desists now that it has been caught red-handed will play little role in any damages the artist can receive. There are no punitive damages available in copyright actions, and statutory damages, which alone provide discretionary enhancements for willful infringement, are not available. The company can continue to infringe with impunity and, at the most, pay only actual damages that leave the unrepentant infringer without an incentive to respect copyright ex ante and effectively granting the infringer a compulsory license. Even if the artist attempts to obtain preliminary injunctive relief, the prospects for success are dubious. By the time he obtains an injunction, its value has diminished significantly: the clothing manufacturer may have moved on to its next line of seasonal clothing. Moreover, obtaining injunctive relief is expensive and the fees for doing so are non-recoupable.

The underlying rationale for this result is particularly problematic and rests on several unfounded assumptions about our registration system. In 2008, the Ninth Circuit addressed the registration-timing issue on damages for the first time with its ruling in *Derek Andrew, Inc. v. Poof Apparel Corp.*[43] The court adopted the reasoning and conclusion of the other circuits that have considered the issue by finding that such an interpretation of section 412 advanced Congress's intent to "promote early registration of copyright" by (1) "provid[ing] copyright owners with an incentive to register their copyright promptly" and (2) "encourag[ing] potential infringers to check the Copyright Officer's database."[44]

Although the statute may not leave sufficient room for alternate interpretations, these rationalizations themselves do not hold up under scrutiny. First, if a court held that each of a series of ongoing infringements constituted a new act of infringement for the purposes of section 412, copyright holders would still have a strong incentive to register. After all, there are numerous other advantages to registration besides qualification for statutory damages and attorneys' fees. Specifically, timely registration serves an important evidentiary function by enabling rightsholders to make infringement cases more easily. For example, registration provides a plaintiff with a prima facie presumption of copyright validity—but only if a work is registered within five years of publication.[45] Thus, plaintiffs have a strong incentive to register on a relatively timely basis in order to enjoy the presumption of validity. Registration also provides proof of the date of creation. This benefit encourages timely registration because, ipso facto, a work's date of registration sets its latest possible date of creation. Thus, a registration certificate dated March 6, 2003, irrefutably establishes the registered work must have been created before March 6, 2003. Such proof can be instrumental in many cases, especially where a defense of independent, or earlier, creation is proffered.

Second, as we explore later, the idea that potential infringers can confidently check the Copyright Office's database for complete registration information is deeply flawed. In short, the entire notion that registration will serve a notice function to potential infringers is a vast exaggeration. Moreover, the consequences of the current reading of section 412 are perverse as, in many instances, it immunizes defendants so they may infringe with impunity.

Of course, it is fair to ask whether a different reading of section 412 by the courts, in which each violation of an exclusive right secured under section 106 constitutes a new infringement for the purposes of section 412, would fare any better. As it turns out, such an alternate reading would lead to a whole new set of policy problems. First, courts would have to address the thorny issue of when one violation ends and the next begins. In the pre-Internet age, it was easier to make such a determination. After all, infringements came in more discrete bits—each day's edition of the newspaper featuring the infringement or each broadcast of an infringement could constitute a new act. But in the nondiscrete world of the Internet, online newspapers and blogs are updated continuously, and websites stream infringing content at all hours of the day. Second, a different reading of section 412 might nullify the entire purpose of the timely registration incentive for statutory damages and attorneys' fees. After all, a plaintiff could wait for an infringement to occur, register, and then sue with a colorable demand for statutory damages and attorneys' fees so long as the defendant violates just a single exclusive right of the plaintiff after the effective date of registration. In the end, however, the shortcomings of an alternative interpretation of section 412 provide further reason to rethink the registration requirement as it pertains to statutory damages and attorneys' fees.

2. The One-Way Risk of a Fees Award

The 1976 Copyright Act disincentivizes unsophisticated artists from vindicating their legal rights through litigation in another way: the one-way risk of an attorneys' fee award. Section 505 gives courts the general discretion to grant fees to a prevailing party in an infringement suit, and frequently courts do so. For example, the Ninth Circuit, billed by Judge Alex Kozinski as "the Court of Appeals for the Hollywood Circuit,"[46] has in the past generally awarded fees to prevailing plaintiffs in copyright suits.[47] However, section 412 of the Act prevents courts from awarding fees to a plaintiff who has not timely registered.[48] This creates a one-way risk for any individual artist attempting to be made whole. Most individual artists do not timely register and are therefore ineligible for attorneys' fees. Yet a prevailing defendant *always* enjoys the potential to recover fees. Thus, without timely registration, if you prevail in your infringement suit, you can never obtain attorneys' fees. But, should you lose, the defendant can recover fees against you.

This state of affairs significantly dissuades the individual artist from pursuing even a clear-cut case of infringement, lest something go wrong at trial. Even in the most obvious case of infringement, there is always a chance the case may go awry due to an error in registration, a difference of opinion over "substantial similarity," or a generous reading of the fair use doctrine by the trier of fact.

For example, errors in registration[49] are commonplace and almost always play a role in a defense to an infringement suit. As Charles Ossola reminds us, parties will often spend hundreds of thousands of dollars in a suit dealing with the inevitable claim of fraud on the Copyright Office based on mistakes in an application for registration. As he explains, "There are almost always mistakes, or at least arguable mistakes [in a registration application], which are invariably discovered during litigation."[50] On occasion, courts have looked askance at such errors, throwing out suits in their entirety, no matter how strong the merits and how blatant the infringement.[51]

3. The Inadequacy of Remedies Absent Timely Registration

Absent access to statutory damages and attorneys' fees, a creator has little meaningful ability to punish an infringer or deter future acts of infringement. As Judge Richard Posner has stated,

> [T]here is no basis in the law for requiring the infringer to give up more than his gain when it exceeds the copyright owners' loss. Such a requirement would add a punitive as distinct from a restitutionary element to copyright damages, and . . . the statute contains no provision for punitive damages.[52]

Posner's conclusion is widely shared. As Nimmer observes, "The cases are clear that exemplary or punitive damages should not be awarded in a statutory copyright infringement action."[53] At first blush, it would appear the Copyright Act provides plenty of room for punitive style damages under the guise of the statutory damages regime and pursuant to the courts' authority to enhance those statutory damages five-fold on the grounds of willful infringement. However, in the vast majority of real-world infringements, untimely registration of a copyright precludes a prevailing plaintiff from recovering statutory damages (or any willfulness enhancement), no matter how egregious the defendant's conduct.

Thus, with punitive damages unavailable, a prevailing unsophisticated creator is left with only actual damages or disgorgement of profits. However, for copyright infringement, actual damages are often speculative and expensive to prove. Moreover, case law interpreting the Copyright Act has specifically excluded psychological injury from the equation for actual damages. Thus, if your artwork is used in an unauthorized manner that is repulsive to you, the modern damages analysis provides you with no relief on these grounds.[54]

Disgorgement of profit can certainly be a useful remedy, but it is often difficult to quantify. Although case law does establish a presumption that all profits stem from the infringing act, it is rebuttable, leading courts to engage in the problematic task of accurate apportionment.[55] Moreover, a defendant will often show no profit. For example, the entertainment industry is notorious for its ability to show a loss on virtually every project, including some of its biggest hits.[56] To scrutinize such troublesome accounting, a plaintiff needs to spend extensive time in discovery without any hope of recovering fees for the effort.

When it becomes too difficult for a plaintiff to demonstrate profit by the defendant from an act of infringement, a few courts have analogized to patent law's reasonable royalty analysis for damages and have allowed the assessment of a hypothetical license value for the unauthorized use of the copyrighted work.[57] But as Nimmer notes, this line of authority is of relatively recent vintage, and only a "smattering" of decisions have explicitly followed the lead of the Seventh Circuit, which first allowed such a recovery in its 1985 ruling.[58] Under this analysis, a court determines ex ante the price upon which a willing licensor and licensee would have agreed for the use. But unlike patents, copyrighted works are not merely commodities. As such, there are many more unwilling copyright licensors than unwilling patent licensors. One's willingness to license one's invention might differ markedly from one's willingness to license one's song. In the realm of patents, for example, there are no holdouts from licensing on the grounds it will diminish the inherent beauty of the invention. The same is not true of copyrighted content, largely because of the personal and artistic content that form its subject matter. Consider the reticence of some major bands to license their music for use in advertising. R.E.M. famously rejected an offer of more than $10 million from Microsoft for use of their tune "It's the End of the World as We Know It (And I Feel Fine)" for the launch of Windows 95—though The Rolling Stones were more than happy to step in and ultimately ended up licensing "Start Me Up" for the use.[59] However, a medical device maker is unlikely to refuse to license its patented technology for a rate far above market.

The one area of potentially meaningful leverage an unsophisticated creator does possess is the threat of injunctive relief. But this leverage is limited in several critical ways. To begin with, the creator must first discover the infringement at the ideal time to effectively utilize the threat of injunctive relief. This occurs on the eve of a product release, when enjoining the distribution of an infringing product is both most feasible and economically painful. Often, however, infringement is not discovered until much later, after the infringer has already enjoyed significant unauthorized use of the work.

Second, the burdens facing a plaintiff seeking injunctive relief in an intellectual property dispute have grown markedly in recent years. Specifically, there is no automatic entitlement to injunctive relief in a copyright dispute, no matter the merits of a claim. Rather, the choice to grant an injunction—either preliminary or permanent—resides within the sound discretion of the trial court.[60] Absent exceptional circumstances, courts used to routinely grant permanent injunctions to prevailing plaintiffs in intellectual property cases. However, starting with dicta in *New York Times Co. v. Tasini*,[61] and culminating in an express statement in *eBay v. Mercantile Exchange*,[62] which ruled on the issue in the patent context, the Supreme Court has abandoned this general rule.[63] By allowing judges the discretion to transform patent, copyright, and trademark protection from property rights to a liability regime, the Court reasserted the importance of a critical element sometimes overlooked in the adversarial setting: the public interest. Courts therefore possess the option to order damages but allow an act of infringement to continue unabated. As the Supreme Court held in *eBay*, "[T]his Court has consistently rejected invitations to replace traditional equitable considerations with a rule that an injunction automatically follows a determination that a copyright has been infringed."[64]

Courts have begun to apply the principals of *eBay* in the context of preliminary injunctions as well. A recent wave of cases has questioned the presumption of irreparable harm all intellectual property plaintiffs used to enjoy when applying for injunctive relief.[65] Of course, there may be plenty of good public policy reasons to make obtaining injunctive relief in intellectual property disputes more difficult both at the preliminary and permanent levels. As Justice Kennedy noted in his *eBay* concurrence:

> When the patented invention is but a small component of the product the companies seek to produce and the threat of an injunction is employed simply for undue leverage in negotiations, legal damages may well be sufficient to compensate for the infringement and an injunction may not serve the public interest. In addition injunctive relief may have different consequences for the burgeoning number of patents over business methods, which were not of much economic and legal significance in earlier times.[66]

Along the same lines, during a widespread outbreak of anthrax, it may not make sense to enjoin an infringing company from distributing lifesaving drugs to the infected. That said, however, the increased difficulty in obtaining injunctive relief in intellectual property disputes dramatically and disproportionately impacts unsophisticated creators seeking to vindicate their rights.

Additionally, with the burden placed on the plaintiff to demonstrate a likelihood of success on the merits, a defendant need only poke sufficient doubt into a single issue (such as registration or ownership) to defeat an application for preliminary injunctive relief. Moreover, even if a court grants an injunction, it can be stayed pending an appeal and, in the end, can only issue after the plaintiff posts a bond.[67] Under the Federal Rules, a court must set the security at an amount sufficient "for the payment of such costs and damages as may be incurred or suffered by any party who is found to have been wrongfully enjoined."[68] Thus, a bond can be especially expensive when seeking to halt the distribution of a valuable product, and the high price can be cost-prohibitive for many plaintiffs.[69] Finally, the attorneys' fees expended to obtain injunctive relief are never recoupable for a plaintiff who has not timely registered an infringed work. In all, therefore, there are numerous shortcomings to the remedies available for plaintiffs whose works are not timely registered but are willfully infringed.

4. Pitfalls for the Unsophisticated Even with Timely Registration: The Inevitable and Wasteful Scrutinization of Registration Applications

At the same time, the registration regime elevates form over substance, leading to a disproportional emphasis on compliance with formalities when one attempts to vindicate one's intellectual property rights. Indeed, the most profoundly time-consuming and taxing aspect of many copyright infringement suits is the inevitable attack lodged by defendants against the propriety of the registration. Though this arguably should be one of the least important aspects of litigation—after all, questions of copyright ownership, validity, and substantial similarity would appear to trump it in significance—registration often becomes a central question because the entire value of the case rides on the issue. If the registration is declared invalid, a plaintiff loses standing to bring the suit and must begin the litigation anew after filing a new registration form. More problematically, if the registration is deemed invalid, the plaintiff loses the right to recover statutory damages and attorneys' fees against the defendant, even if the suit is refiled. Quite simply, valid registration will not have occurred prior to the commencement of infringement.

Because of the value of timely registration, procedural formalities are crucial in copyright infringement litigation, often overshadowing the merits of a case. For a system purportedly seeking to vindicate the legitimate rights of creators, this can be a devastating turn of events. Because statutory damages, attorneys' fees, and even the ability to bring a suit in the first place rely on proper and timely registration, the tendency of some courts to lapse into hyperformalism when scrutinizing registration applications has dramatic consequences. Although there is ample basis to view errors in the registration process forgivingly,[70] many courts have deviated from this scheme—certainly enough to give unsophisticated plaintiffs pause about pursuing an infringement action. Several cases from the federal circuit courts illustrate this cautionary note.

Consider *Raquel v. Education Management Corp.*,[71] an infringement suit involving the rock band Nirvana. In the case, the copyright holder to the song "Pop Goes the Music" had sued, inter alia, Nirvana and its record label, Geffen, for the unauthorized use of the song in Nirvana's music video "About a Girl". The defendants responded by arguing, inter alia, that the plaintiff lacked a proper registration for the work. As it turned out, the plaintiff had filed a copyright registration application for a musical composition and described the "nature of the work" as an "audiovisual work." The reason for this designation seemed plausible enough: the claimant had submitted a videotape of a television commercial in which the claimant's song had been performed. Moreover, the claimant had correctly noted on the registration application that the nature of the authorship claim was "[a]ll music and lyrics and arrangement." Nevertheless, the court invalidated the registration on the grounds the claimant had made a material misrepresentation to the Copyright Office obfuscating information that would have led to the application's rejection. Moreover, the court held the misrepresentation was not inadvertent or innocent, a fact that would ordinarily prevent invalidation. The case drew a vigorous dissent from future Supreme Court Justice Samuel Alito, who charged the majority with irrationally and unfairly elevating form over substance and mandating "a forfeiture of a valid copyright because of a misstatement that the trial court had already labeled inadvertent."[72]

Indeed, the court's concern about intentional misrepresentation appears particularly misplaced when one considers the real facts. The premise underlying the entire opinion—fraud on the Copyright Office—was simply untrue. As it turns out, the Copyright Office was not misled in any way. The Office took pains to announce this when it formally addressed *Raquel* by issuing a statement of policy on Registration of Claims to Copyright.[73] The Copyright Office unequivocally and resoundingly rejected the reasoning of *Raquel*:

> The Copyright Office is issuing this policy statement to clarify that it was not misled in registering the copyright claim in the *Raquel* case, and that the Copyright Office knew that the copyright claim was in a musical work, and not an audiovisual work. The Office is also issuing this statement to clarify that in the "nature of this work" space on Form PA, it has been and continues to be acceptable to describe the physical nature of the deposit submitted with the application.[74]

Despite the Copyright Office's firm rebuke of the holding in *Raquel*, it was too late to help the plaintiff. Moreover, despite the Copyright Office's statement of policy, the ultimate question of registration validity remains in the hands of the courts. As the *Raquel* case and others demonstrate, there is always the risk of invalidation of a registration on relatively minor grounds.[75] Indeed, other circuit courts have also invalidated registrations (although not on such a flimsy basis) because of errors contained in the application forms.[76]

At the turn of the last century, the Register of Copyrights at the time, Thorvald Solberg, expressed his profound distaste for the registration regime and its ability to punish seemingly innocuous errors and omissions with the dramatic loss of substantive rights. In a report to the Librarian of Congress dated December 1, 1903, he wrote,

"[A] system has gradually grown up under which valuable literary rights have come to depend upon exact compliance with these statutory formalities which have no relation to the equitable rights involved, and the question may very well be raised whether this condition should be continued."[77] Over a century later, the same concern continues to resonate.

5. Comparing American and Foreign Infringement Remedies

When one considers the remedies available to any creator under foreign laws, the tremendous disadvantages facing unsophisticated creators in the United States become all the more remarkable. Compare our infringement remedies to those of the United Kingdom and Canada—two countries whose legal regimes are most closely aligned to our own. The United Kingdom has no government registration system at all. And although statutory damages are not available, punitive damages—called "additional" damages—are. The United Kingdom's Copyright, Designs and Patent Act 1988 provides a plaintiff can recover actual damages plus "additional" damages to both deter future infringers and punish defendants who willfully violate a plaintiff's intellectual property rights.[78] Furthermore, prevailing plaintiffs (whether in copyright cases or otherwise) recover attorneys' fees.[79]

Canada similarly lacks a registration requirement. And although the country's remedies are more limited in some ways, they are also more expansive in others. First, any prevailing plaintiff in a copyright infringement suit is entitled to recover statutory damages and attorneys' fees, regardless of the existence or date of any copyright registration.[80] But, to counter this expansion in remedy eligibility, Canadian law limits the amount of statutory damages to a maximum award of CAN\$20,000 per act of infringement[81]— a small fraction of the maximum statutory damages award allowed under American law.[82] In addition, courts have discretion to award exemplary damages to punish infringers and effectively deter future infringements.[83]

Thus, in both Canada and the United Kingdom, sophisticated or unsophisticated creators share an equal footing as far as available remedies for the vindication of their copyright interests go. Additionally, unlike the United States, both the United Kingdom and Canada recognize noneconomic injuries, such as moral prejudice or harm to one's reputation, as cognizable damages in an infringement suit. For example, Directive 2004/48/EC of the European Parliament and of the Council of 29 April 2004 on the enforcement of intellectual property rights instructed Member States to grant judges the authority to fashion infringement awards, when appropriate, based on "moral prejudice"[84] to rightsholders. Pursuant to this directive, the United Kingdom passed the Intellectual Property (Enforcement, etc.) Regulations in 2006.[85] The Regulations asked judges to take into account "all appropriate aspects" of damages, including negative economic consequences and noneconomic factors such as "moral prejudice caused by the infringement."[86] In Germany, for example, authors, photographers, and performers may "recover, as justice may require, a monetary indemnity for the injury caused to them even if no pecuniary loss has occurred."[87] Thus, even in the absence of actual economic damages, German courts can fashion awards based on subjective, noneconomic harms stemming from infringement. Similarly, in Canada, a computation of actual damages, if elected in lieu of statutory damages, can include a claim of noneconomic injury (e.g., harm to a copyright holder's reputation).[88]

All told, the U.S. registration regime fails to protect unsophisticated creators adequately due to the unavailability of statutory damages even for post-registration infringement, the one-way risk of attorneys' fees, and the absence of any punitive or reputational damages. This situation is of even more concern when compared to the state of protection under foreign regimes, including those close to our own.

D. REGISTRATION AND THE FAILURE OF THE NOTICE FUNCTION

Besides putting unsophisticated creators at a profound disadvantage when seeking to vindicate their legal interests, the registration system fails to achieve even its basic function of notice. Despite our rhetorical distaste for copyright formalities, courts and commentators have explained the endurance of the registration regime based on the important notice function it serves. As numerous jurists have asserted, the registration requirement "encourages potential infringers to check the Copyright Office's database" to ascertain protection status.[89] However, this claim is vastly overstated.

At the outset, it is a dubious proposition that potential infringers would even check the database at all, let alone prior to their infringement. Such an assumption may have made marginally more sense in previous centuries when the law provided greater incentives to conduct a registration check. Prior to the enactment of the 1909 Copyright Act, for example, a work did not receive any copyright protection at all unless it was registered prior to, or simultaneous with, first publication.[90] The 1909 Act, which governed until December 31, 1977, reduced this formality somewhat by allowing a statutory copyright so long as a registration took place and a deposit was made "promptly" after publication.[91] Although the promptness requirement was substantially eviscerated with the Supreme Court's 1939 ruling in *Washingtonian Publishing Co. v. Pearson*,[92] delayed registration could give rise to a laches defense preventing enforcement of a copyright.[93] Timely registration remained a requirement until 1964 for the author to have the option to renew a copyright after the first twenty-eight-year term.

Thus, in the past, registration determined the copyright status of many works. Failure to conform to certain formalities, such as providing proper copyright notice on a work, was fatal to the work's protection.[94] As many published works were not registered, renewed, or published with certain notice formalities, there was a decent chance any given work lacked copyright protection. However, copyright now subsists from the moment of creation for all works created after January 1, 1978, meaning that just about any creative work authored in the past few decades enjoys copyright protection.[95] As a result, all creative works are copyrighted and are the potential subject of a lawsuit, regardless of registration status.[96]

At the same time, for works registered prior to 1978, the Copyright Office's Catalog of Copyright Entries is not available in any official online format. It is only accessible by visiting the Copyright Office Public Records Room in Washington, DC, by paying the Copyright Office to conduct a check, or by otherwise accessing a copy. Yet, even after conducting a thorough search, one cannot be sure of a work's copyright status. The Office's own searches produce only a "factual, noninterpretive report"[97] and, as the Office takes pains to caution, no investigation, no matter how comprehensive, can determine copyright status with certainty: "Copyright investigations often involve more than one of these methods [examining the work for proper copyright notice, searching the Copyright

Office catalog, having the Copyright Office make a search for you]. Even if you follow all three approaches, the results may not be conclusive."[98]

Thus, even on the off chance potential infringers do check the Copyright Office's records, they will frequently have difficulty gleaning accurate information about the registration status of a particular work. As regular practitioners know, the Copyright Office's database is not up-to-date. Although registration becomes effective upon the Copyright Office's receipt of a complete application,[99] a copyright registration certificate usually does not issue for several months—until after the Copyright Office has had the opportunity to evaluate and process an application. Even after a certificate is issued, there is an additional delay before the information is entered into the database. Although the Copyright Office's recent move to elective electronic registration may reduce some of these delays, there is still a significant gap between effective registration and the availability of such information on the Copyright Office's database.[100]

Additionally, the Copyright Office database—at least in its most accessible, online form—does not contain a single image or copy of a registered work. Instead, one must search for a work via text alone. Moreover, textual searches yield only the information an applicant has actually provided. Matching a work to a registration can, therefore, represent a task rife with uncertainty. For example, imagine you are a potential infringer who wants to use a photograph documenting the infamous night in 2006 when Hollywood starlets Britney Spears, Lindsay Lohan, and Paris Hilton hit Los Angeles's infamous Sunset Strip to celebrate Britney's divorce from Kevin Federline. That November evening, the paparazzi were on the prowl, and they caught the moment on film. The photographs hit the Internet and caused an immediate sensation, as several candid shots caught Britney *in flagrante commando*. Spears' unfortunate decision to disregard undergarments that evening led to the exposure of her nether regions to the world.

FIGURE 4.2 Britney, Lindsay and Paris, Together at Last.

It also raised two central legal issues. First, it traumatized millions, resulting in a potentially viable action for intentional infliction of emotional distress. Second, and less facetiously, it spurred a wave of copyright infringement. Within hours, thousands of bloggers reproduced the images without authorization so they could feature them on their front pages.

If you were seeking to use the photographs legally, you could have approached one of the sources of the photographs: X17.[101] However, as easy as it would have been to contact X17 and obtain a license (for the right price, of course), it would have been impossible to determine whether the photographs were registered with the Copyright Office. First, as the photographs had just been published, there was no way to know yet about their registration status. Second, even if you were seeking to use the photographs a year later, definitively determining registration status from the Copyright Office would be next to impossible. After all, you can only search by text and not image on the database. And, to make things worse, the work lacks a determinate title. Although movies and music usually have official titles, photographs often do not. Consider some of the most famous images of the twentieth century. With a simple description, most readers will immediately recall the photographs to which I am referring: Mohammed Ali (then Cassius Clay) lording over a defeated Sonny Liston,[102] an unnamed couple kissing jubilantly at celebrations marking the end of World War II in New York,[103] troops raising the American flag on Iwo Jima,[104] the first panoramic color view of planet Earth from space,[105] or the iconic shot of Che Guevara qua revolutionary.[106] But although recognizing these photographs may be easy, ascertaining their registration statuses or their titles is something else altogether.

For example, to check on the registration status of the Che Guevara photo, it would help to know the work is actually titled *Guerrillero Heroico*. Even then, the information you learn might lead you to the wrong conclusion. On the Copyright Officer's website, you would find a registration to the work that was based upon the Uruguay Round Agreement Act (URAA). The URAA restored copyright protection to certain foreign works that as of January 1, 1996, had fallen into the public domain in the United States because of a failure to comply with certain American formalities. The first problem with the registration is that it is unclear to which photograph the registration relates—the original version of the Che Guevara photograph or the more stylized, cropped version of the photograph that is more famous. Moreoever, regardless of which version is relevant, even though the copyright records suggest the photograph is protected, the work is likely in the public domain.

According to the photographer,[107] the original version was first published in Cuba around 1960, where copyright protection for a photograph extended only ten years from the date of first use.[108] Thus, the photograph has fallen into the public domain in Cuba. But even assuming the photograph originally received protection in the United States at the time of its Cuban publication, its present status in the United States is determined by the failure to file a copyright renewal application in the twenty-eighth year after the photograph's publication, a fact that placed the work in the public domain no later than 1988. And even though the URAA restored American copyrights for certain foreign works, the Act only applies to works that are still in copyright in the country of first publication. As the photograph has likely fallen into the public domain in Cuba, it is ineligible for restoration. In a further wrinkle, the URAA may not even be constitutional in the first

FIGURE 4.3 *El Guerrillero Heroica* (Uncropped) by Alberto Korda.

place.[109] Thus, the work is likely in the public domain in the United States, even though its registration form on file with the Copyright Office claims otherwise.[110] The cropped version—to the extent it does not add substantial creativity to the original—is therefore also likely to be in the public domain.[111] Thus, even if you effectively comb through the Copyright Office's registration documents, you might conclude the work is both still in copyright and registered. But, in fact, the work is likely free for anyone to use.

Moreover, even if you definitively conclude no registration under the that name of a copyright owner exists, that does not end the inquiry on registration. Copyrights may also be registered by an exclusive licensee of a work.[112] As a result, determining that a copyright owner has not registered its own work does not conclusively settle the issue of registration and protection.[113] In fact, the work may have been registered by any number of the owners' exclusive licensees, a potentially large pool of entities given the difficulty courts have faced in drawing a clear distinction between exclusive and nonexclusive licensees.[114]

Additionally, many works (including photographs) may be constructively registered if they are published as part of a collection, such as a periodical, that is itself registered. In such cases, the Copyright Office records do not separately list the contents of such collections. As the Copyright Office concedes in its Circular 22, "Individual works such as stories, poems, articles, or musical compositions that were published as contributions to a copyrighted periodical or collection are usually not listed separately by title in our records."[115] Nevertheless, courts have conferred the benefits of registration to such individual works in a variety of circumstances. For example, in *Abend v. MCA, Inc.*, the Ninth Circuit found a magazine publisher's registration of a blanket copyright for a particular issue effectively registered a story within the issue, although the author of the story had conveyed to the publisher only magazine publication rights and retained all other rights, and the author did not separately register any copyright for the story.[116] Thus, the benefits of registration were found to extend to a smaller work contained in a larger work, even when the authors of the two works (the magazine as a whole versus the story itself) were different. Although *Abend* does not deal with the availability of statutory damages and attorneys' fees—it was decided under the 1909 Copyright Act, when timely registration was not a prerequisite for such relief—it does suggest the benefits of a collection's registration could extend to all of the works within the collection. Other courts have made similar suggestions.[117]

In the end, this exhaustive examination of the vagaries of the search process and the law surrounding it leads to an inescapable conclusion: registration status can be difficult to determine with certainty. Returning to our example involving Britney Spears and her night on the town with Paris Hilton and Lindsay Lohan, this point becomes clear. In one of my more dubious professional accomplishments, I actually registered the copyright to a set of these photographs.[118] Late one night, I was left to decide the title of each photograph, including the infamous "upskirt" shots. In an homage to Spears's hit, "Oops! . . . I Did It Again," I briefly contemplated going with *Oops! . . . She Did It Again.* But I ultimately settled on the distinctly less titillating, but eminently more descriptive, appellations *Britney Spears exposes her derriere*[119] and *Britney Spears exposes herself (again)*,[120] so as to increase the possibility (no matter how unlikely) that would-be infringers could in fact identify the registration status of the work. However, as this example illustrates, there is no assurance the title will match the work at all.

FIGURE 4.4 Britney Spears, In Flagrante Commando, under the Careful Watch of the Paparazzi.

All told, the registration requirement—at least as presently implemented—fails its basic notice function. It is doubtful whether would-be infringers would really engage in ex ante consultation of the registration rolls. Even if they did, they would have trouble finding a definitive answer on registration status. For works registered before 1978, registration records are not easily available. For more recent works, the available database is not up-to-date. Information provided in the database is text-only, making it difficult to identify the registration status of certain works. This problem is especially acute for visual works. Moreover, divining the title of some works can prove to be challenging. Furthermore, registration can be achieved not only by a copyright holder but by any of its exclusive licensees, of which there may be several. And works can be constructively registered as a part of a larger work. In short, the registration system remains relatively opaque, thereby undermining its purported utility.

E. REGISTRATION, REMEDIES, AND INTERNATIONAL TREATY OBLIGATIONS

Besides failing its basic notice function, our registration system also runs into a legal concern that has remained largely unscrutinized: it potentially shirks our international treaty obligations. The timely registration requirement for statutory damages and attorneys' fees arguably flouts the tenets of the Berne Convention. Moreover, the potential incompatibility of the U.S. registration regime with international law becomes even clearer when one considers the language of the WIPO Copyright Treaty. These issues are particularly salient at a time when we are taking other countries to task for their failure to honor international copyright obligations. Moreover, it is difficult to call out foreign countries for their alleged disrespect for the value of intellectual property when we do not adequately protect many domestic creators.

The world's oldest international copyright agreement, the Berne Convention for the Protection of Literary and Artistic Works, was first drafted in 1886. But the United States did not accede to the Convention until 1988, more than a century later.[121] In the words of the principal congressional architect of its implementation, the prohibition on formalities is "the central feature of Berne."[122]

Therefore, according to conventional wisdom, Berne's implementation in 1988 eliminated most of the remaining formalities of the American copyright regime. Yet the requirement for timely registration in order to recover statutory damages or attorneys' fees continues to survive. All the while, many observers have blithely rejected any possible conflict between section 412 and the dictates of the Convention. For example, as Ralph Oman (who drafted the Practicing Law Institute's publication *The Impact of Berne on U.S. Copyright Law*) dismissively argues, "[W]e could scotch the requirement of timely registration as a precondition to statutory damages and attorneys' fees, but, whatever the policy arguments pro and con, it is difficult to argue with a straight face that this fringe-benefit is a formality barred by the Berne Convention."[123]

It is certainly possible the registration prerequisite for statutory damages and fees does not violate Berne. After all, it was on that understanding the Berne Convention Implementation Act of 1988 was passed. Before the United States formally enacted the Convention, the State Department put together the Ad Hoc Working Group on U.S. Adherence to the Berne Convention to evaluate areas of American copyright law falling outside the parameters of Berne. The Group's report formed the basis for the Implementation Act, which, in the words of one scholar, took a "minimalist approach to adherence."[124] Upon consideration of whether section 412's registration prerequisite for statutory damages and attorneys' fees constituted an impermissible formality, the Ad Hoc Group glibly concluded that "[s]ection 412 is compatible with Berne since it deals with certain specific remedies rather than the ability to obtain redress at all."[125] Nimmer appears to agree, concluding "Berne imposes a condition that copyright subsistence for works emanating from other member states may not be premised on formal requirements. It does not, however, prohibit formalities as a condition to certain types of remedies, licenses, exemptions, etc."[126]

However, the contrary position—that the statutory damages prerequisite violates Berne's prohibition on formalities—is hardly as implausible as Oman and others may suggest. Here, perhaps, Oman's impressive background comes into play: he spent almost a decade as the Registrar of the Copyright Office, where he led the federal government's efforts to enter the Berne Convention and served as chief counsel of the Senate Subcommittee on Patents, Copyrights, and Trademarks.[127] As a result, he may be disinclined to second-guess his own work by legitimizing questions as to whether our statutory damages and fees scheme complies with Berne. Additionally, Oman's characterization of statutory damages as mere *fringe* benefits is intellectually disingenuous. Rather than a peripheral or secondary feature of copyright law, statutory damages are in practice the only effective means under U.S. law by which plaintiffs can enforce their copyrights in a manner that deters future infringements.

Indeed, there is reason to believe the registration prerequisite for statutory damages and attorneys' fees may actually violate treaty obligations such as the Berne Convention. In relevant part, the Berne Convention dictates "[t]he enjoyment and the exercise of these rights shall not be subject to any formality."[128] These rights include the exclusive right of reproduction of a copyrighted work.[129] Because copyright registration is undoubtedly a formality, the threshold question is whether it affects a copyright holder's "enjoyment and exercise" of rights purportedly secured by the Berne Convention.

Though Oman, the Ad Hoc Group, and Nimmer appear to draw a distinction between copyright subsistence and copyright remedies—arguing Berne prohibits formalities attaching to the former but not the latter—such a conclusion is not inescapable. The language of Berne draws no clear-cut subsistence/remedies dichotomy. Instead, it speaks of the "enjoyment and exercise" of rights, something to which remedies are inextricably related. Consider the most foundational case in American constitutional jurisprudence, *Marbury v. Madison*, which advanced the critical link between the creation of a right and the affordance of a meaningful remedy for its violation.[130] Admittedly, there is no language in the Berne Convention that explicitly requires a Member State to provide prevailing plaintiffs with statutory damages or even attorneys' fees. Indeed, the Convention makes no mention of remedies whatsoever.

However, one can argue—with a straight face, to boot—that enjoyment and exercise of one's exclusive right of reproduction necessarily requires the ability to *deter* infringement.[131] Thus, although Berne may not ban a copyright registration system that serves a procedural end, its language appears to render suspect any copyright registration system that affects substantive rights, including significant remedies. In the absence of an ability to pursue statutory damages and attorneys' fees, there is little deterrent effect in copyright enforcement under American law. Indeed, the worst-case scenario for defendants is they might have to pay damages ex post in an amount similar to what they might have paid for a license ex ante. They may also face an injunction, but not one that issues automatically upon a finding of infringement. Moreover, making attorneys' fees unavailable to a prevailing plaintiff in an infringement case stifles his ability to be made whole for the injury to his rights. Over the years, I have been approached by hundreds of artists who have no viable infringement suit against monied defendants who have undoubtedly and willfully infringed their copyrights. The first question any experienced copyright litigator asks a potential plaintiff-client is: "Were the works registered before the infringement occurred?" If the answer is negative, the artist is often left with only extralegal means, such as moral force or business sanctions (where available), to rectify the wrongdoing.

Furthermore, even if one accepts the view that Berne does not proscribe the existence of formal prerequisites for certain remedies, that does not end the discussion on international obligations as more recent treaties also need to be considered. For instance, the WIPO Copyright Treaty (WCT) calls into serious question the continued viability of the registration prerequisite for statutory damages and attorneys' fees.

The United States played a key role in drafting the WCT, which went into force domestically on March 6, 2002. The WCT serves as an extension to the rights established by the Berne Convention and was passed pursuant to its Article 20.[132] Unlike Berne, the WCT actually makes specific reference to the remedy obligations of "Contracting Parties," mandating the parties "shall ensure that enforcement procedures are available under their law so as to permit *effective action* against any act of infringement of rights covered by this Treaty, including expeditious remedies to prevent infringements and remedies which constitute a *deterrent to further infringements*."[133] For creators who do not timely register, American law provides no punitive damages, statutory damages, or attorneys' fees. With only actual damages or disgorgement of profits left, there is no deterrent effect, and plaintiffs are frequently unable to take effective legal action against infringers.

III. Hierarchy and Reform

The American copyright registration system not only frustrates the ability of many creators to be made whole for even the most egregious infringements of their copyrights, but it also fails to fulfill its basic notice function and possibly violates our international treaty obligations. Nevertheless, efforts to eliminate section 412 or otherwise amend the law have been met with steep resistance; therefore, nothing has been done. Although it is impossible to ascertain precisely why such proposed amendments were never enacted, the hearings surrounding this issue provide clues as to who opposed the elimination of section 412 and why they opposed this change.

As the following analysis reveals, by creating a two-tiered system of protection, the registration requirement constructs a hierarchy of works defined by their violability. Works by sophisticated creators have the opportunity to become part of the commercial canon. Their aura is secured through artificial scarcity perpetuated by copyright law and the dramatic penalties facing infringers for unauthorized exploitations of such works.

Thus, sophisticated creators can dangle copyright's Sword of Damocles over the heads of would-be infringers. Almost any book, periodical, recording, movie, television show, or computer program distributed by a large press, magazine publisher, music label, film studio, broadcast network, or software developer enjoys similar protection, even though many such works may lack continued economic value.[134] The recent wave of high-profile infringement suits involving peer-to-peer file-sharing clarifies this point: the expansive remedies provided by the Copyright Act allow organizations such as the RIAA to hand individual defendants their heads on a platter with more fervor than Salomé's dance (to licensed music, of course).

For an illustration of this concept, consider the case of Jammie Thomas-Rasset, a single mother of four who earned her living working as a natural-resources coordinator for a Native American tribe in Minnesota. In 2005, Thomas was sued by the RIAA for sharing twenty-four songs on the peer-to-peer file-sharing site Kazaa. Initially, the court found Thomas liable for willful copyright infringement in the amount of $222,000. Although the $9250-per-track judgment may seem high, it was far less than the $150,000-per-track statutory damages courts are permitted to award plaintiffs, even in the absence of any proof of actual harm. Ultimately, however, Thomas earned a retrial when the verdict was thrown out based on an error in jury instructions.

Unfortunately for Thomas, things went even worse the second time around. In 2009, a jury returned another judgment against her, this time for the whopping amount of $1.92 million. At $80,000 per song, this is almost a full order of magnitude larger than the earlier verdict. The infringed songs were sold on iTunes at a price of $.99 each, arguably making the ratio between the verdict and the actual damages 80,000 to 1.[135] Ironically, in the context of punitive damages awards, the Supreme Court has ruled that any ratio in excess of ten to one violates the due process clause of the Constitution.[136]

On the other hand, non-registered works—generally those produced by unsophisticated creators such as individual artists—serve as fodder for remix, reinterpretation, transformation, and unauthorized use. These works lack any aura, their violability is not patrolled, and they may be infringed, sometimes even with impunity. As a result, the current system does not uniformly protect the interests of all authors so much as it privileges a certain class of works. The primary beneficiaries of this system are the major players in the copyright industry—the large corporations who are both generators and users of content. A system with more uniformly harsh consequences for infringement would be unfavorable to these players when they are on the receiving end of suits. This is especially so because the law imposes liability on both direct and vicarious infringers, regardless of mens rea (though mens rea can affect the amount of damages in a case of timely registration).[137] A two-tiered system is ideal for these corporations. When they infringe the materials of others—even if they do so willfully—the consequences are relatively benign. Meanwhile, when an outsider infringes their work, the penalties are drastic. The strategic preference of certain sophisticated creators for this dichotomous structure becomes clear when one examines the failed efforts to eliminate section 412 in the early 1990s.

A. SECTION 412 REFORM AND ITS DISCONTENTS

In 1993, Representative William J. Hughes of New Jersey introduced legislation—dubbed the Copyright Reform Act—that, inter alia, would have repealed the registration requirement for standing, statutory damages, and attorneys' fees.[138] The House ultimately passed the bill on November 20, 1993, and again on September 20, 1994.[139] However, the bill died when the Senate failed to act.[140]

The available paper trail provides insight into the various interests that worked to prevent the bill from passing. A number of groups representing libraries or smaller creators (including the Graphic Artists Guild, the American Society of Media Photographers, the Software Publishers Association, the Committee for Library Property Studies, and the American Association of Law Libraries) all spoke in favor of the bill.[141] Just three groups came to speak in opposition,[142] yet the bill never passed. These three groups were, oddly enough, the Association of American Publishers (AAP), the American Association of University Presses (AAUP), and the Authors Guild (AG). The AAP is, in its own words, "the principal trade association of the U.S. book publishing industry."[143] The AAUP is a trade association with more than 130 members worldwide, consisting of both nonprofit academic and scholarly publishers.[144] Finally, despite its name, the AG neither represents most authors nor speaks for them. Indeed, by their own description at the time, the Guild was made up of "6500 published writers—authors of fiction, history, biography, textbooks, periodical articles, short stories and other literary works—and includes winners of the Nobel Prize in Literature, the Pulitzer Prize and countless other literary awards."[145] Their membership numbers have grown since the 1993 hearing,[146] but membership decisions continue to be made on a case-by-case basis upon application. At a minimum, book authors must have published their work with an established American publisher and received a "significant advance" in order to receive consideration.[147] The AG therefore constitutes an elite group of only the most successful commercial authors—individuals who have a strong economic interest in the inviolability of their works. Not surprisingly, their spokesperson at the hearing on the Copyright Reform Act of 1993 was novelist Scott Turow, an author who has profited handsomely from adaptations of his works in a number of contexts.[148]

At first blush, one would think groups representing the interests of publishers and authors would appreciate the ability to vindicate their rights with fewer formalities. However, such groups register their works and therefore already have the opportunity to vindicate their rights to the fullest extent possible under the law. Yet when they are on the receiving end of a lawsuit, they would prefer their opponents not enjoy the full panoply of remedies available. After all, many creators make use of other copyrighted works. With the current registration regime, sophisticated interests get the best of both worlds: the full range of remedies when they are plaintiffs seeking vindication of their intellectual property interests, but incredibly narrow remedies for any plaintiffs seeking to do the same against them, thereby helping them fend off suits for infringement.

Strangely, the forces opposing section 412's repeal dismissed the possibility the existing system might frustrate the ability of copyright holders to vindicate their intellectual property rights. After what it claimed to be "an elaborate process of consultation with its own members and representatives of other writers groups," the Authors Guild concluded:

> Our efforts to find an example of a meritorious claim by a writer that was lost or seriously frustrated under the present system was unsuccessful. Undoubtedly, there must be such cases; but our diligent efforts to study the issue empirically suggest that instances where the lack of statutory damages have prevented writers

from bringing infringement claims are far less widespread than imagined and that the currently available remedies appear to be accomplishing their intended effect.[149]

Unfortunately, it seems the Guild's researchers were not looking particularly hard, as such a claim appears thoroughly disingenuous in light of our prior discussion. Indeed, a simple examination of case law reveals numerous decisions demonstrating just this point.

Take *Deltak, Inc. v. Advanced Systems, Inc.*,[150] a suit resolved a decade before the debate over the Copyright Reform Act of 1993 took place. The litigation involved Deltak's claims of literary infringement, but not of the highbrow variety. Rather, copy from a corporate pamphlet describing programs that taught data processing skills was lifted wholesale by a rival company, Advanced Systems, for use in its brochures. In the suit, Judge Richard Posner, who was sitting by designation, found the defendant had not only infringed plaintiff's copyright, but had done so willfully. On this basis, he noted:

> If Deltak had registered its copyright within the time provided by the Copyright Act, I would have no hesitation in awarding not only the maximum statutory damages [at the time] under section 504(c)(2) of $50,000, but also attorney's fees, which are authorized by section 505 and are frequently awarded in cases of willful infringement even if no actual damages are proved.[151]

Not surprisingly, however, the plaintiff had not timely registered its copyright, and was unable to establish damages with sufficient certainty.[152] The defendant's plan to use Deltak's brochures for its own marketing purposes ultimately failed, and therefore there were no proven profits to disgorge or actual sales lost by the plaintiff.[153] As a result, despite the willful infringement of its works, Posner felt he was left with no alternative but to award the plaintiff *nothing*, despite the verdict in its favor.[154] As the Second Circuit lamented when dealing with the same issue in a different case, the existing section 412 structure can lead to "the anomaly of affording plaintiffs a right without a remedy."[155] These cases represent only the tip of the iceberg because the dictates of section 412 render such infringements—no matter how unabashed—impractical to litigate.

Conversely, opponents of the reform efforts claimed the elimination of section 412 would undermine the legitimate fair use of copyrighted works by spurring on frivolous and vexatious litigation by rapacious rightsholders. As the AAP and AAUP stated:

> We oppose repeal because it would upset the careful and critical balance struck by [§]412 among the interests of authors and publishers of pre-existing works and those who would transform, build upon and make reasonable use of those works. Repeal would discourage legitimate and important activities of historians, biographers, journalists, and other authors and publishers.[156]

Taken at face value and viewed narrowly, the sentiments reflected in this testimony seem to make eminent sense. However, when one considers the positions taken by the AAP and AAUP in litigation and their public representations, and one assesses the situation in the broader context of rights management, things appear quite different.

Unless we make the dubious assumption the AAP and AAUP are somehow more socially responsible and altruistic than other copyright holders, the arguments of these organizations would militate against the availability of statutory damages and fees in *all* infringement suits, lest they encourage frivolous litigation. After all, many of the works to which the AAP and AAUP claim copyright are ones of which historians, biographers, journalists, and other authors and publishers would like to make transformative, accretive, or reasonable use. Nevertheless, the AAP and AAUP were clearly not willing to take such a stand. After all, by timely registering their works, they enjoy dramatic benefits when, as rightsholders, they seek to assert their copyrights and pursue alleged infringers with the threat of statutory damages and attorneys' fees. Indeed, their palaver regarding legitimate educational activities is readily betrayed by their lacks of qualms about opposing the unauthorized use of *their* copyrighted works as primary materials for other historians, biographers, journalists, and researchers in many contexts. As it turns out, the AAP and AAUP have repeatedly asserted that *any* unauthorized use of their works constitutes an act of infringement—and they have demonstrated a willingness to sue on the basis of this principle.

For example, in just the past few years, the major academic publishers have filed dozens of lawsuits across the country against reproduction shops that produce course "readers" used on college campuses on the theory that such packets violate the publishers' copyrights.[157] Although the makers of the course readers undoubtedly profit in their provision of these services, the packets directly serve an educational purpose. Section 107 of the Copyright Act explicitly states, "the fair use of a copyrighted work, . . . for purposes such as . . . teaching (including multiple copies for classroom use), scholarship, or research, is not an infringement of copyright."[158] Section 107's language may be merely preambulary, or it may create a bright-line rule protecting the use of copyrighted materials for teaching and research purposes. But either way, for the concept of fair use to have any meaning, there must be some threshold at which the use of a copyrighted work for such purposes is excused—whether it is the quotation of a single sentence or the unauthorized reproduction of many pages. Nevertheless, the major publishers serving the academic community have vigilantly maintained that any use, no matter how small, by the copy shops requires their authorization and payment through the Copyright Clearance Center—a centralized clearing house for published content.[159] And, in their public statements, it appears this position is not simply limited to copy shops but extends to any unauthorized use of their copyright works. In language that has grown almost de rigueur in the industry, one leading academic publisher warns: "No part of this book may be reprinted or reproduced or utilized in any form or by any electronic, mechanical, or other means, now known or hereafter invented, including photocopying and recording, or in any information storage or retrieval system, without permission in writing from publishers."[160]

More broadly, an examination of copyright stances taken by some sophisticated creators quickly undermines any assumption that they are less likely to engage in extreme and aggressive positions vis-à-vis their purported intellectual property rights. As Jason Mazzone points out, major publishers often claim copyright protection over works that are indisputably in the public domain. Many of these works constitute important primary source materials for historians and others. In a quintessential example of overbearing copyright claims, Mazzone observes a pocket version of the U.S. Constitution sold on the market sternly warns anyone against reproducing the work without written permission from the publisher. As Mazzone quips, "Whatever the Constitution's framers and ratifiers had in mind when they authorized Congress to create copyright law, they surely did not expect that somebody would one day claim a copyright in the Constitution itself."[161]

All told, there is no reason to think sophisticated creators, such as the AAP, AAUP, or AG members, are any more altruistic or socially responsible as to the enforcement of their copyrights than any other rightsholder. As such, drawing a line on the availability of statutory damages and attorneys' fees via the timely registration requirement in order to prevent a tide of frivolous litigation makes little sense. Moreover, by comparing the purported reasoning of such groups as the AAUP and AAP in opposing section 412 reform with their litigation agendas and fair use policies, it becomes reasonable to at least suspect section 412 serves sophisticated creators quite well by granting them expansive rights to use the works of unsophisticated creators without authorization while simultaneously enabling them to enforce their own copyrights with tenacity and severity.

B. HIERARCHY IN HOLLYWOOD

In light of our foregoing discussions, it is natural to ask how artists could fail to register their works. After all, artists dedicate countless years and make many sacrifices to bring their work to fruition, and it may seem surprising they do not take that extra step to obtain full legal protection for it. Part of the problem is that many artists are not aware of the importance of registration. Others do not want to be bothered with paperwork and its apparent complexities. However, it is not simply a matter of ignorance or myopia. For many artists, effective and timely registration is cost-prohibitive. For example, for artists such as photographers who create a large volume of works (only a small number of which may attain high value), registration can be a costly affair.[162] In recent years, the Copyright Office has adopted regulations that allow group registration of some works, but these regulations are highly restrictive.[163] Moreover, many artists are effectively dissuaded from registration by relying on private registration regimes—regimes that grant them some of the benefits of going through the Copyright Office, but not the recovery of statutory damages and attorneys' fees. As we shall see, screenwriters are such a group. At the same time, the field of screenwriting also provides a salient illustration of the modern two-tiered protection system, including its perpetuation of hierarchy and the powers it serves.

In Hollywood, it is no secret screenwriters often feel unappreciated and disenfranchised. Directors are, after all, often viewed as the creative CEOs of movies—their names drive critical discussions about oeuvres and masterpieces. Through the "a film by" credit, directors are designated by fiat as a film's auteur. Similarly, actors serve as the industry's public face and have always represented a key engine of its financial success—at least until recently.[164] And, although it is true a movie cannot get made without a script, the overriding sentiment toward screenwriters is perhaps best captured by one studio mogul's famous musing: "If we could only figure out a way to make movies without writers."[165] In the early days of the industry, some of our finest novelists sought to pay their bills by trying their luck in Tinseltown. The products of these ill-advised ventures by William Faulkner, Nathanael West, James Agee, Ernest Hemingway, and others are notorious.[166] As critic Edmund Wilson would later observe, the failures of Fitzgerald and

FIGURE 4.5 Critic Edmund Wilson, Ready to Do Battle with Hollywood.

West "may certainly be laid partly to Hollywood, with its already appalling record of talent depraved and wasted."[167] The writers often wound up defeated and desolate. To Wilson, however, the result was not surprising: Hollywood was "an intractable magnetic mountain, which twists American fiction askew."[168]

There are, of course, many factors that allow such "twisting" to take place: commercial realities, the multidimensional nature of the moviemaking process, bargaining power disparities, the history of the industry, and the roles of the various guilds representing above-the-line talent such as directors, actors, and writers. However, the "twisting" is also aided by a de facto norm in the industry that is not usually analyzed: the absence of strong copyright protection for scripts.

In Hollywood, paranoia over the unauthorized usurpation of the heart of one's screenplay or treatment runs rampant. And the reason is simple: it happens. Screenwriters have responded, but not with widespread registration of their works with the Copyright Office. Instead, since 1927, the Writers Guild of America, West (WGAW) has administered a registration system for works that is convenient, easy to use, and relatively inexpensive. Unfortunately, it is also largely useless when utilized in lieu of a copyright registration, as it frequently is.

Billed as "the world's number one screenplay and intellectual property registration service,"[169] and the "the industry standard in the creation of legal evidence for the protection of writers and their work,"[170] the WGAW Registry is not entirely without utility. Individuals—both the general public and WGAW members alike—can deposit copies of their works, including screenplays and treatments prepared for radio, film, television, video, interactive media, and other works such as theatrical plays, novels, short stories, poems, commercials, lyrics, drawings, and music, with the WGAW. This helps to establish date of creation by producing a record of a screenplay or treatment being held in deposit by the Guild. This record can be useful should charges of plagiarism, misappropriation, or copyright infringement later emerge.

However, there is no good reason to opt for the WGAW's registration system over that of the Copyright Office. Unfortunately, however, many individuals both inside and outside of the industry do. The reason is not surprising. In a blurb buried within its Frequently Asked Questions section, the WGAW website does disclaim "[r]egistering your work with the WGAW Registry does not take the place of registering with the Library of Congress, U.S. Copyright Office." But the Guild obfuscates the registration issue by eschewing explanation of the dramatic consequences of failing to register a work with the Copyright Office.[171] Moreover, its website states WGAW registration and Copyright Office registration "both create valid legal evidence that can be used in court," thereby promoting a deceptive sense of interchangeability between the two regimes.[172]

However, the two forms of registration are far from equal. Any work capable of being registered with the WGAW is, by its very nature, capable of being registered or pre-registered with the U.S. Copyright Office, as it is an original work of authorship fixed in a tangible medium.[173] Yet the WGAW registration system fails to provide several of the key advantages of registration with the Copyright Office—specifically, the presumption of copyright validity and, most importantly, qualification for statutory damages and attorneys' fees in the event of an infringement suit. Although WGAW registration is less expensive than Copyright Office registration, it is only marginally so.[174]

The result of a world dominated by WGAW registrations is dramatic. The movie studios register their films with the Copyright Office, so infringement of those works is subject to harsh penalties. By contrast, the underlying screenplays, treatments, and outlines are usually registered only with the WGAW. As a result, the screenplay becomes a low-tiered work in the copyright schema, subject to manipulation, reinterpretation, transformation, and even unauthorized exploitation to a degree. It is not a sacred text; its inviolability is not ensured by law. Normatively, some will conclude this is exactly as it should be; others will be appalled. Either way, however, the system constructs a hierarchy of works. In the end, the screenplay is malleable, submissive, and yielding; the movie is untouchable, consecrated, and unassailable. Formality serves function in determining Hollywood's chain of command.

C. CONSECRATION, CRITICAL THEORY, AND MUSIC

The history of the modern music industry also reveals the stratification process emerging from formalities in action. As K.J. Greene has observed, the ostensibly neutral technicalities of our copyright regime undoubtedly exist in a "concrete social milieu"[175] where "not all creators of intellectual property are similarly situated."[176] Often the privileging of certain works takes on the qualities of other social stratifications that divide along lines of class, gender, and race. As Greene argues, inequalities in bargaining power, a fundamental tension between structural components of copyright law and "the oral predicate of Black culture," and discrimination that resulted in the devaluation of Black creative contributions have resulted in the historical disadvantaging of African-American creators, especially African-American musicians.[177] A prominent example is the growth of the modern music industry. Driven by rock 'n' roll, the industry saw much of its early success from the unauthorized exploitation of old blues riffs, many stolen directly from unacknowledged and uncompensated African-American folk artists.[178] Although the resulting musical compositions and sound recordings represent the product of unsanctioned pastiche, the industry continues to vigilantly protect them—not just from wholesale reproduction (as the flood of file-sharing suits demonstrates), but from transformative remixing (as case law on sampling illustrates).

Although sound recordings generally did not receive federal copyright protection until 1972,[179] musical compositions have qualified for protection since 1831.[180] However, for a musical composition to receive a copyright, it had to be fixed in a tangible medium—in other words, it had to be written. This situation resulted in what Keith Aoki terms a "dual economy" of music. Under this system, certain kinds of music (and, therefore, composers) received legal protection, and certain kinds of music (and composers) did not. In general, copyrighted (or copyrightable), notated, written scores were composed by upper middle class-educated whites, while unnotated musical compositions (including those created by or within folk collectives) did not receive copyright protection. Many unprotected works were intertemporal, intergenerational, anonymous, communal, or improvisational in their composition. Thus, in general, those works that arose within collective experiences of slavery, the struggle for freedom, and post-Reconstruction subordination did not receive protection.[181] Indeed, the strictures of our modern copyright regime, with its mystification and fetishization of the Romantic author trope, have often privileged Western forms of (ostensibly) individualistic creation over other modalities.[182]

In recent decades, the widespread dissemination of recording and publishing technology has ensured virtually all creative works are fixed in a tangible medium, thereby avoiding one iteration of the "dual economy" problem identified by Aoki. However, the timely registration requirement has stepped in to enforce a hierarchy of works by distinguishing between sophisticated and unsophisticated creators. Creative works by those at the legal and social margins remain unregistered and therefore unprotected. These intellectual properties become low-tier works, relegated to the status of raw materials subject to remixing, reinterpretation, and transformation. But from these low-tier works come the inviolable commercial products whose iterations are carefully controlled and whose scarcity is assiduously patrolled. Registered and enforced by the RIAA, the commercial product represents a sacred work that cannot be manipulated without authorization of its rightsholders. Thus, the potential socioeconomic and racial dimensions to the cultural hierarchy of copyrighted works live on through the timely registration requirement.

IV. Caveats and Considerations for Reform

As it turns out, American copyright militancy is vastly overstated. Indeed, by comparison to most developed countries, we continue to provide inadequate remedies to a large class of content creators: authors who do not timely register their copyrights. Instead, we practice a two-tiered protection system that privileges sophisticated creators. Their works become sacred, inviolable matter protected from unauthorized exploitation or transformation by a series of remedies that often rise to troubling levels. Meanwhile, the works of unsophisticated creators remain fodder for remix and reinterpretation. Thus, the registration system plays a critical role in perpetuating a sacralization process. While the emergence of mass reproduction and digital dissemination has threatened the consecration of privileged works, our registration regime has rekindled the aura. What technology has undermined, our two-tiered copyright hierarchy has reinstated, at least in part.

Indeed, a close examination of the language and current interpretation of the Copyright Act reveals several difficulties facing unsophisticated creators who seek to vindicate their rights in the United States. First, courts have found section 412 precludes recovery of statutory damages and attorneys' fees when an infringement continues after registration. As a result, an infringer can continue its wrongful activity with impunity if a work is not timely registered at the time of first infringement. Second, unsophisticated creators face a one-way risk of attorneys' fees. Plaintiffs who fail to register their copyright on a timely basis are never eligible to recover their fees even if they prevail in a suit and the infringement is willful.[183] By contrast, defendants are always eligible to recover their fees if they prevail. Third, creators cannot seek punitive or reputational damages, and actual damages are often insufficient to make them whole or to deter future infringement. All told, these factors combine to create a rather bleak enforcement regime for the rights of creators who do not register in a timely manner.

At the same time, however, possible elimination of the timely registration requirement of section 412 could make litigation more profitable, thereby increasing the risk of frivolous suits. As a result, it is important any possible reform of section 412 should not occur in a vacuum, as concomitant changes in several areas are needed.[184] For example, broader general protection of transformative rights (for both sacred and low-tier works), including the implementation of some bright-line rules, would reduce the likelihood of some socially undesirable litigation.[185] Moreover, a limitation on the recovery of statutory damages would conform the remedies regime to constitutional due process dictates that require punitive assessments to bear some reasonable relationship to actual damages.[186] Indeed, the disproportional size of statutory damages, decoupled from any proof of actual damages, may do far more to encourage frivolous litigation than putting all creators—sophisticated and unsophisticated—on a level playing field for remedies. As a result, it may make sense to think about simultaneously reducing the upper range of statutory damage awards and providing better protections for innocent infringers while expanding the availability of statutory damages to all copyright holders, regardless of formalities. We should also consider improving the powers defendants have in fighting meritless infringement claims by considering greater penalties for overreaching copyright claims[187] and making attorneys' fees recovery for prevailing defendants easier to attain.[188]

Thus, any reform of the copyright system that seeks to treat content creators of all stripes on a more equal basis must remain cognizant of the critical need to balance the rights of creators with those of users. With this in mind, the final chapter of the book turns our attention to contemplating what Copyright 2.0 might look like. And, in so doing, we remain cognizant it is not necessarily more copyright or less copyright we need but, rather, *better* copyright.

To get past racism, we must here
take account of race.
There is no other present way.
—McGeorge Bundy, November 1, 1977

In order to get beyond racism, we must first
take account of race.
There is no other way.
—Justice Harry Blackmun, June 28, 1978

The way to end racial discrimination
is to stop discriminating by race.
—Judge Carlos Bea, October 20, 2005

The way to stop discrimination on the basis of race
is to stop discriminating on the basis of race.
—Chief Justice John Roberts, June 28, 2007

5

THE INDIVIDUAL AS REFORMER

In which we contemplate student notetaking as a crime, the constitutional right to play fantasy baseball, purple bananas and dancing toddlers, Slash's criminal record, the drinking of Kool-Aid, the dangers of Krypton, William Shatner as astute cover artist, soiled and haggard orphans, judicial plagiarism, the Boston Strangler, and the possibility of infringing oneself

I. Restoring Balance to Copyright Law

THROUGH THE COURSE of this book, we have examined the individual as an infringer of copyrighted works, a transformer of copyrighted works, a consumer of copyrighted works, and a creator of copyrighted works. As we saw in Chapter 1, individuals can face backbreaking penalties for the most pedestrian activities—a fact exacerbated by the realities of digital life and the growing scope of copyright protections we documented in Chapter 2. Specifically, intellectual property law's regulation of cultural symbols can have a profound impact on consumers of creative works by controlling and mediating identity formation—the subject of our analysis in Chapter 3. Yet, not all works are created equal; creators enjoy differing levels of protection for intellectual properties under the law. Chapter 4 revealed how works by unsophisticated creators can sometimes be used and abused with impunity while the works of sophisticated creators remain subject to harsh and sometimes excessive penalties for their infringement.

In this final chapter, we turn our attention from critiquing the extant copyright regime to examining the issue of reform. We do so by beginning to contemplate what Copyright 2.0 might look like. As we have seen, social, technological, and jurisprudential changes have combined to make our present copyright system increasingly ill-suited for the realities of the digital age, especially for ordinary netizens of the twenty-first century. In the process, the rights of the individual—as user, as transformer, and as creator of copyrighted works—have often suffered. We seek to reverse this trend.

We present our proposals in order of modesty, moving from small (and perhaps realistic) reforms to fundamental (and perhaps less likely) ones. Our policy prescriptions are far from comprehensive, and they do not address each and every concern raised in this book. Indeed, undertaking such an extraordinarily ambitious task would require far more analysis and space. Nevertheless, our thoughts are meant to represent a humble starting point for fostering a dialogue on the issue of holistic reform, especially as we start to consider the enactment of an entirely new copyright code—the first since 1976.

To this end, our reforms fall into three broad categories. Initially, we seek to help restore greater balance between users of and rightsholders to copyrighted content by suggesting a series of reforms that would discourage the kind of overreaching claims of copyright ownership and rights that have grown all too commonplace in recent years. These overreaching claims have negatively impacted expressive rights, stifled political and cultural discourse, controlled personhood development, and restricted the critical dissemination of information. Present law provides few, if any, disincentives for such overreaching claims. Though by no means exhaustive, four reforms—drawn to address the various shortcomings of the present regime explored in this book—could help equalize the playing field by tempering overreaching ownership and rights claims. First, given the increasing importance of the Internet as a vehicle for the distribution of user generated content, we need to provide the Digital Millennium Copyright Act's section 512(f)—the provision that penalizes putative rightsholders who make false representations to effect the takedown of allegedly infringing content online—with more bite. Second, given the massive cost of copyright litigation, it makes sense to provide defendants with the same ability to recover attorneys' fees as sophisticated plaintiffs. As we shall explain, despite nominal lip service to this principle, the courts continue to exercise a dual standard regarding fees in copyright cases. Third, we need to reinstitute penalties for false claims of copyright ownership and rights under federal law. Fourth, we should temper copyright's strict liability regime by providing better defenses and superior damage-mitigation mechanisms for acts of innocent infringement.

We then endeavor to achieve a greater balance between unsophisticated and sophisticated parties by proposing two conjunctive reforms. First, we advocate the repeal of the registration prerequisite of section 412 of the Copyright Act, which requires copyright holders to register their copyrights on a timely basis if they wish to recover attorneys' fees and statutory damages. This, in turn, will allow unsophisticated creators with the power to enforce their rights fully, something that (as we have detailed in Chapter 4) is sorely lacking in the current regime. Second, we propose the maximum allowable statutory damages be substantially decreased and/or limited to some small multiplier of actual damages in order to reduce the in terrorem effect of modern copyright litigation and to temper its more inequitable results. By reducing the value of statutory damages while increasing their availability, we give unsophisticated creators the ability to enforce their legitimate rights as we check outlandish damages penalties that enable sophisticated creators to overstep their rights.

Finally, we aim to restore greater balance between transformative users and creators of copyrighted content. Just as we began the book with a thought experiment, we end with one. This time, instead of evaluating rampant infringement and the widening gap between copyright law and social norms, we imagine a radical change in the nature of copyright law and assess its impact on the fundamental goal of the regime: progress in the arts. Through the course of our analysis, we have documented how the widening ambit of copyright protection has increasingly encroached upon critical First Amendment values, suppressing transformative uses of copyrighted works that advance creativity and free speech rights. To address this problem, we propose an intermediate liability regime for transformative uses of copyrighted works that unshackles expressive activities from the chains of legal interdiction and promotes artistic evolution, all while continuing to allow original creators to profit from the use of their works.

II. Restoring the Balance Between Users and Creators

A. IN TERROREM: COPYRIGHT OVERREACH

As the gedanken experiment at the outset of the book suggested, there are myriad daily activities in the digital age that may technically constitute infringements and create a nightmare of potential liability for ordinary individuals if rightsholders exerted their rights to the maximum extent allowed by law. Of course, most such acts can and should be excused by fair use, an implied waiver defense, or the de minimus doctrine. But such conjecture provides little ex ante comfort to accused infringers, and finding out whether an act will be excused from liability can be an expensive proposition. A putative copyright holder hell-bent on enforcing its rights to the utmost can therefore make life difficult indeed for the unwary and stifle legitimate uses of copyrighted works. The costs of such machinations are not just borne by those individuals threatened with legal action. When such overreaching claims remain consistently unopposed, copyright creep results over time. Outlandish assertions of rights embolden copyright holders, which leads in turn to the chilling of activities that should remain protected under a more balanced regime.

We are literally inundated by false claims of copyright ownership and rights on a daily basis. These aggressive claims are not mere inconveniences: they have serious societal consequences with massive negative externalities. As we shall see, they can choke economic competition, affect the cost of goods and services such as higher education, restrict legitimate fair use rights, and silence free speech. In short, the effects of overbroad copyright claims can be felt in all aspects of modern life, from the political and economic to the social and cultural.

Consider how corporations have increasingly used litigation threats, grounded in tenuous claims of intellectual property rights, to stifle the dissemination of legitimate consumer information and stymie public discourse about important issues. For example, it is an axiomatic principal of copyright law that facts cannot be copyrighted. Yet recent headlines are replete with examples of companies claiming intellectual property rights in just that—facts.

To prevent pricing information from spilling onto the Internet and to deter web surfers from taking full advantage of the information transparency and dissemination possible on a worldwide global network, some corporations have begun to claim a copyright interest in their basic retail data. In 2002, Wal-Mart ended up in a dispute with FatWallet.com, an online forum for consumers to share discounts and pricing information.[1] A FatWallet user had posted details of the products and prices scheduled to appear in advertisements for Wal-Mart's annual Black Friday sale on the day after Thanksgiving. Wal-Mart issued a takedown notification to FatWallet, demanding it remove the post on the grounds it violated Wal-Mart's copyrights. Although Wal-Mart eventually backed down on its attempt to subpoena FatWallet for the identity of the poster, it did manage to get the information removed from the website. Apparently, Wal-Mart has continued its takedown notifications undeterred ever since.[2] Other retailers, such as OfficeMax, Best Buy, and Staples, have used the DMCA for similar purposes.[3] Even if one views such content as not facts (which are wholly uncopyrightable)[4] but rather a compilation of facts (entitled to thin protection given sufficient originality),[5] their unauthorized use is also subject to a strong fair use defense. As such, the tactics of Wal-Mart and other retailers to limit the availability of their pricing information online likely do not have support under the law, but they have succeeded nonetheless because of the threat of litigation.

Interestingly, for-profit corporations have not been alone in advancing these aggressive, if not wholly misguided, interpretations of copyright law. Despite educational missions that would seemingly support information sharing (if not free-market price competition), institutions such as Harvard University have also taken such positions. In 2007, the venerable Harvard Coop, Harvard's official bookstore, started calling the police whenever they noticed a student jotting down the names and prices of books assigned for various courses.[6] Concerned about online price competition, the Coop informed law enforcement officials that these individuals were violating the store's intellectual property—namely, that their book lists, including title and price, were copyrighted.[7] Noting the irony, the *Harvard Crimson* reported "taking notes in class may be encouraged, but apparently it can get you kicked out of the Coop."[8]

Harvard University is not alone in its regressive stance on copyright—a position that increases the cost of higher education. Leading university presses, along with other academic publishers, have asserted overreaching copyright claims that directly lead to increases in the costs of books and other educational materials for students in two ways. First, they have repeatedly taken the position that any unauthorized use of their copyrighted works, no matter how small, constitutes an act of infringement. As such, they maintain even a one-paragraph reproduction of a one thousand-page book could incur liability. To cite a small smattering of examples, books published by Princeton University Press contain a copyright warning dictating "[n]o part of this book may be reproduced in any form . . . without permission in writing from the publisher;" Cengage Learning asserts any republication, reproduction, or redistribution of any content from its works "is prohibited without the prior written consent of Cengage Learning." Pearson Education categorically proclaims dissemination of any "parts" of any of its works "is not permitted," and that materials from its works "should never be made available to students except by instructors using the accompanying text in their classes." Most disappointingly, and despite my own best efforts to convince my publisher's counsel to allow otherwise, the copyright page of this book contains a similarly overreaching statement. All of these statements are untrue as a matter of law and, among other things, entirely ignore the existence of the fair use doctrine, as embodied in section 107 of the Copyright Act.

Second, university presses and other academic publishers regularly engage in a practice Jason Mazzone has dubbed *copyfraud*—the act of "claiming falsely a copyright in a public domain work."[9] In a quintessential yet stunning example of the practice, Mazzone notes a pocket version of the U.S. Constitution sold on the market sternly warns anyone against reproducing the work without written permission from the publisher. As he quips, "Whatever the Constitution's framers and ratifiers had in mind when they authorized Congress to create copyright law, they surely did not expect that somebody would one day claim a copyright in the Constitution itself."[10] It seems that, if it were up to some publishers, even those attempting to use works in the public domain (such as the Constitution) would face liability for copyright infringement. And, the problem is not limited to the Constitution. As Mazzone points out, copyfraud is omnipresent: "False copyright notices appear on modern reprints of Shakespeare's plays, Beethoven's piano scores, greeting card versions of Monet's *Water Lilies*, and even the U.S. Constitution. Archives claim blanket copyright in everything in their collections. Vendors of microfilmed versions of historical newspapers assert copyright ownership. These false copyright claims, which are often accompanied by threatened litigation for reproducing a work without the "owner"'s'

FIGURE 5.1 Copyright 1787?

permission, result in users seeking licenses and paying fees to reproduce works that are free for everyone to use."[11]

The Copyright Clearance Center (CCC), an administrative agency charged by major publishers with the collection of reproduction and other usage fees provides a stunning example of copyfraud in action. Through the CCC, many publishers demand licensing fees for the photocopying of materials that are indisputably in the public domain. Often, these fees are collected from educational institutions and, ultimately, students who are making educational use of these works. In the process, the publishers misrepresent that any use of such works requires permission from and payment to them, when, as a matter of law, it does not. For example, various publishers demand payment via the CCC for the reproduction of any portion of *The Complete Works of Shakespeare* and such classics as Henry David Thoreau's *Walden* (1854), Charles Darwin's *The Expression of the Emotions of Man and Animals* (1872), and Jane Austen's *Sense and Sensibility* (1811). As it turns out, the publishers' ability to demand such payments is highly suspect. William Shakespeare (1564–1616) lived before the passage of the Statute of Anne (1710), the world's first modern copyright act. Copyright law therefore did not even exist when Shakespeare authored his plays and poems and, as a result, his works never enjoyed copyright protection and have always belonged to the public domain. Similarly, Austen's *Sense and Sensibility* and Darwin's *The Expression and Emotions of Man and Animals* never enjoyed protection in the United States. They were first published in the United Kingdom, and British authors did not receive copyright protection in the United States until 1891. Finally, works such as those of Thoreau (which were published before 1923) no longer possess copyright protection in the United States as their terms have expired. These are but a few examples of the rampant practice of demanding licensing fees for the use of public domain materials. All told, it is unknown how many millions of dollars the major publishing companies wrest from college students each year for the photocopying of works which are, in fact, not copyrighted. However, among other things, these improper claims undoubtedly contribute to the rapidly increasing cost of higher education.

Meanwhile, claims of copyright ownership in e-mails and other correspondence have also grown, with some dizzying effects. Indeed, tenuous copyright assertions have even extended to the very notifications through which suit is threatened. An overly aggressive cease-and-desist letter to a sympathetic defendant can generate a firestorm of bad publicity for the author's client, especially in the Internet age. As a result, (suddenly publicity shy) lawyers have begun to claim copyrights in their letters to prevent the unauthorized dissemination of these missives by their recipients.

For example, in 2007 a furniture outlet named DirectBuy learned several websites contained comments about the company and its services (calling it a "scam" and a "nightmare") that it considered defamatory. The websites, it turns out, were consumer information pages that allowed users of infomercial products to provide reviews, commentary, and criticism regarding the products and their producers' sales tactics. DirectBuy's attorneys, Dozier Internet Law, P.C., promptly fired off a cease-and-desist to the websites' owner. The letter was rather mundane, except for its conclusion, which warned: "Please be aware that this letter is copyrighted by our law firm, and you are not authorized to republish this in any manner. Use of this letter in a posting, in full or in part, will subject you to further legal causes of action."[12] Of course, such a tack was nothing more than a thinly veiled attempt to preclude the negative publicity DirectBuy's cease-and-desist letter might yield and to stifle the websites' free speech rights. Ostensibly, the strategy paid dividends. According to DirectBuy's attorneys, no one had ever dared publish their cease-and-desist letters before.[13] In the end, however, the owner of the websites refused to be intimidated, and his attorneys, the Public Citizen Litigation Group (PCLG), placed the cease-and-desist letter prominently on its website, daring Dozier to litigate the issue.[14] Dozier never sued.

Meanwhile, entertainment content is replete with overreaching claims that ultimately chill legally protected activities. For example, sports fans are all too familiar with the requisite copyright warnings that accompany every televised event. For years, at least once during each major league baseball game, an announcer has dutifully informed viewers "This copyrighted telecast is presented by authority of the Office of the Commissioner of Baseball [and/or INSERT YOUR FAVORITE TEAM NAME]. It may not be reproduced or retransmitted in any form, and the accounts and descriptions of this game may not be disseminated, without the express written consent of [INSERT YOUR FAVORITE TEAM NAME]."[15] Other professional sports leagues broadcast similarly stern admonishments. Parries the National Football League, "This copyrighted telecast is property of the NFL, any rebroadcast, retransmission or any other use of this telecast without the express written permission of the NFL is strictly prohibited."[16]

Of course, there is nothing particularly unusual about a corporation trumpeting its rights. However, the gross inaccuracy of these legal conclusions is particularly troubling. With their uncompromising air of certitude and authority, these bold declarations radically misrepresent the law and the rights the leagues enjoy.

First, the copyright warnings entirely neglect the existence of the fair use doctrine, which allows the unauthorized use of broadcasts to occur without liability under certain conditions. Firmly embedded in the federal Copyright Act and, quite arguably, a constitutionally mandated First Amendment check on the copyright monopoly, fair use allows exploitation of creative works for such purposes as commentary or criticism without the permission of the copyright holder. For example, unauthorized use of MLB footage to demonstrate the changing physique of the average slugger through the years for a presentation on performance-enhancing drugs (PEDs) might well constitute fair use.[17] In such circumstances, a user would possess a complete defense to charges of copyright infringement, even in the face of explicit demands by MLB to make no use of its footage of Barry Bonds, Mark McGwire, and Rafael Palmeiro. The copyright warnings of MLB and the NFL conveniently omit any mention of the fair use rights all members of the public enjoy. Such a tack recalls glib efforts by other segments of the content-creation industry to downplay or entirely gloss over fair use rights. As we have seen, publishers routinely insist any exploitation of a work, no matter how small, requires a license.[18] And, as we saw in the Introduction, Hollywood and the RIAA appear to feel similarly in their educational efforts to combat movie and music piracy.

Second, while the leagues' copyright warnings prohibit any unauthorized retransmissions, the law says otherwise. For example, the Copyright Act specifically allows both cable and satellite operators to retransmit over-the-air broadcasts without the authorization of copyright holders, so long as the operators pay a statutory license.[19] In some cases, such as the retransmission of over-the-air broadcasts of local television stations by cable and satellite operators, the license is virtually royalty-free.[20]

Third, the leagues' apparent recognition of only express, written permissions stands on shaky legal ground. Admittedly, federal copyright law requires that any *exclusive* license be in writing.[21] However, as courts have repeatedly recognized, an individual can obtain a nonexclusive license to exploit a copyrighted work either orally or by conduct, even in the absence of any express written consent.[22]

Fourth, MLB's attempt to propertize all "accounts" of a game under the aegis of copyright subject matter is deeply problematic. Major League Baseball undoubtedly owns a copyright to particular descriptions of its game by its broadcasters. But the phrasing of MLB's copyright statement suggests a claim of ownership to something more. Indeed, MLB's recent litigation posture confirms this suspicion. Over the past few years, MLB has asserted property rights in player names and statistics and has demanded fantasy baseball operators obtain a license for the right to market their services to the public. In short, MLB has sought to profit more directly from the rapidly increasing popularity of fantasy baseball, a sizeable fraction of the $1.5 billion fantasy sports industry.[23]

Although MLB had been able to wrest licenses from most operators, negotiations between MLB and a Missouri fantasy baseball company, CBC Distribution, broke down in 2005. CBC sued MLB in federal court, seeking declaratory relief for its right to use player names and statistics without a license.[24] Ultimately, CBC prevailed, as the trial court rejected both MLB's copyright and right of publicity claims.[25] The Eighth Circuit agreed, finding the names and statistics of baseball players were information "in the public domain."[26] In June 2008, the Supreme Court denied MLB's petition for certiorari, effectively ending the dispute at least within the Eighth Circuit (for copyright law) and in Missouri (for right of publicity law).[27] Thus, according to the only reported decision on the matter, MLB does not have an intellectual property right to its players' names and statistics. Undeterred, however, MLB implicitly continues to claim this right in such representations as its copyright warning.

The copyright reach of the leagues has grown so expansive that, like DirectBuy, they have even fought unauthorized reproduction *of their own legal warnings*. Attorney and academic Wendy Seltzer found this out firsthand when she posted a brief snippet from Super Bowl XLI on YouTube so students in her class could hear the NFL's copyright warning for themselves. Seltzer was using the video as an educational tool to demonstrate the ways in which entities overreach in claims about their intellectual property rights. The demonstration went far "better" than Seltzer could have ever imagined. Within days, YouTube had received a takedown demand from the NFL, which claimed Seltzer's posting of the clip infringed its copyright. YouTube acceded to preserve its ISP safe harbor from liability under the Digital Millennium Copyright Act.[28] But refusing to be intimidated, Seltzer struck back with a counter-notification under section 512(g)(3) (which enabled YouTube to restore the clip to its server for public performance) by which she effectively challenged the NFL to take her to court.[29]

The NFL attempted another takedown notification, but ultimately backed down and, apparently unwilling to test its infringement theory in court, never filed suit. However, few potential copyright defendants are as well versed in their legal rights as Wendy Seltzer, and even fewer are willing to take their chances against a multibillion-dollar corporation. Surprisingly, the NFL did not ultimately pursue action against Seltzer for subsequently reproducing their DMCA takedown demand to YouTube on her website.[30] It was, after all, the unauthorized reproduction of a creative work.

Despite Seltzer's bold stand, individuals in her position possess only limited means to combat overreaching claims. Even though making such fraudulent claims effectively chills a wide swath of protected activity, there is little relief available against the deception. The Copyright Act therefore effectively incentivizes the propagation of such false information, with such overreaching statements of law serving as a powerful vehicle to extend the breadth of the copyright monopoly without any adverse consequences.

B. REFORMING COPYRIGHT'S IN TERROREM REGIME

1. Modifying Section 512(f)'s Good Faith Requirement

Upon cursory examination, the DMCA appears to provide relief against rightsholders who, like the NFL in the Seltzer situation, overreach in their demands to Internet Service Providers for the takedown of allegedly infringing materials online. Specifically, the DMCA creates a cause of action against those who "knowingly materially misrepresent[] . . . that material or activity is infringing"[31] in an online takedown notification. Typically, a person challenging a takedown notification will argue the copyright owner knowingly materially misrepresented having "a good faith belief that use of the material in the manner complained of is not authorized," as required under section 512(c)(3)(A)(iv).

However, as it turns out, judicial interpretation of the mental state required to prove such a knowing material representation has made success on a section 512(f) action under the DMCA improbable. For example, the leading case on section 512(f)'s mens rea requirement, *Rossi v. MPAA*,[32] held the "good faith belief" requirement was entirely subjective, not objective: "A copyright owner cannot be liable simply because an unknowing mistake is made, even if the copyright owner acted unreasonably in making the mistake. Rather, there must be a demonstration of some actual knowledge of misrepresentation on the part of the copyright owner."[33] Though such a reading may be consonant with Congress's intent, it makes for bad policy.

A party issuing a takedown notice can escape section 512(f) liability by possessing a subjective, good faith belief the activity about which it complains constitutes infringement. This raises a veritable Kool-Aid defense—if you have drunk the content-creation industry's Kool-Aid and believe there is no such thing as fair use, you cannot be held liable under section 512(f), no matter how objectively unreasonable your belief.

Take the infamous *Lenz v. Universal* case. The dispute began when, on February 7, 2007, Stephanie Lenz uploaded a twenty-nine-second home video that featured her toddler son bouncing around to the sounds of Prince's 1984 hit "Let's Go Crazy," which was playing in the background. Lenz was using YouTube as a convenient way to share the footage with family and friends. However, another party—Universal—quickly took an interest in the video. As the owner of sound recording copyright for "Let's Go Crazy," Universal promptly sent YouTube a takedown notification under section 512(c)(3)(A), claiming the video infringed the company's copyright in the sound recording. Universal's uncompromising desire to force the removal of a sweet (mainstream audiences apparently did not realize the child was dancing to a song replete with references to phone sex and "purple bananas") recording of a son taken by his mother gained widespread media attention. After several rounds of procedural machinations, Lenz ultimately filed suit against Universal claiming, inter alia, that Universal had made a knowing material misrepresentation to YouTube that her video infringed Universal's copyright.

Initially, Lenz's complaint was dismissed for failing to allege "a knowing misrepresentation."[34] Lenz proceeded to amend her complaint, and, in an issue of first impression, the court did find a takedown notification under the DMCA must take into consideration the fair use doctrine.[35] As the court opined, "In order for a copyright owner to proceed under the DMCA with 'a good faith belief that use of the material in the manner complained of is not authorized by the copyright owner, its agent, or the law,' the owner must evaluate whether the material makes fair use of the copyright."[36] But, even so, the court admitted instances of liability under section 512(f) are rare, given the subjective bad faith standard: "Although there may be cases in which such considerations will arise, there are likely to be few in which a copyright owner's determination that a particular use is not fair use will meet the requisite standard of subjective bad faith required to prevail in an action for misrepresentation under 17 U.S.C. § 512(f)."[37] As such, the odds of Lenz prevailing on her section 512(f) action remain exceedingly low. Indeed, it appears one can avoid section 512(f) liability by simply drinking the Kool-Aid unabashedly—so long as you truly believe the voices of the maximalists, who have virtually read the fair use doctrine out of the Copyright Act, your takedown notification will qualify as one made in good faith for the purposes of section 512(f).

Courts have further enervated the vigor of section 512(f) by limiting the damages and fees remedies allowed under the provision. The section provides victims of takedown notifications brought in bad faith are entitled to recover damages caused by and attorneys' fees incurred because of the takedown.[38] But courts have read the scope of recoverable damages and fees narrowly, finding damages must be "proximately caused by the misrepresentation to the service provider and the service provider's reliance on the misrepresentation"[39] (as opposed to "all damages that occur as a 'but for' result of the misrepresention"[40]) and that only fees related to pre-litigation activity ("i.e., in drafting and issuing the counter notice") are recoverable—not all fees for litigating a section 512(f) claim itself.[41]

The state of the law on section 512(f) is emblematic of the unbalanced nature of our present copyright regime. Misrepresentations of infringement by putative rightsholders require subjective bad faith to be actionable. Meanwhile, as we shall see, no state of mind—no matter how innocent—can protect a defendant from liability on allegations of infringement. This imbalance between plaintiffs and defendants in copyright suits is also notable in the broader infringement-litigation context with respect to remedies such as attorneys' fees.

2. Equalizing Grants of Attorneys' Fees Under Section 505

Beyond just Internet takedowns, there are broader reforms that can attach to all copyright disputes to equalize the playing field between users and creators, consumers and rightsholders. For example, the courts' interpretation of the attorneys' fees provisions of the Copyright Act have played a role in failing to stem the tide of overreaching copyright claims. Under section 505 of the Copyright Act, prevailing parties can, at the court's discretion, recover attorneys' fees. On the surface, such a provision would appear to dissuade plaintiffs from pursuing meritless claims of infringement lest the defendants receive their fees as a prevailing party. However, despite the absence of any statutory language distinguishing between prevailing plaintiffs and defendants, courts have historically applied a bifurcated standard on the fees question, depending on which side has prevailed. In short, defendants face greater difficulty in recovering fees, even in relatively one-sided cases. As the cost of litigation is one of the most salient factors preventing individuals from fighting overreaching copyright claims, reform of the recovery of attorneys' fees is a necessary step to equalizing the playing field between content owners and users.

Prior to 1994, many courts—including the copyright-rich Second and Ninth Circuits—explicitly adopted an unbalanced approach to the award of fees under section 505. Courts would routinely grant fees to prevailing plaintiffs [42] but deny them to prevailing defendants absent a finding of frivolousness or bad faith—an exacting standard.[43] As the D.C. Circuit stated in 1987, "[C]ourts generally have agreed that defendants are entitled to fees . . . only when the claims are frivolous or are brought in bad faith."[44]

Things appeared to change in 1994 when *Fogerty v. Fantasy, Inc.* reached the Supreme Court. In the case, Credence Clearwater Revival (CCR)'s old record label, Fantasy, sued the band's lead singer, John Fogerty, for copyright infringement. The case garnered immediate headlines because of one unusual fact—Fogerty was being accused of effectively infringing himself. Specifically, Fantasy charged that Fogerty's solo work "The Old Man Down the Road" infringed his CCR classic "Run Through the Jungle," whose copyright Fantasy owned. Due to the acrimony between the two sides (Fogerty and Fantasy's owner, Saul Zaentz, had a famous falling out, and the suit was one among several disputes between them), the case went all the way to trial, where a jury ultimately ruled in favor of Fogerty. As a prevailing defendant, Fogerty then sought recovery of his attorneys' fees, and the appeal (which ended up before the Supreme Court) concerned the proper standard courts should apply in analyzing recovery of fees under section 505.[45] In the case, the Supreme Court overruled the predominant practice of the time and rejected the dual standard for fees outright, ordering hereafter "[p]revailing plaintiffs and prevailing defendants are to be treated alike"[46] under section 505. Reasoned the Court, "Because copyright law ultimately serves the purpose of enriching the general public through access to creative works, it is peculiarly important that the boundaries of copyright law be demarcated as clearly as possible. To that end, defendants who seek to advance a variety of meritorious copyright defenses should be encouraged to litigate them to the same extent that plaintiffs are encouraged to litigate meritorious claims of infringement."[47] Although the Court eschewed any particular test of the provision of fees, preferring an imprecise reliance on "equitable discretion,"[48] it did reference a nonexclusive list of factors, including "frivolousness, motivation, object unreasonableness (both in the factual and in the legal components of the case) and the need in particular circumstances to advance considerations of compensation and deterrence,"[49] that lower courts might consider. Regardless of what standard was used, the Court insisted prevailing plaintiffs and defendants be treated evenhandedly.

However, upon an examination of infringement decisions since 1994, it appears a dual standard continues to prevail. For example, despite the Supreme Court's edict in *Fogerty*, lower courts often continue to grant fees routinely to prevailing plaintiffs. The Ninth Circuit—home of Hollywood and the entertainment industry—has continued to award fees to them as a general matter of right. For example, in the remarkable and ironically named *Krypton* opinion from 1997,[50] the Ninth Circuit held "a plaintiff in a copyright action is generally awarded fees by virtue of prevailing in the action."[51] Although the case was decided some three years *after* the Supreme Court's *Fogerty* decision, the Ninth Circuit never cited that case and inexplicably ignored its core holding. There is also no plausible basis to think the Ninth Circuit accidentally overlooked *Fogerty*. Indeed, the *Krypton* opinion shows the Ninth Circuit was quite familiar with *Fogerty*—on several occasions during the course of the ruling, the Ninth Circuit refers to its own (overruled) decision in *Fogerty* for non-fees-related propositions.[52]

Meanwhile, post-*Fogerty*, defendants continue to be denied fees "absent bad faith motivation (such as to dominate the market in question), hard-ball tactics [such as discovery abuse] . . . or objective unreasonableness (such as pursuing a claim against a defendant after dismissal of the identical claim against a co-defendant)."[53] Thus, to receive fees, the defendant must demonstrate almost extraordinary gall and bad judgment by the plaintiff. Take *Bond v. Blum*,[54] for example. In the case, the plaintiff was an author who had written an autobiographical manuscript detailing the murder of his father when the plaintiff was 17. His ex-wife managed to obtain a copy of the manuscript and produced it as an exhibit in custody proceedings to demonstrate her former husband would not provide an environment suitable for children. Plaintiff then sued his ex-wife and her law firm for copyright infringement, arguing (rather absurdly) that they had engaged in the unauthorized reproduction of his copyrighted manuscript. The court found the defendants' use of the manuscript squarely protected by the fair use doctrine and awarded fees on the grounds the infringement case was "not a close one."[55] It further found the suit to be frivolous and motivated by a desire to suppress the underlying facts of the plaintiff's work—not to protect the creative expression embodied in the manuscript.

Similarly, a defendant was granted fees in *Hofheinz v. AMC Products*[56] when bad faith motivation for the litigation came to light. In the case, a widow retracted what appeared to be a grant of permission for the use of certain materials in a documentary when she did not like the movie's final cut. She then sued for infringement. The court awarded fees on the grounds the case was brought for improper purposes. Specifically, the timing of the objection strongly suggested an ulterior motive to ensure the documentary showcased her husband in a more favorable light. As such, the court found the claim "objectively unreasonable" and frivolous, thereby warranting an award of fees to the defendant.[57]

However, absent such egregious behavior by a plaintiff, a defendant usually does not receive fees. Consider the predicament of notorious appropriation artist Jeff Koons. His encounters with the court system epitomize the troubles facing a defendant who raises legitimate fair use defenses. In 1989, in *Rogers v. Koons*, Koons was famously sued—and lost—in an artistic appropriation case involving his unauthorized transformation of a photograph into a satirical sculptural work.[58] In the suit, the court rejected Koons's fair use defense and found him liable for copyright infringement.[59] Although the suit did not produce a reported decision on Koons's liability for the plaintiffs' attorneys' fees under section 505, the court strongly hinted at their likely recoverability, styling Koons's actions in an unfavorable light and noting the plaintiff was a good candidate for the extra-ordinary relief (such as enhanced statutory damages) available to owners of infringed copyrighted works that are timely registered.[60]

Several years later, Koons found himself in court again. In *Blanch v. Koons*,[61] the plaintiff owned the copyright to a photograph entitled *Silk Sandals by Gucci*—a commercial work used in advertising. Koons usurped the image, reproducing a portion of it for his painting *Niagara*, which had been commissioned by Deutsche Bank. This time, however, the court found Koons's actions protected by the fair use doctrine as a form of transformative appropriation. Koons then petitioned the court for fees as a prevailing defendant, but his request was denied.[62] As the court reasoned, the suit was neither frivolous nor brought in bad faith.[63] Such a result is typical post-*Fogerty*. As Nimmer notes, "[M]ost courts deny fees to prevailing defendants when the plaintiffs' claims were neither frivolous nor motivated by bad faith. By the same token, there is typically no award of fees in cases involving issues of first impression or advancing claims that were [not] objectively unreasonable."[64]

Interestingly, the *Blanche* decision added a warning to Koons. The court reasoned that, as an appropriationist artist, Koons knowingly took the risk of copying works by others even though the Copyright Act had ultimately protected him. Unconcerned with the chilling effect such a ruling might have on future fair use in the arts, the court unsympathetically commented "appropriation artists can expect

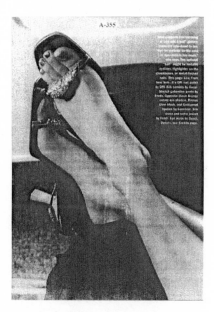

FIGURE 5.2 *Silk Sandals by Gucci.*

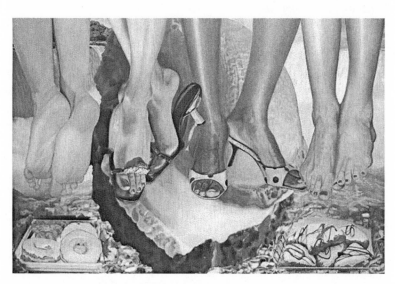

FIGURE 5.3 *Niagara* by Jeff Koons.

that their work may attract lawsuits. They must accept the risks of defense, including the time, effort, and expenses involved."[65] However, such a result fails to make Koons whole. In winning the case and successfully fending off charges of copyright infringement, Koons still found himself out-of-pocket for over one million dollars in attorneys' fees and costs.[66] Thus, only the most wealthy celebrity artists could afford to fight even when a meritorious fair use defense exists.

Thus, in the *Rogers* and *Blanche* cases, we have two copyright infringement claims involving issues of fair use and the appropriationist works of Jeff Koons. In the first—where liability was established—the plaintiff was likely to get fees. In the second—where liability was denied and the fair use defense accepted—the defendant was unable to recover fees. In effect, despite the admonitions of the Supreme Court to the contrary, a dual standard for grants of fees apparently continues to prevail.

This continuing asymmetry between plaintiffs and defendants does not merely affect artists making transformative uses of copyrighted content; it can suppress core political speech rights as well. Consider the case of Michael Savage, the conservative talk show host who sued the Council on American–Islamic Relations (CAIR) when CAIR excerpted approximately four minutes of his two-hour broadcast of October 27, 2007 without authorization. During the broadcast, Savage deemed the Koran to be "a book of hate" and referred to Muslims as "throwbacks" who should be deported "without due process," declaring "I don't want to hear one more word about Islam." Savage then told Muslims to "Take your religion and shove it up your behind. I'm sick of you," and he exhorted his fans to "Speak it out at the supermarket! Tell them what you think of Islam. Tell them what you think of Muslims. Tell them what you think of these things." Savage's shocking religious invective drew widespread criticism and excerpts of the broadcasts were appended to an Internet article put out by CAIR, an advocacy group whose mission is to promote understanding of Islam and to protect the civil liberties of Muslim-Americans. Entitled *National Radio Host Goes on Anti-Muslim Tirade*, the article critiqued Savage's Islamophobic vitriol and encouraged "radio listeners of all faiths to contact companies that advertise on Michael Savage's nationally syndicated radio program to express their concerns about the host's recent anti-Muslim tirade."[67] In short, the use of Savage's broadcast appeared to be a quintessential form of commentary and criticism, immunized from liability both under the strictures of copyright law's fair use doctrine and the First Amendment's protection of core political speech. Savage, however, felt CAIR had illicitly impinged on his exclusive dominion over his intellectual property and sued the organization for copyright infringement in a California federal district court.

The court quickly dispensed with the suit, granting a motion for judgment on the pleadings pursuant to Federal Rule of Civil Procedure 12(c) on the basis that CAIR's actions were protected by the fair use doctrine as a matter of law.[68] Nevertheless, the court denied CAIR's subsequent motion for attorneys' fees. Although the court admitted "Plaintiff's Copyright Act claim was never strong and was litigated anemically,"[69] the court simply and unilaterally concluded the defendant was not entitled to an award of fees,[70] an opinion it affirmed upon a motion for reconsideration by the defendant.[71]

By denying CAIR's motion for fees, the court failed to disincentivize overreaching claims. So it was not surprising that shortly thereafter, Savage attempted to silence other groups, once again using intellectual property claims as the basis. Indeed, the impact of the court's refusal to grant CAIR fees became readily apparent only a few weeks later when Savage reignited his attempts to leverage his copyrights into a vehicle for silencing his critics.[72] This time, Savage targeted Brave New Films, which had snagged one minute of Savage's comments—a quarter of CAIR's use—as part of a media piece they had prepared on his anti-Muslim views and posted on YouTube. Despite the court's ruling of fair use over the exact same footage in the CAIR case, Savage's company, Original Films, claimed its rights had been infringed and filed a takedown notice with YouTube pursuant to the DMCA. YouTube removed the video just as Brave New Films had taken out a full-page advertisement in the *New York Times* with a link to the video. The blow to Brave New Films was significant as the takedown thoroughly neutered the power of its concentrated outreach campaign. Although Brave New Films ultimately sued so that it could have its use of the video restored, the damage had already been done. In the end, Savage's behavior went undeterred when the court, without much comment, declined to award CAIR its fees. Yet the purpose of section 505 is not just to make the infringed whole but to vindicate the rights of noninfringers dragged by overbearing plaintiffs to court. In this latter goal, it is failing.

In addition, many infringement suits that are successfully fended off by defendants are further immunized from a grant of fees under section 505. For example, in many circuits, if a case is dismissed for lack of standing (e.g., brought on a false claim of copyright ownership), a court is precluded from granting fees under section 505 on the theory the court lacks continuing subject matter jurisdiction over the case and the defendant has not prevailed on the merits.[73] Barring the unusual imposition of Rule 11 sanctions,[74] such a result protects misguided plaintiffs from awards of fees against them even for weak claims of infringement over works for which they do not actually possess rights. As we have seen through the course of our analysis in this book, attorneys' fees constitute a substantial part of the monetary value of an infringement suit. As infringement suits are both tremendously costly to prosecute and defend against, reforming the availability of attorneys' fees makes a critical difference in leveling the playing field in infringement litigation.

3. Creating a Federal Cause of Action for False Copyright Ownership and Rights Claims

The fact that federal courts arguably lack standing to even consider whether to grant fees against a plaintiff who lacks actual ownership of an allegedly infringed work highlights the need for our next proposed reform: the creation of a federal cause of action that provides damages against individuals and entities who make false claims of copyright ownership. Such a reform will also provide potential relief to individuals facing overreaching copyright claims that are not subject to section 512(f), which only applies in limited contexts for online takedown notifications.

In the past, Jason Mazzone has proposed that Congress amend the Copyright Act to create a cause of action against copyfraud. More broadly, however, it would make sense to penalize false statements about the nature of an owner's rights as well. Indeed, there is precedent for such a move. The Copyright Act currently penalizes (albeit lightly) a failure by publishers to disclaim copyright in portions of a work embodying government works.[75] More pointedly, the Patent Act provides a potent (perhaps too much so) cause of action against the false marking of a product as patented.[76]

There are also long-forgotten historical analogues for combating false copyright claims, but these are scarcely mentioned in modern literature. Starting in 1802 with the first amendment to the Copyright Act, federal law began to provide a cause of action for "false entry of copyright." According to the new statute, "If any person or persons . . . shall print or publish any book, map, chart, musical composition, print, cut, or engraving, not having legally acquired the copyright thereof, and shall insert or impress that the same hath been entered according to act of Congress, or words purporting the same, every person so offending shall forfeit and pay one hundred dollars; one moiety thereof to the person who shall sue for the same, and the other to the use of the United States, to be recovered by action of debt, in any court of record having cognizance thereof."[77] In effect, the provision served as a private attorney general statute that split recoveries for violations evenly between the plaintiff and the U.S. government. It remained on the books throughout the nineteenth century and served as a significant part of the federal copyright scheme. For example, the 1831 Copyright Act had only sixteen sections, one of which was dedicated entirely to the "false entry of copyright" claim. The provision was also harsh in its application, doling out strict liability against violators. As an article appearing in a 1857 edition of *The New York Times* noted, although an error might be "caused by carelessness and inadvertence, . . . that none the less exposes the parties to the penalties."[78]

However, at the dawn of the twentieth century, the power of the false-entry provision eroded significantly. The provision was radically altered in the 1909 Copyright Act when Congress added a requirement of "fraudulent intent" and eliminated the qui tam nature of the claim. Instead of allowing a private cause of action, enforcement was left entirely to government discretion and deterrence took the form of a misdemeanor publishable by a fine of between $100 and $1000. On January 1, 1978, the provision entirely disappeared with the enactment of the 1976 Copyright Act.

Not surprisingly, therefore, recent decades have seen increasingly dubious copyright claims wrecking havoc with the legitimate rights of the public to access uncopyrightable factual information, to exploit creative works that have fallen into the public domain, and to make fair use of copyrighted works that remain under legal protection. The reenactment of a qui tam federal cause of action for any objectively unreasonable and false claim to copyright ownership or rights over a work could help equalize the playing field between users and creators of works. As we have seen, infringing users pay a high price under the law for their violation of a copyright holder's exclusive rights secured under 17 U.S.C. § 106. There is no reason why purported rightsholders should not pay a high price for violating the rights of users protected under the First Amendment, the fair use doctrine, and other provisions of the Copyright Act that protect the public interest by circumscribing the ambit of property rights held by copyright owners.

4. Revitalizing Recognition of the Innocent Infringer

a. Reforming Copyright's Strict Liability Regime

Finally, as noted earlier, one of the most inequitable and unbalanced aspects of our copyright regime is its strong embrace of strict liability. There is no mens rea requirement in copyright. Thus, everyone in the chain of supply can be held hostage to claims of infringement, a particularly pernicious state of affairs in the digital era where works can pass through multiple agents and contact points before getting to an end user. Moreover, in a networked world where we all violate copyright law multiple times a day, the risk of penalties—even for innocent infringements—can be staggering.

During copyright's early years from 1790 through 1909, knowledge was a required element of any cognizable infringement claim. As a result, accidental infringement was excused from liability. Things began to change, however, with the passage of the 1909 Copyright Act and Judge Learned Hand's famous decision in *Hein v. Harris*,[79] where he rejected a composer's defense that he had never heard the song he had purportedly infringed. Hand wrote that "whether or not the defendant, as he alleges, had never heard the complainant's song, when he wrote his chorus, the chorus certainly is an infringement, and the complainant under his copyright is entitled to protection."[80] Within two decades, the Supreme Court affirmed this proposition explicitly when it determined "intention to infringe is not essential under the [1909] Act" for the purposes of establishing liability.[81]

Thus, modern copyright law has no mens rea requirement. Specifically, a defendant's knowledge of his or her infringing actions is utterly irrelevant for the purposes of liability for direct infringement.[82] At first blush, the harshness of this rule appears to be tempered by a corollary principle: although "innocent" infringement cannot defeat the fact of liability, state of mind can still be a relevant factor in the assessment of damages, thereby reducing the amount of one's liability. However, even there, the defense's limitations are notable. Courts can reduce statutory damages only to $200 (from a minimum of $750) for each act of innocent infringement. But, such a reduction is entirely within a court's discretion, and a court can still order statutory damages in the amount of $30,000 per act of innocent infringement if it so pleases. Moreover, the meager limitation on statutory damages for innocent infringers is not matched by reduction in actual damages. Whether one's infringement is entirely innocent or ridden with wanton willfulness, liability for actual damages remains the same.[83]

For example, George Harrison famously found himself on the receiving end of an infringement suit for copying The Chiffons' 1963 doo-wop hit "He's So Fine" with his stately and saturnine spiritual "My Sweet Lord," which was released in 1970. Harrison claimed he had independently written the musical composition and that he had no knowledge of The Chiffons' work. Although the court purported to accept Harrison's factual allegations, it nevertheless found him liable on a theory he had subconsciously pilfered "He's So Fine."[84] Reasoned the court:

> I conclude that the composer, in seeking musical materials to clothe his thoughts, was working with various possibilities. As he tried this possibility and that, there came to the surface of his mind a particular combination that pleased him as being one he felt would be appealing to a prospective listener; in other words, that this combination of sounds would work. Why? Because his subconscious knew it already had worked in a song his conscious mind did not remember. Having arrived at this pleasing combination of sounds, the recording was made, the lead sheet prepared for copyright and the song became an enormous success. Did Harrison deliberately use the music of He's So Fine? I do not believe he did so deliberately. Nevertheless, it is clear that My Sweet Lord is the very same song as

He's So Fine with different words, and Harrison had access to He's So Fine. This is, under the law, infringement of copyright, and is no less so even though subconsciously accomplished.[85]

Thus, although Harrison was effectively held to be an innocent infringer, the court found damages against him in the amount of $1,599,987.[86]

The absence of effective innocent-infringer mitigations also leads to a multi-defendant strategy often exploited in litigation by plaintiffs: as state of mind is irrelevant to liability and copyrighted works typically flow through numerous steps in the supply chain, a litigant can sometimes sue an endless number of defendants for a given act of infringement. For example, if someone produces a motion picture from my screenplay without authorization, my potential claim for relief lies not only against the producer of the movie, but myriad other parties as well, including the studio for distributing the movie, theater chains for exhibiting it, manufacturers of the actual DVD and soundtrack for reproducing it, television stations for publicly displaying it, rental chains for distributing it, and toy manufacturers for creating derivatives based on it. Most, if not all, of these defendants may have no reason whatsoever to suspect they have engaged in any wrongdoing. Perhaps no amount of reasonable due diligence could have alerted them to the potential liability. Nevertheless, liability attaches.

Of course, these defendants often have indemnification agreements that temper the inconvenience of being hauled to court. Nevertheless, these agreements are not always useful—especially if the indemnifier has gone belly-up. Moreover, the threat of dragging one's economic partners to court—even if indemnification agreements are in place—can disrupt business relationships. Finally, the ability to hale a potentially endless parade of defendants from the supply chain to court for even trivial violations of which they had no knowledge or even reason to know raises questions of fundamental equity.

The deterioration of the innocent infringement defense has come at a particularly inopportune time. As Tony Reese argues, because more creative materials are subject to copyright protection and the exclusive rights held by copyright owners are less circumscribed than they used to be, the risk of accidental infringement has grown substantially over the past century.[87] In addition, the Internet age brings us into contact with copyrighted works at unprecedented rates. With digital technology, the tools for the reproduction, derivatization, distribution, public display, and public performance of copyrighted works lie at our fingertips. This fuels innocent infringements—a risk made plain by the hypothetical scenario involving Professor John in Chapter 1. There is no reason John should face up to $4.544 billion in liability per year as his acts of innocent infringement should be subject to defenses that limit to a reasonable level the maximum damages he can be assessed.

Indeed, despite the rhetoric of the MPAA and RIAA, it is not always easy to identify when one is downloading legally or illegally. For consumers of a certain age or level of inexperience with the Internet, iTunes and Grokster may not appear very different from one another, and, in the wake of the rash of litigation over online downloading, such users may steer clear of Internet distribution altogether.[88] Moreover, although the provision of music or movie downloads for free may indicate a site's legitimacy, this fact alone is not dispositive. Some sites that provide downloads for a price—such as the infamous

Russian site, allofmp3.com—may be doing so without proper permission of rightsholders, so using these sites could result in infringement liability for a consumer. At the same time, some sites provide downloads for free and may be doing so with the permission of rightsholders. Indeed, the offering of free product is a tactic that is not limited to unknown artists as even established acts sometimes offer their sound recordings gratis to consumers. Additionally, it is well known that the major record labels cooperate with blogs to promote their music and often give these blogs permission to provide the download of free tracks along with their recommendations to influence tastemakers and generate hype for a new release.[89]

Record label EMI recently found itself in a quandary precisely because of this practice. EMI had filed a copyright infringement suit against mp3tunes.com for its "Sideload" product, which enables users to add songs found on the Internet to virtual storage lockers for later use. But, it turns out many of the songs EMI claimed mp3tunes.com was infringing were actually being given away for free, with permission of EMI, all over the Internet.[90] As this example suggests, it can be difficult for users to ascertain whether a website truly has permission to distribute the copyrighted work. Due to the strict liability nature of our copyright regime, users frequently face unwitting infringement liability, a growing problem scholar Ned Snow has dubbed "copytraps."[91]

b. The Ease of Innocent Infringement: Examples from the Annals of Supreme Court Jurisprudence

All told, our legal regime has grown increasingly intolerant of innocent infringements—infringements that occur unwittingly and regularly. Indeed, one need look no further than our nation's highest court for a reminder that the copyright regime's current position on accidental infringement is excessively rigid. Though charged with the faithful observance and interpretation of the law, Supreme Court justices are not immune from violations of the law, especially when dealing with copyrighted materials. As it turns out, two of the most famous turns of phrase from recent Supreme Court jurisprudence are quite arguably the products of innocent infringement. And, in both cases, the words were lifted without so much as a proper acknowledgement.

In *Regents of the University of California v. Bakke*,[92] a rejected medical school applicant sued the University of California on the grounds its race-conscious admissions policy violated the Fourteenth Amendment's equal protection clause and constituted an impermissible form of discrimination. Although the Supreme Court struck down the particular policy at issue, holding it represented a racial quota system that could not withstand constitutional scrutiny, the Court narrowly permitted the use of race as a "plus" factor in the holistic review of a candidate's application for admission to institutions of higher learning.[93] Justice Harry Blackmun's opinion in the case, in which he concurred in part and dissented in part, found no constitutional infirmity in the challenged admissions policy. Reasoned Blackmun: "In order to get beyond racism, we must first take account of race. There is no other way."[94]

Blackmun's poignant defense of race-conscious policies became famous. Less famous, however, is its origin. It turns out Blackmun's striking evocation was the direct result of innocent infringement. In November 1977, McGeorge Bundy had written a piece for the *Atlantic Monthly*. Titled *The Issue Before the Court: Who Gets Ahead in America*, and published just before oral arguments were held before the Supreme Court, the essay previewed the *Bakke* case and presented a strong defense of affirmative action. Near the end of Bundy's analysis, we find a curiously familiar phrase: "To get past racism, we must here take account of race. There is no other present way."[95]

It is not mere speculation that Blackmun borrowed his words from Bundy rather than independently generating them on his own. As longtime Supreme Court reporter Linda Greenhouse reminds us, Blackmun was meticulous in his recordkeeping and would log every article he perused, noting the date upon which he read each piece.[96] As it turned out, one of his law clerks, Keith P. Ellison, had given him a copy of Bundy's article. And in Blackmun's files (which were released after his death), his copy of the Bundy article possessed numerous check marks at the margins plus the notation "Read 5-6-78." The *Bakke* decision was issued six weeks later on June 28, 1978, but Blackmun did not include any footnote or citation to Bundy. As Greenhouse concludes, "Whether Blackmun was even aware, by the time [the *Bakke* decision] was issued, . . . that he had borrowed those words is unclear. In any event, the thought behind the words was now, beyond a doubt, his own."[97] Thus, in issuing one of the more notable declarations in the recent annals of Supreme Court jurisprudence, Justice Blackmun also managed to become an innocent infringer. According to current copyright law, his infringement is not excused by the absence of intent on his part. No matter how subconscious or unconscious, Blackmun's actions would risk liability.

In this regard, Blackmun is not alone among the Bretheren. More recently, Chief Justice John Roberts engaged in some innocent infringement of his own, and with no less a famous edict. In 2007, the Supreme Court considered a constitutional challenge to the use of race-conscious admissions policies at a secondary school in Seattle. In a 5–4 vote, the Court struck down the policy as a violation of the equal protection clause. Chief Justice Roberts issued the Court's plurality decision, in which he announced in the opinion's penultimate and most famous line, "The way to stop discrimination on the basis of race is to stop discriminating on the basis of race."[98]

Roberts' folksy, tautological edict instantly gained widespread notoriety—both good and bad. But the maxim's origins, which were attributed to Roberts as he had not cited to any source, received far less attention. As it turns out, the line came straight from a dissent Judge Carlos Bea had written when the U.S. Court of Appeals for the Ninth Circuit had heard the case some two years earlier. Mused Bea, "The way to end racial discrimination is to stop discriminating by race."[99] Chief Justice Roberts' words were unmistakably borrowed—so much so that, in a subtle jab, Justice Breyer called him out for his failure to cite to Bea. In his dissenting opinion in the same case, Breyer tacitly noted Roberts' oversight by directly quoting Bea's original language (and not Roberts' rendition) and by calling the line "the plurality's slogan."[100]

Fortunately for Justice Blackmun, McGeorge Bundy was not litigious; and lucky for Justice Roberts, Judge Bea's words were part of a government work and therefore exempted from copyright protection. Nevertheless, the point endures: innocent infringement abounds, among even the most law-abiding citizens engaged in the most high-minded of professional pursuits. The cases of Justice Blackmun and Justice Roberts reveal how the traditional dichotomy drawn between the right to make one's own speech and the right to make someone else's speech is excessively facile. Moreover, they highlight the dangers of a copyright regime that imposes strict liability and fails to make appropriate adjustments for innocent acts that may technically constitute infringement.

II. Restoring the Balance Between Sophisticated and Unsophisticated Parties

Besides seeking to restore the balance between users and creators of copyrighted materials, our reform proposals aim to more evenly protect sophisticated and unsophisticated parties dealing with creative works. As we have seen in our analysis in Chapter 4, the current copyright regime frequently enables sophisticated parties to flout copyright law when they draw on the intellectual properties of unsophisticated parties without authorization or payment. Yet when the copyrighted works of sophisticated parties are violated, infringers typically pay a steep (if not grossly punitive) price. To remedy this asymmetrical situation, we propose eliminating the registration requirement as a prerequisite to qualify for attorneys' fees and statutory damages so that unsophisticated creators are on a level playing field with the content creation industry as far as protection of their intellectual property rights goes. Simultaneously, we would reduce the maximum size of statutory damages awards and/or limit the ratio of statutory damages to actual damages. Thus, although unsophisticated creators would be better able protect their rights, we would concurrently limit the inequitable, harsh consequences of the enforcement regime against users of copyrighted content.

A. TEMPERING THE SIZE OF STATUTORY DAMAGES AWARDS

As we have seen, by using formalities, the 1976 Copyright Act has actually created two distinct tiers of effective protection for copyrighted works. Sophisticated, regular creators (generally corporations in the content-creation industries) timely register their works and therefore enjoy generous remedies against infringers, including the recovery of reasonable attorneys' fees and the assessment of statutory damages—which can rise to the whopping rate of up to $150,000 per willful act of infringement.[101] Absent any proof of actual damages, such plaintiffs can elect statutory damages that quickly create the possibility of a multimillion-dollar judgment in their favor.

Armed with the threat of statutory damages and attorneys' fees, representatives of the content-creation industry can dangle copyright's Sword of Damocles over the heads of unauthorized users of their works. Almost any book, periodical, recording, movie, television show, or computer program put out by a large press, magazine publisher, music label, film studio, broadcast network, or software developer enjoys similar protection, even though many such works may lack continued economic value.[102] The result is an in terrorem effect where the threat of litigation can prostrate all but the most well-funded (or foolhardy) defendants.

The specific congressional intent behind the statutory damages regime is punitive and meant to impose an additional cost on caught infringers to deter future acts of infringement, both by the defendant and others. In general, this makes eminent sense as there should be some level of statutory damages available. First, it can be difficult to prove actual damages in some copyright cases, yet there may be a public policy reason to show we take copyright seriously and to dissuade infringement. More pressingly, without the availability of statutory damages, one could not adequately dissuade infringement. Absent some form of statutory or punitive damages, potential infringers would usurp the works of others with impunity, knowing that, in a worst case scenario, they may only have to pay the licensing fee they should have paid at the outset.

But the problem emerges when statutory damages begin to dramatically exceed actual damages, often by several orders of magnitude. Such a result is not only inequitable but, quite arguably, unconstitutional. Under modern due process jurisprudence, punitive damages have to bear a reasonable relationship to actual damages. Ironically, in the context of punitive damages awards (usually against large corporate defendants), the Supreme Court has ruled that any ratio in excess of ten to one typically violates the due process clause of the Constitution.[103] Yet, to date, copyright law continues to exist in a vacuum, apparently immune from the implications of such constitutional restraints on damages awards.[104] The absurdity is abundant when one compares the results of relevant cases. In *BMW v. Gore*, for example, the Supreme Court struck the award of $2 million in punitive damages against a car manufacture for tortious conduct that resulted in $4000 in actual damages—a ratio of 500 to 1. In *State Farm v. Campbell*, the Supreme Court struck a $145 million punitive damages award on $1 million in actual damages—a ratio of 145 to 1.

Meanwhile, however, the annals of copyright jurisprudence are replete with judgments assessing statutory damages awards in wild excess of actual damages, and even awarding them where there are likely no actual damages. Consider *UMG Recordings, Inc. v. MP3. Com, Inc.*[105]—the source of the largest statutory damages award on record. An early pioneer in the online music sphere, mp3.com developed an innovative service called "Beam-It." Users of the service (which was free) could access their home libraries of music and play them anywhere in the world so long as they had an Internet connection. Offered in the days before the iPod and postage stamp-sized terabyte hard drives, Beam-It was one of the first products to allow consumers true global music portability. To ensure users could only access music they actually owned, Beam-It used a verification system: users would insert their purchased CDs, one by one, into their computers and the Beam-It service would verify the album. Once verified, the users could access the album as it was situated on mp3.com's servers. And therein lay the problem. To make the service viable, especially in the day when wholesale transfer of one's music library to a digital locker was not possible due to available file transfer speeds, mp3.com began to make digital copies of as many CDs as it could as part of its private library. It was these recordings that were literally played back when a user accessed his or her digital locker. UMG, among others, took exception, claiming the act was an unauthorized reproduction of sound recordings to which they held a copyright. They sued and won big. Although there was *no evidence* whatsoever mp3.com profited from the service and there was *no showing that actual damages had been suffered by the plaintiffs,* the court awarded statutory damages in the amount of $25,000 per infringed CD, resulting in a remarkable $53.4 million judgment for the plaintiffs. The innovative Beam-It service was effectively dead on arrival, and mp3.com was financially crippled by the judgment. Yet all the company had done was enable protected space-shifting—allowing users who had legitimately purchased sound recordings to listen to these recordings anywhere they could find an Internet connection. In effect, the judgment not only imposed disproportionate penalties on mp3.com, it also stifled the development of an innovative new technology.

In the infamous *Feltner* case, C. Elvin Feltner, Jr. and his corporation, Krypton International, became delinquent in paying royalty payments pursuant to a license they had to broadcast several television programs owned by Columbia Pictures, including *Who's the Boss, Silver Spoons,* and *T.J. Hooker.* Nevertheless, Feltner continued to broadcast the shows. In total, he broadcast 440 episodes of the television programs, and a federal district court awarded Columbia statutory damages in the amount of $20,000 per act—a whopping $8.8 million.

Felter appealed the judgment all the way to the U.S. Supreme Court, arguing the issue of damages should have been submitted to a jury rather than determined by a judge. The Court agreed, reversing the judgment on a constitutional technicality. Although admitting Congress had solely intended statutory damages awards to be determined by a judge, the Court ruled this power violated the Seventh Amendment, which "provides a right to a jury trial on all issues pertinent to an award of statutory damages under section 504(a) of the Copyright Act."[106] As such, statutory damages are now squarely within the sole province of the jury—something Congress never intended or approved. As an aside, the consequences of such a dramatic shift in procedure are evident when one considers the nature of judge-led versus jury-led decisions. Although the amount of a statutory damages award is committed to the discretion of the decision maker, when judges rendered the decision, they used precedent as a guide for such determinations.[107] But now that the decision is within the exclusive province of a jury, no guidance is provided. As David Nimmer points out, the jury, unlike the judge, "has no institutional mechanism for distinguishing and relying on precedent from other cases."[108] Thus, despite Feltner's triumph before the nation's highest court, he may have done more damage than good to future defendants. In addition, the reversal of the judgment against Feltner turned out poorly for Feltner himself.

The Pyrrhic nature of Feltner's victory before the Supreme Court was soon apparent: on remand, he fared almost four times worse. His Seventh Amendment argument succeeded in vacating a judge's $8.8 million statutory damages award against him. But, at the retrial, the issue of damages went before a jury, and this time resulted in a whopping $31.68 million verdict against him ($72,000 for each of 440 acts of infringement).[109]

The actual damages to Columbia from Feltner's actions were a small fraction of the ultimate, multimillion-dollar damages award. Statutory damages awards are frequently divorced entirely from actual damages. Yet the practice of awarding statutory damages in wild excess of actual damages is commonplace in copyright jurisprudence and frequently unquestioned. Indeed, the *Feltner* opinion never raised the specter of a due process concern.

Admittedly, Feltner is hardly a sympathetic character. He was a sophisticated businessman with knowledge of copyright law, possessed no semblance of a fair use defense to shield his actions, and, as the court noted, 415 of his 440 infringed works were aired after Columbia had sued him, suggesting spectacular willfulness in his misdeeds.[110] But it is not just commercial users, such as broadcasters and technology providers, who are suffering from disproportionate statutory damages awards as individual users found to infringe in their homes for even personal-use purposes face similar penalties. The recent wave of high-profile infringement suits involving peer-two-peer file sharing make this point clear. In Chapter 4, we discussed the case of Jammie Thomas-Rasset, the single mother of four who was hit with a $1.92 million verdict for sharing twenty-four copyrighted songs on a peer-two-peer network. But Thomas-Rasset is not alone, as thousands of individuals have faced similar suits brought by the Recording Industry Association of America and its members.

For example, Joel Tenenbaum, a doctoral candidate at Boston University, found himself on the receiving end of a bankrupting judgment in the amount of $645,000 in statutory damages for infringing the rights to thirty songs in the course of peer-two-peer file-sharing.[111] With the price of the infringed songs on iTunes at ninety-nine cents each, the ratio between Tenenbaum's statutory damages verdict and the actual damages arguably incurred stood at approximately 22,500 to 1.[112] By contrast, in due process challenges to punitive damages verdicts, the Supreme Court has struck as unconstitutional awards with comparatively meager 500 to 1 and 145 to 1 ratios.

In one way, Thomas and Tenenbaum should consider themselves lucky: at least they did not face criminal charges. Once applied only to massive, sophisticated underground bootlegging operations generating profits at the expense of legitimate industry, criminal copyright charges are increasingly being brought against isolated individual infringers. Consider the case of Jack Yates, a twenty-eight-year-old who worked for a duplication company charged with making promotional copies of the Mike Myers movie *The Love Guru* shortly before its general release in 2008. Yates made the mistake of burning an extra copy of the movie—a copy that eventually made its way onto the Internet, where according to prosecutors it was allegedly downloaded more than 85,000 times. Yates was charged with criminal copyright infringement and sentenced to six months in a federal prison. As industry gossip site TMZ noted, "It may be the dumbest move of all time: A man risking his personal freedom, public humiliation and his entire career—all because he wanted to illegally burn a copy of 'The Love Guru.' As if sitting through the flick wasn't punishment enough."[113]

Or witness the fate of Kevin Cogill, a blogger who posted nine tracks from Guns N' Roses' long-awaited album *Chinese Democracy* on his website shortly before the songs' release in 2008. At the urging of Geffen Records, his home was raided and he was arrested at *gunpoint* for violating federal copyright law.[114] In early 2009, after he pled guilty to the charges it was reported federal prosecutors would be seeking a six-month prison term.[115] He had faced a potential five-year prison term and a $250,000 fine.[116] The raid and arrest even received support from Slash, the ex-guitarist for Guns N' Roses who famously left

FIGURE 5.4 Sheriff Slash.

the band more than a decade ago after a feud with lead singer Axl Rose. "I hope he rots in jail," Slash ranted. "It's going to affect the sales of the record, and it's not fair. The Internet is what it is, and you have to deal with it accordingly, but I think if someone goes and steals something, it's theft." Slash's ire was particularly ironic and noteworthy given his own extensive record of illegal conduct—including drug dealing and numerous acts of theft—for which he has never done significant prison time.[117]

B. PROTECTING UNSOPHISTICATED CREATORS

The absurdity of the present statutory regime comes into focus when one compares the results when the works of sophisticated versus unsophisticated creators are infringed. Infringe works from sophisticated creators who have timely registered their content with the Copyright Office and you may find yourself like Jammie Thomas-Russet, Joel Tenenbaum, Jack Yates, Elvin Feltner, or Kevin Cogill: on the receiving end of a bankrupting, multimillion-dollar judgment for infringement and/or jail time, even though there may have been no profit accrued from your actions or any proof of actual damages to the plaintiffs. By sharp contrast, infringe the work of an unsophisticated creator with impunity as you frequently remain insulated from litigation and liability.

Thus, to restore the balance between unsophisticated and sophisticated parties, we also propose the elimination of section 412's registration prerequisite for eligibility for attorneys' fees and statutory damages. There are certainly some risks to repealing the registration requirement. First, the registration requirement advances the ability of individuals and corporations to engage in activity akin to efficient breaches of contracts—at least in theory. However, to engage in an efficient infringement, one must be aware of one's rights and potential liabilities ex ante. Unfortunately, as we have seen, the copyright system does not enable this as there is no good way to know if a work is registered and therefore entitled to enhanced protection. One can know when a work is registered, but it is difficult to conclude with assurance that a work is *not* registered. Thus, the value of making efficient breaches available through the registration scheme is heavily dissipated.

Additionally, elimination of the timely registration requirement for statutory damages and fees eligibility could certainly lead to some problems, especially if it is enacted without other significant changes to our infringement and remedies regime. As Jon Baumgarten and Peter Jaszi have argued, repeal of section 412 might indeed increase copyright litigation, especially of the frivolous variety.[118] Such a threat should not be taken lightly, specifically in an era where there exist far too many overreaching copyright claims and the disparity between copyright norms and laws have left us all vulnerable to infringement litigation for countless daily activities.[119] Indeed, in recounting the threat that copyright enforcement run amuck can inflict on our daily lives, we have recognized the benefits that accrue to society from many works not being registered and, therefore, remaining ineligible for attorneys' fees and statutory damages. By making infringement litigation more profitable for more rightsholders, we certainly risk an uptick in litigation by giving even plaintiffs with petty claims more leverage.

However, there is good reason to think reform will not unleash a tide of frivolous litigation, especially when such reform is accompanied by stronger limitations in the range of available statutory damages and superior defenses for innocent infringement. First, such a position presumes the existing holders of copyright interests that are timely registered—so they have statutory damages and fees as a remedy—are less likely to pursue frivolous litigation than the masses. As we have already discussed,[120] this assumption is relatively untenable. Second, we have direct experience suggesting otherwise. Specifically, under the pre-1976 regime, fees and statutory damages were available to all regardless of registration, and a registration requirement for standing to bring a suit was largely eviscerated by the Supreme Court's decision in *Washington v. Gray* in 1937. Despite this, no boom in litigation (especially of the frivolous variety) resulted. Moreover, no other country has a registration requirement. Yet we have not witnessed a flood of frivolous copyright litigation either pre-1976 or in other countries, especially those sharing common legal traditions.[121] Indeed, the disproportional size of our statutory damages (which have grown dramatically since 1976), decoupled as they are from any proof of actual damages, may do far more to encourage frivolous litigation than putting all creators— sophisticated and unsophisticated—on a level playing field as far as remedies go.

III. Restoring the Balance Between Transformers and Creators

Finally, we present a fairly radical proposal to address one of the most fundamental problems with our existing copyright regime: although copyright exists for the express purpose of advancing progress in the arts, it does not always do so. In fact, as we have identified, the core doctrinal changes in copyright law over the past century and a half, particularly the fair use test, have altered copyright, taking it from its utilitarian bent to a more natural-law-oriented regime. In turn, copyright has increasingly stifled express rights, in the process impeding progress in the arts. Although we do not seek to return copyright to its eighteenth and early nineteenth century moorings, we advance an intermediate liability proposal that can unshackle and encourage transformative activity, thereby advancing freedom of speech and promoting artistic innovation.

A. THE PROBLEM WITH FAIR USE: TRANSFORMATION, PROGRESS IN THE ART, AND FREE SPEECH

As we have seen in Chapters 2 and 3, copyright law inextricably touches upon the First Amendment, affecting the expressive rights and personhood development of individuals. Courts have historically charged the fair use doctrine with the duty of reconciling any potential clash of copyright protection with free speech rights. However, as we have argued, fair use has failed to do its job. Far from vindicating the rights of the public to access and utilize copyrighted works in a way that promotes progress in the arts, the fair use doctrine has actually promulgated a vision of copyright that has fetishized the natural-law property rights of authors over the utilitarian goal of the regime.

According to the courts, fair use is a central vehicle for the incorporation of First Amendment concerns in copyright law. For example, in its most salient pronouncements on copyright doctrine, the Supreme Court has explained away any clash between free speech rights and copyright by arguing any tension can be handled through intrinsic limits on copyright, including fair use and the idea/expression dichotomy. As the Court explained in *Eldred v. Ashcroft*, "[C]opyright's built-in free speech safeguards are generally adequate to address [any conflict with free speech rights]."[122] Similarly, in rejecting a First

Amendment argument in *Harper & Row Publishers, Inc. v. Nation Enterprises*, the Supreme Court ruled the Copyright Act already embodied First Amendment protections through its "distinction between copyrightable expression and noncopyrightable facts and ideas, and the latitude for scholarship and comment traditionally afforded by fair use."[123]

As a result, courts have systematically denied the clash between free speech rights and copyright protections. What is particularly salient about this dismissal is the way in which it is laden in the discourse of property rights, signaling the hegemony of a natural-rights vision of copyright over an instrumentalist view and the concomitant immunization of copyright law from First Amendment scrutiny. There is no clash because, as the district court in *Eldred v. Reno* wrote, "[T]here are no First Amendment rights to use the copyrighted works of *others*."[124] Similarly, in only somewhat more demure language, the Supreme Court in *Eldred v. Ashcroft* contended "[t]he First Amendment securely protects the freedom to make—or decline to make—one's own speech; it bears less heavily when speakers assert the right to make *other people's speeches*."[125] With this pronouncement, Justice Ginsburg, writing for the majority, espoused a sharply natural-rights vision of copyright by drawing a clear distinction between the right we have to make our "own speech" under the First Amendment and our significantly curtailed ability to borrow "other people's speeches."[126]

But the notion there is an easy differentiation between one's own speech and the speech of others is an assumption fraught with trouble because all copyrighted speech inevitably builds upon the speech of others. As Benjamin Kaplan notes, "Education . . . proceeds from a kind of mimicry, and 'progress,' if it is not entirely an illusion, depends on generous indulgence of copying."[127] The creative process is inherently iterative. As Jessica Litman has eloquently argued:

> All authorship is fertilized by the work of prior authors, and the echoes of old work in new work extend beyond ideas and concepts to a wealth of expressive details. Indeed, authorship is the transformation and recombination of expression into new molds, the recasting and revision of details into different shapes. What others have expressed, and the ways they have expressed it, are the essential building blocks of any creative medium. If an author is successful at what she does, then something she creates will alter the landscape a little. We may not know who she is, or how what she created has varied, if only slightly, the way things seem to look, but those who follow her will necessarily tread on a ground distorted by her vision. The use of the work of other authors in one's own work inheres in the authorship process.[128]

Moreover, although there may be little doubt that in some cases an accused infringer is merely making the speech of others (as in *Eldred*, where the accused infringer adopted, word-for-word, the writings of others), as we saw in Chapter 2, there are a multitude of transformative instances where accused infringers have combined the fruit of another's intellectual labor with their own to create something new and original. Such uses not only muddy the notion of speech ownership, they can also contribute to progress in the arts.

Yet, as we have discussed, fair use—the ostensible vehicle for protecting expressive rights and the public domain in copyright jurisprudence—has failed to do its job. Simply put, under the fair use test, courts cannot give free speech interests appropriate weight.

The nature of the fair use test, which envisions copyright as a strong natural-law property interest, precludes such balancing. Far from checking the scope of copyright protections in order to protect the expressive interests of the public, the fair use test has actually served to expand (rather than diminish) the copyright monopoly, thereby undermining the utilitarian goals of the Copyright Clause. Specifically, as we illustrated in Chapter 2, the fair use test prevents those who engage in many forms of transformative use from escaping liability from copyright infringement. Hence, modern copyright law has impeded original and socially useful speech. At the same time, other elements of the fair use test have unjustifiably suppressed free speech interests.

First, the expressive rights of a copyright user, embodied in the transformative use doctrine, constitute only a meager fraction of the fair use test, playing a role in only one of the section 107 factors: "the purpose and character of the use."[129] On a rhetorical level, transformative use has grown increasingly important in the fair use calculus in recent years. In *Campbell v. Acuff-Rose*,[130] the Supreme Court extensively cited and adopted the reasoning of Judge Pierre Leval's influential article, *Toward a Fair Use Standard*,[131] in which Leval advocates making transformative use a stronger consideration in the fair use test.[132] However, in all but the case of parody, those engaging in transformative uses have not found solace in the fair use doctrine.[133] The courts have generally permitted unlicensed transformative uses solely for modalities such as parody, which inherently necessitate a derivative user conjure up the original work. As the *Campbell* Court concluded, "Parody needs to mimic an original to make its point . . . whereas satire can stand on its own two feet."[134] This formulation of the transformative use component of the section 107 balancing test is laden in the discourse of property rights, allowing borrowing only when conditions *require* it. Such a view casts fair use, rather than copyright, as a privilege.

Moreover, even if one is fairly confident a particular expressive use is protected as fair use, one can never be sure: the jurisprudence in the fair use arena is notoriously unpredictable.[135] The line between idea and expression, which bears directly on fair use matters,[136] is particularly problematic. As Learned Hand once conceded, "Nobody has ever been able to fix that boundary, and nobody ever can."[137] Moreover, by the fair use statute's own admissions, the four factors listed are not comprehensive.[138] There is also little consistency in the way the various four (or more) factors are weighed.[139] Wildly disparate outcomes on similar fact patterns have resulted, making copyright cases hard to decipher and reconcile.[140] For example, as Rebecca Tushnet points out, "After decades of litigation, it is still difficult to tell when and whether one can photocopy copyrighted materials, even for scientific research."[141]

The capricious outcome of fair use cases has, of course, been previously observed.[142] However, it is particularly troubling in light of the free speech implications involved (and the courts' denials thereof). It is axiomatic that cases implicating free speech interests require heightened judicial scrutiny of legislative action and acute concern over the potential chilling effects vague rules and overbroad regulations can have on the exercise of First Amendment rights.[143] However, when such issues ostensibly fall under the aegis of intellectual property law, the impact of overbroad regulations and vague rules on the chilling of speech are frequently ignored.[144] There is little doubt the nebulous fair use standards have prompted and will continue to prompt self-censorship in the private realm. Potential infringers will be unwilling and unable to bear the substantial costs of litigation as well as the risk of liability, even where it does not or should not exist.[145] The result not only suppresses free speech but also hinders the progress of the arts. This risk is particularly exacerbated by the massive statutory damages available under copyright law.[146] The exorbitance of these penalties inhibits anyone but the most bold and well-financed potential infringers from relying upon a fair use defense.[147]

Finally, fair use is an affirmative defense. As we saw in Chapter 2, prior to the development of the fair use doctrine, courts viewed acts of borrowing, if they were sufficiently transformative, as *noninfringing* uses. In other words, the burden of persuasion remained on the copyright holder to demonstrate the work was infringing and not transformative. Under *Folsom* and its progeny, once a prima facie showing of borrowing was made, the burden shifted to the alleged infringers to demonstrate their use was excusable. Thus, a party justifying use bears the burden of persuasion at trial on all issues involved in a fair use analysis.[148] Despite the plaintiff's alleged burden of showing a likelihood of success on the merits to obtain injunctive relief, some courts have even placed the burden of persuasion on the defendant for any fair use defense at the preliminary injunction phase.[149] Again, this rule stands in stark contrast to the typical judicial tack when dealing with free speech interests: prior restraints are strongly disfavored and presumptively invalid.[150] Given the social utility of transformative uses in advancing the arts, it is unusual these burdens are not reversed, especially as First Amendment rights are involved.

B. RECONCILING FIRST AMENDMENT RIGHTS AND COPYRIGHT PROTECTION: AN INTERMEDIATE LIABILITY PROPOSAL

All told, fair use's four-part balancing test and the century and a half of precedent interpreting it have combined to limit the possible responses of courts. The statutory scheme of the present regime forces courts to choose between two extreme options: infringement or fair use. If courts find infringement, hefty statutory damages often ensue—up to $150,000 per willful act—that are often well in excess of actual damages. However, if courts find fair use, an unauthorized user of a copyrighted work is able to exploit (without permission or payment) the work of another with impunity, thereby free riding on the creative success of the original author. This zero-sum regime has ultimately precluded courts from effectively balancing First Amendment and intellectual property considerations. Meanwhile, this harsh binary is particularly troublesome given the broad statutory definition of a derivative work and the fact that transformative uses—uses that advance dissemination of creative works with new meanings, expression, and messages—typically fail to qualify for fair use protection under the current balancing test.

Just as the modern torts revolution precipitated the evolution of comparative liability that overrode the harsh binary features of prior negligence doctrine, copyright law could benefit from the introduction of an intermediate liability option that can simultaneously advance First Amendment rights and the utilitarian goals of the federal copyright regime. Specifically, free expression issues become most pressing in the copyright arena when transformative uses—uses that "add[] something new, with a further purpose or different character, altering [an original creative work] with new expression, meaning, or message"—are made of creative works.[151] Transformative, or productive, uses of copyrighted works that would otherwise constitute infringements should be made exempt from statutory or actual damages. Such uses should be deemed per se noninfringing. However, commercial exploitation of transformative works would be subject to an accounting of profits—profits that would, as a default rule, be evenly split between the author of the original work and the transformative user.

Several benefits would accrue from such an intermediate liability option. First, courts would be discharged from the harsh choice between massive infringement liability and fair use—a binary that has prevented courts from fully addressing the free speech issues inherent in copyright enforcement. For transformative users of copyrighted works, liability would never exceed profitability; consequently, free expression rights would not be denied because of monetary concerns. This limitation of liability would in turn advance key First Amendment interests. Moreover, such an intermediate liability option also advances the original, utilitarian vision of the federal copyright system—the maximization of dissemination of creative works to the public so as to advance progress in the arts.[152] Meanwhile, copyright owners would continue to receive reasonable payments for the commercial exploitation of their works.

1. The Proposal

a. The Basics

Under the intermediate liability alternative, a court would first determine whether a work is infringing. If the work infringes, a defendant could proffer two defenses— fair use and transformative use. The fair use defense would continue to function as it currently does, providing immunity from liability for individuals meeting the four-part balancing test delineated in section 107 of the Copyright Act. Thus, such practices as time shifting would remain protected and insulated from liability,[153] as would other nontransformative activities (including some forms of photocopying for noncommercial academic purposes) that have been deemed fair use. Pursuant to the fair use doctrine, those engaging in such uses would be absolved of payment or apportionment.

However, if a defense of fair use fails, defendants can elect the intermediate liability option by arguing they have engaged in transformative use of the copyrighted work. To do so, they must have properly registered their work as a transformative use with the Copyright Office. Drawing upon the Supreme Court's reigning definition, a use is transformative if it "adds something new, with a further purpose or different character, altering the first [work] with new expression, meaning, or message."[154] To assist in this determination, the Copyright Office would issue guidelines that define certain categories of use as transformative, thereby providing ex ante guidance on what constitutes transformative use.[155]

Under this new intermediate liability option, transformative uses would include, inter alia, parody, satire, digital sampling, and appropriationist modern art, as each of these activities draws upon copyrighted works to create a new work of art imbued with new expressions that criticize or illuminate our values, assess our social institutions, satirize current events, or comment on our most notorious cultural symbols. For uses that emerge with the development of new technologies, the Copyright Office would engage in a public comment and consideration system akin to the liability exemption system provided under the Digital Millennium Copyright Act.[156] The Copyright Office would also retain discretion to add to the categories of uses determined to be "transformative."

For all such transformative uses registered with the Copyright Office, intermediate liability would attach. The resulting transformative use would be exempt from actual and statutory damages as well as injunctive relief.[157] Thus, the law would permit the creation and dissemination of transformative works without the consent of the author of the original work from which the transformative use drew. By default, however, the original author of the copyrighted work and the transformative user of that work would evenly divide all profits resulting from the commercial exploitation of the transformative work.[158]

Upon cursory examination, the decision to create a default position of even profit apportionment appears somewhat arbitrary. After all, under the Coase theorem, assuming zero transaction costs, the same outcome will result regardless of initial legal entitlement.[159] However, two grounds subvert the traditional Coasian admonishment regarding the irrelevance of initial entitlement distributions and support such a default position. First of all, the Coasian world is, of course, characterized by a lack of transaction costs.[160] By contrast, the world of copyright permissions is replete with transaction costs, especially given the absence of a centralized clearinghouse for effectuating licensing and the nebulous and poorly documented chains of copyright title. Given the free speech issues inherent in transformative use of copyrighted works, a default position allowing, rather than proscribing, transformative uses is warranted.

Second, although the Coasian world does not necessarily view the refusal of certain parties to deal as being a market failure,[161] the presence of such parties undermines progress in the arts. As we have documented previously, the world of copyright licensing is characterized by many parties that simply decline to permit transformative uses of their works, even if they might derive substantial economic advantages from such licensing. As such holdouts impede the availability of transformative uses to society—uses the Supreme Court has deemed accretive to the central goal of copyright to advance progress in the arts[162]—a default position that facilitates transformative use is preferable to the current system (which discourages it).

What is critical here is not the value judgment that may be signified through a choice to divide profits evenly between the original copyright owner and the transformative user. Indeed, if debate over the issue warrants a different balance—say 90 percent to 10 percent in favor of the original copyright owner, or 10 percent to 90 percent in favor of the transformative user—so be it. What is key is the creation of a liability option that subverts the harsh choice presently faced by the courts. Currently, if a court finds infringement, then ownership of the transformative use is divided 0 percent to 100 percent in favor of the original copyright owner. By contrast, if a court finds fair use, ownership of the transformative use is divided 0 percent to 100 percent in favor of the transformative user. The default position of even profit division can easily be contracted around, but it creates a reasonable starting point for negotiations between the original copyright owner and the transformative user. Specifically, by creating a default position of profit sharing, the intermediate liability regime limits original copyright owners from discriminating between favorable and unfavorable transformative uses of their copyrighted works.

Most importantly, noncommercial users would be free to appropriate copyrighted works for transformative purposes without compensation. Thus, the proposed regime unburdens precisely the type of speech that has historically received the greatest protection under

First Amendment jurisprudence—noncommercial expression. Meanwhile, commercial users would be able to appropriate copyrighted works for transformative purposes for a price that grows only in proportion to the profit earned from exploitation of the work. Thus, liability would never exceed profitability, thereby advancing constitutionally protected expressive freedoms. Taken together, such a scheme would alleviate free speech concerns, encourage transformative uses that promote progress in the arts, and maintain the economic incentives for authors to create and disseminate their works.

b. Clarifications and Limitations

A similar theory has been proposed in the model for the Xanadu project, which envisioned the creation of a digital library and hypertext publishing system where users could link to the works of others and create their own derivative works.[163] Theodor Nelson, the progenitor of Xanadu, asked copyright owners to waive their derivative rights when placing their work on the system in return for receipt of royalties for derivative creations; royalties would be shared between the author of the original work and the individual making use of the original work to create a derivative product.[164]

In a sense, therefore, the intermediate liability proposal is similar to considering an original creator and a transformative user as joint authors of a derivative work, where each individual holds a joint tenancy in the copyright and evenly splits the profits from the exploitation of the work.[165] However, the intermediate liability scheme has several key advantages over the imposition of joint authorship. First, it diminishes the uncertainty problem afflicting wholesale judicial determination of transformative use by setting out, ex ante, the types of uses deemed transformative for the purposes of intermediate liability. Certainly, courts can review these determinations, but the findings of the Copyright Office would be entitled to heavy deference. Second, this proposal routes around the profound judicial reluctance to divide ownership of copyright by putting the issue in the hands of the Copyright Office. Finally, the proposal avoids one of the implications of joint authorship—that the original creator both authorized and collaborated in the creation of the transformative work. Under the intermediate liability proposal advanced here, a transformative work cannot be attributed to the original author unless the original author requests it. Trademark law will take an increasingly important role under such a regime to ensure an absence of confusion regarding the origin of copyrighted works.

For example, if I write a satire of the 2008 elections based on *Star Wars*, I can make use of the storyline, characters (e.g., Yoda, Darth Vader, Luke Skywalker), and terms (e.g., *Jedi, lightsaber, Star Wars*) from the movie series, but I cannot attribute my satire to George Lucas. If anything, a disclaimer on my work should make it clear it is an unauthorized derivative work. However, George Lucas, as the original copyright holder to *Star Wars*, would be entitled to a presumptive 50 percent of any profits resulting from the creation of my work.

It is also important to note the limits of this proposal. As we demonstrated in Chapter 3, a use need not be transformative to possess a valuable purpose.[166] Sometimes, as in the case of classroom duplication, providing copies of copyrighted works serves a significant social end.[167] Moreover, a number of existing limitations on the copyright monopoly serve important free speech interests without advancing transformative use rights. These constraints include the idea/expression dichotomy, denial of copyright to government works, first-sale doctrine, compulsory licenses, liability exemptions for schools and libraries, merger doctrine, and lack of a broad performance right for sound recordings.[168] Interests in pure copying will continue to be served by application of the fair use test and the existing limits on the copyright monopoly, as bolstered by the reforms we have suggested in Parts I and II of this chapter as a means to restore balance between users and creators and between unsophisticated and sophisticated parties. Meanwhile, the intermediate liability proposal addresses the transformative use problem in copyright law.

The intermediate liability scheme proposed here is not without several immediate concerns on implementation, workability, and incentivization grounds. Each of these three areas is addressed in turn.

c. Implementation

i. Enactment of the Intermediate Liability Scheme

Of course, statutory change will undoubtedly be difficult. Robert Merges has characterized the history of intellectual property rights over the past one hundred years as a century of "solicitude" by corporate interests bent on maximizing monopoly-like protections for their intellectual properties.[169] Simply put, the derivative rights doctrine provides the content-creation industries with an economic boon that—Panglossian optimism aside—they are unlikely to give up without a massive fight. Nevertheless, this does not obviate the need to consider doctrinal alternatives to the modern copyright regime, especially in light of its increasing clash with expressive interests.

Moreover, in recent years, the public has demonstrated increasing awareness of the impact of the modern copyright regime on expressive freedoms and basic daily activities. Additionally, just as the boom in peer-to-peer file-sharing has benefited many companies (including cable and DSL operators, computer and hard drive manufacturers, and consumer electronics providers),[170] there are also powerful corporate interests that could benefit from the types of revisions advanced here. Companies that sell the technological tools for making transformative uses would stand to profit from a regime that expanded transformative rights. Greater "fair use" rights could also inure to the long-run economic benefit of the content-creation industry. Despite losing the *Sony v. Universal* decision and famously warning "the VCR is to the American film producer and the American public as the Boston strangler is to the woman home alone,"[171] the entertainment industry did not suffer a precipitous demise when it failed in its efforts to outlaw the VCR. In fact, the legality of the VCR and the DVD and the deeming of time shifting as fair use have vastly expanded revenue-generation opportunities for the Hollywood studios; they now earn more profit from DVD/video rental and sales than from theatrical ticket sales.[172] Thus, a coalition of consumer rights groups, technology manufacturers, and innovative content providers could provide support for the adoption of the intermediate liability proposal.

ii. Rethinking the Derivative Rights Doctrine

Adoption of an intermediate liability scheme would inextricably necessitate a reexamination of the derivative rights doctrine. As the Supreme Court argued in *Campbell*, the creation and dissemination of transformative works advances the constitutional goal of progress in the arts.[173] However, the broad exclusive right of copyright owners to prepare derivative works has swallowed up the ability of transformative users to escape infringement liability, thereby undermining the key goal of the federal copyright regime.

Commenting on an Illinois court's blunt rejection of a transformative use claim by the creator of a guidebook on Beanie Babies on the grounds such an activity violated the derivative works rights of the Beanie Baby creators,[174] Matthew Bunker reminds us that "[C]reating a derivative work is at least suggestive of some transformation. When coupled with the addition of new information and interpretation regarding the toys, the claim at least deserves serious judicial analysis."[175]

However, the strictures of section 106 of the Copyright Act do not allow for such analysis as they unequivocally provide copyright owners with the exclusive right to "prepare derivative works based upon the copyrighted work."[176] Although original copyright laws protected solely against slavish reproduction of an entire work, modern copyright law expansively protects the actual copyrighted work itself (whether borrowed in part or whole), nonliteral elements of the copyrighted work, and any derivative works based upon the copyrighted work. Thus, translations and abridgements, formerly considered transformative uses of a copyrighted work and therefore per se noninfringing, are now categorized as derivative works that come under the exclusive right of a copyright owner under section 106.[177] Indeed, section 101 of the Copyright Act defines a *derivative work* as "a work based upon one or more preexisting works, such as a translation, musical arrangement, dramatization, fictionalization, motion picture version, sound recording, art reproduction, abridgment, condensation, or any other form in which a work may be recast, *transformed*, or adapted."[178] This definition, which implicates transformative uses as derivative ones, undermines the very viability of a transformative use defense in copyright law.

As copyright historically evolved from the narrow right to forbid duplication of one's original work to a broader right to interdict (irrespective of form) any borrowing of the elusive intellectual essence of one's original work, an artificial hierarchy of works emerged to rationalize the expansion of an author's property right.[179] Appealing to the romantic notion of authorship as a flash of genius, this hierarchy presented "some works . . . as inherently superior due to their supposed originality, [and] relegated [other works] to the now, by definition, inferior status of derivatives."[180] This unchallenged hierarchy—which began to take shape in the nineteenth century—begs reconsideration on two important grounds: the important role of transformative use in the advancement of the arts, and the value of transformative use on expressive grounds.

To revitalize the role of transformative use in copyright jurisprudence, the derivative works doctrine must therefore be reexamined. Naomi Voegtli, for one, has suggested fine-tuning the definition of derivative works so that they constitute "either (1) a work based significantly upon one or more pre-existing works, such that it exhibits little originality of its own or that it unduly diminishes economic prospects of the works used; or (2) a translation, sound recording, art reproduction, abridgment, and condensation."[181] Contrary to the existing definition of derivative work, a revised definition must draw a distinction between uses that are transformative and those that are merely derivative. The first part of the Voegtli definition accomplishes this goal by simply defining a derivative work as a non-transformative use of someone else's copyrighted work. The adoption of such a definition of derivative work would go a long way toward reconciling the inherent conflict between the present definition of derivative works and the viability of transformative use defenses to infringement. The second part of Voegtli's definition represents a catch-all for potentially transformative uses that, for public policy reasons, may be deemed to nevertheless infringe under the derivative rights doctrine. Potentially transformative uses the courts feel would not sufficiently advance progress in the arts could be placed under the second part of the derivative works definition. Quite simply, we should ask ourselves whether translations, sound recordings, art reproductions, abridgements, condensations, and other heretofore unknown manipulations of copyrighted works in the digital age are sufficiently accretive to progress in the arts that we want to encourage their dissemination without fear of infringement liability. Inevitably, adoption of the intermediate liability proposal advanced here will require wholesale reconsideration of the derivative right—a doctrine whose expansive terms have contributed heavily toward the growing tension between copyright and expressive rights.

d. Workability

i. Defining Transformative Use

Even after adoption, the intermediate liability standard for transformative uses of copyrighted works will not be without potential workability challenges.[182] For example, some observers have speculated that defining transformative use would necessarily implicate the Copyright Office and the courts in the business of judging the quality of artistic works.[183] As Justice Holmes explained a century ago, "It would be a dangerous undertaking for persons trained only to the law to constitute themselves final judges of the worth of [a work], outside of the narrowest and most obvious limits."[184] However, determining what constitutes transformative use need not be commensurate to an assessment of whether the use of a copyrighted work in question is in good or bad taste, whether the message (or lack thereof) of the allegedly infringing work is agreeable, or whether the result of the alleged infringement is sublime. As the California Supreme Court stated in its adoption of transformative use as a doctrinal limitation on the right of publicity:

> In determining whether the work is transformative, courts are not to be concerned with the quality of the artistic contribution—vulgar forms of expression fully qualify for First Amendment protection. On the other hand, a literal depiction of a celebrity, even if accomplished with great skill, may still be subject to a right of publicity challenge. The inquiry is in a sense more quantitative than qualitative, asking whether the literal and imitative or the creative elements predominate in the work.[185]

Thus, in the copyright context, to ascertain transformative use, the Copyright Office and the courts would examine whether something new and creative, possessing the ability to contribute to progress in the arts, has been developed through the allegedly infringing use.[186] Thus, slavish imitation of a copyrighted work, even if accomplished with great skill, would not qualify as transformative. But, even vulgar transmogrifications of a copyrighted work, if infused with creative and original elements, would qualify. As the Supreme Court has conceded, although "transformative use is not absolutely necessary for a finding of fair use . . . the goal of copyright, to promote science and the arts, is generally furthered by the creation of transformative works."[187] As advancement of the arts represents the chief goal of copyright protection, we must inevitably make some judgments about the types of derivative works that benefit progress and the types that do not.

Naturally, drawing the line between transformative and non-transformative uses is laden with subjectivity. However, making such a determination in the administrative and judicial contexts is both feasible and less troublesome than the muddled fair use test critiqued here and elsewhere. As noted earlier, a transformative use test is consistent with the utilitarian origins of the Copyright Clause of the Constitution; such prominent consideration of transformative use would raise progress in the arts to the forefront of the copyright calculus. Further, adoption of a transformative use test would help alleviate the growing clash between copyright law and free speech rights.

This proposal does not dictate a return to the same judgments as our predecessors about what constitutes transformative use. Perhaps we will not view the act of translation or abridgement as sufficiently transformative or accretive to progress in the arts to warrant intermediate liability under the proposed regime. However, because of the strong expressive component latent in transformative works and the high potential of transformative works to advance progress in the arts, transformative value should lie at the heart of our consideration in carving out an exception to traditional copyright liability. Both the dictates of the First Amendment and the Copyright Clause warrant explicit assessment of the progressive value of each use of copyrighted works—be it a form of postmodern art, digital sampling, or some heretofore unknown technological manipulation. Indeed, as Jay Daugherty has argued, transformative uses can contribute to progress in the arts in two guises: trans*expressive* uses (where an original work is utilized for a new form of expression), and trans*purposive* uses (where an original work is set to a new purpose).[188] Although various observers might disagree as to whether uses of a copyrighted work may amount to transexpressive or transpurposive, it is a worthwhile debate for us, as a society, to have. And, it is critical we provide transexpressive and transpurposive users of copyright works with ex ante protection from infringement liability in order to foster progress in the arts.

ii. Moral Rights and the Potential for Market Glut

Under the intermediate liability regime, the public could make transformative uses of copyrighted works with impunity. This raises two critical and related concerns. First, the proposal might precipitate a glut of derivative works on the market that would undermine the value, both economically and artistically, of the original works. Second, creators would lose control over the products of their imagination—including the very characters, plotlines, visuals, and semantics they perceive as extensions of themselves.[189] As Samuelson and Glushko succinctly state, "Authors often regard their writings as expressions of their personalities. Any tampering with their texts may be viewed by such authors as a 'mutilation' of the work, as objectionable as if someone had the effrontery to walk up to you and cut your hair without your permission."[190]

The effective functioning of the section 115 compulsory mechanical license[191] over the past century not only diffuses both of these concerns but also illustrates the tremendous social benefit that can accrue from the ability to make unauthorized transformative uses of the copyrighted works of others.[192] Under the existing copyright regime, the creator of the original work holds the exclusive right to reproduce a copyrighted work and to prepare any derivatives of it. However, since 1909, music compositions have enjoyed an exception to this rule. Section 115 of the Copyright Act provides that anyone can record a cover version of a copyrighted, nondramatic musical composition and distribute copies of it.[193] No permission is required from the original composer; cover artists need only provide the copyright owner or the Copyright Office with notice of their intentions to record a cover song[194] and pay a per-album fee fixed by a royalty panel.[195] Although full transformative use of musical compositions cannot be made under the statute, cover artists are free to tinker with the composition to adapt it to a particular musical genre: "a compulsory license includes the privilege of making a musical arrangement of the work to the extent necessary to conform it to the style or manner of interpretation of the performance involved."[196] Thus, without any authorization from the original artist, Limp Bizkit can record a thrash-metal version of George Michael's pop song "Faith"; Luna a dreamy, lo-fi cover of Guns N' Roses's "Sweet Child O' Mine"; William Shatner a loungy take on Pulp's alternative rock classic "Common People"; and Dynamite Hack an acoustic folk-rock rendition of N.W.A.'s gangsta rap "Boyz N tha Hood."

In fact, as the history of modern music has demonstrated, the public, musicians, and music industry have benefited tremendously from the availability of the compulsory mechanical license. Although Bob Dylan is a remarkable songwriter and musician, there are few who would consider his renditions of "All Along the Watchtower" and "Mr. Tambourine Man"—two songs he both composed and recorded—superior to the covers of those songs by Jimi Hendrix and the Byrds, respectively. Hendrix's version of "All Along the Watchtower" helped launch him into rock's pantheon; it also secured the place of Dylan's composition in rock history. The availability of a section 115 license therefore enabled Hendrix to expand his popularity and introduced a whole new audience to the works of both Dylan and Hendrix.

Despite its seemingly perennial platform advocating strong copyright protection, the recording industry has ardently supported maintenance of the compulsory mechanical license scheme. The music industry's view of the compulsory mechanical license stands in stark contrast to its position on other copyright issues. In hearings before the House Committee on the Judiciary in 1967, the recording industry argued "performers need unhampered access to musical material on nondiscriminatory terms. . . . [T]he 1909 statute adopted the compulsory license as a deliberate anti-monopoly condition on the grant of [copyright]. . . . They argue that the result has been an outpouring of recorded music, with the public being given lower prices, improved quality, and a greater choice."[197] At a minimum, we should ask ourselves whether the same logic might apply to motion pictures, literary works, and other copyrightable subject matter.

On this issue, there is a body of favorable experience. Although the mechanical licensing scheme applies only to musical compositions, the public enjoys unadulterated access to any creative works once the work's copyright term expires. In the United States, almost any work published prior to 1923 has fallen into the public domain and can be used and abused without fear of infringement. Yet, we have not witnessed an avalanche of derivative works that undermine the artistic integrity and vision espoused by these original works. Moreover, the only harm to the commercial market for these original works has stemmed not from the universal ability to make transformative uses of these works, but because the works can now be slavishly reproduced without running afoul of copyright laws.

According to ardent protectionists such as Jack Valenti, former president of the Motion Picture Association of America:

A public domain work is an orphan. No one is responsible for its life. But everyone exploits its use, until that time certain when it becomes soiled and haggard, barren of its previous virtues. Who, then, will invest the funds to renovate and nourish its future life when no one owns it?[198]

However, the practices of Valenti's own industry undermine the credibility of his claim. Neither the works of Jane Austen nor of William Shakespeare have become soiled or haggard: the interest in their novels and plays continues to thrive, and their works continue to enjoy such high popular regard that Hollywood studios have based numerous movies on them. Ultimately, the works of Jane Austen are not any less revered, meaningful, or commercially successful because of Alicia Silverstone's *Clueless*, and Shakespeare is none the worse because of the Julia Stiles vehicle, *O*. Indeed, unauthorized transformative uses of copyrighted works can even reignite the meaning and value of the original works. Take, for example, JibJab's brilliant use of Woodie Guthrie's "This Land Is Your Land" in satirizing George W. Bush and John Kerry during the 2004 presidential elections.[199] The satire not only provided both amusement and meaning to millions who saw it, but it also brought renewed attention to Guthrie's song and his oeuvre. Interestingly, the creators of the satire faced the threat of an infringement suit from the owners of the publishing rights to Guthrie's song. Ultimately, the threats were dropped after the Electronic Frontier Foundation learned the publisher's copyright in the Guthrie song had likely lapsed and it had therefore fallen into the public domain.[200]

Finally, the proposal advanced here would not unilaterally wrest power from the hands of artistic innovators. Although the intermediate liability option will diminish the control that creators have in one sense, it will expand control in another. Though the ambit of the right to exclude would shrink so that creators could no longer prevent recoding[201] of their copyrighted works, artists would simultaneously enjoy an expanded palette of expressive possibilities, including the right to engage in transformative uses of all existing copyrighted works.

iii. Audience Interests in Semiotic Stability

According to critics of reform, an expansive transformative use regime not only threatens the moral rights of artists, it undermines interests consumers of copyrighted works have in their sustained integrity. In a provocative article[202] that draws on the work of Landes and Posner,[203] Justin Hughes has cast light upon a latent cost stemming from the dissemination of transformative uses: the harm copyright audiences suffer when a work loses the stability of its meaning. Thus, Hughes suggests many theorists have wholly ignored the vast positive social externalities that accrue from preserving the stability of cultural images. As Hughes rhetorically asks, "What justifies concern for the gay artist who wants to print postcards of John Wayne wearing pink lipstick but no concern for the young, heterosexual army recruit who wants to identify with a stable image of John Wayne?"[204]

Though thought-provoking, Hughes's critique suffers from a fatal flaw: audience interests in stability of meaning are fundamentally different from interests advancing transformative use. In a regime where transformative uses are presumptively not allowed, the expressive interests of those making the transformative use and the personhood interests of those consuming such uses are necessarily suppressed. By contrast, when transformative uses are allowed, the stability of cultural hieroglyphics is not necessarily undermined. Indeed, as Hughes himself concedes,[205] many cultural icons that have fallen into the public domain (and are therefore subject to free recoding), including Shakespeare, the Statue of Liberty, and the Mona Lisa, have retained their core meanings. Moreover, as Mark Lemley points out, audience interests in stable cultural iconography probably apply only to a small subset of copyrighted works that have achieved widespread dissemination.[206] Thus, when weighing competing utilities between regimes favoring and restricting transformative uses, it makes sense to err on the side of an expansive right to recode.

To this effect, market competition can best guide the clash between core and fluid meaning and the societal returns they provide. Rather than using artificially granted monopolies to create a static intellectual property semiotic, copyright policy should allow transformative uses to compete against original meanings. In short, if the stability interest in John Wayne's representation of the quintessence of rugged American heterosexuality and morality outweighs the aggregate utility that stems from the recoding of John Wayne's image, the marketplace of ideas will dictate it.

e. Preserving Economic Incentives for Artistic Creation and Dissemination

Finally, the adoption of an intermediate liability standard for transformative uses would not undermine the ability of authors to recoup their investment in a work or to earn a reasonable royalty. First, as Pierre Leval notes, "[T]he more the appropriator is using the material for new transformed purposes, the less likely it is that appropriative use will be a substitute for the original."[207] As such, transformative works do not interfere with the rightful economic market of the original copyright creator. This observation recalls the words of the California Supreme Court, which has noted that "when a work contains significant transformative elements, it is not only especially worthy of First Amendment protection, but it is also less likely to interfere with the economic interest protected by the right of publicity."[208] The same logic holds for copyrighted works.

Admittedly, content creators would no longer enjoy the windfall that has come from the derivative rights doctrine. However, the intermediate liability standard for transformative uses still enables authors to profit substantially from the commercial exploitation of their creative works. Transformative uses of copyrighted works would no longer constitute infringement, but a copyrighted work could not be commercially appropriated without compensation, as the creator of the copyrighted work from which an appropriator draws would, as a default rule, earn half the profits from the exploitation of the transformative end product.

The effect on the incentives to create and disseminate knowledge are likely minimal. Once again, the experience of the compulsory mechanical license is instructive. Section 115 certainly diminishes the rights of musical composers vis-à-vis the rights of other content creators. Under current law, individuals are not free to film their own remake of George Lucas's *Star Wars* or write their own sequel to F. Scott Fitzgerald's *The Great Gatsby*; yet anyone can record and distribute for profit their own interpretation of the Beatles's "Yesterday," regardless of how odious the cover might seem to Paul McCartney. Indeed, once a musical composer releases a song to the world, he no longer possesses the right to control who can take that song and make it her own. Nevertheless, modern copyright discourse contains little outcry from musical composers about individuals taking their songs, violating the moral rights to their artistic creations, profiting unfairly from the commercial exploitation of their lyrics and music, and grotesquely bowdlerizing the integrity and vision of their works. The suggestion a musician would withhold public release of his musical composition because he knows that, under existing law, others can cover the song with impunity simply does not pass the laughter test. In a similar vein, given the commercial incentives that will still remain for the dissemination of copyrighted works even under the intermediate liability scheme, artists of all stripes will continue to release their material to the public.

Shackled by the fair use doctrine, courts have been unable to address fully the First Amendment issues inextricably interwoven in the fabric of copyright law. After all, copyrighted works are not just a form of property; they are also the primary means through which modern individuals exercise their expressive rights. Our proposal for a new intermediate liability standard that would apply to transformative uses would provide a much-needed alternative to the harsh dichotomy of existing law, which forces courts to categorize any unauthorized use of a copyrighted work as either an infringement (in which case the use is subjected to weighty statutory damages), or a fair use (in which case the use is excused from any liability whatsoever). Additionally, by morphing copyright from a property regime to a liability regime in this regard, we address the hold-out problem, where rightsholders either refuse to give permission for their works to be used in transformative ways or do so only upon payment of monopolistic rents. Early copyright jurisprudence gave special protection to transformation as such uses contributed to the underlying goal of the federal copyright system—progress in the arts—and supported expressive rights. By targeting transformative uses, the intermediate liability regime will encourage progress in the arts, rekindle the utilitarian underpinnings of copyright law as envisioned by the Framers, and advance the protection of vital free speech interests while still retaining important economic rewards for the creators of copyrighted content.

IV. Toward a Copyright 2.0

The proposals presented here are far from perfect or comprehensive solutions to the issues we have raised throughout the course of the book. And although some changes would be relatively simply to implement, other policy prescriptions would face numerous challenges, including thorny questions over definitional concerns and heated fights with entrenched interests who benefit from the current state of affairs. Nevertheless, the vast doctrinal and technological changes that have occurred in recent decades warrant a serious discussion about copyright reform. After all, in an information society where the use of cultural symbols and knowledge and the undertaking of expressive activities are inevitably regulated by the strictures of copyright law, the state of that law is of increasing relevance to us all. With this in mind, we have advanced several proposals that will help restore greater balance between users and creators, sophisticated and unsophisticated parties, and transformers and creators. At the very least, these suggestions represent a small step toward developing a regime that better fosters and protects both creativity and individual expression. Ultimately, however, change will not happen without even greater public awareness about copyright and its impact on even the most routine aspects of our lives. With so much at stake, therefore, the individual—reified for so long as an infringer, a transformer, a consumer, and a creator—must become something else entirely: a reformer.

All animals are equal but some animals are
more equal than others.
—George Orwell, *Animal Farm* (1945)

CONCLUSION

Copyright, Consecration, and Control

In which we contemplate music as torture, famous standoffs at papal nunciatures, Hollywood's founders as outlaws, Uncle Sam as a DJ, Vegas musicals, Ashley Wilkes's sexual orientation, Captain Kirk's reincarnation, and Holden Caulfield's maturation

ALTHOUGH THE DIRECT subject matter of this book is copyright law, its implicit focus and potential implications are much broader. Specifically, our analysis speaks to the critical role of our intellectual property regime in mediating social, political, and economic rights. By regulating the dissemination of knowledge and patrolling access to cultural symbols, copyright law has become an increasingly important force in the construction of our information society. In the process, copyright law serves a broader hegemonic project, shaping public discourse and impacting power relationships between sovereigns and their subjects, corporations and individuals, and entrenched interests and surging parvenus.

As John Fiske writes, "Popular culture always is part of power relations; it always bears traces of constant struggle between domination and subordination, between power and various forms of resistance to it or evasions of it."[1] Thus, it is not surprising that intellectual property laws that control access to and use of popular culture are a function of power relations. Specifically, intellectual property laws increasingly inform the way in which social order is maintained in the twenty-first century. In the early 1970s, cultural theorist Pierre Bourdieu introduced the concept of cultural reproduction to explain the processes through which the dominant class retained its power.[2] Drawing on the example of schooling in modern society, he argued educational institutions function largely to preserve hegemonic interests by perpetuating the reproduction of the cultural and social values of the elite.[3] Bourdieu's work on cultural reproduction has inspired waves of scholarship in the social sciences, but has generated little accompanying interest in the legal academy, especially in the field of intellectual property. Yet the notion of cultural reproduction is instrumental to understanding the consequences of intellectual property laws on knowledge/power systems. The work of Bourdieu and his progeny suggests the inviolate recitation of the cultural production of entrenched social forces is a profound vehicle for the inculcation of a set of values and symbols that consolidate existing power structures. If that is the case, the act of imperfect reproduction, or of customization, of cultural production can translate into an act of subversion or reproduction of the existing social order in a particular form. These acts of differentiation and similitude, or the acts of imperfect reproduction and customization, are carefully regulated by intellectual property laws. And, the selective protection granted to cultural production under the guise of copyright unveils the role of intellectual property law in shaping social relations, molding identities, enforcing dominant values, and controlling expressive rights. Copyright's procedural and substantive rules therefore serve as a key vehicle for the discursive exertion of knowledge/power systems on individuals. This understanding implicitly informs the analysis throughout the course of the book and directly impacts the reform proposals advanced in the last chapter. After all, to paraphrase George Orwell, although all copyrighted works are equal, it turns out some are more equal than others.

I. IP as Hegemonic Battleground

For many years, intellectual property doctrine has served as a key battleground for the struggle between entrenched economic interests and emerging competitors. An examination of historical conflicts between intellectual property maximalists and minimalists makes this point clear. As Larry Lessig has argued, many of the same industries that now lobby heavily for strong intellectual property rights established themselves precisely because of their flagrant, unauthorized exploitation of the intellectual property of others.[4] Thus, the very powers now advocating copyright maximalism were borne of infringement during their formative years.

For more than a century, the fledgling American publishing industry benefited from the ability to reproduce the works of foreign authors—especially those from Britain—without paying a penny in royalties.[5] Cable television blossomed because of retransmission of the signals (i.e., the copyrighted content) of the major networks without authorization or payment.[6] Hollywood became the center of the motion picture universe when Louis Mayer famously travelled to the West Coast to seek better weather and reduce production costs.[7] Less famously, Mayer and his cronies were seeking to evade the watchful eye of Thomas Edison and his attorneys.[8] Edison, it turned out, owned numerous patents for technology used by the burgeoning film industry—and filmmakers were eager to save money by evading his licensing demands.[9] In short, Hollywood became the global capital of the entertainment industry because of infringement. Major studios such as Walt Disney have long profited by drawing upon the rich tradition of folktales without compensating anyone for their exploitation.[10] And, as we have seen, the modern music industry saw much of its early success from the unauthorized exploitation of old blues riffs, many stolen directly from unacknowledged African-American folk artists.[11]

We continue to see the clash between prior creators and emerging innovators in action today. For example, leading Internet sites are pushing the line on copyright law as they challenge the dominion of traditional content creators. Web 2.0 outfits such as YouTube

FIGURE 6.1 An Early Version of Thomas Edison's Motion Picture Projection Technology.

thrive on "user-generated content"—much of which consists of either the copyrighted works of third parties or works by users that, without authorization, integrate the copyrighted works of third parties.[12] These third parties are frequently the major movies studios and record labels. To date, Web 2.0 companies have shielded themselves from liability through the precarious provisions of the DMCA safe harbor for Internet Service Providers who host user-generated content. However, those provisions are under attack by such traditional media conglomerates as Viacom, who claim YouTube illegitimately free rides on the backs of content creators whose works provide the value that makes YouTube a top online destination.[13]

Besides its role as a central battleground in the struggle between emerging and mature industries, intellectual property also mediates the relationship between sovereigns and their subjects. One can witness this power dynamic at play in some recent encounters between governments and copyright law.

A. GUANTANAMO'S GREATEST HITS: MUSIC, TORTURE, AND COPYRIGHT LAW

Consider the curious case of the use of music by the federal government at the American military base at Guantanamo Bay and the subsequent response by the recording industry. Shortly after taking office in 2009, President Barack Obama stated he would bring to an end to the use of Guantanamo Bay as a detention camp for enemy combatants in the war on terrorism.[14] With the eventual closing of the facility, a number of rather controversial policies would presumably also come to an end. Of those practices, one of the more unusual was the military's arguably infringing use of music on the prisoners.[15] The soundtrack to Guantanamo Bay, it turns out, was replete with copyrighted songs meant to addle and unnerve, especially on repeat, but to which the government apparently possessed no rights to perform.[16]

As a preliminary matter, the playlist at Guantanamo was filled with interesting choices. For example, it included "Fuck Your God"—a particularly bizarre selection considering the Bush Administration's religiosity and the federal government's position (through the FCC) on the use of indecent language in other contexts. Guantanamo Bay's Top Ten List—the songs most frequently played to interrogate prisoners—featured a perverse smorgasbord of heavy metal, children's music, and (seemingly) patriotic stadium rock:

1. "Enter Sandman"–Metallica
2. "Bodies"–Drowning Pool
3. "Shoot to Thrill"–AC/DC
4. "Hell's Bells"–AC/DC
5. "I Love You" (from the *Barney and Friends* children's television show)
6. "Born in the USA"–Bruce Springsteen
7. "We Are The Champions"–Queen
8. "Babylon"–David Gray
9. "White America"–Eminem
10. "Sesame Street" (theme from eponymous children's television show)[17]

Thankfully, the Cure's "Killing an Arab" (no matter what its existentialist, Camusian roots) was not on the list.

Of course, the music-as-weapon policy was not entirely new. In 1989, General Manuel Noriega, a reputed opera lover,[18] was holed up in a Papal nunciature in Panama City, seeking refuge with the Vatican after American forces had invaded his country. In response, American military officials bombarded him incessantly with loud rock and pop, including such songs as "Nowhere to Run" and "Smugglers Blues."[19] In 1993, the ATF and FBI famously blared heavily distorted music[20] and recordings of rabbits being slaughtered[21] during the infamous standoff with the Branch Davidians in Waco, Texas. The origins may go even further back than 1989. One military official, retired U.S. Air Force Lieutenant Colonel Dan Kuehl, located the policy's spiritual genesis in the Bible, commenting: "Joshua's army used horns to strike fear into the hearts of the people of Jericho. His men might not have been able to break down literal walls with their trumpets, but the noise eroded the enemy's courage."[22]

Politics aside and whatever its origins, the government's music policy in Guantanamo raised a key copyright issue: it appeared the government was not paying the appropriate public performance licenses needed to play the music. But, the response from artists was mixed. James Hetfield of Metallica appeared to condone the practice, though he did mention the government had neither asked his permission nor paid him royalties. Ironically, Metallica has led the fight against unauthorized downloading of its music on the Internet. But speaking about the use of his music by the U.S. government in Fallujah, Hetfield commented, "If the Iraqis aren't used to freedom, then I'm glad to be part of their exposure."[23]

Not everyone was so enthusiastic, however. As Trent Reznor of Nine Inch Nails wrote, "It's difficult for me to imagine anything more profoundly insulting, demeaning and enraging than discovering music you've put your heart and soul into creating has been used for purposes of torture."[24] Reznor also threatened legal action: "If there are any legal options that can be realistically taken they will be aggressively pursued, with any potential monetary gains donated to human rights charities."[25] However, it appears Reznor never followed up on this threat. In contraposition to Metallica, Reznor has served as a powerful voice opposing the RIAA lawsuits against unauthorized Internet downloading.[26]

Although a few individual artists have raised concerns about the apparent infringement, the industry itself has remained relatively silent. The RIAA appears to have no qualms about suing children and grandmothers for engaging in peer-to-peer file sharing, but it does not seem as enthusiastic about pursuing infringement charges against the federal government, despite the brazen unauthorized public performance of the songs.[27]

Admittedly, the infringement issue does raise some complexities. The most immediate question that comes to mind is whether and how U.S. copyright law might apply in Guantanamo in the first place. After all, it is an axiomatic principal of American copyright law that it has no extraterritorial application.[28] And, as the Bush Administration maintained in constitutional challenges to its Guantanamo detention policy, the territory was not considered U.S. soil in any sense of the word. Specifically, the government claimed it did not exert sovereignty over Guantanamo Bay and, therefore, U.S. law did not apply there.[29] Ultimately, however, the Supreme Court rejected this argument in *Boumediene v. Bush*, finding the United States had exerted de facto sovereignty through its "complete and uninterrupted" exercise of "absolute and indefinite" control over Guantanamo for almost a century.[30]

Arguably, the federal Copyright Act applies in any territory over which the United States exerts sovereignty. However, to avoid any issue of ambiguity, most U.S. territories have an express statute that enables application of federal copyright laws.[31] For example, the Copyright Act applies in the Panama Canal Zone through operation of section 391 of the Panama Canal Code, which provides "The patent, trade-mark, and copyright laws of the United States shall have the same force and effect in the Canal Zone as in continental United States, and the district court is given the same jurisdiction in actions arising under such laws as is exercised by United States district courts."[32] Guantanamo Bay does not appear to have such a provision in place. Thus, post-*Boumediene*, there is still some question about the application of American copyright protection in Guantanamo.

However, one can potentially circumvent this problem in two ways. First, if a part of the infringing activity occurs in the United States (e.g., perhaps the recordings are selected in the United States for unauthorized public performance in Guantanamo Bay), parties in the United States who contributed to the infringing activity can be held liable under American copyright law.[33] Second, if one distinguishes *Boumediene* and argues the terms of the lease for Guantanamo between Cuba and the United States determine the issue, Cuba is the territorial sovereign, and unauthorized performance would represent a violation of Cuban law.[34] Given these facts, it is surprising that not a single one of the myriad rockers with a penchant for all things Che Guevara has reveled at the prospect of suing the U.S. government for infringement under Cuban copyright law.

The lack of action by composers and record labels has effectively granted the federal government unfettered rights to take the works of various recording artists and cast them in unfamiliar lights and contexts, thereby lending some of these compositions' meanings entirely at odds with the intentions of their authors. Consider Bruce Springsteen's "Born in the U.S.A." Through its bleak portrait of a Vietnam veteran forgotten by his own country, the song presents a poignant critique of societal inequities and our tragic failure to properly honor the men and women of the armed forces for their sacrifices. Played at Guantanamo Bay, however, the song takes on an entirely different significance—at least to its intended audience of soldiers and detainees. With the imprimatur of DJ Uncle Sam, the song's seemingly jingoistic, anthemic chorus takes center stage. In the process, the tune transforms into a patriotic paean rather than a biting attack on the false promises of the American dream, and it serves as an effective aural device to demarcate the insider (American and non-terrorist)/outsider (terrorist and non-American) divide separating the soldiers and detainees. Indeed, a central distinction between detainees taken to Guantanamo Bay and held indefinitely without charges and those brought to the United States and entitled to full due process rights was initially based on a detainee's citizenship/birth status.[35] If you were, indeed, lucky enough to be born in the U.S.A., you were entitled to fundamentally different rights than those who were not. Thus, besides setting a patriotic tone and asserting the base's status as a distinctly American space, the blaring of the song over the Guantanamo loudspeakers also serves as a stark reminder to the detainees of how much the accidents of birth can affect one's fate.

All told, the unauthorized use of Springsteen's "Born in the U.S.A." allows the government to reengineer the meaning of the song almost entirely, transforming it from an ironic, caustic critique of our societal failures to a bold assertion of national pride and prowess. And, it is the absence of infringement litigation (for the government alone) that enables this radical semiotic recasting of the work to take place. Indeed, at a time when the recording industry is suing individual users for millions of dollars for unauthorized peer-to-peer downloading—an effort supported by the federal government with legislation that has provided heightened statutory damages and increased criminal enforcement of copyright laws—the recording industry has remained quiet about the federal government's use of copyrighted recordings at Guantanamo Bay. Meanwhile, the federal government has shown no compunction about making such uses, regardless of the potential infringement.

B. THE EXEMPTION OF STATE GOVERNMENTS FROM INFRINGEMENT LIABILITY

Despite the deafening silence of the recording industry's response to the unauthorized use of music at Guantanamo Bay, it remains true the federal government can be held liable for copyright infringement—at least in theory. By sharp contrast, under current law, state governments enjoy absolute immunity from claims of infringement. Consequently, state governments can make unauthorized use and abuse of copyrighted works with impunity as they suffer no adverse legal consequences. Although the way in which our laws arrived at this state of affairs is mired in constitutional complexity, it does point to the existence of a remarkable loophole from infringement liability for state governments.

Under the Eleventh Amendment, states enjoy sovereign immunity from suits brought in federal court by citizens of another state or of a foreign country.[36] Although the actual text does not grant a state protection from suits brought by its own citizens in federal court, the Supreme Court has interpreted the Eleventh Amendment to also include immunity from such claims,[37] a view most recently reaffirmed by a narrow 5–4 margin.[38]

As federal courts have exclusive jurisdiction over copyright claims,[39] the Supreme Court's interpretation of the Eleventh Amendment and the principle of sovereign immunity has historically foreclosed application of copyright law to states. This is the case even though the language of section 501(a) of the Copyright Act is written broadly, seemingly holding "anyone" who violates certain exclusive rights of a copyright holder liable for infringement.[40] However, the Supreme Court has held sovereign immunity must be closely guarded and, therefore, can only be abrogated through a valid exercise of congressional power achieved through "unmistakably clear language."[41]

With section 501(a) of the Copyright Act seemingly insufficient in clarity, Congress sought to end this loophole for the states in 1990 by passing the Copyright Remedy Clarification Act (CRCA). The CRCA made it clear, in no uncertain language, that states could be held liable for acts of copyright infringement.[42] Thus, the CRCA tried to abrogate by federal statute the Eleventh Amendment immunity of states from copyright claims. Subsequently, Congress passed similar legislation to eliminate state immunity from federal trademark and patent infringement claims by enacting the Trademark Remedy Clarification Act (TRCA)[43] and the Patent and Plant Remedy Clarification Act (PPRCA).[44]

However, the Supreme Court has rebuked these efforts to hold states accountable for violations of intellectual property law. Although the Court has conceded Congress can abrogate state sovereign immunity pursuant to section 5 of the Fourteenth Amendment,[45] such exercises of power by Congress must meet the "congruence and proportionality" test enunciated in *City of Boerne v. Flores* for the invocation of Congress's remedial power to enforce substantive rights guaranteed under the due process clause.[46] Thus, to abrogate a state's sovereign immunity by statute, Congress must not only make its intentions unequivocal, it must also identify the specific property rights the states are taking away without due process of law and then tailor its legislative scheme to remedying this violation.[47] To warrant an abrogation of sovereign immunity, therefore, Congress must first demonstrate an unremediated pattern of massive and widespread infringement by the states.

According to the Supreme Court, Congress has failed to do so—at least with respect to trademark and patent infringement. Thus, the High Court struck both the TRCA and the PPRCA as unconstitutional.[48] And although the Supreme Court has not considered the validity of the CRCA, all lower courts to weigh in on the matter have drawn on the Supreme Court's treatment of the TRCA and PPRCA to hold the CRCA constitutionally infirm as well.[49]

Thus, as of today, states can willfully infringe copyright law without risk of legal liability. The immunity enjoyed by the states contrasts sharply with the massive liability faced by individuals for relatively common and widespread acts of infringement. Individuals unlucky enough to come under the gaze of the content-creation industries face back-breaking penalties and potentially bankrupting judgments. They can even end up in jail. In short, the very acts for which the states enjoy absolute immunity can ruin people's lives. At the very least, the vast disparity in treatment for similar acts raises fundamental questions of equity. More pointedly, it reveals a broader and more systematic structuring of copyright law to support entrenched social, political, and economic interests, either at the expense of or in contraposition to treatment of the unsophisticated or less powerful.

II. Of Procedure and Substance: The Modern Hierarchies of Protection

Thus, copyright law represents a key battleground in power relations (especially in the twenty-first century) as various societal actors struggle for the rights to control, regulate, and manipulate cultural content. Old industries use intellectual property enforcement to resist competition from start-ups. Sovereigns benefit from intellectual property exemptions (both legal and practical) that enable their free use and reinterpretation of cultural content. And corporations draw on intellectual property rights to ensure the consecration of their creative output. However, not all cultural content is treated the same way. The particular structure of copyright law in doling out differing levels of protection to creative works represents a key aspect of broader domination and subordination practices. Under our copyright regime, some works become beatified as sacred texts while others remain subject to unadulterated manipulation and reinterpretation. This process of stratification and sacralization represents an instrumental part of a wider historical project involving the protection of elite culture and the regulation of social boundaries. Indeed, both procedural and substantive aspects of copyright doctrine drive the process.

A. *LOVE* AND LAW: THE MODERN CLASH

To illustrate copyright's role in the sacralization process, consider the example of the *Love* project, released by The Beatles in 2006. A Grammy Award-winning soundtrack compilation album and a Cirque du Soleil show playing exclusively in Las Vegas, *Love* featured an innovative remixing and reinterpretation of approximately 130 different recordings by the band. Yet it was not without its critics. While giving the soundtrack an "A," *Entertainment Weekly* commented the album "flirts with heresy by remixing and remodeling the most sacrosanct pop canon of the 20th century" but that "[y]ou could figure it as a sop to today's interactive mash-up culture."[50]

In *All Together Now*, the documentary that followed the creation of the *Love* show and soundtrack, Paul McCartney waxes eloquent about the majestic and transformative nature of the remixes in *Love* and how they allow listeners to experience The Beatles in an entirely new manner. In an ostensible nod to musical democracy, he rejects calls of heresy, noting audiences can always play the group's old albums if they want to hear the original songs in their unadulterated form. McCartney's view of *Love* is entirely laudatory, as he takes pains to convey the project allows audiences to reexamine and reinterpret The Beatles in a provocative and meaningful way.

No matter what McCartney's words, however, one cannot help but question the depth of his sentiments. After all, he does not appear ready to open the marketplace to others who might be capable of taking The Beatles' oeuvre in innovative and expressive directions. Far from it, in fact. As it turns out, only two people in the world were given the right to engage in such a remarkable reinterpretive journey with the works of The Beatles: trusted producer George Martin and his son Giles. And although the project had no direct involvement from either of the surviving Beatles, Paul and Ringo,[51] it did require a smidgeon of vital input: approval. Because of the exclusive rights secured under the Copyright Act, the ability to conduct a remix depended entirely on receiving permission from Paul McCartney, Ringo Starr, Yoko Ono, and Olivia Harrison. Moreover, if anyone besides the

Martins had attempted the feat, they would have faced a multimillion-dollar suit for the unauthorized creation of a derivative work.

Witness the response to the wildly popular *Grey Album*, which preceded *Love* by two years. A mashup by Danger Mouse that remixed Jay-Z's *The Black Album* with numerous samples from *The White Album* by The Beatles, *The Grey Album* was motivated by the same creative and artistic spirit purportedly fueling *Love*. And, according to many observers, it succeeded brilliantly. Among other things, the work was named by *Entertainment Weekly* as the Top Album of 2004.[52] However, unlike *Love*, *The Grey Album*'s very existence was illegal,[53] if not criminal.[54] Music label EMI, acting with the apparent blessing of The Beatles, responded not with *love* but with *law*. Attorneys attempted to wipe the recording out of existence by serving online distributors with the usual stream of cease-and-desist letters threatening infringement litigation.[55] And although there are pockets of the Internet where you can still download copies of *The Grey Album*, you will never find it mass distributed at retail stores.

With the tools of copyright law put to use, sacred works can remain relatively inviolable, subject only to reinterpretation when the masters themselves deem a project worthy (artistically, monetarily, or otherwise). In other words, the sacred work is shielded from the open marketplace through the derivative rights doctrine that forbids mongrelization in all forms. As Max Weber once noted, stratification or status order comes into being when certain ideals, material goods, or opportunities are "directly withh[e]ld from free exchange by monopolization, which may be effected either legally or conventionally."[56] This observation applies with force to the state-granted monopoly that is intellectual property. Comments Lawrence Levine, "When Shakespeare, opera, art, and music were subject to free exchange, as they had been for much of the nineteenth century, they became the property of many groups, the companion of a wide spectrum of other cultural genres, and thus their power to bestow distinction was diminished, as was their power to please those who insisted on enjoying them in privileged circumstances, free from the interference of other cultural groups and the dilution of other cultural forms."[57] But when taboos emerge—whether based on the emergence of a new set of norms or the expanding scope of copyright law—works remain intentionally unadulterated, consecrated in a static state that perpetuates their elite status.

The power of The Beatles and their business partners to control the destiny (and maintain the "aura") of their musical compositions for a lifetime plus seventy years is, of course, a carefully designed feature of the copyright system.[58] As we have explored more fully in prior chapters, in the context of sampling sound recordings, courts have been especially enthusiastic about protecting rightsholders against unauthorized users. In so doing, they have chosen to deny any semblance of a fair use defense to litigants.[59]

Thus, if you try to pull a stunt such as *Love*, no matter how much it may constitute a labor of love, the potential consequences could be severe. First, under existing law, you will almost certainly be liable for infringement. Second, the penalties could be devastating. The Beatles' works are, quite naturally, timely registered and eligible for enhanced remedies in the event of infringement: statutory damages of up to $150,000 per act of willful infringement[60] (of which there would be at least 130 if one replicates the *Love* project) and recovery of reasonable attorneys' fees.[61] Consequently, even without causing any cognizable actual damage or making any actual profits from the unauthorized exploitation of The Beatles' works, individuals trying to make their own version of *Love* could face damages in excess of $20 million—$19,500,000[62] plus fees and costs. Progress, even in the arts, has a price, but it need not be that high.

It is not just The Beatles, of course, who can dangle copyright's Sword of Damocles over the heads of would-be appropriationists. Almost any book, periodical, recording, movie, television show, or computer program put out by a large press, magazine publisher, music label, film studio, broadcast network, or software developer enjoys similar protection, even though many such works may lack continued economic value.[63]

B. COPYRIGHT REGISTRATION AND THE SACRALIZATION OF CULTURAL PRODUCTION

But, not all works receive the heightened level of protection enjoyed by musical compositions and sound recordings released by the major labels or movies produced and distributed by the major Hollywood studios. The hierarchies of protection effectively afforded under federal copyright law are constructed, inter alia, through seemingly innocuous procedures (such as the registration requirement)[64] and the ostensibly aesthetically neutral application of substantive rules (such as the fair use doctrine or the idea/expression dichotomy).

For example, as we saw in Chapter 4, our existing copyright regime uses ostensbly neutral formalities to create two distinct tiers of protection for copyrighted works. Sophisticated, regular creators (generally corporations in the content-creation industries) timely register their works and therefore enjoy generous remedies against infringers. Thus, the inviolability of their works is ensured through a combination of potentially draconian penalties, including sizable statutory damages,[65] attorneys' fees awards,[66] and even criminal sanctions.[67] Absent any proof of actual damages, such plaintiffs can elect statutory damages that quickly create the possibility of a multimillion-dollar judgment in their favor. By sharp contrast, unsophisticated creators (generally individual creators and artists) do not timely register their works and are often left with little except moral force to vindicate their intellectual property rights. They are denied the ability to recover attorneys' fees, even if the defendants' infringing conduct continues after registration. Moreover, they are ineligible for statutory damages and can collect only actual damages, which are both difficult to prove and often of limited value. In short, they are left without adequate mechanisms to enforce their exclusive rights purportedly granted through the Copyright Act.

Of course, the idea that access to legal counsel and adherence to certain legal formalities can improve the effective scope of one's rights is certainly not novel or surprising. But, the consequences in copyright law are particularly dramatic, virtually determining the rights to and in cultural production. Sophisticated, economically powerful interests receive full protection for their creative works, making their cultural production sacred and inviolable. The act of Bourdieuian cultural reproduction is therefore controlled and patrolled by copyright law—with the hallowed works of elites subject to use and reuse only with proper authorization and payment. Meanwhile, the output of the rest of society does not receive such beatification. For unsophisticated players, their production becomes fodder for remix, reinterpretation, and re-commercialization, all without authorization or payment. Thus, although the law purports to grant copyright protection to any work of authorship with minimal creativity fixed in a tangible medium, whether made by Manet or the Man on the Street, that is not the case. All works and creators are not treated alike as the formalities of the registration requirement establish a hierarchy of protected and less protected works, the untouchable and the readily manipulable. The resulting gestalt enables dominant social forces to usurp freely (both metaphorically and literally) the creative content of the masses for their own use while simultaneously enjoying the ability to prevent any unauthorized use of their privileged creative content. Within the confines of this regime, it is the underclass that typically ends up with minimal protection:

- It is the African-American blues musician who, just two generations ago, saw his riffs and melodies appropriated by the burgeoning modern music industry to "develop" rock 'n' roll. As his creative efforts helped develop a multibillion-dollar marketplace, he watched from the economic sidelines, unable to vindicate the legal rights to his intellectual property because he had failed to conform to the procedural strictures of copyright law.

- It is the unheralded rural landscape painter whose evocative depictions of nature are used to decorate and set the mood for the outdoorsy, Western-themed catalog of a major retailer. Although her work is used without permission or payment, her failure to register on a timely basis leaves her without meaningful remedies if she threatens to pursue legal action.

- It is the screenwriter—the least valued of Hollywood's traditional above-the-line creative triumvirate[68]—who followed industry protocol by registering his screenplay with the Writers Guild of America (WGA) and then found original dialogue and a unique action sequence from his work in the summer's leading blockbuster. Though his work was used without authorization or payment, he finds himself without meaningful remedies to pursue legal action because registration with the WGA fails to provide the legal benefits of registration with the U.S. Copyright Office.[69]

- It is the dance choreographer, whose uniquely sequenced moves make their way into the new music video for a leading pop star. Having failed to register her choreography on a timely basis with the U.S. Copyright Office, she is unable to recover statutory damages and attorneys' fees, making legal action of dubious worth.

- It is the developing-world tailor whose original designs are noticed by New York fashionistas who integrate them into the new season's latest haute couture offerings in the Western world. The tailor has never heard of the U.S. Copyright Office. Even if he had, he would not have the funds to afford registration, which would amount to the equivalent of a year's salary. Although the tailor's creative efforts are driving "innovation" in the fashion world, he will not enjoy any of the resulting monetary benefits.

- It is the small businesswoman who drafts effective copy for a marketing pamphlet only to see it copied wholesale by a competitor. In the absence of timely registration, legal action makes no practical sense. She finds herself holding "a right without a remedy."[70]

- It is the solo architect whose structural design plans for an industrial building integrating green photovoltaic technology are utilized by a multinational corporation to save itself the cost of generating its own plans. In the unlikely event the architect catches the infringement and sues, she will, at best, likely recover only the value of the plans in the first place. Facing no punitive consequences for its illicit conduct, the multinational corporation has every incentive to infringe. Absent timely registration, the architect is without meaningful remedies, especially when one considers the (non-recoupable) cost of litigation.

- It is the stylings of graffiti artists in urban corridors whose renderings eventually make their way into the newly sacrilized work of the modern art world's latest sensation (whose multimillion-dollar originals and "affordable" limited edition prints are carefully controlled and regulated) in order to obtain the Benjaminian aura that generates value in the art marketplace.

All the while, back-breaking penalties face those who would touch without permission the copyrighted works of the modern music industry, the major Hollywood studios, the elite art world, or the fashion industry, even when these are built on the unprotected works of others. By controlling the manipulation and transformation of cultural content through its hierarchical system of protection, copyright law's registration requirement plays a significant role in mediating identity formation, regulating social networks, and controlling expressive rights as it determines the ways in which we can and cannot interact with the seminal semiotic signposts of our civilization.

C. AESTHETIC JUDGMENT AS HEGEMONIC PROJECT

Besides copyright's procedural rules, its seemingly innocuous and neutral substantive provisions also regulate the bodily integrity of sacred and privileged texts, patrol cultural reproduction, and impact identity development in the service of dominant social forces. Throughout the decades, courts have repeatedly emphasized the aesthetic neutrality of their decision-making calculus in copyright matters. Yet this rhetoric of aesthetic neutrality is readily belied by judicial decisions imbued with cultural and political biases that inevitably determine the level of protection granted to copyrighted works.

1. The Myth of Aesthetic Neutrality

On the surface, courts have historically maintained a steadfast commitment to aesthetic neutrality in their copyright jurisprudence. Consider Justice Oliver Wendell Holmes's enduring and foundational admonition in the 1903 Bleistein case. Cautioning judges to expurgate aesthetic judgments from the courtroom, Holmes (writing for the majority of a divided Supreme Court) found no reason to deny copyright protection to an advertisement featuring renderings of circus performers, despite its prosaic commerciality.[71] Rejecting the view of the defendants and the lower courts, Holmes asserted the perceived aesthetic value of a work could not and should not determine its copyrightability.[72] In theory, therefore, commercial copy would receive the same protection as high art. Reasoned Holmes in his classic formulation of the matter: "It would be a dangerous undertaking for persons trained only to the law to constitute themselves final judges of the worth of pictorial illustrations, outside of the narrowest and most obvious limits."[73]

On the surface, judges have heeded Holmes's advice, and the rhetoric of aesthetic neutrality is a dominant trope in modern copyright jurisprudence. As Robert Gorman notes,

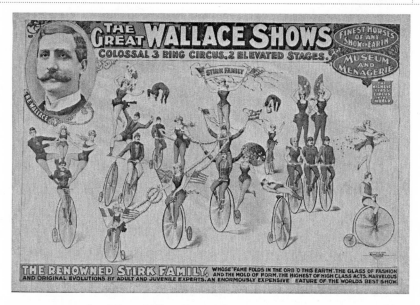

FIGURE 6.2 A Great Wallace Shows Advertisement at Issue in *Bleistein*.

"It is indeed the rare judge who purports to assess, in explicit terms, whether the art, literature or music before it is good or bad."[74] Courts have frequently agreed—at least in theory. One need look no further than the emphatic language of the Seventh Circuit: "[J]udges can make fools of themselves pronouncing on aesthetic matters."[75]

Yet for all this rhetorical solicitude, courts inevitably make aesthetic judgments when approaching copyright cases. In his groundbreaking work on the subject, Alfred Yen argues the palaver of aesthetic neutrality has belied the common judicial practice of assessing aesthetics factors in deciding fundamental issues of copyright law.[76] To illustrate this point, Yen examines seminal jurisprudence on the issue of originality, the useful arts doctrine, and substantial similarity. At a certain level, copyright hermeneutics necessarily implicate aesthetic considerations. For example, the Constitution's Copyright Clause—which appears to limit copyright protection to the extent it promotes "the Progress of Science and useful Arts"[77]—virtually demands such "aesthetic determinations."[78] In addition, judges have introduced aesthetic considerations into the copyright calculus in a variety of ways through doctrines having their origins in the common law. For example, determining a productive or transformative use under the first factor of the fair use defense elevates certain types of work (e.g., parody) over other types of work (e.g., satire).[79] Construing conceptual severability for the purposes of distinguishing between works of applied art (which receive copyright protection) and works of industrial design (which do not) inevitably involves aesthetic judgments about what constitutes art and what defines the proper relationship between form and function needed to secure legal protection. All told, as Gorman comments, "[I]t is not at all rare to find courts addressing the question, 'what is art?' And it is quite common to find copyright courts assessing—sometimes covertly, sometimes openly—whether a work has merit, worth or social value."[80]

The consequences of such aesthetic adjudications are far-reaching. As Yen argues, they inextricably affect the type of works we as a society receive from our artists. After all, economically motivated artists might "prefer creating works that meet the aesthetic judgments of judges because other works would either not get the benefits of copyright protection or wind up being suppressed."[81] Even more fundamentally, however, aesthetic judgments can serve to both maintain and preserve existing power structures. The seemingly neutral laws of copyright therefore have the potential to create a hierarchy of culture that serves hegemonic interests.

Consider the application of the fair use doctrine. In Chapter 2, we discussed the dangers of its unpredictability, its role in revitalizing a natural-law vision of copyright, and its part in impeding transformative uses that advance progress in the arts. Here, we tease out another potentially adverse consequence from its operation. Specifically, we examine the way in which application of the fair use doctrine (in combination with other copyright principles) has violated ostensible norms of aesthetic neutrality with its role deciding which works will remain consecrated and hallowed and which works will not. With a narrow reading of fair use, a court can protect a work from remix, reinterpretation, and unauthorized mutilation. In short, it can preserve a work's aura, inviolability, and canonic status and promote its economic value to its rightsholder. With a broader reading of fair use, a court can open the floodgates for the work's use and abuse. Indeed, if the time has come for a work to be metaphorically rejected from the modern canon, there is perhaps no more defining moment than when that work loses its strong copyright protection in court. A careful exegesis of copyright jurisprudence reveals that aesthetic decisions, driven by implicit cultural and political considerations, can dramatically affect the fair use calculus.

To illustrate this point, it is instructive to compare the results of two high-profile copyright infringement suits involving canonical literary works, unauthorized derivatives, and claims of fair use. The first suit involved Alice Randall's *The Wind Done Gone*, an unauthorized follow-up to Margaret Mitchell's *Gone with the Wind*. The second suit involved John David California's *60 Years Later*, an unauthorized send-up of J.D. Salinger's *Catcher in the Rye*.

2. The Consecration Done Gone: The Decanonization of *Gone with the Wind* and the
   Battle to Depict the Antebellum South

In the first suit, *Suntrust v. Houghton Mifflin*,[82] the estate of Margaret Mitchell sued to enjoin publication of Alice Randall's *The Wind Done Gone* on the grounds it constituted an unauthorized derivative work based on *Gone with the Wind*. The main conceit of Randall's novel was its recasting of the *Gone with the Wind* story and world from the point of view of the African-American slaves and mulattos rather than the white aristocrats. In Randall's work, Ashley Wilkes is gay, interracial sexual relationships are discussed, and the travails of daily life for the victims of the South's rigid and racist social hierarchy are vividly depicted.

A district court initially enjoined publication of *The Wind Done Gone*, accepting the Mitchell estate's contention that it constituted an infringing work and rejecting Randall's fair use defense. Specifically, the trial judge found *The Wind Done Gone* was a sequel and not a parody, and therefore not the type of transformative use granted fair use protection. The tenor of the judge's opinion is particularly revealing. It begins by immediately emphasizing *Gone with the Wind*'s place in the cultural canon and its commercial significance—both noting its "widespread acclaim" and its impressive sales in the "tens of millions."[83] These facts are, of course, largely irrelevant to any aesthetically neutral analysis of infringement and fair use. But, they set the tone for the court's opinion, which reflects a strong deference to the work's favored aesthetic status: its presumed import and its cultural and economic value.

The existing body of fair use precedent all but mandates that parodic works enjoy exemption from infringement liability. The key portion of the trial court's decision therefore comes when it characterizes *The Wind Done Gone* as not primarily a parody, but a sequel or some other form of unauthorized derivative work. While acknowledging the book has numerous parodic elements, the court somehow divines "the book's overall purpose is to create a sequel to the older work and provide Ms. Randall's social commentary on the antebellum South."[84] The court's attempt to segregate the parodic elements of the work from the sequel-like elements is difficult to understand when the two concepts are not at all mutually exclusive and, quite often, intertwined. For example, Mel Brooks's classic *Spaceballs* is in some senses both an unauthorized sequel to and parody of *Star Wars*. Indeed, the dialectic that casts parody in opposition to sequel is, at its core, an aesthetic judgment. As a parody, the work is presumed to be transformative and, consequently, entitled to fair use protection for its contribution to progress in the arts. As a sequel, the work is seen as nothing more than an effort to free ride off of the copyrighted work of another. In this sense, the court conflates its analysis of commercialism with its analysis of transformative use, later concluding "the purpose of putting the key characters of *Gone with the Wind* in new settings is to entertain and sell books to an active and ready-made market for the next *Gone with the Wind* sequel."[85] To the court, Alice Randall is nothing more than a leech sucking economic value away from Mitchell's genius. But, at some level, all parodies can be portrayed as such. After all, they all rely upon the original and its status as a recognized work to a particular audience.

As it turns out, a careful parsing of the court's decision reveals the sequel/parody distinction and conclusion stem from an implicit aesthetic judgment about the inviolability of *Gone with the Wind*. As the court tautologically posits, "If the defendant is permitted to publish *The Wind Done Gone*, an unauthorized derivative work, then anyone could tell the love story of *Gone with the Wind* from another point of view and/or create sequels or prequels populated by Ms. Mitchell's copyrighted characters without compensation to the Mitchell Trusts."[86] With these words, the court presupposes the latter result simply cannot obtain (despite the existence of the fair use doctrine that plainly creates no such hard and fast rule). Put another way, the court assumes—and thereby ensures—the work must remain inviolate. As a sacred text, *Gone with the Wind* should be protected from unauthorized individuals telling the story from a different point of view.

Consecration is at the heart of the court's concern because a world where the sacred text has been defiled is unimaginable: "By killing two core characters from *Gone With the Wind* and marrying off another, *The Wind Done Gone* has the immediate effect of damaging or even precluding the Mitchell Trusts' ability to continue to tell the love story of Scarlett and Rhett."[87] Ready literally, the court's admonition fails to distinguish between real life—where an individual's death typically precludes the possibility of resurrection—and fiction—where no such limitations exist. The statement not only reflects a startling failure of imagination by the court (doubtlessly provoked by the inability to envision the bastardization of the consecrated work), but also does not hold weight empirically. For example, the *Star Trek* franchise has continued to thrive in telling the stories of Captain Kirk, Mr. Spock, and the U.S.S. *Enterprise* despite both Kirk[88] and Spock[89] having been killed at various points during the *authorized* movies. Moreover, audiences can readily discern between authorized and unauthorized sequels of a franchise, but if they cannot, that is something the federal Lanham Act could help police through its prohibition of unfair competition and false advertising.

Of course, the Scarlett and Rhett characters do not die just because Alice Randall says they do. But, what the court really fears is *The Wind Done Gone* will sound not the literal death knell for the characters, but for *Gone with the Wind*'s untouchability. Stripped of unadulterated idealization, the work and its characters can no longer survive in the exact form they once possessed. Thus, it is not whether the work is a parody or sequel that truly appears to animate the court's decision: it is destruction of the work's romanticism—a romanticism that is grounded in a distinctly whitewashed vision of the antebellum South that painfully ignores the harsh realities of life for that society's under-class. Thus, the court's read on copyright law, driven by aesthetic judgments, has an impact on the discourse about what is perhaps the most famous and popular vision of Southern life during the years of slavery. Through the district court's opinion, copyright law preserves a hegemonic vision of the South that has historically prevailed in the American conscious.

By sharp contrast, the Eleventh Circuit found *The Wind Done Gone* protected by the fair use doctrine and the First Amendment and reversed the district court's injunction. Despite its differing logic, however, the Eleventh Circuit's opinion was similarly influenced by aesthetic judgments. To the Eleventh Circuit, criticism, ridicule, and even scorn for a work serves as a social good that trumps any harm it may do to a copyright holder's economic rights. Citing the Ninth Circuit's *Fisher* case that immunized "When Sonny Sniffs Glue" from liability as a parody of "When Sunny Gets Blue," the court's concurring opinion by Judge Marcus asserts "[d]estructive parodies play an important role in social and literary criticism and thus merit protection even though they may discourage or discredit an original author."[90] Works are not to be treated as sacred cows, and the preservation of immutability does not serve public interests. "Because the social good is served by increasing the supply of criticism—and thus, potentially, of truth," posits the court, "creators of original works cannot be given the power to block the dissemination of critical derivative works."[91]

In particular, the Eleventh Circuit found *Gone with the Wind* especially ripe for deconstruction. And this becomes a critical point when considering identity interests and how the copyright holders may draw on intellectual property rights as a means to preserve and maintain existing power structures, visions of inclusion and exclusion, and critical historical narratives. The Eleventh Circuit specifically singles out the Mitchell Estate's control of prior authorized derivative works and its desire to limit certain themes as a basis *for*, rather than *against*, its ruling. In sharp contrast to the district court, which sought to retain the aesthetic integrity of Mitchell's saccharine depiction of Dixie and protect it from unwanted mutilation, the appeals court viewed Mitchell's work as one ripe for (if not outright in need of) deconstruction. As the court takes pains to point out, the Mitchell Estate was particularly horrified at the idea that the *Gone with the Wind* milieu might be adulterated with depictions of interracial relationships or homosexuality. Indeed, the court quotes the Mitchell Estate as having told a potential writer for the authorized sequel for *Gone with the Wind*: "You're not going to like this, but the estate will require you to sign a pledge that says you will under no circumstances write anything about miscegenation or homosexuality."[92] Ultimately, therefore, the court's decision sought to vindicate Randall's right to transform "Ashley Wilkes into a homosexual" and to "depict[]. . . interracial sex, and . . . multiple mulatto characters."[93]

All told, the struggle over the scope of the *Gone with the Wind* copyright becomes one over the right to present an alternate vision of Old Dixie, using the familiar terrain of the romanticized antebellum South to bring long-suppressed issues of race, class, and even sexual orientation to the forefront of the story. In the end, the Eleventh Circuit found the preliminary injunction enjoining publication of *The Wind Done Gone* constituted "an unconstitutional prior restraint"[94]—not just of free speech broadly speaking, but of the right to challenge the idealized notions of the old South that have historically resided in the national subconscious precisely because of such works as *Gone with the Wind*. To the Eleventh Circuit, the time had come to decanonize *Gone with the Wind* with the loss of its inviolability.[95] The decision to do so stemmed from aesthetic judgments supporting the subversive power of Randall's broadside in novel form.[96] Painfully out of sync with more modern views, *Gone with the Wind* had to face the fact that the time to lose its consecrated status had come.

3. *60 Years Later*: J.D. Salinger and the Preservation of the Canon

A revealing contrast emerges when one considers the ultimate outcome of *The Wind Done Gone* suit—which effectively excommunicated *Gone with the Wind* from the category of sacred text—to the more recent controversy involving the unauthorized send-up of *The Catcher in the Rye*, entitled *60 Years Later: Coming Through the Rye* and purportedly authored by one John David California. In 2009, shortly before his passing, J.D. Salinger came out of hiding (at least legally speaking) to seek an injunction restraining publication of *60 Years Later* on the grounds it constituted a blatant infringement of his copyright.[97] The defendant objected, claiming fair use and First Amendment protection.

The district court issued the injunction sought by Salinger after finding he was likely to prevail on the merits of the case. On appeal, the Second Circuit affirmed the holding.[98] A central part of the decision came when the court distinguished the suit involving *The Wind Done Gone*. Specifically, the court opined *The Wind Done Gone* was clearly a parody— thereby entitling it to a fair use defense—while *60 Years Later* was a sequel. But, as we discussed earlier, *The Wind Done Gone*'s purported status as a parody, sequel, or both is wrought with complexity. And, at a minimum, it was a close call, with the U.S. District Court for the Northern District of Georgia ruling one way and the Eleventh Circuit ruling the other.

Moreover, there were several key facts that actually should have given *60 Years Later* a *better* fair use defense than *The Wind Done Gone*. First, with respect to the fourth (and most important, according to some courts) fair use factor—market harm—*The Wind Done Gone* was certainly more damaging to the Margaret Mitchell Estate's *economic* interests than *60 Years Later* was to J.D. Salinger's. Specifically, the Margaret Mitchell Estate had actually demonstrated a clear interest in entering the market to create derivative works based on *Gone with the Wind*. In 1991, they authorized publication of a sequel titled *Scarlet*. And, at the time of the *Suntrust* case, they had entered into a contract authorizing a possible second sequel. Indeed, St. Martin's Press had paid dearly for the privilege of publishing the latter (to the tune of seven figures). By sharp contrast, whatever the moral offense to Salinger, the publication of *60 Years Later* did not raise the same specter of economic harm as did the publication of *The Wind Done Gone*. After all, Salinger was a notorious recluse who had categorically refused to publish anything for the past half century. He never indicated any interest in publishing a sequel to *Catcher in the Rye*. *60 Years Later* was therefore highly unlikely to dilute a derivative market in which Salinger had no desire whatsoever to participate. Admittedly, the jurisprudence applying the market harm test has suggested injury to potential markets is enough for a plaintiff to prevail on this element of the fair use test. The *Salinger* court noted as much: "[A]lthough Salinger has not demonstrated an interest in publishing a sequel or other derivative work of *Catcher*, ... the Second Circuit has previously emphasized that it is the 'potential market' for the copyrighted work and its derivatives that must be examined, even if the 'author has disavowed any intention to publish them during his lifetime,' given that an author 'has the right to change his mind' and is 'entitled to protect his opportunity to sell [derivative works].'"[99] But, potential must at least be plausible and, at the end of the day, it is utterly disingenuous to read Salinger's suit as an attempt to preserve his right to change his mind should he decide to enter the market for derivative works.

Second, large parts of *The Wind Done Gone* actually retold the story from *Gone with the Wind*, thereby engaging in more actual borrowing, both literal and structural, than *60 Years Later* did from the *Catcher in the Rye*. *The Wind Done Gone* even appropriated entire sentence structures from the original work. As an example, the first line of *The Wind Done Gone* reads "She was not beautiful, but men seldom recognized this, caught up in the cloud of commotion and scent in which she moved," while *Gone with the Wind* begins, "Scarlett O'Hara was not beautiful, but men seldom realized it when caught by her charm."[100] *60 Years Later* certainly used the Holden Caulfield character from *Catcher in the Rye* and his history, but its plotline is grounded in metacommentary and features a fictionalized J.D. Salinger himself, who narrates part of the novel, haunted by his Caulfield character and wishing to bring him back to life only to kill him. In fact, the *Salinger* ruling was particularly notable to the publishing industry, which announced it was the first time a court in the Second Circuit had found copyright protection extended to a single character who had appeared in a single work.[101]

Nevertheless, while *The Wind Done Gone* ultimately received fair use protection, *60 Years Later* was enjoined from publication. And aesthetic judgments on the relative value of unauthorized derivative works appear to have made a key difference in the court's decision to issue the injunction. Consider the only mention the *Salinger* court makes of the overarching goals of the copyright system. Seeking to reconcile its ruling with copyright's role in promoting progress in the arts, the *Salinger* court reasoned "some artists may be further incentivized to create originals due to the availability of the right *not* to produce any sequels."[102] As a first matter, the court's speculation on this point strains all credulity. But regardless of how one feels about the bizarre conjecture that the right not to produce sequels can incentivize creation, it is clear the court's statement rests on a tacit aesthetic judgment: that it is better to preserve (ex post) the incentive to create *The Catcher in the Rye* than it is to stimulate the creation of unauthorized sequels.

The calculus here is fairly remarkable; the court chooses to enjoin *definitely* the publication of unauthorized derivatives—works that could contribute to progress in the arts—on the *chance*, based on idle speculation, that some artists may create more because they can rest secure in the knowledge that no one can create sequels of their works. The hierarchy at play is simple: the original work implicitly trumps the sequel(s) and/or derivatives, especially those of the unauthorized variety. Certainly, for every *Godfather II* and *Return of the Jedi*, there are dozens of *Blues Brothers 2000s*. But in deciding the fate of *The Wind Done Gone*, the Eleventh Circuit certainly did not seem bothered by this possibility as it adopted a radically different aesthetic judgment of the unauthorized derivative. At a more subconscious level, in the context of our times, it perhaps feels less wrong to allow someone to skewer the dated artistic vision of Margaret Mitchell than to permit the bastardization of the revered masterworks of The Beatles or the adulteration of J.D. Salinger's beloved Holden Caulfield.

In the end, the decision to open up *Gone with the Wind* to *The Wind Done Gone* effectively freed the literary property—and, more generally, the popular interpretation of a critical era in our nation's history—to different narratives and perspectives. Thus, the battle over copyright protection can often become a battle over identity politics and personhood interests and a clash between the hegemonic power of cultural reproduction and subversive effects of semiotic disobedience.[103] Through both procedural rules and substantive doctrines, our intellectual property laws can use registration requirements and aesthetic judgments to achieve something much broader than merely "progress of the arts." Instead, by consecrating meaning and value, patrolling cultural hierarchy, and regulating the semiotic signposts of our society, intellectual property transcends its small corner of the legal universe and plays a fundamental role in shaping social structures and regulating individual behavior as part of a broader hegemonic project.

IV. The Future of Infringement Nation

In 2010, copyright turned three hundred years old. From its humble origins as a limited form of intellectual property protection relevant to only a small segment of society, copyright has grown dramatically in both its scope and relevance. With the mass dispersion of digital technology and the growth of the Internet, copyright law now impacts our lives on a daily basis by determining how we consume creative cultural content and by regulating some of our most basic expressive activities, from the words we can say to the melodies we can sing and the images we can paint. One need look no further than the headlines in recent years, which have featured landmark copyright litigation involving literary franchises such as the *Harry Potter* series and *The Catcher in the Rye*, appropriationist art by Jeff Koons and Shepard Fairey, paparazzi photographs and news reporting bloggers, fantasy sports, popular songs used in political campaigns, and file-sharing on the Internet.

This book has traced the history and evolution of copyright law and its profound impact on the lives of ordinary individuals in the twenty-first century. Using the trope of the individual in five different copyright-related contexts—as an *infringer, transformer, consumer,* and *creator* of copyrighted works and as a *reformer* of copyright law—we have charted the changing contours of our copyright regime and assessed its vitality in the digital age. In the process, we have questioned some of our most basic assumptions about copyright law.

In Chapter 1, we illustrated the unseemly amount of liability an average person rings up in a single day—a result that runs counter to our norms and highlights the inherent danger in the current law for its potential to make criminals of us all. Each of us is an infringer, especially in an era where we all have access to a global printing press in the form of a networked computer.

In Chapter 2, we examined the origins of our copyright system and focused on the counterintuitive role of the fair use doctrine in fundamentally swaying our regime toward a natural-rights vision of copyright that privileges the inherent property interests of authors in the fruits of their labor over the utilitarian goal of maximizing progress in the arts. As such, the rights of the individual as a transformer of copyrighted works have shrunk markedly over the past century and a half.

With Chapter 3, we emphasized it is not only transformative uses of copyrighted works that have important implications for individuals. Rather, there are important expressive interests at play in even the unauthorized use of copyright works—uses that are increasingly coming under the scope of liability as technology and copyright law continue to change.

In Chapter 4, we turned our attention from the individual as a consumer of copyrighted content to the individual as a creator of copyrighted content. In the process, we revealed the surprisingly low level of protection American copyright law grants many creators, and we examined how seemingly innocuous procedural formalities have shaped the nature of copyright protection in the United States and established a hierarchy of cultural content.

Finally, in Chapter 5, we focused on the individual as a reformer. In the process, we advanced several proposals to help restore greater balance between users of and rightsholders to copyrighted content, between unsophisticated and sophisticated parties, and between transformative users and original creators.

Throughout the course of the book, we have witnessed the broader political import of copyright law on the exertion of social regulation and control. Intellectual property rights regulate the reproduction and manipulation of cultural content in a way that serves knowledge/power systems. Copyright law therefore represents a key situs in the battle for social control among sovereigns and their subjects, corporations and individuals, and entrenched interest groups and young upstarts. In the course of our analysis, we have examined how the structure of our intellectual property regime advances subordination practices by carefully establishing a hierarchy of cultural texts, thereby fostering certain forms of use while discouraging (if not outright banning) other acts of semiotic disobedience. Lying at the heart of discursive struggles over cultural reproduction, inculcation, and meaning, intellectual property laws—in both their procedural and substantive guises—have dramatic consequences for social relations, especially in the twenty-first century.

In the end, copyright has the power to shape the fundamental structure of our information society. The stakes at play in any copyright reform process are therefore critical. This is true not just for the content-creation industries, policy wonks, or intellectual property scholars. It is a matter of importance for us all.

Notes

1. 17 U.S.C. § 102(a) (setting out the categories of "works of authorship" falling within the subject matter of copyright).

2. Madhavi Sunder, *IP³*, 59 STAN. L. REV. 257, 263 (2006).

3. *Id.*

4. Madhavi Sunder, *Intellectual Property and Identity Politics: Playing with Fire*, 4 J. GENDER RACE & JUST. 69, 70 (2000).

5. Tim Wu, *Tolerated Uses*, 31 COLUM. J. L. & ARTS 617, 618 (2008).

6. Reno v. ACLU, 521 U.S. 844, 850 (1997) (quoting ACLU v. Reno, 929 F. Supp. 824, 844 (E.D. Pa. 1996)).

7. *See, e.g.*, ROBERT ZUCCARO, "DOW, 30,000 BY 2008!" WHY IT'S DIFFERENT THIS TIME (2001).

8. *See, e.g.*, DAVID ELIAS, DOW 40,000: STRATEGIES FOR PROFITING FROM THE GREATEST BULL MARKET IN HISTORY (1999); JAMES K. GLASSMAN & KEVIN A. HASSETT, DOW 36,000: THE NEW STRATEGY FOR PROFITING FROM THE COMING RISE IN THE STOCK MARKET (1999); CHARLES W. KADLEC, DOW 100,000: FACT OR FICTION (1999).

9. *See* Jack L. Goldsmith, *Against Cyberanarchy*, 65 U. CHI. L. REV. 1199, 1200–01 (1998). As Goldsmith argues, regulation skeptics

> make three basic errors. First, they overstate the differences between cyberspace transactions and other transnational transactions. . . . Second, the skeptics do not attend to the distinction between default laws and mandatory laws. . . . Third, the skeptics underestimate the potential of traditional legal tools and technology to resolve the multijurisdictional regulatory problems implicated by cyberspace. Cyberspace transactions do not inherently warrant any more deference by national

regulators, and are not significantly less resistant to the tools of conflict of laws, than other transnational transactions.

Id.

10. John Perry Barlow, A Declaration of the Independence of Cyberspace (Feb. 8, 1996), http://homes.eff.org/~barlow/Declaration-Final.html. The manifesto opens: "Governments of the Industrial World, you weary giants of flesh and steel, I come from Cyberspace, the new home of Mind. On behalf of the future, I ask you of the past to leave us alone. You are not welcome among us. You have no sovereignty where we gather." *Id.*

11. *See, e.g.,* Ashcroft v. ACLU, 535 U.S. 564, 584–85 (2002) (upholding the Child Online Protection Act's use of local contemporary community standards, despite objections from the plaintiffs that, inter alia, the standard was quixotic in light of the inherently national, if not transnational, nature of Internet publication and distribution).

12. *See, e.g.,* Digital Millennium Copyright Act, 17 U.S.C. §§ 1201–1205 (2006) (providing criminal penalties against, inter alia, anyone who traffics in devices that circumvent digital rights management measures taken by copyright holders).

13. *See* LAWRENCE LESSIG, CODE AND OTHER LAWS OF CYBERSPACE 175 (2006); Pamela Samuelson, *The Copyright Grab*, WIRED, Jan. 1996, at 135.

14. *See* LESSIG, *supra* note 13, at 175; Samuelson, *supra* note 13, at 191.

15. *See* James Boyle, *The Second Enclosure Movement and the Construction of the Public Domain*, 66 LAW & CONTEMP. PROBS. 33, 34–37, 40–41 (2003).

16. Sonny Bono Copyright Term Extension Act, Pub. L. No. 105-298, § 102(g), 112 Stat. 2827, 2827–28 (1998) (codified at 17 U.S.C. §§ 301–304 (2006)).

17. Lawrence Lessig, *The Balance of Robert Kastenmeier*, 2004 WIS. L. REV. 1015, 1018.

18. Mary LaFrance, *Authorship and Termination Rights in Sound Recordings*, 75 S. CAL. L. REV. 375, 375 (2002).

19. Under the Copyright Act, a work made for hire is either "a work prepared by an employee within the scope of his or her employment" or "a work specially ordered or commissioned" through a written agreement for use in one of nine statutory categories: "as a contribution to a collective work, as a part of a motion picture or other audiovisual work, as a translation, as a supplementary work, as a compilation, as an instructional text, as a test, as answer material for a test, or as an atlas." 17 U.S.C. § 101. Thus, it is unclear whether sound recordings made by nonemployees can ever constitute works made for hire.

20. Works made for hire enjoy copyright protection for 120 years from creation or 95 years from publication, whichever comes first. *Id.* § 302(c). All other works receive protection that lasts until seventy years after the death of the last surviving author. *Id.* § 302(a)–(b).

21. *See id.* § 203(a).

22. *Id.* As Mary LaFrance notes, individual recording artists who create their works as employees of their own loan-out corporations also risk having their termination rights waived as the sound recordings are likely considered works made for hire. LaFrance, *supra* note 18, at 403–04.

23. Of course, such an assignment is only meaningful to the extent musicians are considered in the first place to be the authors of a sound recording. One could argue that, by literally fixing the music in a tangible medium, the record labels are actually the authors of sound recordings as they literally press the "record" button. *See, e.g.,* Cmty. for Creative Non-Violence v. Reid, 490 U.S. 730, 737 (1989) (deeming the author is "the party who actually creates the work, that is, the person who translates an idea into a fixed, tangible expression entitled to copyright protection"); Taggart v. WMAQ Channel 5, 57 U.S.P.Q.2d 1083, 1086 (S.D. Ill. 2000)

(finding plaintiff interviewee had no copyright interest in an interview by defendant, a broadcasting station, and noting "[t]herefore, if anyone was the 'author,' it may very well have been the cameraman who fixed the ideas into a tangible expression, the videotape").

24. Notification of the termination must be given at least two years (but no more than ten years) prior to the termination date. 17 U.S.C. § 203(a)(4)(A).

25. The termination right itself is subject to an exemption for derivative works contained in 17 U.S.C. § 304(c).

26. LaFrance, *supra* note 18, at 375–76.

27. *See, e.g.,* Jonathan Lethem, *The Ecstasy of Influence: A Plagiarism,* HARPER'S MAG., Feb. 2007, at 57 (critiquing our existing copyright regime's suppression of transformative use and appropriationist art); D. T. Max, *The Injustice Collector,* THE NEW YORKER, June 19, 2006, at 34 (documenting the overzealous copyright enforcement of the James Joyce Estate); Richard A. Posner, *On Plagiarism,* ATLANTIC MONTHLY, Apr. 2002, at 23 (discussing notions of plagiarism and arguing that in some instances we could use "more plagiarism!"); James Surowiecki, *Righting Copywrongs,* THE NEW YORKER, Jan. 21, 2002, at 27 (critiquing copyright term extensions).

28. *See, e.g.,* Shloss v. Sweeney, 515 F. Supp. 2d 1083 (N.D. Cal. 2007). After receiving a nasty cease-and-desist letter from the Estate of James Joyce, Stanford professor Carol Shloss (with the help of the Center for Internet and Society) filed a declaratory relief action in federal court to affirm her fair use rights to quote Joyce's works for academic purposes without payment or permission. She not only obtained that right, but her attorneys won a fee award of more than $325,000.00 for their efforts in vindicating her fair use rights. *Id.*

29. *See, e.g., Assessing the Impact of the Copyright Royalty Board Decision to Increase Royalty Rates on Recording Artists and Webcasters: Hearing Before the H. Comm. on Small Business,* 110th Cong. (2007) (statement of Richard Eiswerth, President, Cincinnati Public Radio), *available at* http://www.house.gov/smbiz/hearings/hearing-06-28-07-internet-radio/testimony-06-28-07-eiswerth.pdf (addressing a Mar. 2, 2007 decision by the Copyright Royalty Board that increased royalty expenses for both commercial and noncommercial webcasters).

30. Exemption to Prohibition on Circumvention of Copyright Protection Systems for Access Control Technologies, 71 Fed. Reg. 68,472 (Nov. 27, 2006) (codified at 37 C.F.R. pt. 201) (enacting, pursuant to 17 U.S.C. § 1201(a)(1), the recommendation of the Register of Copyrights to add a record six new DMCA exemptions).

31. Copyright Act of 1909 §§ 10, 12 (codified as amended at 17 U.S.C. 11, 61 Stat. 652 (1947)) (repealed by Copyright Act of 1976, Pub. L. No. 94-553, 90 Stat. 2541). Although the "promptness" requirement was substantially eviscerated with the Supreme Court's 1939 ruling in *Washingtonian Publishing Co. v. Pearson,* 306 U.S. 30 (1939), delayed registration could give rise to a laches defense preventing enforcement of a copyright. *See, e.g.,* Kontes Glass Co. v. Lab Glass, Inc., 250 F. Supp. 193 (D.N.J. 1966), *aff'd,* 373 F.2d 319 (3d Cir. 1967) (arguing delay in registration may create a defense of laches); Samet & Wells, Inc. v. Shalom Toy Co., 185 U.S.P.Q. 36 (E.D.N.Y. 1975) ("the delay in filing the copyright notice may prevent plaintiff from complaining of any [infringing] turtles which were sold [prior to filing of registration]").

32. Timely registration remained a requirement until 1964 for the renewal of a copyright after the first twenty-eight-year term.

33. Copyright Act of 1909 § 10 (codified as amended at 17 U.S.C. 11, 61 Stat. 652 (1947)) (repealed by Copyright Act of 1976, Pub. L. No. 94-553, 90 Stat. 2541). 2-7 MELVILLE B. NIMMER & DAVID NIMMER, NIMMER ON COPYRIGHT § 7.14 [A][1] (2008) (describing how failure to

observe proper notice requirements on a work used to lead to its dedication to the public domain). *See, e.g.*, Neimark v. Ronai & Ronai, LLP, 500 F. Supp. 2d 338, 341 (S.D.N.Y. 2007) (noting "works published without a copyright notice prior to the enactment of the Berne Convention on March 1, 1989 are injected into the public domain and thus lose any copyright protection to which they might otherwise have been entitled").

34. Save the Music & Creative Commons: Proceedings Before the U.S. Copyright Office at 13 (Mar. 25, 2005), http://www.copyright.gov/orphan/comments/OW0643-STM-CreativeCommons. pdf (Comments of Creative Commons and Save the Music).

35. 17 U.S.C. § 102. Technically, protection attaches regardless of the observance of any formalities such as registration. But, as we shall see later, registration still impacts the remedies a plaintiff enjoys in copyright litigation and, in turn, determines substantive rights. *See* 17 U.S.C. § 412.

36. *Id.*

37. This fact is exacerbated by the status of fair use as an affirmative defense, which places the burden of proof on the user. *See* John Tehranian, *Et Tu, Fair Use? The Triumph of Natural-Law Copyright*, 38 U.C. Davis L. Rev. 465, 495 (2005).

38. Chris Anderson, The Long Tail: Why the Future of Business is Selling Less of More 10 (2006).

39. *See* Matthew Sag, *Piracy: Twelve Year-Olds, Grandmothers, and Other Good Targets for the Recording Industry's File Sharing Litigation*, 4 Nw. J. Tech. & Intell. Prop. 133, 146 (2006).

40. 17 U.S.C. § 504(c)(2).

41. *See* 17 U.S.C. §§ 101 (defining a performance as public if it takes place somewhere "open to the public or at any place where a substantial number of persons outside of a normal circle of a family and its social acquaintances is gathered"), 106(4) (granting to a copyright holder of a musical composition the exclusive right to publicly perform the work). There is, of course, an ambiguity as to how far the "public performance" right extends. A traffic light at a crowded intersection could well be the site of a public performance from a person's car if the windows are rolled down. Admittedly, section 110(4) of the Copyright Act exempts from liability certain "performance[s] of a nondramatic literary or musical work otherwise than in a transmission to the public, without any purpose of direct or indirect commercial advantage and without payment of any fee or other compensation for the performance to any of its performers, promoters, or organizers." 17 U.S.C. § 110(4). But this exemption is limited to instances where there is no indirect commercial advantage and, if someone is using their vehicle for work purposes, it could be viewed as an office on wheels where the unauthorized performance does, in fact, serve some indirect commercial purpose. Moreover, one's own rendition of a musical composition, especially if fixed in any tangible medium, could be viewed as the creation of an unauthorized derivative work.

42. *See Kwik-Fit Sued Over Staff Radios*, BBC News, Oct. 5, 2007, http://news.bbc.co.uk/1/hi/scotland/edinburgh_and_east/7029892.stm (last visited Dec. 6, 2007).

43. The public performance right is already regarded as "[o]ne of the greatest sources of revenue in the music industry." Woods v. Bourne Co., 60 F.3d 978, 983–84 (2d Cir. 1995) (citation omitted).

44. Although initially reported as a "merit badge," the program was actually for a "merit patch." *See* BoingBoing, *Boy Scouts Shill for MPAA with Copyright Merit Badge*, http://www. boingboing.net/2006/10/20/boy_scouts_shill_for.html.

45. *L.A. Boy Scouts New Merit Badge: "Respect Copyrights,"* S.F. Chronicle, Oct. 20, 2006, *available at* http://www.sfgate.com/cgi-bin/article.cgi?file=/news/archive/2006/10/20/entertainment/e110452D84.DTL.

46. Press Release, Motion Picture Association of America, Los Angeles Area Boy Scouts Collaborate with MPAA to Teach Young People about Respecting Copyrights (Oct. 20, 2006) (*available at* http://www.mpaa.org/press_releases/boy%20scouts%20press%20release.pdf).

47. Nate Anderson, *Boy Scouts Get MPAA Approved Merit Badge*, Oct. 20, 2006, *available at* http://arstechnica.com/news.ars/post/20061020-8044.html.

48. *See* Archived Captain Copyright Comic Panel from http://www.captaincopyright.ca/ Kids/Comic4.aspx, *available at* http://en.wikipedia.org/wiki/File:Captain_copyright.jpg.

49. *See* Lessons for Grades 1–3, http://web.archive.org/web/20060613141526/www. captaincopyright.ca/Teachers/Grade1-3.aspx

50. http://web.archive.org/web/20060619082731/www.captaincopyright.ca/Teachers/ Docs/ GR_3-6_Act_5.pdf.

51. BoingBoing, Canadian Copyright Agency Launches Kids' Propaganda Campaign, http:// boingboing.net/2006_06_01_archive.html (reporting on the contents of the now-defunct website at http://www.captaincopyright.ca/Ipnotice.aspx).

52. For example, as Professor Michael Geist (an expert on Canadian copyright law) pointed out about the Captain Copyright program: "There is no reference to user rights, which are particularly relevant in the education context. . . . Our children need to develop love for learning, a passion for creativity, and appreciation of art and science. The exercises that are offered do not provide any of that. Instead they reduce Canadian copyright to levels not seen before. They are so shameful that they should not be included in any classroom in the country." Michael Geist, *Captain Copyright*, May 31, 2006, http://www.michaelgeist.ca/ content/view/1275/125/.

53. http://web.archive.org/web/20070203012806/http://www.captaincopyright.ca/.

54. *Id.* §§ 504(c)(2), 506; 18 U.S.C. § 2319 (providing criminal penalties against certain copyright infringers). The $4.544 billion figure assumes that for the purposes of tallying statutory damages, the number of works infringed (83) are multiplied by the maximum award for willful infringement ($150,000 per infringed work) and by 365 days. I also assume that neither acquiescence nor fair use defenses excuse the conduct.

55. Wheaton v. Peters, 33 U.S. 591 (1834) (featuring a battle between two Supreme Court reporters over copyright claims to synopses of Court decisions).

56. Stowe v. Thomas, 23 F. Cas. 201 (C.C.E.D. Pa. 1853) (Harriet Beecher Stowe sued the author of an unauthorized German translation of Stowe's celebrated work, *Uncle Tom's Cabin*, for copyright infringement).

57. Folsom v. Marsh, 9 F. Cas. 342, 345 (C.C.D. Mass. 1841) (No. 4901).

58. *See, e.g.*, Bridgeport Music, Inc. v. Dimension Films, 383 F.3d 390, 398 (6th Cir. 2004) (holding that any unauthorized sample of a sound recording, no matter how small, constitutes copyright infringement: "Get a license or do not sample"); Grand Upright Music, Ltd. v. Warner Bros. Records, Inc., 780 F. Supp. 182 (S.D.N.Y. 1991) (sternly warning would-be samplers with the cautionary words of the Eighth Commandment: "Thou shalt not steal"); Jarvis v. A & M Records, 827 F. Supp. 282, 288–92 (D.N.J. 1993).

59. *See, e.g.*, Rogers v. Koons, 960 F.2d 301 (2d Cir. 1992) (finding modern artist Jeffrey Koons's kitschy mutilation of a photograph featuring a couple and some puppies to create a satire of suburban American aesthetic sensibilities infringed the copyright of the original photographer).

60. Walt Disney Prods. v. Air Pirates, 581 F.2d 75, 753 (9th Cir. 1978) (finding an edgy comic book series featuring a "rather bawdy depiction of the Disney characters as active members of a free thinking, promiscuous, drug ingesting counterculture" infringed Disney's copyrights).

61. Dr. Seuss Enters., L.P. v. Penguin Books USA, Inc., 109 F.3d 1394 (9th Cir. 1997) (finding a satire of the O.J. Simpson trial based on *The Cat in the Hat* infringed Dr. Seuss's copyright).

62. Paramount Pictures Corp. v. Carol Publ'g Group, 11 F. Supp. 2d 329 (S.D.N.Y. 1998) (finding a book that analyzed, mocked, and satirized all things *Star Trek* violated Paramount's copyright in the television show).

63. Donald Barthelme, *The Genius*, FORTY STORIES 18 (1989).

64. LUDWIG WITTGENSTEIN, TRACTUS LOGICO-PHILOSOPHICUS 68 (1974).

65. Jorge Luis Borges, *The Library of Babel*, FICCIONES (1994).

66. San Francisco Arts & Athletics, Inc. v. United States Olympic Comm., 483 U.S. 522 (1987).

CHAPTER 1

1. 17 U.S.C. § 504(c)(2). As we see later, this requires (among other things) timely registration by the copyright holders and a finding of willfulness.

2. 17 U.S.C §§ 102(a)(1), 106(1), 501(a).

3. The total represents a maximum award of $150,000 per act of willful infringement, 17 U.S.C. § 504(c)(2), multiplied by twenty acts of infringement.

4. 17 U.S.C §§ 102(a)(1), 106(1), 501(a).

5. 17 U.S.C. §§ 102(a)(5), 102(a)(8), 106(2), 501(a).

6. *Id.* §§ 102(a)(1), 106(4), 501(a).

7. 17 U.S.C. § 202.

8. *Id.* §§ 102(a)(5), 106(1), 106(3), 106(5), 501(a). See the discussion *infra* note 31 and accompanying text regarding unpublished works and implied licenses.

9. *Id.* §§ 102(a)(5), 106(1), 501(a).

10. 17 U.S.C. §§ 102(a)(5), 106(5), 501(a).

11. *Id.* § 503(a).

12. *Id.* § 503(b).

13. Credit must go to Daniel Rosenthal for this quip.

14. 17 U.S.C. § 503(b).

15. Time Warner claims copyright ownership over the lyrics to "Happy Birthday" and vigorously enforces its purported exclusive rights based thereon. *See, e.g.*, KEMBREW C. MCLEOD, FREEDOM OF EXPRESSION: RESISTANCE AND EXPRESSION IN THE AGE OF INTELLECTUAL PROPERTY 15–18 (2007).

16. 17 U.S.C. §§ 102(2), 106(1), 106(4), 501(a).

17. 17 U.S.C. §§ 102(5), 106(1), 501(a).

18. 17 U.S.C. §§ 102(1), 102(5), 106(1), 106(3), 106(5), 501(a). As previously unpublished works, the materials featured in *Found* are subject to only severely limited fair use rights. *See infra* notes 27–29 and accompanying text.

19. *See* MGM Studios Inc. v. Grokster, Ltd., 545 U.S. 913, 930 (2005) ("One infringes contributorily by intentionally inducing or encouraging direct infringement . . . ."). By subscribing to *Found*, John is quite arguably encouraging and materially contributing to *Found*'s acts of infringements by making them profitable.

20. 17 U.S.C. § 504(c)(2).

21. *Id.* §§ 504(c)(2), 506; 18 U.S.C. § 2319 (providing for criminal penalties against certain copyright infringers). The $12.45 million figure assumes that, for the purposes of tallying statutory damages, one uses the number of works infringed (83) and multiplies it by the

maximum award for willful infringement ($150,000 per infringed work). I also assume that neither an acquiescence nor fair use defense excuses the conduct.

22. In addition, the damages analysis above does not include the sizeable attorneys' fees for which a defendant might be responsible, even if there is only a minimal finding of damages. Courts have routinely demonstrated their willingness to award attorneys' fees that far exceed statutory or actual damages in a case, often by a ratio of greater than 10 to 1. *See, e.g.*, Princeton Univ. Press v. Michigan Document Servs., Inc., 869 F. Supp. 521, 523–24 (E.D. Mich. 1994) (awarding plaintiff $326,318.52 in attorneys' fees and costs on a statutory damages award of $30,000); Branch v. Ogilvy & Mather, Inc., 772 F. Supp. 1359 (S.D.N.Y. 1991) (awarding plaintiff $116,700 in attorneys' fees on a damages award of $10,001); Landsberg v. Scrabble Crossword Game Players, Inc., 212 U.S.P.Q. 159 (C.D. Cal. 1980) (awarding plaintiff $233,026.27 in attorneys' fees on lost profits award of $87,086.47). As one court that granted $326,318.52 in attorneys' fees on a statutory damages award of just $30,000 put it: "Although the statutory damages awarded are significantly less than the attorney fees sought, the court notes the success achieved is more than the financial gain and that the recovery of fees is necessary to protect copyright law and to encourage the litigation of meritorious infringement claims." *Princeton Univ. Press*, 869 F. Supp. at 523–24.

23. 17 U.S.C § 102(a)(1).

24. Feist Publ'ns, Inc. v. Rural Telephone Servs. Co., 499 U.S. 340 (1991).

25. 17 U.S.C § 106(1).

26. 17 U.S.C. § 501(a).

27. Harper & Row v. Nation Enters., 471 U.S. 539 (1985).

28. New Era Publ'ns Int'l, ApS v. Henry Holt & Co., 873 F.2d 576 (2d Cir. 1989) (emphasis added).

29. Salinger v. Random House, Inc., 811 F.2d 90 (2d Cir. 1987).

30. 17 U.S.C. § 202.

31. *Salinger*, 811 F.2d at 94–95.

32. *See, e.g.*, Gershwin Publ'g Corp. v. Columbia Artists Mgmt., Inc., 443 F.2d 1159, 1162 (2d Cir. 1971) (imposing contributory liability when defendant has knowledge of an infringement and materially contributes to it and imposing vicarious liability when a defendant has the right and ability to control the activities of an infringer and gains a direct financial benefit from these activities).

33. *See* Mark Bartholomew & John Tehranian, *The Secret Life of Legal Doctrine: The Divergent Evolution of Secondary Liability in Trademark and Copyright Law*, 21 BERKELEY TECH. L.J. 1363, 1369–70 (2006).

34. Sony Corp. v. Universal City Studios, 464 U.S. 417 (1984).

35. MGM Studios Inc. v. Grokster, Ltd., 545 U.S. 913 (2005).

36. *Id*. at 936–937.

37. *See* Bartholomew & Tehranian, *supra* note 33, at 1369–70.

38. 17 U.S.C § 106(1).

39. 17 U.S.C § 501(a).

40. 17 U.S.C. § 107 (emphasis added).

41. *See, e.g.*, Princeton Univ. Press v. Michigan Document Servs., Inc., 99 F.3d 1381 (6th Cir. 1996); Am. Geophysical Union v. Texaco, 37 F.3d 881 (2d Cir. 1994), *superseded by* 60 F.3d 913 (2d Cir. 1994); Duffy v. Penguin Books, 4 F. Supp. 2d 268 (S.D.N.Y. 1998); Television Digest, Inc. v. U.S. Tel. Ass'n, 841 F. Supp. 5 (D.D.C. 1993); Basic Books, Inc. v. Kinko's Graphics Corp., 758 F. Supp. 1522 (S.D.N.Y. 1991).

42. *Princeton Univ. Press*, 99 F.3d 1381.

43. *Id.*

44. *Id.* (Martin, J., dissenting).

45. Castle Rock Entm't, Inc. v. Carol Publ'g Group, Inc., 955 F. Supp. 260, 271 (S.D.N.Y. 1997) (emphasis added); *see also* Campbell v. Acuff-Rose Music, Inc., 510 U.S. 569, 591–93 (1994).

46. 960 F.2d 301 (2d Cir. 1992).

47. *Id.* at 312.

48. Seuss Enters., L.P. v. Penguin Books USA, Inc., 109 F.3d 1394 (9th Cir.), *cert. dismissed*, 521 U.S. 1146 (1997).

49. *Id.* at 1403.

50. *Id.* at 1400–01.

51. *Id.*

52. 955 F. Supp. 260 (S.D.N.Y. 1997).

53. 430 F.3d 888, 890 (7th Cir. 2005).

54. 17 U.S.C. § 110(1).

55. *See, e.g.*, Christopher A. Harkins, *Tattoos and Copyright Infringement: Celebrities, Marketers, and Businesses Beware of the Ink*, 10 Lewis & Clark L. Rev. 313 (2006) (using the infringement suit involving NBA star Rasheed Wallace's tattoo as the starting point for analyzing the minefield of ink-related copyright issues).

56. Among other things, O'Neal famously rescued a gay man being assaulted by a group of thugs because of his sexual orientation. He also paid for the funeral of Shaniya Davis after being touched by her tragic murder, which resulted from her mother trafficking her to settle a drug-related debt.

57. 17 U.S.C. § 503(b).

58. There is little doubt that the recording of the moment could invoke copyright liability, as an unauthorized reproduction of the song has been made in violation of 17 U.S.C. § 106(1). In addition, the restaurant may face liability for the unauthorized public performance of the song. On one hand, performance of the song might be exempted from liability under 17 U.S.C. § 110(4), which immunizes certain "performance of a nondramatic literary or musical work otherwise than in a transmission to the public, without any purpose of direct or indirect commercial advantage and without payment of any fee or other compensation for the performance to any of its performers, promoters, or organizers." *Id.* As Nimmer argues, "It would seem that, under normal circumstances, restaurants do not compensate staff 'for the performance.' It therefore follows that, in institutions charging no admission fee, the waiters' song likewise does not excite copyright liability." 2-8 Melville B. Nimmer & David Nimmer, Nimmer on Copyright § 8.15 (2006); *see also* Davis v. The Gap, Inc., 246 F.3d 152, 173 (2d. Cir. 2001) (noting, in dicta, that the de minimus doctrine would likely immunize the singing of "Happy Birthday to You" at a public restaurant). On the other hand, as Roger Brauneis points out in responding to Nimmer, section 104 immunization requires there be no "direct or indirect commercial advantage" and "one could make an argument that there is an 'indirect commercial advantage' to making it known that waiters will bring out a piece of cake with a candle on it and sing 'Happy Birthday to You,' namely, the sale of the cake, and perhaps of dessert more generally and even of the entire meal, for people who want to celebrate a birthday at a restaurant, yet want the celebration to include the singing of 'Happy Birthday to You' along with the other traditional trappings." Roger Brauneis, *Addenda and Errata*, http://http://docs.law.gwu.edu/facweb/rbrauneis/happybirthdayaddenda.htm.

59. Time Warner traces the copyright back to its registration date of 1935, meaning the song was scheduled to have fallen into the public domain in 1991—two twenty-eight-year terms after 1935. However, the Copyright Act of 1976 extended subsisting terms by an additional nineteen years. The Copyright Term Extension Act of 1998 then added an additional twenty years, thereby giving "Happy Birthday" protection until at least 2030—at least in theory.

60. Robert Brauneis, *Copyright and the World's Most Popular Song*, 56 J. COPYRIGHT SOC'Y U.S.A. 335 (2009).

61. There was some litigation during the 1930s and 1940s, but that was related to the melody, which was presumably under copyright protection only until 1949. *Id.*

62. *See supra*, note 59.

63. *See, e.g.*, McLeod, *supra* note 15, at 15–18.

64. THE CORPORATION (Big Picture Media Corp. 2003).

65. Federal copyright law has been this way since at least 1931, when the Supreme Court foreclosed as a defense to copyright infringement liability the absence of mens rea. In the relevant suit, ASCAP (the American Society of Composers, Authors and Publishers) brought suit against a hotel operator in Kansas City. *See* Buck v. Jewell-LaSalle Realty Co., 283 U.S. 191 (1931). The hotel provided radio receivers to guests so that publicly available over-the-airwave broadcasts could be piped into their rooms from the hotel's master receiver. After finding the retransmission of a public broadcast constituted a "public performance" in violation an exclusive right granted to copyright holders (and potentially a "for-profit" one at that), *id.* at 198, the Court deemed mens rea wholly irrelevant to the issue of liability under the Copyright Act, holding "Intention to infringe is not essential" for copyright liability. *Id.*

66. Although state of mind does not affect liability under copyright law, it can reduce some of the damages.

67. However, for contributory liability, knowledge (whether actual or imputed/constructive) is required.

68. Bright Tunes Music Corp. v. Harrisongs Music, Ltd., 420 F. Supp. 177 (S.D.N.Y. 1976).

69. 2-8 MELVILLE B. NIMMER & DAVID NIMMER, NIMMER ON COPYRIGHT § 8.01 (2006).

70. Grand Upright Music Ltd. v. Warner Bros. Records, Inc., 780 F. Supp. 182, 183 (S.D.N.Y. 1991).

71. Bridgeport Music, Inc. v. Dimension Films, 383 F.3d 390, 398 (6th Cir. 2004).

72. 126 F.3d 70 (2d Cir. 1997).

73. *Ringgold* is hardly an outlier. In *Weismann v. Freeman*, the defendant had been sued for distributing nine copies of a syllabus for a medical review course for use in a lecture, even though the allegedly infringing copies of the syllabus were collected at the end of the lecture. Although the trial court had entered a verdict for the defendant, the Second Circuit found infringement and reversed. Weissmann v. Freeman, 868 F.2d 1313 (2d Cir. 1989); Weissmann v. Freeman, 684 F. Supp. 1248 (detailing the facts of the alleged infringement).

74. 126 F.3d at 77–78.

75. 239 F.3d 1004 (9th Cir. 2001).

76. On the original Napster, users were free to simply act as "leeches" and download music from other people's computers without reciprocating or opening up their file folders to other users.

77. 239 F.3d at 1015.

78. 227 F.3d 1110, 1117–18 (9th Cir. 2000), *cert. denied*, 532 U.S. 958 (2001).

79. 227 F.3d at 1117–18.

80. *See, e.g.,* Williams v. Columbia Broad. Sys., Inc., 57 F. Supp. 2d 961 (C.D. Cal. 1999), *vacated by consent,* 1999 WL 1260143 (C.D. Cal. Dec. 21, 1999) (finding "spirit message" from Army unit broadcast during 1997 Army/Navy football game, which featured animated clay "Sailor Bill" that drew on copyrighted Mr. Bill character, constituted fair use because, inter alia, use was quasi-noncommercial).

81. *See, e.g.,* Gershwin Publ'g Corp. v. Columbia Artists Mgmt., Inc., 443 F.2d 1159, 1162 (2d Cir. 1971).

CHAPTER 2

1. Tyler T. Ochoa & Mark Rose, *The Anti-Monopoly Origins of the Patent and Copyright Clause,* 49 J. COPYRIGHT SOC'Y U.S.A. 675 (2002).

2. *See* Folsom v. Marsh, 9 F. Cas. 342 (C.C.D. Mass. 1841).

3. *Id.* at 348.

4. U.S. CONST. art. I, § 1, cl. 8.

5. Statute of Anne, 1710, 8 Ann., c. 19 (Eng.).

6. *Id.*

> [T]he author of any book or books already composed, and not printed or published, or that shall hereafter be composed, and his assignee or assigns, shall have the sole liberty of printing and reprinting such book and books for the term of fourteen years, to commence from the day of first publishing the same, and no longer.

Id.

7. "[A]fter the expiration of the said term of fourteen years, the sole right of printing or disposing of copies shall return to the authors thereof, if they are then living, for another term of fourteen years." *Id.*

8. The Statute of Anne stated:

> [T]he author of any book or books already printed, who hath not transferred to any other the copy or copies of such book or books, share or shares thereof, or the bookseller or booksellers, printer or printers, or other person or persons, who hath or have purchased or acquired the copy or copies of any book or books, in order to print or reprint the same, shall have sole right and liberty of printing such book and books for the term of one and twenty years, to commence from the said tenth day of April, and no longer.

Id.

9. *See* 2 JOHN LOCKE, TWO TREATISES ON CIVIL GOVERNMENT 24–51, 305–06 (1924). For a further examination of competing theories of property (including those of John Locke) and their influence on legal thought, see Margaret Jane Radin, *Property and Personhood,* 34 STAN. L. REV. 957 (1982).

10. Ochoa & Rose, *supra* note 1, at 683.

11. 8 Ann., c. 19.

12. MARK ROSE, AUTHORS AND OWNERS: THE INVENTION OF COPYRIGHT 45 (1993).

13. *See* WILLIAM BLACKSTONE, 2 COMMENTARIES ON THE LAWS OF ENGLAND 405–06. *See also* Hannibal Travis, *Pirates of the Information Infrastructure: Blackstonian Copyright and the*

First Amendment, 15 BERKELEY TECH. L.J. 777, 782–83 (2000) (arguing the Blackstonian vision of copyright embraced an author's "'sole and despotic dominion' over a given work, a right of 'total exclusion' asserted in perpetuity against any attempt to imitate the sentiments, vary the disposition, or derive any social or economic value from a work").

14. Donaldson v. Becket, 98 Eng. Rep. 257 (H.L. 1774).

15. *See* BENJAMIN KAPLAN, AN UNHURRIED VIEW OF COPYRIGHT 13 (1966).

16. *See* Irah Donner, *The Copyright Clause of the U.S. Constitution: Why Did the Framers Include It with Unanimous Approval?*, 36 AM. J. LEGAL HIST. 361, 361 (1992); Edward C. Walterscheid, *To Promote the Progress of the Useful Arts: The Background and Origin of the Intellectual Property Clause of the United States Constitution*, 2 J. INTELL. PROP. L. 1, 26–27 (1994).

17. THE FEDERALIST NO. 43 (James Madison).

18. U.S. CONST. art. I, § 8, cl. 8.

19. *See* Donald L. Doernberg, *"We the People": John Locke, Collective Constitutional Rights, and Standing to Challenge Government Action*, 73 CAL. L. REV. 52, 57 (1985).

20. *See* 1 Copyright Act of 1790, ch. 15, § 1, 1 Stat. 124 (repealed 1831) (emphasis added).

21. Of course, this policy choice also reflected profoundly protectionist impulses.

22. *See* Zechariah Chafee, Jr., *Reflections on the Law of Copyright: I*, 45 COLUM. L. REV. 503, 506–11 (1945); Diane Leenheer Zimmerman, *Information as Speech, Information as Goods: Some Thoughts on Marketplaces and the Bill of Rights*, 33 WM. & MARY L. REV. 665, 704 (1992).

23. *See, e.g.*, John O. McGinnis, *The Once and Future Property-Based Vision of the First Amendment*, 63 U. CHI. L. REV. 49, 80 (1996) (arguing the Framers' paramount purpose for the Copyright Clause was to protect the "individual's natural property in his information"). McGinnis and other scholars who take such a position on the Framers' intent ignore the instrumentalist language of the Copyright Clause, its significant temporal and utilitarian limits (by sharp contrast to material property rights), the Framers' profound skepticism of monopolies, the influence of the English experience with the Statute of Anne, and the historical context of its promulgation.

24. *See* Stephen Breyer, *The Uneasy Case for Copyright: A Study of Copyright in Books, Photocopies, and Computer Programs*, 84 HARV. L. REV. 281, 291 (1970).

25. Letter from Thomas Jefferson to Isaac McPherson (Aug. 13, 1813), *in* 13 THE WRITINGS OF THOMAS JEFFERSON 333–34 (Albert Ellery Bergh ed., 1907) (emphasis added).

26. JAMES MADISON, WRITINGS 756 (Jack N. Rakove ed., 1999).

27. 33 U.S. (8 Pet.) 591 (1834).

28. *Id.* at 664–68.

29. *Id.* at 653.

30. *Id.* at 661.

31. *Id.* ("Congress, then, by this act, instead of sanctioning an existing right, as contended for, created it. This seems to be the clear import of the law, connected with the circumstances under which it was enacted.").

32. *Id.* at 653.

33. *See* Ochoa & Rose, *supra* note 1, at 675.

34. *Wheaton*, 33 U.S. at 657 ("That an author, at common law, has a property in his manuscript, and may obtain redress against any one who deprives him of it, or by improperly obtaining a copy endeavours to realise a profit by its publication, cannot be doubted.").

35. *See, e.g.*, 17 U.S.C. § 104(a) (2004).

36. Samuel D. Warren & Louis D. Brandeis, *The Right of Privacy*, 4 HARV. L. REV. 193, 193 (1890).

37. *Id.* at 205 (emphasis added).

38. L. Ray Patterson, Folsom v. Marsh *and Its Legacy*, 5 J. INTELL. PROP. L. 431, 445 (1998).

39. *See, e.g.*, Stowe v. Thomas, 23 F. Cas. 201 (C.C.E.D. Pa. 1853); Newbery's Case, 98 Eng. Rep. 913 (Ch. 1773); Gyles v. Wilcox, 26 Eng. Rep. 489 (Ch. 1740); Burnett v. Chetwood, 35 Eng. Rep. 1008–09 (Ch. 1720).

40. *Burnett*, 35 Eng. Rep. at 1009.

41. KAPLAN, *supra* note 15, at 10–12.

42. As Kaplan argues, the rule that emerged in this time was "if the accused book was a work of authorship, it could not at the same time infringe." *Id.* at 10.

43. *Stowe*, 23 F. Cas. at 201.

44. *Id.* at 201 (noting Stowe's attorney stated "[t]he question is novel").

45. *Id.* at 202 & n.2.

46. *Id.* at 202.

47. *Id.* at 201.

48. *Id.* at 206.

49. *Id.* at 208.

50. *Id.* at 206.

51. *Id.* at 207.

52. *Id.*

53. Gyles v. Wilcox, 26 Eng. Rep. 489 (Ch. 1740).

54. *Id.* at 490.

55. *Id.*

56. Lord Hardwicke ultimately recommended the case to arbitration, where the plaintiff lost. *See* KAPLAN, *supra* note 15, at 11.

57. Newbery's Case, 98 Eng. Rep. 913 (Ch. 1773).

58. KAPLAN, *supra* note 15, at 12 (quoting *Newbery's Case*, 98 Eng. Rep. at 913). Hawkesworth's work was itself based on a reconstruction of the original journals of several notable explorations, including Captain James Cook's first circumnavigation of the globe. *Id.*

59. *Id.*

60. *Id.*

61. *See, e.g.*, Story v. Holcombe, 23 F. Cas. 171, 173 (C.C.D. Ohio 1847) (No. 13,497) (finding "[a] fair abridgment of any book is considered a new work, as to write it requires labor and exercise of judgment").

62. *See* Wheaton v. Peters, 33 U.S. 591, 651 (1834) ("An abridgement fairly done, is itself authorship, requires mind; and is not an infringement, no more than another work on the same subject."). The plaintiffs, however, argued the Condensed Reports at issue in the case did not constitute an abridgement: "The [defendant's] Condensed Reports have none of the features of an abridgement, and the work is made up of the same cases, and no more than is contained in Wheaton's Reports." *Id.* at 652.

63. *See* Folsom v. Marsh, 9 F. Cas. 342, 345 (C.C.D. Mass. 1841) (No. 4901) (noting a "real, substantial condensation" of work did not constitute an act of infringement so long as "intellectual labor and judgment [was] bestowed thereon"). As we shall see, however, this affirmation was somewhat disingenuous as the opinion fundamentally altered copyright law. *See infra* Section II.A.

64. Of course, it was not just norms that supported such uses of Shakespeare. An absence of legal prohibitions also encouraged remixing activities.

65. LAWRENCE LEVINE, HIGHBROW/LOWBROW: THE EMERGENCE OF CULTURAL HIERARCHY IN AMERICA 88 (1988).

66. KATHERINE K. PERSON, OPERA ON THE ROAD: TRAVELLING OPERA TROUPES IN THE UNITED STATES, 1825–1860 (2001); LEVINE, *supra* note 65.

67. LEVINE, *supra* note 65, at 89–90.

68. *Folsom*, 9 F. Cas. at 342.

69. *Id.*

70. *Id.* at 348. According to Justice Story, in deciding questions of infringement, courts should "look to the nature of and objects of the selections made, the quantity and value of the materials used, and the degree in which the use may prejudice the sale, or diminish the profits, or supersede the objects, of the original work." *See id.* This test is closely replicated in the current fair use provisions of the Copyright Act. *See* 17 U.S.C. § 107 (2004).

71. *See, e.g.*, Matthew D. Bunker, *Eroding Fair Use: The "Transformative" Use Doctrine After Campbell*, 7 COMM. L. & POL'Y 1, 1 (2002) (praising fair use as "one of the most important limits on the monopoly of copyright owners over the use of their copyrighted expression").

72. Patterson, *supra* note 38, at 431.

73. *Id.*

74. *Id.*

75. *Id.* at 432.

76. The 255-page statistic excludes official documents and documents that had appeared in publication prior to Sparks's own use.

77. Folsom v. Marsh, 9 F. Cas. 342, 345 (C.C.D. Mass. 1841) (No. 4901).

78. *Id.* at 349.

79. *Id.*

80. *Id.* at 348.

81. *Id.* at 349 (quoting Lewis v. Fullarton, 48 Eng. Rep. 1080, 1081 (K.B. 1839)).

82. Travis, *supra* note 13, at 821 n.223. As Travis notes, "Blackstone's work [had] been in the public domain due to the 1790 Copyright Act's reservation of its protections to U.S. citizens." *Id.*

83. Folsom v. Marsh, 9 F. Cas. 342, 345 (C.C.D. Mass. 1841) (No. 4901).

84. *Id.*

85. *See* 17 U.S.C. § 107 (2004). The modern fair use test balances these (nonexclusive) four factors to determine when an individual or corporation can make use of copyrighted works without permission or payment.

86. 17 U.S.C. § 107(2) (2001).

87. *Id.* § 107(3).

88. *Id.* § 107(4).

89. Patterson, *supra* note 38, at 442.

90. 10 F. Cas. 1035 (C.C.D. Mass. 1839) (No. 5728).

91. *Id.* at 1038.

92. *See id.* at 1038–39.

93. Emerson v. Davies, 8 F. Cas. 615 (C.C.D. Mass. 1845) (No. 4436).

94. *Id.* at 619.

95. *Id.*

96. Travis, *supra* note 13, at 819.

97. *See id.* at 819.

98. *See id.*

99. Copyright Act of 1870, ch. 230, § 86, 16 Stat. 198 (1870).

100. *Id.* The Act provided "authors may reserve the right to dramatize or to translate their own works." *Id.*

101. *See, e.g.,* Twin Peaks Prod., Inc. v. Publ'ns Int'l, Ltd., 996 F.2d 1366, 1370 (2d Cir. 1993) (finding defendants' book about the television program *Twin Peaks* infringed copyrights in teleplays for series); *cf.* Castle Rock Entm't, Inc. v. Carol Publ'g Group, Inc., 955 F. Supp. 260, 268 (S.D.N.Y. 1997) (holding the *Seinfeld Aptitude Test,* a trivia book on all things Seinfeld, constituted unauthorized derivative work that infringed Castle Rock's copyright in the *Seinfeld* television program).

102. See, for example, the suit by Scholastic, the owner of the Harry Potter copyright, against the *New York Daily News,* which published a synopsis of the plot of the then-forthcoming *Harry Potter and the Order of the Phoenix.* Keith J. Kelly, *Scholastic Sues Daily News for $100M in "Pottergate,"* N.Y. POST, June 19, 2003, at 37.

103. *See* Feist Publ'ns, Inc. v. Rural Tel. Serv. Co., 499 U.S. 340, 352–57 (1991).

104. Mark A. Lemley, *Romantic Authorship and the Rhetoric of Property,* 75 TEX. L. REV. 873, 895–96 (1997).

105. *See id.* at 895 n.123.

106. *See* Travis, *supra* note 13, at 826.

107. Lemley, *supra* note 104, at 898 n.126.

108. *See* Stewart E. Sterk, *Rhetoric and Reality in Copyright Law,* 94 MICH. L. REV. 1197, 1198 (1996) ("The notion that according copyright protection to architectural works will generate more creative architecture, for instance, is manifestly ridiculous. Even in [other] situations where instrumental justifications [for protection] remain plausible, their foundation is often shaky.").

109. *See* 17 U.S.C. § 302(a), (c), § 304 (2004).

110. Even the majority's decision in *Eldred v. Ashcroft* suggests this point. *See* 537 U.S. 186, 208 (2003) (noting "we are not at liberty to second-guess congressional determinations and policy judgments of this order, however debatable or arguably unwise they may be. Accordingly, we cannot conclude that the CTEA—which continues the unbroken congressional practice of treating future and existing copyrights in parity for term extension purposes—is an impermissible exercise of Congress' power under the Copyright Clause.").

111. Copyright Act of 1831, ch. 16, 4 Stat. 436.

112. Copyright Act of 1870, ch. 230, 16 Stat. 198.

113. *See* Copyright Act of 1909, ch. 320, 35 Stat. 1075. The Act gave authors the exclusive right to "translate the copyrighted work into other language or dialects, or make any other version thereof, if it be a literary work; to dramatize it if it be a nondramatic work; to convert it into a novel or other nondramatic work if it be a drama; to arrange or adapt it if it be a musical work; to complete, execute, and finish it if it be a model or design for a work of art." *See id.* § 1(b).

114. *See* 17 U.S.C. § 106(2) (2004).

115. Under the current (1976) Copyright Act, a derivative work is "a work based upon one or more pre-existing works, such as a translation, musical arrangement, dramatization, fictionalization, motion picture version, sound recording, art reproduction, abridgment, condensation, or any other form in which a work may be recast, transformed, or adopted. A work consisting of editorial revisions, annotations, elaborations, or other modifications which, as a whole, represent an original work of authorship, is a 'derivative work.'" *See* 17 U.S.C. § 101 (2004).

116. *See* Sterk, *supra* note 108, at 1215–17 (1996).

117. On a related note, some theorists have challenged even the idea that copyright encourages innovation and creation. As Mark Nadel notes, very few creators ever reap significant financial rewards from copyright protections. *See* Mark S. Nadel, *Questioning the Economic Justification for Copyright* at 39, *available at* http://www.serci.org/2003/nadel.pdf. In the winner-take-all entertainment, publishing, and software industries, only a precious few creators achieve extraordinary wealth through a hit record or bestseller. In these superstar-driven markets, copyright protection may simply enable publishers to support larger marketing campaigns and greater rents for powerful talents; these marketing costs and rents may well dissipate all of the increased revenues generated by copyright protection. Thus, borderline creators will never enjoy greater profits from copyright protection. *See id.* However, Nadel carries his point too far. Although actual financial rewards go to very few, it is possible the promise and potential of huge financial rewards encourage individuals to create art. Thus, like a lottery effect, the promise of huge rewards may still incentivize artistic creation. Admittedly, the existence of derivative rights may further add to the incentives. However, the magnitude of this effect is uncertain, and it may be more than offset by another effect noted by Nadel—the backward-bending labor supply curve. *See id.* at 10.

118. *Id.*

119. *See* William M. Landes & Richard A. Posner, *An Economic Analysis of Copyright Law*, 18 J. Legal Stud. 325, 354 (1989).

120. *See* Sterk, *supra* note 108, at 1216–17.

121. *See id.* at 1217.

122. *See* Nadel, *supra* note 117, at 10.

123. *See* Jane C. Ginsburg, *Creation and Commercial Value: Copyright Protection of Works of Information*, 90 Colum. L. Rev. 1865, 1890 (1990); *see also* Kalem Co. v. Harper Bros., 222 U.S. 55, 61–62 (1911); Dam v. Kirk La Shelle Co., 175 F. 902, 907–09 (2d Cir. 1910) (holding the defendant's play infringed the plaintiff's right to dramatize his story, even though the play borrowed only the story's central incident and contributed events, characters, and dialogue of its own); Daly v. Palmer, 6 F. Cas. 1132, 1134–38 (S.D.N.Y. 1868) (No. 3552).

124. *Daly*, 6 F. Cas. at 1132.

125. *Id.* at 1133.

126. *Id.* at 1138.

127. Lawrence Levine, Highbrow/Lowbrow: The Emergence of Cultural Hierarchy in America 72 (1988).

128. *Id.* at 139.

129. For example, as symphonic music made the transition from mainstream to highbrow, "the masterworks of the classic composers were to be performed in their entirety by highly trained musicians on programs free from the contamination of lesser works or lesser genres, free from the interference of audience or performer, free from the distractions of the mundane; audiences were to approach the masters and their works with proper respect and proper seriousness, for aesthetic and spiritual elevation rather than mere entertainment was the goal." *Id.* at 146.

130. Of course, with Shakespeare in the public domain, anyone can make use of his works and bastardize the language, plots, characters, and themes in any way one wants. But, norms depressed such activity, thereby leading to Shakespeare's eventual transition from the peoples' playwright to a leading symbol of highbrow culture. Copyright law achieves the same function as those prior norms by interdicting the mongrelization of protected works.

131. *See* Negativland, *Fair Use*, http://www.negativland.com/fairuse.html.

132. COMTE DE LAUTRÉAMONT, POÉSIES (1870).

133. Anna Nimus, *Copyright, Copyleft and the Creative Anticommons*, *available at* http://subsol.c3.hu/subsol_2/contributorso/nimustext.html.

134. *Id.*

135. Marcel Duchamp, *L.H.O.O.Q.* (1919).

136. Marcel Duchamp (as R. Mutt), *Fountain* (1917).

137. Peter Schjeldahl, *Hope and Glory: A Shepard Fairey Moment*, THE NEW YORKER (Feb. 23, 2009).

138. Fairey v. The Associated Press, No. 09-CV-1123 (S.D.N.Y. Feb. 4, 2009).

139. Simply witness the language of the Copyright Clause, the antimonopolistic origins of American copyright law, and the early jurisprudence on copyright, including the unequivocal holding of the Supreme Court in *Wheaton*.

140. Grand Upright Music, Ltd. v. Warner Bros. Records, Inc., 780 F. Supp. 182, 183 (S.D.N.Y. 1991).

141. *Id.*

142. Though, if allowed with permission, digital sampling will not enable plaintiffs to gain the exclusive benefit of any use of their copyright works.

143. Bridgeport Music, Inc. v. Dimension Films, 383 F.3d 390, 398 (6th Cir. 2004).

144. *Id.*

145. *See* Jarvis v. A & M Records, 827 F. Supp. 282, 288–92 (D.N.J. 1993).

146. Stowe v. Thomas, 23 F. Cas. 201, 206 (E.D. Pa. 1853).

147. *See* UMG Recordings, Inc. v. MP3.com, Inc., 92 F. Supp. 2d 349, 352 (S.D.N.Y. 2000).

148. A cognizable trespass claim at common law has, of course, no actual damages requirement.

149. Patterson, *supra* note 38, at 451.

150. 17 U.S.C. § 107(1) (2000).

151. 510 U.S. 569 (1994).

152. *See* Pierre N. Leval, *Toward a Fair Use Standard*, 103 HARV. L. REV. 1105, 1111 (1990).

153. The *Campbell* Court, citing Leval's work, emphasized the importance of transformative use in the copyright infringement calculus and the need to determine whether "the new work merely 'supersedes the objects' of the original creation, or instead adds something new, with a further purpose or different character, altering the first with new expression, meaning, or message." *See Campbell*, 510 U.S. at 579 (citations omitted).

154. *Id.* at 578–80.

155. Rebecca Tushnet, *Copyright as a Model for Free Speech Law: What Copyright Has in Common with Anti-Pornography Laws, Campaign Finance Reform, and Telecommunications Regulation*, 42 B.C. L. REV. 1, 26 (2000).

156. Naomi A. Voegtli, *Rethinking Derivative Rights*, 63 BROOKLYN L. REV. 1213, 1216 (1997).

157. Rogers v. Koons, 960 F.2d 301 (2d Cir. 1992).

158. Although Koons is well known for his art work, he is perhaps most famous for his notorious and short-lived marriage to Italian porn star (and member of Italian Parliament) Cicciolina.

159. Martin Garbus, *Lolita and the Lawyers*, N.Y. TIMES BOOK REV., Sept. 26, 1999, at 35.

160. *Koons*, 960 F.2d at 310.

161. *See* Dr. Seuss Enters., L.P. v. Penguin Books USA, Inc., 109 F.3d 1394, 1401 (9th Cir. 1997).

162. 510 U.S. 569 (1994).

163. *Id.* at 579.

164. *See, e.g.*, Pierre N. Leval, *Copyright in the Twenty-First Century:* Campbell v. Acuff-Rose: *Justice Souter's Rescue of Fair Use*, 13 CARDOZO ARTS & ENT. L.J. 19 *(1994)* (praising elevation of transformation in fair use analysis with the Supreme Court's decision in *Campbell*).

165. *See, e.g.*, Laura G. Lape, *Transforming Fair Use: The Productive Use Factor in Fair Use Doctrine*, 58 ALB. L. REV. 677 (1995) (decrying elevation of transformation in fair use analysis with the Supreme Court's decision in *Campbell*). As Lape argues, "The productive use doctrine is not a traditional part of fair use analysis; it stands in the way of sensible application of fair use and should be abandoned as a doctrinal dead-end." *Id.* at 724.

166. *Compare Campbell*, 510 U.S. at 569 (finding fair use in 2 Live Crew's parody of Roy Orbison's song *Pretty Woman*), *with* Rogers v. Koons, 960 F.2d 301 (2d Cir. 1992) (finding no fair use in Jeffrey Koons's satirical use of Art Rogers's *Puppies* photograph).

167. *Campbell*, 510 U.S. at 580–81.

168. *Id.* at 580.

169. It is possible the Court's parenthetical language does leave a limited protective berth for satire:

> [W]hen there is little or no risk of market substitution, whether because of the large extent of transformation of the earlier work, the new work's minimal distribution in the market, the small extent to which it borrows from an original, or other factors, taking parodic aim at an original is a less critical factor in the analysis, and looser forms of parody may be found to be fair use, as may satire with lesser justification for the borrowing than would otherwise be required.

Id. at 580 n.14.

170. Paul Hirshson, *Names and Faces*, BOSTON GLOBE, July 22, 1989, at 7. *But see* Suntrust Bank v. Houghton Mifflin Co., 268 F.3d 1257, 1277 (11th Cir. 2001) (Marcus, J., concurring) (noting "[p]arodies and caricatures . . . are the most penetrating of criticisms").

171. *See infra.*

172. Naomi A. Voegtli, *Rethinking Derivative Rights*, 63 BROOK. L. REV. 1213, 1227–28 (1997).

173. 11 F. Supp. 2d 329 (S.D.N.Y. 1998).

174. *Id.* at 335–36.

175. *Id.*

176. BUNKER, *supra* note 71, at 12–13.

177. *Paramount Pictures*, 11 F. Supp. 2d at 335.

178. Dr. Seuss Enters., L.P. v. Penguin Books USA, Inc., 109 F.3d 1394 (9th Cir. 1997), *cert. dismissed*, 521 U.S. 1146 (1997).

179. 109 F.3d at 1403.

180. *Id.* at 1401.

181. *See infra.*

182. *Dr. Seuss*, 109 F.3d at 1403 (reasoning "[b]ecause, on the facts presented, [the defendants'] use of *The Cat in the Hat* original was non-transformative, and admittedly commercial, we conclude that market substitution is at least more certain, and market harm may be more readily inferred").

183. *Id.*

184. *Id.* at 1400–01.

185. Castle Rock Entm't, Inc. v. Carol Publ'g Group, Inc., 955 F. Supp. 260 (S.D.N.Y. 1997). On appeal, the district court's finding of infringement (and no fair use) was affirmed, but the

Second Circuit held the trivia book was not even transformative. Castle Rock Entm't, Inc. v. Carol Publ'g Group, Inc., 150 F.3d 132, 147 (2d Cir. 1998) ("since *The SAT* has transformed *Seinfeld*'s expression into trivia quiz book form with little, if any, transformative purpose, the first fair use factor weighs against defendants").

186. *Castle Rock*, 955 F. Supp. at 268 (quoting Campbell v. Acuff-Rose Music, Inc., 510 U.S. 569, 578 (1994)).

187. *Castle Rock*, 955 F. Supp. at 268.

188. *Id.* at 272.

189. *Id.* at 271.

190. *Id.* at 270.

191. The fourth factor assesses the "effect of the use upon the potential market for or value of the copyrighted work." 17 U.S.C. § 107(4) (2000).

192. *Castle Rock*, 955 F. Supp. at 271; *see also* Campbell v. Acuff-Rose Music, Inc., 510 U.S. 569, 591–93 (1994).

193. This was not the only error committed by the *Castle Rock* and *Dr. Seuss* courts. As David Nimmer notes, the problematic interpretation of the fair use balancing test in both cases also went hand in hand with erroneous application of the substantial similarity doctrine. *See* David Nimmer, *Codifying Copyright Comprehensibly*, 51 UCLA L. REV. 1233, 1242 nn.63–66 (2004).

194. Warner Bros. Entm't Inc., v. RDR Books, 575 F. Supp. 2d 513 (S.D.N.Y. 2008).

195. *Id.* at 543 (citing Castle Rock Entm't, Inc. v. Carol Publ'g Group, Inc., 150 F.3d 132, 141 (2d Cir. 1998)).

196. *Warner Bros.*, 575 F. Supp. at 546.

197. *Id.* at 551.

198. 17 U.S.C. § 107(1) (2000).

199. A & M Records, Inc. v. Napster, Inc., 239 F.3d 1004, 1015 (9th Cir. 2001).

200. *See* Worldwide Church of God v. Philadelphia Church of God, Inc., 227 F.3d 1110, 1117–18 (9th Cir. 2000), *cert. denied*, 532 U.S. 958 (2001) (holding that giving away thirty thousand free copies of a religious work constituted a commercial activity because the defendant "profited" from the use of the work by attracting new members who ultimately contributed to the organization by tithing).

201. 17 U.S.C. § 107(4) (2000).

202. *See* Stewart v. Abend, 495 U.S. 207, 238 (1990); Harper & Row v. Nation Enters., 471 U.S. 539, 566 (1985).

203. 17 U.S.C. § 107 (2000).

204. *But see* Am. Geophysical Union v. Texaco Inc., 60 F.3d 913, 926 (2d Cir. 1994) (suggesting *Campbell*'s omission of language emphasizing the fourth factor as being the most important may indicate abandonment of the idea that "any factor enjoys primacy").

205. Cory Doctorow, *Argentine Philosophy Prof Faces Prison Time for Posting Unofficial Translations of Out of Print Derrida Texts*, http://www.boingboing.net/2009/03/23/argentine-philosophy.html (Mar. 23, 2009). Although this example is from Argentina, U.S. copyright law also provides for criminal sanctions for the willful infringement of copyright for "purposes of commercial advantage or private financial gain." 17 U.S.C. § 506(1)(A).

206. Andrés Hax, *Francia impulsó la baja de un sitio argentino que difundía obras filosóficas*, http://www.clarin/.com/diario/2009/02/08/sociedad/s-01867515.htm (Feb. 8, 2008).

207. KENNETH MUIR, THE SOURCES OF SHAKESPEARE'S PLAYS (1978); James D. A. Boyle, *The Search for an Author: Shakespeare and the Framers*, 37 AM. U. L. REV. 625, 629 (1988).

208. Boyle, *supra* note 207, at 628.

209. NIRVANA, *Smells Like Teen Spirit, on* NEVERMIND (Geffen Records 1991).

210. THOMAS PYNCHON, GRAVITY'S RAINBOW (Viking ed., 1973). A book that is much more frequently cited and discussed than read, *Gravity's Rainbow* has been simultaneously hailed as a masterpiece and dismissed as utter nonsense. Winner of the National Book Award, the novel was also unanimously recommended for a Pulitzer Prize by the Pulitzer jury. However, the Pulitzer trustees overturned the decision on the grounds the work was turgid and unintelligible. *See* WILLIAM GADDIS, AGAPE AGAPE 61 (2002).

211. PYNCHON, *supra* note 210, at 538.

212. *Id.*

213. NIRVANA, *supra* note 209.

214. PYNCHON, *supra* note 210, at 538.

215. NIRVANA, *supra* note 209.

216. *See* Bright Tunes Music Corp. v. Harrisongs Music, Ltd., 420 F. Supp. 177 (S.D.N.Y. 1976).

217. A similar dynamic—Bobby Fischer's status as a fugitive—enabled Paramount Studios to greenlight the movie *In Search of Bobby Fischer*, despite the notorious ambiguity of laws protecting the right of publicity. I am grateful to David Nimmer for pointing this out. *See* SEARCHING FOR BOBBY FISCHER (Paramount Pictures 1993).

218. *See* John Yewell, *Tracking Thomas Pynchon Through Space and Time, available at* http://www.metroactive.com/papers/metro/10.01.98/cover/lit-pynchon-9839.html (noting efforts of CNN and *New York Magazine*, among others, to track down Pynchon).

219. *See* Jules Siegel, *Who Is Thomas Pynchon . . . and Why Did He Take Off with My Wife?,* PLAYBOY, Mar. 1977, at 97.

220. *Id.*

221. Daniel Kahneman, Jack L. Knetsch, & Richard H. Thaler, *Experimental Tests of the Endowment Effect and the Coase Theorem,* 98 J. POL. ECON. 1325, 1342 (1990) (noting the endowment effect holds "the value that an individual assigns to [objects] appears to increase substantially as soon as that individual is given the object"). *See also* Russell Korobkin, *The Endowment Effect and Legal Analysis,* 97 Nw. U. L. Rev. 1227 (2003).

222. Steffen Huck, Georg Kirchsteiger, & Jörg Oechssler, *Learning to Like What You Have—Explaining the Endowment Effect,* 115 ECON. J. 689, 689 (2005).

223. *See, e.g.,* Charles R. Plott & Kathryn Zeiler, *Asymmetries in Exchange Behavior Incorrectly Interpreted as Prospect Theory* (June 2005). American Law & Economics Association Annual Meetings. American Law & Economics Association 15th Annual Meeting. Working Paper 63, *available at* http://law.bepress.com/alea/15th/art63 (arguing the endowment effect is largely a product of experiment design and vastly exaggerated).

224. Kahneman et al., *supra* note 221.

225. *Id.*

226. *See, e.g.,* Am. Metro. Enters. of New York, Inc. v. Warner Bros. Records, 389 F.2d 903, 905 (2d Cir. 1968) (noting copyright infringement presumptively causes irreparable harm for which there is no adequate remedy at law). This automatic presumption typically comes into play when copyright holders seek injunctive relief from courts.

227. *See* James Surowiecki, *The Permission Problem,* THE NEW YORKER, Aug. 11, 2008.

228. A. Michael Warnecke, *The Art of Applying the Fair Use Doctrine: The Postmodern-Art Challenge to the Copyright Law,* 13 REV. LITIG. 685, 701 (1994) (observing an endowment effect would cause copyright holders to demand more for access to their work than would otherwise be predicted).

229. D.T. Max, *The Injustice Collector*, THE NEW YORKER, June 19, 2006.

230. *Id.*

231. *Id.*

232. *Id.*

233. *See, e.g.*, Olunfunmilayo B. Arewa, *Copyright on Catfish Row: Musical Borrowing*, Porgy and Bess, *and Unfair Use*, 37 RUTGERS L.J. 277 (2006); Rebecca Ganz, *Portrait of an Artist's Estate as a Copyright Problem*, 41 LOYOLA L. REV. 739 (2008) (discussing the permission holdout problems that have emerged with a number of prominent literary and musical estates); Leval, *supra* note 152, at 1107 (referring to the "widow censor" problem that emerges when a scholar "who wishes to quote personal papers of deceased public figures . . . must satisfy heirs and executors . . . after the subject's death. When writers ask permission, the answer will be, 'Show me what you write. Then we'll talk about permission.' If the manuscript does not exude pure admiration, permission will be denied").

234. Frank P. Darr, *Testing an Economic Theory of Copyright: Historical Materials and Fair Use*, 32 B.C. L. REV. 1027, 1046 (1991).

CHAPTER 3

1. R.E.M., IN TIME: THE BEST OF R.E.M. (Warner Bros. 2003) (liner notes for *Everybody Hurts*).

2. LUDWIG WITTGENSTEIN, TRACTATUS LOGICO-PHILOSOPHICUS § 5.6, at 149 (C.K. Ogden trans., 1922) (emphasis in original omitted).

3. JORGE LUIS BORGES, *The Library of Babel*, in FICCIONES 79 (Anthony Kerrigan ed., Grove Press 1962) (1956). In his celebrated short story, *The Library of Babel*, Borges imagines an endless library with books containing every possible ordering of letters, spaces, and punctuation marks. *Id.* Although most of the books in the library are apparent nonsense, volumes within the library contain, among other things:

> the minute history of the future, the autobiographies of the archangels, the faithful catalogue of the Library, thousands and thousands of false catalogues, a demonstration of the fallacy of these catalogues, a demonstration of the fallacy of the true catalogue, the Gnostic gospel of Basilides, the commentary on this gospel, the commentary on the commentary of this gospel, the veridical account of your death, a version of each book in all languages, the interpolations of every book in all books.

Id. at 83.

4. Joseph P. Liu, *Copyright Law's Theory of the Consumer*, 44 B.C. L. REV. 397, 398–99 (2003) (noting "despite this recognition of a general consumer interest, rather little has been written about the precise shape and scope of this interest" and "[t]he Copyright Act itself scarcely mentions consumers—indeed it contains no consistent generic term to refer to those who consume copyrighted works—and the literature has generally followed suit").

5. By "consumer" or "user," I refer to anyone who makes use of copyrighted content, not simply those who purchase copyrighted material or receive authorized access. As Joseph Liu observes, the word "consumer" is particularly apropos, as it emphasizes a focus on uses of copyrighted works that are literally consumptive, and not necessarily productive, in nature. *See* Liu, *supra* note 4, at 400 ("[C]opyright law and commentary contain no universally accepted generic term for those who access, purchase, and use—i.e., 'consume'—copyrighted

works. I am consciously choosing the term 'consumer,' rather than a more neutral term like 'user,' 'the public,' or 'audience,' in part because I wish to focus on those uses that are literally consumptive rather than productive in nature, and the term roughly captures this distinction." (footnotes omitted)).

6. *Id.* at 399. As Joseph Liu argues, copyright doctrine seeks to "ensur[e] that conditions exist for a functioning market in copyrighted works," by forbidding, inter alia, unauthorized reproduction of protected works and creating economic incentives for the distribution of such works. In the process, therefore, it implicitly supports a theory of passive consumption by simply ensuring that copyrighted works, much like potato chips, athletic shoes, and bottled water, are supplied to users like any other consumer good. *Id.* at 402–04. At the same time, copyright doctrine also recognizes the fact that new creative works can often come from the use/consumption of old works. As such, copyright makes room for such efforts through features such as the idea/expression dichotomy, the fair use doctrine (especially its protection for transformative uses), and the limited term of protection. *Id.* at 405–06.

7. *Id.* at 406–07.

8. *Id.* at 411.

9. *Id.* at 415.

10. *See* Rebecca Tushnet, *Copy This Essay: How Fair Use Doctrine Harms Free Speech and How Copying Serves It*, 114 YALE L.J. 535, 545–46 (2004).

11. "If The Sopranos or Queer as Folk have a significant impact on our culture," argues Tushnet, "then access to those programs improves a person's ability to participate in making and interpreting that culture. There could be a problem for democracy when copyright owners set prices so high that some people can't read or watch what many others do." *Id.*

12. *Id.* at 565 (noting "'copying promotes democracy by literally putting information in citizens' hands") (citing David Owen, *Power to the People: The Photocopier*, L.A. TIMES, Aug. 10, 2004, at B13.

13. For example, Tushnet points out "the implementation of music into a home video can help to explain how one feels and what one values" and "most Americans can probably recall some song, book, or movie that seemed so perfectly expressive of their own lives that they identified completely with it and would even explain themselves to other by reference to that work." 114 Yale L.J. at 565.

14. *See* John Tehranian, *All Rights Reserved? Reassessing Copyright and Patent Enforcement in the Digital* Age, 72 U. CIN. L. REV. 45, 52 (2003) (noting how digital technology is creating an even more pronounced distinction between physical and intellectual property).

15. For example, one need look no further than the considerable increase in the purchases of smartphones, which allow consumers ubiquitous access to intellectual property. *See* Lance Whitney, *Cell Phone, Smartphone Sales Surge*, CNET (May 19, 2010, 10:01 AM), http://news.cnet.com/8301-1035_3-20005359-94.html.

16. Liu, *supra* note 4, at 409.

17. Here, I use the term "semiotic devices" to refer to a signaling device that conveys and expresses information about aspects of an individual's identity.

18. *See* John Tehranian, *Et Tu, Fair Use? The Triumph of Natural Law Copyright*, 38 U.C. DAVIS L. REV. 465 (2005) (documenting the struggle between natural law and utilitarian conceptions of copyright law through the years).

19. *See, e.g.*, Thomas Jefferson, Letter from Thomas Jefferson to Isaac McPherson (Aug. 13, 1813), *in* THE WRITINGS OF THOMAS JEFFERSON 326, 333–34 (Albert Ellery Bergh ed., 1907) ("If nature has made any one thing less susceptible than all others of exclusive property, it is

the action of the thinking power called an idea, which an individual may exclusively possess as long as he keeps it to himself; but the moment it is divulged, it forces itself into the possession of everyone. . . . He who receives an idea from me, receives instruction himself without lessening mine. . . . That ideas should freely spread from one to another over the globe, for the moral and mutual instruction of man . . . seems to have been peculiarly and benevolently designed by nature. . . ."); James Madison, Detached Memoranda, *in* JAMES MADISON: WRITINGS 745, 756 (Jack N. Rakove ed., 1999) ("The Constitution of the U.S. has limited [monopolies] to two cases, the authors of Books, and of useful inventions, in both which they are considered as a compensation for a benefit actually gained to the community as a purchase of property which the owner otherwise might withhold from public use. There can be no just objection to a temporary monopoly in these cases: but it ought to be temporary, because under that limitation a sufficient recompense and encouragement may be given.").

20. U.S. CONST. art I,§ 8, cl. 8 (granting, with explanation, Congress the power to "promote the Progress of Science and useful Arts, by securing for limited Times to Authors and Inventors the exclusive Right to their respective Writings and Discoveries"); *see also* Copyright Act of 1790, ch. 15, 1 Stat. 124, 124 (1790) (repealed 1831) ("*An Act for the encouragement of learning*").

21. *See* JOHN LOCKE, THE SECOND TREATISE OF GOVERNMENT paras. 25–51, at 16–30 (Thomas P. Peardon ed., The Liberal Arts Press 1952) (1690). For a further examination of competing theories of property, including those of John Locke, and their influence on legal thought, see Margaret Jane Radin, *Property and Personhood*, 34 STAN. L. REV. 957 (1982).

22. *See* 2 WILLIAM BLACKSTONE, COMMENTARIES ON THE LAWS OF ENGLAND 1 (1766).

23. JOHN LOCKE, THE SECOND TREATISE OF GOVERNMENT para. 27, at 17 (Thomas P. Peardon, ed., The Liberal Arts Press 1952) (1690).

24. To Blackstone, natural law gives authors the right to deny any unauthorized use of their literal words and even styles and sentiments. An author "has clearly a right to dispose of [his work] as he pleases, and any attempt to take it from him, or vary the disposition he has made of it, is an invasion of his right to property." *See* 2 BLACKSTONE, *supra* note 22, at 405–06; *see also* Hannibal Travis, *Pirates of the Information Infrastructure: Blackstonian Copyright and the First Amendment*, 15 BERKELEY TECH. L.J. 777, 783 (2000) (arguing that a Blackstonian vision of copyright embraces the author's "'sole and despotic dominion' over a given work, a right of 'total exclusion' asserted in perpetuity against any attempt to imitate the sentiments, vary the disposition, or derive any social or economic value from a work." (quoting 2 WILLIAM BLACKSTONE, COMMENTARIES ON THE LAWS OF ENGLAND 400, 405 (1766)).

25. Margaret Jane Radin, *Property and Personhood*, 34 STAN. L. REV. 957, 977–78 (1982) (noting that Hegel's various insights—"the notion that the will is embodied in things"; the idea that freedom, in the form of rational self-determination, is "only possible in the context of a group (the properly organized and fully developed state)"; and the view of "objective community morality in the intuition that certain kinds of property relationships can be presumed to bear close bonds to personhood"—provide a strong case in favor of property for personhood).

26. *See id.* at 960–61 ("Once we admit that a person can be bound up with an external 'thing' in some constitutive sense, we can argue that by virtue of this connection the person should be accorded broad liberty with respect to control over that 'thing.'. . . [T]here is such a thing as property for personhood because people become bound up with 'things.'"). It is important to note that Radin's influential work did not embrace wholesale propertization without reservations. While she urged strong property rights for certain items bound in personhood, she cautioned that "[s]ome objects may approach the fungible end of the continuum so that the justification for protecting them as specially related to persons disappears." *Id.* at 1005.

27. *Id.* at 972.

28. *See* Cyrill P. Rigamonti, *The Conceptual Transformation of Moral Rights*, 55 AM. J. COMP. L. 67 (2007) (arguing it "has long been a basic tenet of comparative copyright theory that American and European copyright systems differ primarily in their attitudes towards the protection of moral rights of authors. . . . [W]hile the exclusive rights contained in the U.S. Copyright Act were limited to 'economic' rights . . . the copyright statutes of France, Germany, and Italy also included 'moral' rights designed to protect the non-economic interests of authors in their works."). *Id.*

29. *See* Berne Convention for the Protection of Literary and Artistic Works, art. 6bis(1) Sept. 9, 1886, 25 U.S.T. 1341, 828 U.N.T.S. 221 ("Independent of the author's economic rights, and even after the transfer of the said rights, the author shall have the right to claim authorship of the work and to object to any distortion, mutilation or other modification of, or derogatory action in relation to, the said work, which would be prejudicial to his honor or reputation.").

30. 537 U.S. 186 (2003). In the suit, Eric Eldred, an Internet publisher, challenged the constitutionality of the Sonny Bono Copyright Term Extension Act ("CTEA"), which had extended all subsisting copyrights by an additional twenty years. Copyright Term Extension Act, Pub. L. No. 105-298, 112 Stat. 2827 (1998). The CTEA prevented a number of works scheduled to lose their copyright protection from entering the public domain between 1998 and 2018. Chris Sprigman, *The Mouse That Ate the Public Domain, the Copyright Term Extension Act, and Eldred v. Ashcroft*, FINDLAW, Mar. 5, 2002, http://writ.news.findlaw.com/ commentary/20020305_sprigman.html. Eldred and the other plaintiffs relied upon the entry of works into the public domain for their activities. *Eldred*, 537 U.S. at 193. Eldred, for example, owned Eldritch Press, a website where he would make public domain works available to the public without cost. Sprigman, *supra*.

31. 17 U.S.C. §§ 302(a), 302(c), 304 (2006).

32. *Eldred*, 537 U.S. at 192.

33. *Id.* at 194.

34. *Id.* at 218–19.

35. *Id.* at 221 (emphasis added).

36. For example, George Harrison, whom Beatles fans would surely defend as a creator of the first order, was famously and successfully found liable for subconscious infringement when he purportedly usurped key elements from the Chiffons-1963 hit "He's So Fine" in composing his song "My Sweet Lord". *See* Bright Tunes Music Corp. v. Harrisongs Music, Ltd., 420 F. Supp. 177 (S.D.N.Y. 1976).

37. *Eldred*, 537 U.S. at 242–43 (Breyer, J., dissenting).

38. *Id.* at 243.

39. *Id.* at 244.

40. *See id.* at 267 ("[I]f an author expects to live 30 years after writing a book, the copyright extension (by increasing the copyright term from 'life of the author plus 50 years' to 'life of the author plus 70 years') increases the author's expected income from that book—i.e., the economic incentive to write—by no more than about 0.33%."); *see also id.* at 254–55 ("Using assumptions about the time value of money provided us by a group of economists (including five Nobel prize winners), . . . it seems fair to say that, for example, a 1% likelihood of earning $100 annually for 20 years, starting 75 years into the future, is worth less than seven cents today . . . .What potential Shakespeare, Wharton, or Hemingway would be moved by such a sum? What monetarily motivated Melville would not realize that he could do better for his

grandchildren by putting a few dollars into an interest-bearing bank account?" (internal citations omitted)).

41. *Id.* at 250.

42. *Id.* at 222–23 (Stevens, J., dissenting).

43. *Id.* at 226–27.

44. *See, e.g.*, Radin, *supra* note 25, at 1015 (noting that the case is strongest for recognizing personhood interests in property "where without the claimed protection of property as personal, the claimants' opportunities to become fully developed persons in the context of our society would be destroyed or significantly lessened, and probably also where the personal property rights are claimed by individuals who are maintaining and expressing their group identity."); Robert C. Bird & Lucille M. Ponte, *Protecting Moral Rights in the United States and the United Kingdom: Challenges and Opportunities Under the U.K.'s New Performances Regulations*, 24 B.U. INT'L L.J. 213, 217–218 (2006) (noting that moral rights are premised on the protection of an artist's personhood interests and the idea that "the artistic person cannot ever be separated fully or distinctly from her creative works.").

45. *Eldred*, 537 U.S. at 194–96 (detailing the history of copyright terms under federal law). Admittedly, however, extension terms were dependent on the author's survival at the time of renewal eligibility. *Id.* at 201 n.6. For example, under the 1790 Copyright Act, a copyright lasted fourteen years and could be extended for another fourteen years if, and only if, the author both survived the initial term and applied for the renewal. Copyright Act of 1790, ch. 15, § 1, 1 Stat. 124 (repealed 1831).

46. Copyright Term Extension Act, Pub. L. No. 105-298, 112 Stat. 2827 (1998).

47. JAMES BOYLE, SHAMANS, SOFTWARE, & SPLEENS: LAW AND THE CONSTRUCTION OF THE INFORMATION SOCIETY 51–60 (1996); James Boyle, *The Search for an Author: Shakespeare and the Framers*, 37 AM. U. L. REV. 625, 629 (1988); Peter Jaszi, *Toward a Theory of Copyright: The Metamorphoses of "Authorship,"* 1991 DUKE L.J. 455, 455–63 (1991).

48. *See* 15 U.S.C. 1125(a) (prohibiting false designations of origin and false advertising likely to cause consumer consumer confusion). The Lanham Act's prohibitions against false designations of origin and false advertising have been read to include moral rights-style claims against mutilation and false attribution. *See, e.g.*, Gilliam v. ABC, 538 F.2d 14 (2d Cir. 1976) (holding that the unauthorized bowdlerization of several *Monty Python* episodes by ABC could give rise to a cognizable legal claim against the broadcaster under the Lanham Act). As the *Gilliam* court reasoned:

> American copyright law, as presently written, does not recognize moral rights or provide a cause of action for their violation, since the law seeks to vindicate the economic, rather than the personal, rights of authors. Nevertheless, the economic incentive for artistic and intellectual creation that serves as the foundation for American copyright law cannot be reconciled with the inability of artists to obtain relief for mutilation or misrepresentation of their work to the public on which the artists are financially dependent. Thus courts have long granted relief for misrepresentation of an artist's work by relying on theories outside the statutory law of copyright, such as contract law or the tort of unfair competition. Although such decisions are clothed in terms of proprietary right in one's creation, they also properly vindicate the author's personal right to prevent the presentation of his work to the public in a distorted form.

Id. at 24 (internal citations omitted).

49. *See* Visual Artists Rights Act of 1990, 17 U.S.C. § 106A (2006) (granting rights of integrity and attribution for certain works of visual art).

50. Jaszi, *supra* note 47.

51. A sympathetic appeal to the fundamental personhood interests that artists have in the products of their intellectual creation has often been raised when artists and writers—Mark Twain and Charles Dickens in bygone eras, Don Henley and Sheryl Crow in recent years— have famously appeared before Congress or directly lobbied the public for statutory reform. *See, e.g., The Copyright Term Extension Act of 1995: Hearing on S. 483 Before the Senate Judiciary Committee*, 104th Cong. 56 (1995) (statement of Don Henley) ("I cut, shape, refine, and position each word and each note until I have crafted a song that I believe is true. My songs are an expression *of who I am and what I stand for*, and the laws which govern the results of my endeavors demand that people respect my work.") (emphasis added).

52. James Boyle, *Enclosing the Genome: What the Squabbles over Genetic Patents Could Teach Us*, 50 ADVANCES IN GENETICS 97, 119 (2003).

53. Madhavi Sunder, *Intellectual Property and Identity Politics: Playing with Fire*, 4 J. GENDER, RACE & JUST. 69, 71–72 (2000).

54. Madhavi Sunder, *IP³*, 59 STAN. L. REV. 257, 260 (2006) (noting "[s]cholars in both economics and law are unable to make economic sense of new [intellectual property] rights").

55. *See, e.g.*, Pierre N. Laval, *Toward a Fair Use Standard*, 103 HARV. L. REV. 1105, 1124 (1990) ("The utilitarian concept underlying the copyright promises authors the opportunity to realize rewards in order to encourage them to create.").

56. *See, e.g.*, Neil W. Netanel, *Why Has Copyright Expanded? Analysis and Critique, in* 6 NEW DIRECTIONS IN COPYRIGHT LAW 3, 24 (Fiona Macmillan ed., 2007) (noting the intertwining of labor-desert theory with a romantic notion of the author to rationalize greater protectionism).

57. *See, e.g.*, Robert C. Bird, *Moral Rights: Diagnosis and Rehabilitation*, 46 AM. BUS. L.J. 407, 410 (2009) (discussing moral rights protection as premised on the notion that "artistic creation is not merely a product that can be bought or sold but rather it is a direct reflection on the author's personality, identity, and even his or her 'creative soul'").

58. Julie E. Cohen, *The Place of the User in Copyright Law*, 74 FORDHAM L. REV. 347, 349 (2005).

59. *Id.*

60. *Id.* at 373.

61. Sunder, *supra* note 53, at 70.

62. *See, e.g.*, Cohen, *supra* note 58; Tushnet, *supra* note 10; Liu, *supra* note 4.

63. We also eschew a constitutional heuristic, opting to address the raised concerns within the four corners of copyright doctrine by identifying and focusing on the specific features of our copyright regime—both extant and emerging—that result in the inadequate attention given to user interests in the formation and expression of identity. For example, in urging expanded protection for personal uses of copyrighted works, Rebecca Tushnet focuses on the idea that copies (even unauthorized) can constitute a form of speech that should be protected under the First Amendment. Tushnet, *supra* note 10, at 590 ("We should struggle against the impulse to tell only one story about . . . how copyright interacts with the First Amendment. Sometimes a copy is just a copy; other times it is vitally important speech."). Yet for all of its potential and merit, this approach has largely failed in practice as courts have generally rejected independent constitutional scrutiny of copyright on free speech grounds. Jennifer Rothman, *Liberating Copyright: Thinking Beyond Free Speech*, 95 CORNELL L. REV. 463, 478 (2010). Interestingly, courts have appeared more receptive to conducting independent constitutional scrutiny of right of publicity claims. *See, e.g.*, Cardtoons, L.C. v. Major League

Baseball Players Ass'n, 95 F.3d 959, 972 (10th Cir. 1996) (upholding the free speech rights of trading card company to sell parody baseball cards without the permission of the major league players featured on the cards, despite a right of publicity claim). Moving beyond the free speech paradigm, Jennifer Rothman has proposed that the Fourteenth Amendment might serve as a vehicle to vindicate the fundamental liberty interests at play in the use of cultural content. Rothman, *supra* note 63, at 478. Rothman "situate[s] certain types of uses of copyrighted works—identity-based uses—in the context of long-standing substantive due process protections for identity and personhood," *id.* at 475, and argues that limitations of such uses should be subject to heightened scrutiny as they interfere with "liberty" interests protected under the Fourteenth Amendment. *Id.* at 494. In making this substantive due process argument, she provides a creative mechanism to challenge intellectual property maximalism, and gives an alternative constitutional voice to the identity interests of users. *Id.* However, a Fourteenth Amendment challenge faces numerous hurdles. Above all, to be subject to a substantive due process analysis, the allegedly fundamental liberty at stake must be "objectively, 'deeply rooted in this Nation's history and tradition.'" Washington v. Glucksberg, 521 U.S. 702, 720–21 (1997) (quoting Snyder v. Massachusetts, 291 U.S. 97, 105 (1934)). This is an exacting standard, even if it has evolved, as Rothman argues, to require only fealty to general principals rather than specific rights. Rothman, *supra* note 63, at 504 ("the Supreme Court in *Lawrence v. Texas* rejected the narrowly articulated test from *Washington v. Gluckberg* that restricted substantive due process rights only to those that are specifically rooted in history and tradition. *Lawrence* made clear that the historical and traditional grounding of the *specific* right, e.g., homosexual sodomy, is less important than the theoretical grounding of those specific rights in the broader context of historically embraced *principles* such as intimate association or personal autonomy."). While there may be perfectly good reasons to view copyright-related limitations on our rights of intimate association, cultural, linguistic and religious autonomy, and mental integrity as violations of the Fourteenth Amendment, there is little precedent to prevent courts from dismissing the constitutionalization of these interests with the exact same logic they have used to dispense with First Amendment challenges to copyright: by arguing that the Reconstructionists never recognized any incompatibility between the Fourteenth Amendment and copyright, that the two doctrines have co-existed happily for almost a sesquicentennial, and that while you have a right to make your own identity, one does not attain the right to free-ride on the identity or identity interests of others. *See* Eldred v. Ashcroft, 537 U.S. 186, 221 (2003) (rejecting a First Amendment challenge to copyright term extensions by finding that, while you have the right to make your own speech under the First Amendment, you do not necessarily have a constitutional right to make the speech of others). There is also intense skepticism about the increasing reliance on substantive due process to constitutionalize the protection of certain liberties. *See, e.g.,* Washington v. Glucksberg, 521 U.S. 702, 756 (Souter, J., concurring) (acknowledging the "skepticism of those who find the Due Process Clause an unduly vague or oxymoronic warrant for judicial review of state substantive law"); ROBERT H. BORK, SLOUCHING TOWARDS GOMORRAH 31, 118-19 (1996) (decrying substantive due process as a "momentous sham" that constitutes undemocratic legislating from the bench); JOHN HART ELY, DEMOCRACY AND DISTRUST 14–21 (1980) (challenging the legitimacy of substantive due process on the grounds that, inter alia, the very concept is an inherent contradiction in terms, much like "green pastel redness"). Thus, it is entirely possible (and even likely) that the judiciary would reject arguments that user rights to copyrighted property are deeply rooted in our country's history and tradition, and involve fundamental liberty interests on the same grand scale as choices involving abortion, *Roe v. Wade*, 410 U.S. 113 (1973), contraception, *Griswold v. Connecticut*, 381 U.S. 479 (1965), sexual conduct, *Lawrence v. Texas*, 539 U.S. 558 (2003), medical treatment, Cruzan v. Dir., Mo. Dep't of Health, 497 U.S. 261 (1990), child rearing, *Wisconsin v. Yoder*, 406 U.S. 205 (1972), and marriage, *Loving v. Virginia*, 388 U.S. 1 (1967). Thus, while there may be little danger that substantive due process will be entirely eliminated anytime soon, there is strong reason to believe the doctrine will not enjoy such a dramatic expansion as to include the identity interests of users of copyrighted material.

64. GEORG WILHELM FRIEDRICH HEGEL, PHILOSOPHY OF RIGHT para. 44, at 41 (T. Knox trans., Oxford University Press 1942) (1821).

65. As Hegel posits, "A person must translate his freedom into an external sphere in order to exist as Idea. Personality is the first, still wholly abstract, determination of the absolute and infinite will, and therefore this sphere distinct from the person, the sphere capable of embodying his freedom, is likewise determined as what is immediately different and separable from him . . . . As the concept in its immediacy, and so as in essence a unit, a person has a natural existence partly within himself and partly of such a kind that he is related to it as to an external world." *Id.* at paras. 41, 43.

66. ERVING GOFFMAN, ASYLUMS: ESSAYS ON THE SOCIAL SITUATION OF MENTAL PATIENTS AND OTHER INMATES 18–21(1961).

67. Ellen J. Langer & Judith Rodin, *The Effects of Choice and Enhanced Personal Responsibility for the Aged: A Field Experiment in an Institutional Setting*, 34 J. PERSONALITY & SOC. PSYCHOL. 191, 191 (1976).

68. *Id.* at 193–94.

69. *Id.* at 194.

70. *Id.*

71. *Id.* at 193–94.

72. *Id.* at 197; Ellen J. Langer & Judith Rodin, *Long-Term Effects of Control-Relevant Intervention with the Institutionalized Aged*, 35 J. PERSONALITY & SOC. PSYCHOL. 897, 899–900 (1977).

73. *See* Frequently Asked Questions, SCION, http://www.scion.com/#faq_main (listing mission statement as "[t]o satisfy a trendsetting youthful buyer through distinctive products and an innovative, consumer-driven process" and presenting "The Scion Promise," which states the "[s]tandards that are at the heart of the Scion culture" are "Openness Flexibility Personalization").

74. Joe Mandese, *The Art of the Brand Name: Zenith Uses Canvass as Media*, MEDIAPOST NEWS, http://publications.mediapost.com/index.cfm?fuseaction=Articles.san&s=42524&Nid=19928&p=337411.

75. *See* Niko Koppel, *Are Your Jeans Sagging? Go Directly to Jail*, N.Y. TIMES, Aug. 30, 2007, at G1, *available at* http://www.nytimes.com/2007/08/30/fashion/30baggy.html (noting the hip-hop look, replete with sagging pants, "is worn as a badge of delinquency, with its distinctive walk conveying thuggish swagger and a disrespect for authority.").

76. *See* Amanda Marcotte, *Nothing New About Gender-Bending Fashion*, DOUBLE X (Nov. 19, 2009 2:55 PM), http://www.doublex.com/blog/xxfactor/nothing-new-about-gender-bending-fashion.

77. JOHN FISKE, UNDERSTANDING POPULAR CULTURE 4 (1989).

78. *Id.*

79. *Id.*

80. *Id.*

81. *Id.* at 4-5.

82. 17 U.S.C. § 106(1)–(6) (2006).

83. 15 U.S.C. §§ 1114, 1125 (2006).

84. 17 U.S.C. § 106(4)–(5).

85. *Id.* § 202 (noting ownership of copyright is separate and apart from ownership of a tangible work that embodies a copyright).

86. For example, movie studios frequently encourage potential viewers to interact with upcoming releases through a film's website. In the case of the popular *Twilight Saga*, consumers can download wallpapers, widgets, and instant messaging icons. Twilight: The Movie, http://www.twilightthemovie.com (last visited Sept. 11, 2010). Furthermore, the website encourages consumers' creation of their own *Twilight* "virtual characters" through the cyber-community of habbo.com. *See* Andrew Stewart, *'Twilight' to Get a Virtual World*, VARIETY (Sept. 2, 2009, 12:05 PM), http://www.variety.com/article/VR1118008022.html?categoryId=1009&cs=1.

87. R.E.M., IN TIME: THE BEST OF R.E.M. (Warner Bros. 2003) (liner notes for "Everybody Hurts").

88. Colin McGinn, *The Musical Mystery*, N. Y. REV. BOOKS, Mar. 6, 2008, *available at* http://www.nybooks.com/articles/archives/2008/mar/06/the-musical-mystery/ (reviewing OLIVER SACKS, MUSICOPHILIA: TALES OF MUSIC AND THE BRAIN (2008)).

89. THE LIVES OF OTHERS (Sony Classic Pictures 2007).

90. *Id.*

91. *Id.*

92. *Id.*

93. *Id.*

94. John Podhoretz, *Nightmare Come True*, THE WEEKLY STANDARD, Mar. 12, 2007, *available at http://www.weeklystandard.com/Content/Public/Articles/000/000/013/360jfrwt.asp?page=2.*

95. KURT VONNEGUT, MOTHER NIGHT, at v (Dell Publishing 1999) (1961). Vonnegut went on to warn, "so we must be careful about what we pretend to be." *Id.*

96. JEAN BAUDRILLARD, THE CONSUMER SOCIETY 25 (Sage Publications 1998) (1970); *see also* F. Vigneron & L.W. Johnson, *A Review and a Conceptual Framework of Prestige-Seeking Consumer Behavior*, 1999 ACAD. OF MARKETING SCI. REV. 1, 4, *available at* http://www.amsreview.org/articles/vigneron01-1999.pdf.

97. *See generally* THORSTEIN VEBLEN, THE THEORY OF THE LEISURE CLASS (Random House 1934) (1899) (coining the term "conspicuous consumption" to refer to the act of using one's consumption activities to manifest social power); Stephen Wearing & Betsy Wearing, *Smoking as a Fashion Accessory in the 90s: Conspicuous Consumption, Identity and Adolescent Women's Leisure Choices*, 19 LEISURE STUD. 45, 46 (2000) (defining *conspicuous consumption* as "the purchase of goods for display as a means of asserting privilege and status").

98. DON SLATER, CONSUMER CULTURE AND MODERNITY 132 (1997).

99. *Id.*

100. Since 2006, media conglomerate News Corp. has owned MySpace. *See News Corp in $580m Internet Buy*, BBC NEWS (July 19, 2005, 9:03 AM), http://news.bbc.co.uk/2/hi/business/4695495.stm.

101. Facebook, http://www.facebook.com (last visited Sept. 11, 2010).

102. *See* Mark Bartholomew, *Advertising and Social Identity*, 58 BUFF. L. REV. 931, 942 (2010) (noting how MySpace users decorate their pages with trademarks to reflect identity interests).

103. *See supra*, note 97.

104. *See* Brandon23baller, *LeBron James Rapping*, YOUTUBE (Jan. 21, 2010), http://www.youtube.com/watch?v=sDMReUKuApE&feature=fvw.

105. 17 U.S.C. § 105 17 U.S.C. § 105 (2006) (deeming that "[c]opyright protection under this title is not available for any work of the United States Government. . . .").

106. As section 105 of the Copyright Act provides, the exemption for copyright in federal government works does not "preclude[]" the federal government "from receiving and holding copyrights transferred to it by assignment, bequest, or otherwise." *Id.*

107. *Id.*

108. Provided the changes or additions possess the requisite originality, a new copyright can be secured for the revised flag. *See, e.g.*, Waldman Publ'g Corp. v. Landoll, Inc., 43 F.3d 775, 782 (2d Cir. 1994) (noting that, to qualify for protection as a derivative work and to be separately copyrightable, the derivative must contain "a distinguishable variation that is more than merely trivial" and that "[t]he test of originality is concededly a low threshold"). Of course, the new copyright would only extend to the new elements in the flag.

109. The language of section 105 only refers to "any work of the United States Government." 17 U.S.C. § 105. So, for example, although federal statutes such as the United States Code are not protected by copyright law, states and municipalities have occasionally asserted copyright protection over their laws. In 2008, for example, Oregon's Office of Legislative Counsel began sending out cease and desist letters to a number of online entities such as Justia and PublicResource.org, claiming infringement of the Oregon Revised Statutes. *See* Cory Doctorow, *Oregon: Our Laws Are Copyrighted and You Can't Publish Them*, BOINGBOING (Apr. 15, 2008, 10:26 PM), http://www.boingboing.net/2008/04/15/oregon-our-laws-are.html.

110. The government would need to circumvent the provisions of section 109(c), which allow certain automatic display rights for owners of a legitimate copy of a copyright worked, but that might be accomplished by characterizing every "sale" of a flag as merely a license, subject to certain terms and conditions. *See* 17 U.S.C. § 109(c) (2006).

111. Copyright law, of course, provides plaintiffs who have timely registered their copyrighted works with the option of recovering statutory damages, even in instances where actual damages did not occur or would be impossible to prove. *Id.* § 501(c)(1).

112. Fair use, of course, could theoretically protect many interests, including the personhood interests discussed herein, by shielding individuals from liability over claims of copyright infringement. However, the fair use protections are inadequate in practice for a number of reasons. Among others, fair use is notoriously ambiguous, provides no *ex ante* protection against costly copyright litigation, and constitutes an affirmative defense for which a defendant bears the burden of proof. *See generally*, Tehranian, *supra* note 18. Moreover, most of the fair use factors focus on what is being taken from a rightsholder, rather than on what kind of use is being made of the work. As such, the fair use test, as presently constituted, adopts a strong natural-law vision of authorial rights. *Id.* at 508.

113. 17 U.S.C. § 106(2) (2006).

114. Texas v. Johnson, 491 U.S. 397 (1989).

115. United States v. Eichman, 496 U.S. 310 (1990).

116. Eldred v. Ashcroft, 537 U.S. 186, 221 (2003).

117. For example, in *Munoz v. Albuquerque* the Ninth Circuit affirmed an Alaskan federal district court's decision that the mounting of purchased art works on a tile constituted the creation of a derivative work in violation on the Copyright Act. Munoz v. Albuquerque A.R.T. Co., 38 F.3d 1218 (9th Cir. 1994) (not for publication), *aff'g* 829 F. Supp. 309 (D. Alaska 1993); *see also* Mirage Editions, Inc. v. Albuquerque A.R.T. Co., 856 F.2d 1341 (9th Cir.1988), *cert. denied*, 489

U.S. 1018 (1989); *but see* Lee v. A.R.T. Co., 125 F.3d 580 (7th Cir. 1997) (rejecting the logic of *Munoz* and *Mirage Editions*).

118. *See, e.g.*, Gilliam v. Am. Broad. Co., 538 F.2d 14, 21 (2d Cir. 1976) (finding "the unauthorized editing of the underlying work, if proven, would constitute an infringement of the copyright in that work similar to any other use of a work that exceeded the license granted by the proprietor of the copyright").

119. 17 U.S.C. § 120(b) (2006) ("Notwithstanding the provisions of section 106(2), the owners of a building embodying an architectural work may, without the consent of the author or copyright owner of the architectural work, make or authorize the making of alterations to such building, and destroy or authorize the destruction of such building.").

120. *See Eldred*, 537 U.S. at 221.

121. *See* 17 U.S.C. § 201 (2006) (vesting ownership in a copyright and, with it, the exclusive rights secured thereunder in the author of the work unless the work is a work-made-for-hire).

122. *See id.* § 106 (granting the owner of a copyright the exclusive right to reproduce, derivatize, distribute, publicly perform, and publicly display the work).

123. *Id.* § 302(a) (granting individual authors a copyright term of their lifetime plus seventy years).

124. Anne Barron, for example, argues "[i]t has become commonplace of critical legal scholarship that copyright's primary social function is to give form to a 'Romantic' aesthetic; that the key doctrinal features of copyright law—especially the concept of authorship—have been crucially shaped by this aesthetic; and that the law of copyright is centrally oriented towards promoting forms of cultural production that comply with the core values of the Romantic movement." Anne Barron, *Copyright Law and the Claims of Art*, 4 INTELL. PROP. Q. 368, 368 (2002). *See also* Shuba Ghosh, *Enlightening Identity and Copyright*, 49 BUFF. L. REV. 1315, 1317 (2001) (noting "[c]opyright law is premised on the assumption of the 'romantic author'—the lone genius creates valuable expression"); Peter Jaszi, *On the Author Effect: Contemporary Copyright and Collective Creativity, in* THE CONSTRUCTION OF AUTHORSHIP: TEXTUAL APPROPRIATION IN LAW AND LITERATURE 29, 35 (Martha Woodmansee & Peter Jaszi eds., 1994) (positing "[t]he instance of 'moral rights' is but one example of how the Romantic conception of 'authorship' is displaying a literally unprecedented measure of ideological autonomy in legal context").

125. For example, Jessica Litman argues, "All authorship is fertilized by the work of prior authors, and the echoes of old work in new work extend beyond ideas and concepts to a wealth of expressive details. Indeed, authorship *is* the transformation and recombination of expression into new molds, the recasting and revision of details into different shapes. What others have expressed, and the ways they have expressed it, are the essential building blocks of any creative medium. If an author is successful at what she does, then something she creates will alter the landscape a little. We may not know who she is, or how what she created has varied, if only slightly, the way things seem to look, but those who follow her will necessarily tread on a ground distorted by her vision. The use of the work of other authors in one's own work inheres in the authorship process." Jessica Litman, *Copyright as Myth*, 53 U. PITT. L. REV. 235, 243–44 (1991).

126. J.M. Costa & E. Heuvelink, *Introduction: The Tomato Crop and Industry, in* TOMATOES 1, 2 (Ep Heuvelink ed., 2005).

127. The tomato was often confused with the deadly nightshade. *Id.*

128. Jefferson was a pioneer in the growing of tomatoes. *See, e.g.*, ANDREW F. SMITH, THE TOMATO IN AMERICA: EARLY HISTORY, CULTURE, AND COOKERY 28 (1994).

129. According to Silvano Serventi and Francois Sabban, the "first concrete references to the use of pasta in Italy only date back to the thirteenth or fourteenth century." SILVANO SERVENTI & FRANÇOISE SABBAN, PASTA: THE STORY OF A UNIVERSAL FOOD 10 (Antony Shugaar trans., Columbia Univ. Press 2002) (2000).

130. As Harold McGee notes, "It's a story often told, and often refuted, that the medieval traveler Marco Polo found noodles in China and introduced them to Italy." HAROLD MCGEE, ON FOOD AND COOKING: THE SCIENCE AND LORE OF THE KITCHEN 571 (Scribner 2004) (1984).

131. *See* Theopolis Fair, *Asia and Latin America in the Context of World History*, *in* ASIA IN WESTERN AND WORLD HISTORY 782, 787 (Ainslie T. Embree & Carol Gluck eds., 1997) (noting that "[b]efore 1492 black pepper was widely used, but native Americans used a totally unrelated plant of many colors, shapes and intensities. . . . The cooks of the subcontinent adopted these American peppers and cayennes and incorporated them into their dishes.").

132. K. Pushkaran, *Genetic Diversity of Bananas in South India with Specific Reference to Kerala*, *in* BANANAS AND FOOD SECURITY 199, 200 (Claudine Picq et al., eds., 1998).

133. *See* MICHAEL T. MURRAY, JOSEPH PIZZORNO & LARA PIZZORNO, THE ENCYCLOPEDIA OF HEALING FOODS 224 (2005).

134. 2 RICHARD M. JUANG, AFRICA AND THE AMERICAS: CULTURE, POLITICS, AND HISTORY 74 (2008) (noting corn is native to the Americas, and was introduced to Africa around 1500).

135. Roland Barthes, *The Death of the Author*, *in* IMAGE, MUSIC, TEXT 142, 146 (1977).

136. Christian G. Stallberg, *Towards a New Paradigm in Justifying Copyright: An Universalistic–Transcendental Approach*, 18 FORDHAM INTELL. PROP. MEDIA & ENT. L.J. 333, 337 (2008).

137. Elinor Mills, *Authors Guild Sues Google over Library Project*, CNET News, (Sept. 20, 2005, 3:12 PM), http://news.cnet.com/2100-1030_3-5875384.html.

138. Alex Pham, *Google to Allow Booksellers to Profit from Digital Library*, L.A. TIMES, Sept. 11, 2009, at B3 (noting Google continues to operate its Google Book project and has "opened its vast digital books archive to rival retailers who can access the books and sell them online").

139. In its most well-known form, "The Serenity Prayer" reads: "God grant me the serenity to accept / the things I cannot change, / courage to change the things I can, / and wisdom to know the difference." Fred R. Shapiro, *Who Wrote the Serenity Prayer?*, YALE ALUMNI MAGAZINE, July–Aug. 2008, at 34, 36, *available at* http://www.yalealumnimagazine.com/issues/2008_07/serenity.html.

140. *Id.* at 35.

141. *Id.* at 37–38. Interestingly, the prior versions of the Prayer unearthed by Shapiro were by women, all of whom were involved in some sort of volunteer or educational activity. Elisabeth Shifton, *It Takes a Master to Make a Masterpiece*, YALE ALUMNI MAGAZINE, July–Aug. 2008, at 40, *available at* http://www.yalealumnimagazine.com/issues/2008_07/serenity.html.

142. In this sense, Niebuhr may have been no different from George Harrison, who was famously found liable for subconscious infringement. *See supra* note 36.

143. Shapiro, *supra* note 139, at 39. Elizabeth Sifton, Niebuhr's daughter, has adamantly denied Shapiro's allegations. Among other things, in an intervention entitled *It Takes a Master to Make a Masterpiece*, she argues the Prayer must have come from a gifted practitioner from a particular theological context who could only have been her father. Interestingly, the title of her article immediately plays into our most romantic notions of authorship, which seek to reduce creation to a lone genius rather than to the iterative and accretive contributions of many. Shifton, *supra* note 141, at 40–41.

144. In 2009, Duke researcher Stephen Goranson found a citation to Niebuhr as being the Prayer's author in a Christian students newsletter published in 1937. Laurie Goodstein, *Serenity Prayer Skeptic Now Credits Niebuhr*, N.Y. TIMES (Nov. 27, 2009). Shapiro responded "[t]he new evidence does not prove that Reinhold Niebuhr wrote [*The Serenity Prayer*], but it does improve the likelihood that he was the originator," and he lists "The Serenity Prayer" under Niebuhr's name in the most recent edition of *The Yale Book of Quotations*. *Id.*

145. This assumes he conformed to the strictures of the 1909 Copyright Act governing at the time and filed the necessary renewal to keep the copyright in effect.

146. 17 U.S.C. § 110(3) (2006).

147. Thomas Cotter, *Accommodating the Unauthorized Use of Copyright Works for Religious Purposes under the Fair Use Doctrine and Copyright Act § 110(3)*, 22 CARDOZO ART & ENT. L.J. 43, 59 n.70 (2004).

148. The Code of Federal Regulations defines "[f]iction; nonfiction; poetry; textbooks; reference works; directories; catalogs; advertising copy; and compilations of information" as nondramatic literary works, but does not mention anything about prayers. 37 C.F.R. § 202.3(b) (1)(i) (2008).

149. Cotter, *supra* note 147, at 60.

150. U.S. CONST. amend. I.

151. 17 U.S.C. § 110(3).

152. 17 U.S.C. § 106(4) (granting to a copyright holder the exclusive right for a work's public performance).

153. *See* HAMILTON B., TWELVE STEP SPONSORSHIP: HOW IT WORKS 125 (1996).

154. *See* Thomas F. Cotter, *Gutenberg's Legacy: Copyright, Censorship, and Religious Pluralism*, 91 CALIF. L. REV. 323, 335 n.47 (2003) ("In the United States, religious works have constituted a significant portion of the works registered by copyright owners from the creation of federal copyright system in 1790.").

155. *See, e.g.,* Worldwide Church of God v. Phila. Church of God, Inc., 227 F.3d 1110 (9th Cir. 2000) (reversing a district court's finding of fair use and holding that the reproduction and dissemination of a religious text entitled *Mystery of the Ages*, the copyright to which was held by the Worldwide Church of God, constituted copyright infringement by a splinter group using the text in the course of worship); Religious Tech. Ctr. v. Henson, No. 97-16160, 1999 WL 362837 (9th Cir. June 4, 1999) (affirming liability of defendant for copyright infringement of the Church of Scientology's work entitled *NOTs 34*); Urantia Found. v. Maaherra, 895 F. Supp 1329 (D. Ariz. 1995) (rejecting defendant's First Amendment defense to plaintiff's claims of copyright infringement in religious works).

156. *See* 15 U.S.C. §§ 1114(1)(a), 1125(a) (2006) (proscribing uses in commerce of a mark that are likely to cause consumer confusion with a senior mark); *id.* § 1125(c) (proscribing uses in commerce of a mark that are likely to cause dilution (i.e., blurring or tarnishing) of a famous mark).

157. *See* 17 U.S.C. §§ 102(a), 106(1)–(6) (2006) (securing certain exclusive rights for the authors of "original works of authorship fixed in any tangible medium of expression").

158. 36 U.S.C. § 380(c) (1982) (current version at 36 U.S.C. § 220506(a) (2006)).

159. Amateur Sports Act, 36 U.S.C. § 220506.

160. S.F. Arts & Athletics, Inc. v. U.S. Olympic Comm., 483 U.S. 522, 525–27 (1987).

161. *Id.* at 528.

162. *Id.* at 533 (quoting Zacchini v. Scripps-Howard Broad. Co., 433 U.S. 562, 575 (1977)).

163. *See* 15 U.S.C. §§ 1114(1)(a), 1125(a) (2006) (requiring a likelihood of consumer confusion and use in commerce for a trademark holder to prevail in a federal infringement action).

164. Although trademark law provides intellectual property protection of certain phrases and even single words, such protection is unavailable for generic terms, 15 U.S.C. § 1052(f) (2006), and is typically limited to cases where consumer confusion might result. *Id.* § 1066 (allowing denial of a trademark application if the mark so resembles a previously registered mark that it would be likely "to cause confusion or mistake or to deceive"). Of course, the consumer confusion rationale of trademark law has already begun to fade as the courts have expanded the reach of trademark protection in recent years, and as states have granted anti-dilution protections to certain "strong" trademarks. *See, e.g.,* N.Y. Gen. Bus. L. § 360-L (McKinney 2009). Also, Congress has amended the Lanham Act to include special anti-dilution protection for famous marks. *See* Federal Trademark Dilution Act of 1995 § 3, 15 U.S.C. § 1125(c).

165. As an aside, there were several levels of irony in the Supreme Court's *SFAA* decision. First of all, the Court upheld a statute assigning ownership of the term *Olympic* to the *United States* Olympic Committee when it was the Greeks who had actually "invented" the term. If anyone were to own a monopoly on the term, one might fairly question why it was not an Hellenic organization. Secondly, the SFAA's Gay Olympics were probably more true to the original Olympics than their modern, corporate incarnation. Like the ancient Greek games, the Gay Olympics included openly gay participants and involved pure amateurs rather than professional athletes.

166. Int'l Olympic Comm. v. S.F. Arts & Athletics, Inc., 789 F.2d 1319, 1321 (9th Cir. 1986) (Kozinski, J., dissenting from denial of petition for rehearing and suggestion for rehearing en banc).

167. Jim Buzinski, *In Beijing Olympics, Only 10 Openly Gay Athletes*, OUTSPORTS.COM (August 5, 2008, 9:56 PM), http://www.outsports.com/os/index2.php?option=com_content&task=view&id=111&pop=1&page.

168. 403 U.S. 15, 16–17 (1971).

169. *Id.* at 26.

170. *Id.*

171. *Id.*

172. *See N.J. Lawmakers OK Civil Unions, Not Same-Sex Marriage,* CNN.COM (Dec. 14, 2006 6:34 PM), http://www.cnn.com/2006/POLITICS/12/14/same.sex/index.html (noting that gay and lesbian advocates decried a decision by the New Jersey legislature that gives gay and lesbian couples the privileges of marriage, but uses the term "civil unions" to describe the partnership).

173. *See* Brown v. Bd. of Educ., 347 U.S. 483, 494–05 (1954) (finding "separate educational facilities are inherently unequal").

174. *See, e.g.,* Rafaela von Bredow, *Brazil's Pirahã Tribe: Living without Numbers or Time,* SPIEGEL ONLINE (May 3, 2006), http://www.spiegel.de/international/spiegel/0,1518,414291,00.html.

175. *See, e.g.,* NOAM CHOMSKY, ASPECTS OF THE THEORY OF SYNTAX 25 (1965); STEVEN PINKER, THE LANGUAGE INSTINCT 43 (1994).

176. BENJAMIN WHORF, LANGUAGE, THOUGHT, AND REALITY 65–73 (John B. Carroll ed., 1956).

177. WITTGENSTEIN, *supra* note 2, § 5.6, at 149.

178. von Bredow, *supra* note 174; *see also* John Colapinto, *The Interpreter: Has a Remote Amazonian Tribe Upended Our Understanding of Language?*, THE NEW YORKER, April 16, 2007, at 120.

179. von Bredow, *supra* note 174.

180. Peter Gordon, *Numerical Cognition Without Words: Evidence from Amazonia*, SCIENCE, Oct. 15, 2004, at 496, *available at* http://faculty.tc.columbia.edu/upload/pg328/GordonSciencePub.pdf.

181. *Id.* As it turns out, their numerical linguistics is somewhat more nuanced. Dan Everett now states the term *hoi* (with a falling tone), which was thought to mean "one," was more elastic in its meaning and actually referred to "a small size or amount." Similarly, the term *hoi* (with a rising tone), which was thought to mean "two," was more elastic in its meaning and actually referred to "a somewhat larger size or amount." Colapinto, *supra* note 178.

182. *Id.*; *see also* Elizabeth Davies, *Unlocking the Secret Sounds of Language: Life Without Time or Numbers*, THE INDEPENDENT, May 6, 2006, http://www.independent.co.uk/news/science/unlocking-the-secret-sounds-of-language-life-without-time-or-numbers-477061.html (noting Dan Everett's failed attempt to teach the Pirahã how to count).

183. Eldred v. Ashcroft, 537 U.S. 186, 194 (2003) (detailing the history of copyright terms under federal law).

184. 17 U.S.C. § 302(a) (2006).

185. *See supra*, Part I.B.

186. Under the 1790 Copyright Act, a copyright lasted fourteen years and could be extended for another fourteen years if, and only if, the author both survived and applied for a renewal term of an additional fourteen years. Copyright Act of 1790, ch.15, § 1, 1 Stat. 124, 124 (1790).

187. Marion Sinclair, "Kookaburra Sits in the Old Gum Tree" (1934).

188. *See, e.g.*, DAN FOX, WORLD'S GREATEST CHILDREN'S SONGS 56 (2008) (including "Kookaburra" as one of the world's eighty-eight most popular and best loved children's songs).

189. James Madden, *Judge's Ruling a Win for Men at Work*, THE AUSTRALIAN July 7, 2010, at 3 (referring to the song as the "country's de facto national anthem").

190. James Madden, *Men at Work Avoid Big Royalties Payout over Origins of Land Down Under*, THE AUSTRALIAN, July 6, 2010, *available at* http://www.theaustralian.com.au/news/nation/men-at-work-avoid-big-royalties-payout-over-origins-of-hit-song-land-down-under/story-e6frg6nf-1225888404948.

191. *Id.*

192. Men at Work, "Down Under" (1981)

193. *Id.*

194. *Id.*

195. *See* 17 U.S.C. § 504(c)(2) (2006) (providing for the assessment of statutory damages of up to $150,000 per act of willful infringement, regardless of actual damages or profit stemming from the acts of the defendant).

196. Historically, there would be little question that, following a determination of liability, a court would enjoin further sales of an infringing product, as courts used to routinely grant permanent injunctions to prevailing plaintiffs in intellectual property cases, absent exceptional circumstances. *See, e.g.*, Am. Metro. Enters. of N.Y.C., Inc. v. Warner Bros. Records, Inc., 389 F.2d 903, 905 (2d Cir. 1968) ("A copyright holder in the ordinary case may be presumed to suffer irreparable harm when his right to the exclusive use of the copyrighted material is invaded."). However, in recent years, the Supreme Court has seemingly mandated a dramatic shift from this general rule. *See* eBay Inc. v. MercExchange, L.L.C., 547 U.S. 388, 391 (2006)

(explicitly rejecting adoption of a "general rule that courts will issue permanent injunctions against patent infringement absent exceptional circumstances"); New York Times Co., Inc. v. Tasini, 533 U.S. 483, 505 (2001) (finding in dicta that, under the Copyright Act, "it hardly follows from today's decision [finding infringement] that an injunction against [infringing use of the copyrighted works in question] . . . must issue"). By allowing judges the discretion to transform patent, copyright, and trademark protection from property rights to a liability regime, the Court reasserted the importance of a critical element sometimes overlooked in the adversarial setting: the public interest. *eBay Inc.*, 547 U.S. at 391. Courts therefore possess the option to order damages but allow an act of infringement to continue unabated. Noted Justice Kennedy in his *eBay* concurrence:

> When the patented invention is but a small component of the product the companies seek to produce and the threat of an injunction is employed simply for undue leverage in negotiations, legal damages may well be sufficient to compensate for the infringement and an injunction may not serve the public interest. In addition injunctive relief may have different consequences for the burgeoning number of patents over business methods, which were not of much economic and legal significance in earlier times.

eBay, 547 U.S. at 396–97 (Kennedy, J., concurring). Nevertheless, injunctive relief still generally follows an infringement verdict.

197. Kim Arlington, *Infringement Down Under*, THE SYDNEY MORNING HERALD, Feb. 10, 2010, http://www.smh.com.au/news/entertainment/music/men-at-works-down-under-ripped-off-kookaburra-court/2010/02/04/1265151932344.html.

198. Notes Matthew Westwood, an arts journalist in Australia, "It's a very typical Australian sound—a bush sound. That's why I think it's really mean-spirited to say, 'Hey, this is theft,' if it's something that comes from nature." Neda Ulaby, *A Kookaburra Causes Trouble 'Down Under'*, NPR MUSIC (Dec. 1, 2009), http://www.npr.org/templates/story/story.php?storyId=120984958.

199. *See supra* note 97 and accompanying text.

200. *See, e.g.*, Australia-United States Free Trade Agreement, U.S.-Aus., art. 17, May 18, 2004, 118 Stat. 919 (granting an additional twenty-year term to Australian copyrights).

201. As Justice Breyer has rhetorically asked: "How will extension help today's Noah Webster create new works 50 years after his death?" Eldred v. Ashcroft, 537 U.S. 186, 255 (2003) (Breyer, J., dissenting).

202. *Id.* at 251.

203. 17 U.S.C. § 107 (2006).

204. STEVEN ROGER FISCHER, A HISTORY OF READING 59 (2003).

205. *Id.* at 58.

206. *Id.* ("Every ship that put in at Alexandria, one of the world's major ports, had to hand over for copying any scrolls it was carrying. Greek Egypt's ambassadors borrowed scrolls from other Greek libraries for copying. . . . Many Greeks gave scrolls to the Library, while others lent theirs to be copied. Some fraudsters even sold Library officials apocryphal treatises by 'Aristotle' (only centuries later proved to be forgeries).").

207. *Id.*

208. Barbara Krasner-Khait, *Survivor: The History of the Library*, HISTORY MAG. (Oct./Nov. 2001), *available at* http://www.history-magazine.com/libraries.html. Legend has it that, in many cases, the original was kept and it was a mere copy that was returned. *Id.*

209. Here, of course, we use the word "infringement" as it is understood under modern law.

210. James Burke recounts this story in the television series *Connections: Death in the Morning* (Season One, Episode Two, 1978).

211. Krasner-Khait, *supra* note 208.

212. Section 109(a) of the Copyright Act codifies the first sale doctrine, which was first enunciated by the Supreme Court in *Bobbs-Merrill Co. v. Straus*, 210 U.S. 339, 350 (1908) (holding "the copyright statutes, while protecting the owner of the copyright in his right to multiply and sell his production, do not create the right to impose, by notice, such as is disclosed in this case, a limitation at which the book shall be sold at retail by future purchasers, with whom there is no privity of contract"). Notably, section 109 exempts computer programs and sound recordings from certain aspects of the first sale doctrine. 17 U.S.C. § 109(b).

213. 17 U.S.C. § 106(3).

214. *See* Henry Sprott Long III, Note, *Reconsidering the "Balance" of the "Digital First Sale" Debate: Re-Examining the Case for a Statutory Digital First Sale Doctrine to Facilitate Second-Hand Digital Media Markets*, 59 ALA. L. REV. 1183, 1191 (2008) (noting the software industry's prevalent use of "click-wrap" licenses).

215. 17 U.S.C. § 109(a).

216. *See* Long, *supra* note 214, at 1191.

217. *See, e.g.*, ProCD v. Zeidenberg, 86 F.3d 1447, 1453–55 (7th Cir. 1996) (upholding the validity and enforceability of a "shrink wrap license" on a CD-ROM despite claims that the license was preempted under the Copyright Act).

218. *See* Joshua Crum, *The Day the (Digital) Music Died: Bridgeport, Sampling Infringement, and a Proposed Middle Ground*, 2008 BYU L. REV. 943, 949–50 (2008).

219. *Id.* at 949 (noting that "[u]pon gaining independence from Britain, most states instituted their own copyright schemes under the Articles of Confederation").

220. Gillian K. Hadfield, *The Economics of Copyright: A Historical Perspective*, in THE ECONOMICS OF INTELLECTUAL PROPERTY 129, 138–39 (R. Towse & R.W. Holzhauer eds., 2002).

221. ALAN STORY, STUDY ON INTELLECTUAL PROPERTY RIGHTS, THE INTERNET, AND COPYRIGHT 48 (2002).

222. *See id.*

223. *Id.*

224. *Id.*

225. For example, the Library of Congress has instituted a "Preserving Creative America" initiative designed to archive creative content in digital form. *Digital Preservation Program Makes Awards to Preserve American Creative Works*, THE LIBRARY OF CONGRESS (Aug. 3, 2007), http://www.loc.gov/today/pr/2007/07-156.html.

226. According to Iomega, the company that invented the Zip drive, "On March 24, 1995, Iomega shipped the first Zip drive. . . . The Zip drive became one of the fastest selling, most successful peripherals in the history of computing. . . . [T]he Zip product line generate[d] $1.2 billion in sales annually from 1997 through 1999." *Iomega: 25 Years of Storage Technology Leadership*, IOMEGA (last visited Sept. 15, 2010), http://www.iomega.com/25years/index.html.

227. *See* 17 U.S.C. § 106 (2006) (setting out the exclusive rights to which a copyright holder is entitled under federal law).

228. Under the 1909 Copyright Act (and the 1790 and 1831 Acts that preceded it), publication was a prerequisite for federal copyright protection. *See* Paul Goldstein, *Federal System Ordering of the Copyright Interest*, 69 COLUM. L. REV. 49, 51 (1969) (writing, prior to the enactment of the 1976 Copyright Act, that "[p]ublication defines . . . not only the line separating common

law from statutory copyright but, as well, the traditional border between state and federal competence over the copyright interest").

229. Harper & Row v. Nation Enter., 471 U.S. 539, 554 (1985) (holding there is a heavy presumption against fair use of unpublished works).

230. *See, e.g.*, 17 U.S.C. § 115 (2006) (limiting the compulsory mechanical license to published musical compositions).

231. 1 MELVILLE B. NIMMER, NIMMER ON COPYRIGHT § 2.02 (1978). *See, e.g.*, CAL. CIV. CODE § 980 (Deering 1941)) ("The author of any product of the mind, whether it is an invention, or a composition in letters or art, or a design, with or without delineation, or other graphical representation, has an exclusive ownership therein, and in the representation or expression thereof, which continues so long as the product and the representations or expressions thereof made by him remain in his possession.") (amended 1947).

232. This is, of course, no longer the case. With the operation of section 303 of the Copyright Act, common law copyright protection for works that had never been published or registered was eliminated as of January 1, 2003. 17 U.S.C. § 303 (2006).

233. Copyright Act of 1909, § 23, 35 Stat. 1075 (1909) (extending federal copyright protection to an initial term of twenty-eight years with a one-time renewal term of twenty-eight years, dating from the first publication with proper notice).

234. 17 U.S.C. § 106 (2006).

235. Fortnightly Corp. v. United Artists Television, Inc., 392 U.S. 390, 393–95 (1968) (footnotes omitted).

236. 17 U.S.C. § 106(4) (limiting the performance right to those performances that are public).

237. Twentieth Century Music Corp. v. Aiken, 422 U.S. 151, 155 (1975).

238. *See* 17 U.S.C. § 106(1)–(6).

239. *See id.*

240. Arguably, ever-expanding secondary infringement doctrine might someday result in a knowing payment for an illegal copy of a copyrighted work constituting sufficient material contribution to infringement as to support a finding of liability against a purchaser (but not mere possessor) of an unauthorized copy.

241. *See, e.g.*, OR. REV. STAT. § 819.300 (2009) ("A person commits the offense of possession of a stolen vehicle if the person possesses any vehicle which the person knows or has reason to believe has been stolen. . . . The offense described in this section, possession of a stolen vehicle, is a Class C felony.").

242. *See, e.g.*, CONN. GEN. STAT. § 21a-279(a)(2009) (stating that those convicted of a first-time offense of possession of narcotics can face up to seven years imprisonment and up to a $50,000 fine).

243. Miller v. California, 413 U.S. 15, 19–20 (1973). Under *Miller*, a work cannot be deemed obscene and, therefore, banned by the government unless a trier of fact determines that:

> (a) "the average person, applying contemporary community standards" would find that the work, taken as a whole, appeals to the prurient interest; (b) . . . the work depicts or describes, in a patently offensive way, sexual conduct specifically defined by the applicable state law; and (c) . . . the work, taken as a whole, lacks serious literary, artistic, political, or scientific value.

Id. at 24 (internal citations omitted).

244. 394 U.S. 557 (1969). Importantly, the Supreme Court has refused to extend the *Stanley* exception to child pornography. As a result, punishing creation, distribution, *and* possession of child pornography is constitutionally permissible. *See* New York v. Ferber, 458 U.S. 747, 765 (1982) (rejecting a First Amendment challenge to a law proscribing child pornography).

245. *Stanley*, 394 U.S. at 564 ("fundamental is the right to be free, except in very limited circumstances, from unwanted governmental intrusions into one's privacy").

246. *Id.* ("[T]he Constitution protects the right to receive information and ideas. . . . This right to receive information and ideas, regardless of their social worth . . . is fundamental to our free society.").

247. *See, e.g.,* Roth v. United States, 354 U.S. 476, 485 (1954) ("[O]bscenity is not within the area of constitutionally protected speech or press"), *abrogated on other grounds by* Memoirs v. Massachusetts, 383 U.S. 413 (1966), *as recognized in* Marks v. United States, 430 U.S. 188, 193 (1977).

248. *See, e.g.,* Eldred v. Ashcroft, 537 U.S. 186, 221 (2003).

259. *Stanley*, 394 U.S. at 565.

250. Miller v. California, 413 U.S. 15, 24 (1973).

251. *Stanley*, 394 U.S. at 565.

252. Mark Bartholomew & John Tehranian, *The Secret Life of Legal Doctrine: The Divergent Evolution of Secondary Liability in Trademark and Copyright Law*, 21 BERKELEY TECH. L.J. 1363, 1365 (2006).

253. *See* Jay Dratler, Jr., *Common-Sense (Federal) Common Law Adrift in a Statutory Sea, or Why* Grokster *was a Unanimous Decision*, 22 SANTA CLARA COMP. & HIGH TECH. L.J. 413, 419 (2006).

254. *See* 17 U.S.C. § 1201(c)(2) (2006) ("Nothing in this section shall enlarge or diminish vicarious or contributory liability for copyright infringement in connection with any technology, product, service, device, component, or part thereof.").

255. *See* H.R. REP. No. 94-1476, at 61 (1976), *reprinted in* 1976 U.S.C.C.A.N. 5659, 5674 ("The Exclusive rights accorded to a copyright owner under section 106 are 'to do and to authorize' any of the activities specified in the five numbered clauses. Use of the phrase 'to authorize' is intended to avoid any questions as to the liability of contributory infringers. For example, a person who lawfully acquires an authorized copy of a motion picture would be an infringer if he or she engages in the business of renting it to others for purposes of unauthorized public performance.").

256. *Inwood Laboratories Inc. v. Ives Laboratories Inc.*, 456 U.S. 844 (1982) represents the seminal case in secondary trademark liability jurisprudence. In *Ives*, the Supreme Court confirmed the application of secondary liability principles to trademark law by holding that a trademark owner could hold the manufacturer of a generic drug contributorily liable for the actions of pharmacists. *Id.* at 853–54. Although not elaborating on the justification for importing tort principles into the federal trademark regime, the Court affirmed that liability for trademark infringement can extend past those who actually "use" a protected mark as it imposed indirect liability on Inwood. *Id.* at 853–54. Similarly, in *Kalem Co. v. Harper Bros.*, 222 U.S. 55, 63 (1911), the Supreme Court affirmed the application of secondary liability doctrines to copyright infringement. The Court held the producer of an unauthorized film dramatization of the copyrighted book *Ben Hur* was liable for his sale of the film to middlemen who arranged for the film's commercial exhibition. *Id.* The Court explained that although the producer did not take part in the final act of infringement—the exhibition of the infringing film to paying customers—his contribution was sufficient to make him secondarily liable. *Id.* Although *Ives*

and *Kalem Co.* involved contributory liability claims, the decisions imply that both types of secondary liability theories—contributory and vicarious—are available to copyright and trademark plaintiffs.

257. Perfect 10, Inc. v. Visa Int'l Serv. Ass'n, 494 F.3d 788, 794–95, 800 (9th Cir. 2007).

258. *See* Gershwin Publ'g Corp. v. Columbia Artists Mgmt., Inc., 443 F.2d 1159, 1162 (2d Cir. 1971).

259. *See id.*

260. For example, the Ninth Circuit has suggested a more lax standard for considering whether a third party has materially contributed to an act of infringement "in the context of cyberspace," since "services or products that facilitate access to websites throughout the world can significantly magnify the effects of otherwise immaterial infringing activities." Perfect 10, Inc. v. Amazon.com, Inc., 487 F.3d 701, 728 (9th Cir. 2007); *see also* Mark Bartholomew, *Cops, Robbers, and Search Engines: The Questionable Role of Criminal Law in Contributory Infringement Doctrine*, 2009 B.Y.U. L. REV. 783, 792 (2009).

261. *See, e.g.*, Fonovisa, Inc. v. Cherry Auction, Inc., 76 F.3d 259, 264 (9th Cir. 1996).

262. RCA Records v. All-Fast Sys., Inc., 594 F. Supp. 335, 336–37 (S.D.N.Y. 1984).

263. *Fonovisa*, 76 F.3d at 264 (finding contributory liability where defendants provided "space, utilities, parking, advertising, plumbing, and customers" to direct infringers).

264. *Id.*

265. Religious Tech. Ctr. v. Netcom On-line Commc'n Servs., Inc., 907 F. Supp. 1361, 1375 (N.D. Cal. 1995).

266. *See* 17 U.S.C. § 512 (2006).

267. *See* Metro-Goldwyn-Mayer Studios, Inc. v. Grokster, Ltd., 545 U.S. 913, 930 (2005).

268. Perfect 10, Inc. v. Visa Int'l Serv. Ass'n, 494 F.3d 788 (9th Cir. 2007).

269. *Id.* at 810–25.

270. *Id.* at 811–16.

271. *Id.* at 816–22.

272. *Id.* at 801.

273. Salinger v. Colting, 641 F. Supp. 2d 250 (S.D.N.Y. 2009), *aff'd, by* 607 F.3d 68 (2d Cir. 2010).

274. In 2008, Mattel brought a billion dollar copyright suit to protect its stumbling Barbie line from upstart challenger MGA, maker of the Bratz dolls, an edgy line of alternative playthings for young girls introduced in 2001. Bryant v. Mattel, No. CV 04-9049 SGL (RNBx). 2008 U.S. Dist. LEXIS 107208 (2008); *see* Edvard Pettersson & Heather Burke, *Mattel Wins Millions if Bratz Born in Barbie's Family*, May 13, 2008, *available at* http://www.bloomberg.com/apps/news?pid=20601109&sid=ajNk6SgVwXOo ("Barbie, originally all-blonde and all-suburban, has had a place on toy shop shelves since 1959. Since the advent of Bratz in 2001, sales have slipped. Mattel reported April 21 that U.S. Barbie sales fell in the first quarter by 12 percent."); Pallavi Gogoi, *Mattel's Barbie Trouble*, BUSINESS WEEK, July 18, 2006, *available at* http://www.businessweek.com/bwdaily/dnflash/content/jul2006/db20060717_170105.htm (noting eleven consecutive quarters of decreased sales for the Barbie franchise). Although the initial verdict for Mattel and the permanent injunction issued against MGA were later vacated on appeal, for a time, MGA could produce or market virtually no dolls in Bratz, as they would be considered an infringement of Mattel's rights. *See* Mattel, Inc. v. MGA Entertainment, Inc., 616 F.3d 904 (9th Cir. 2010).

275. *See, e.g.*, Complaint, Blackwell Publ., Inc. v. Miller, No. 07-12731 (E.D. Mich. June 28, 2007), 2007 U.S. Dist. Ct. Pleadings LEXIS 8893.

276. For example, the Complaint in *Blackwell Publ, Inc. v. Miller* states that, "by providing the means of reproduction and charging for their use [the Defendant] is just as much engaged in infringement as if its own employees made the copies, and its conduct constitutes willful infringement." *Id.* ¶ 29.

277. Princeton Univ. Press v. Michigan Document Servs., 99 F.3d 1381, 1383 (6th Cir. 1996).

278. Metro-Goldwyn-Mayer Studios, Inc. v. Grokster, Ltd., 545 U.S. 913, 930 (2005) (internal citations omitted).

279. Quite simply, some sort of reproduction of the copyrighted work must exist for the work to be transmitted from the originating party's network to the receiving party's network.

280. *See, e.g.,* Cartoon Network LP v. CSC Holdings, Inc., 536 F.3d 121, 131 (2d Cir. 2008), *cert. denied,* 129 S.Ct. 2890 (2009) (holding that when a user requests a digital copy of a television broadcast to be transmitted to his or her digital video recording device, the user has engaged in an act of reproduction in defiance of section 106(1)).

281. 2 NIMMER & NIMMER § 8.02(c) (Matthew Bender rev. ed. 2010) ("[S]ubject to the privilege of fair use, and subject to certain other exemptions, copyright infringement occurs whenever an unauthorized copy . . . is made, even if it is used solely for the private purposes of the reproducer.") (footnotes omitted).

282. *Compare* 17 U.S.C. § 106(1)–(2) (2006) (requiring no public component to an act of reproduction or distribution to trigger violation of a copyright holder's exclusive rights), *with* 17 U.S.C. § 106(3)–(5) (2006) (requiring public performance or display or distribution to the public to trigger violation of a copyright holder's exclusive rights).

283. Using IP addresses, the RIAA famously sued approximately 18,000 individuals for infringing file sharing over the course of a five-year litigation campaign. *See* David Kravets, *Copyright Lawsuits Plummet in Aftermath of RIAA Campaign,* WIRED (May 18, 2010, 1:24 PM), http://www.wired.com/threatlevel/2010/05/riaa-bump/.

284. 1 ENCYCLOPEDIA OF NINETEENTH-CENTURY PHOTOGRAPHY 365 (John Hannavy ed., 2007).

285. 17 U.S.C. § 106(1) (2006). It arguably implicates another section 106 right as well: the right of public display. *Id.* at § 106(5). However, if the site is closed off to all but family members, arguably no *public* display is occurring.

286. Although the copyright holder may have given you ownership of the actual photograph, she has not assigned the copyright to you absent a written agreement. *See* 17 U.S.C. § 204(a) (requiring all transfer of copyright ownership to be "in writing and signed by the owner of the rights conveyed or such owner's duly authorized agent"). As a result, though one might argue an implied license has been given to copy the photograph, that is far from clear.

287. *See* Matthew Fagin, Frank Pasquale, & Kim Weatherall, *Beyond Napster: Using Antitrust Law to Advance and Enhance Online Music Distribution,* 8 B.U. J. SCI. & TECH. L. 451, 477–78 (2002).

288. *See* Rebecca Tushnet, *My Library: Copyright and the Role of Institutions in a Peer-to-Peer World,* 53 UCLA L. REV. 977, 1015 (2006) ("The DMCA outlaws unauthorized access in almost all circumstances, and copyright owners assert that they have total control over the terms of access, even if that involves getting rid of copyright law's limits on exclusive rights. Such limits include not just statutory fair use and statutory exceptions but even rights that copyright law does not give to owners, such as the right to control lending or private performance.").

289. *See* 17 U.S.C. § 106 (granting no unilateral exclusive "use" right to copyright holders and prohibiting only non-public actions that involve reproduction or derivation).

290. 17 U.S.C. § 1201(a)(1).

291. 17 U.S.C. § 1204(a)(1) (providing for fines of up to $500,000 and imprisonment of five years for a first offense that is willful and "for purposes of commercial advantage or private financial gain").

292. The widespread failure to give proper acknowledgement to McKenzie's directorial genius is probably a function of the fact that he does not exist. He is merely a creation of Costa Botes and Peter Jackson and is featured in their wry mockumentary on the discovery of McKenzie's long-lost masterpiece, *Forgotten Silver* (WingNut Films 1995). Following its broadcast in 1995, *Forgotten Silver* ignited widespread controversy after news reports about the long-forgotten McKenzie began to appear in legitimate publications touting the key role of this New Zealander in the history of film. Botes and Jackson ultimately had to offer a mea culpa to the citizens of their country à la Orson Welles and *War of the Worlds*. *See* MERCURY THEATER ON THE AIR: WAR OF THE WORLDS (CBS radio broadcast Oct. 30, 1938).

293. The professor could conceivably get around the anti-circumvention provisions of the DMCA. Although the DMCA bans the circumvention of *access control* measures, it does not ban the circumvention of *copy control* measures. *Compare* 17 U.S.C. § 1201(a)(1)–(2) (prohibiting the circumvention of access control measures and prohibiting the trafficking in technology designed to circumvent access controls), *with* 17 U.S.C. § 1201(b) (prohibiting the trafficking in technology designed to circumvent copy controls). According to the legislative history, Congress intended to allow individuals who had lawfully acquired a copy of a work the right to make copies of that work, regardless of the digital rights management technologies appended to it. *See* United States v. Elcom Ltd., 203 F. Supp. 2d 1111, 1120–21 (N.D. Cal. 2002) (noting Congress intended to preserve fair use rights of individuals who had lawfully obtained a copy). Thus, if the professor were to merely circumvent copy control measures, rather than access control measures, he would, in theory, not face liability: he could potentially do this by making a new copy of *Salomé* each time he wanted to watch the movie.

294. *Anti-Counterfeiting Trade Agreement*, ELECTRONIC FRONTIER FOUNDATION, http://www.eff.org/issues/acta (positing "disturbingly little information has been released about the actual content of the agreement").

295. For an examination of the broader history and significance of ACTA, see Eddan Katz & Gwen Hinze, *The Impact of the Anti-Counterfeiting Trade Agreement on the Knowledge* Economy: *The Accountability of the Office of the U.S. Trade Representative for the Creation of IP Enforcement Norms Through Executive Trade Agreement*, 35 YALE J. INT'L L. ONLINE 24 (2009), http://www.yjil.org/pubs/online/item/4-the-impact-of-acta-on-the-knowldge-ec.pdf.

296. Gwen Hinze, *Leaked ACTA Internet Provisions: Three Strikes and a Global DMCA*, ELECTRONIC FRONTIER FOUNDATION (Nov. 3, 2009), http://www.eff.org/deeplinks/2009/11/leaked-acta-internet-provisions-three-strikes-and-.

297. *See id.*

298. *See* Steven Seidenberg, *The Record Business Blues*, 96 A.B.A. J. 55, 59 (2010) (noting a "huge outcry" against the three-strikes provision and that a key concern "is that throwing people off the Internet for online infringement of copyrights would be a draconian step in an increasingly digital world").

299. Kathy McGraw, *ACTA: Why You Should Be Concerned*, DRM NEWS (Feb. 6, 2010), http://www.thedrmnews.com/miscellaneous/acta-why-you-should-be-concerned/("While it appears that the final 'strike' of complete disconnection must be administered by a judge, it is uncertain what sort of proof, if any, would be required.").

300. Greg Sandoval, *Grandma Endures Wrongful ISP Piracy Suspension*, CNET NEWS (Feb. 1, 2010, 4:00 AM), http://news.cnet.com/8301-31001_3-10444879-261.html?tag=mncol;mlt_related.

301. *Id.*

302. *Id.*

303. *Id.*

CHAPTER 4

1. Walter Benjamin, *The Work of Art in the Age of Mechanical Reproductions*, in ILLUMINATIONS (Hannah Arendt ed., Harry Zohn trans. 1968).

2. *Id.* at 224.

3. *Id.* at 221.

4. *See, e.g.,* Robert W. Sweeny, *Three Funerals and a Wedding: Simulation, Art Education, and an Aesthetics of Cloning*, 31 VISUAL ARTS RES. 60 (2005) (discussing Benjamin's theory in the context of mediating the relationship between art and developing technologies); LIZ WELLS, PHOTOGRAPHY: A CRITICAL INTRODUCTION (2004) (discussing Benjamin's argument that changes brought about by mechanical reproduction precipitated a sea change in attitudes toward the arts, especially photography); Najmeh Khalili, *Walter Benjamin Revisited: The Work of Cinema in the Age of Digital (Re)production*, OFFSCREEN, Oct 31, 2003, *available at* http://www.horschamp.qc.ca/new_offscreen/new_media.html (discussing digital media theory in light of Benjamin's work).

5. For every action, there is an equal and opposite reaction. *See* Isaac Newton, *Mathematical Principles of Natural Philosophy*, in THE AGE OF REASON 108 (Louise L. Snyder ed., 1955).

6. 17 U.S.C. § 106(1) (2006) (granting copyright holders the exclusive right to make any type of reproduction of a protected work).

7. 17 U.S.C. §§ 106(4)–(5) (2006).

8. *See* 17 U.S.C. §§ 103, 106(2) (2006).

9. Christian G. Stallberg, *Towards a New Paradigm in Justifying Copyright: An Universalistic-Transcendental Approach*, 18 FORDHAM INTELL. PROP. MEDIA & ENT. L.J. 333, 337 (2008).

10. *See, e.g.,* BÉNÉDICTE CALLAN, PIRATES ON THE HIGH SEAS: THE UNITED STATES AND GLOBAL INTELLECTUAL PROPERTY RIGHTS 1 (1998) (noting that, in recent years, the United States has "cast itself as the great proponent of intellectual property rights worldwide").

11. One might argue it is unsurprising, any aspect of our legal regime would privilege repeat players, but copyright law does so with extreme vigor. And the particular privileges copyright law grants go against conventional wisdom on the subject.

12. *See, e.g.,* Grand Upright Music, Ltd. v. Warner Bros. Records, Inc., 780 F. Supp. 182, 183 (S.D.N.Y. 1991) (concluding, upon considering the propriety of digital sampling without authorization, that "[t]hou shalt not steal").

13. *See, e.g.,* WTO, China—Measures Affecting the Protection and Enforcement of Intellectual Property Rights, http://www.wto.org/english/tratop_e/dispu_e/cases_e/-ds362_e.htm (last visited Oct. 25, 2009) (summarizing the conflict between the United States and China over the adequacy of latter country's intellectual property protection and enforcement mechanisms).

14. *See* David E. Miller, *Combating Copyright Infringement in Russia: A Comprehensive Approach for Western Plaintiffs*, 33 VAND. J. TRANSNAT'L L. 1203 (2000) (noting American corporations lose millions of dollars each year as a result of the illegal reproduction and sale of copyrighted goods in Russia).

15. Henry Hansmann & Marina Santilli, *Authors' and Artists' Moral Rights: A Comparative Legal and Economic Analysis*, 26 J. LEGAL STUD. 95, 95–97 (1997).

16. *See, e.g.*, Lawrence A. Beyer, *Intentionalism, Art and the Suppression of Innovation: Film Colorization and the Philosophy of Moral Rights*, 82 Nw. U. L. REV. 1011, 1047, 1052–54 (1988) (arguing the moral right of integrity subverts both buyer and seller freedom in market transactions involving copyrighted works); Stephen L. Carter, *Owning What Doesn't Exist*, 13 HARV. J.L. & PUB. POL'Y 99, 101 (1990) (noting the moral rights doctrine runs counter to traditional property rights notions by telling owners of paintings, films, and other works they "should not have the right to do with their possessions as they wish").

17. Peter K. Yu, *The Copyright Divide*, 25 CARDOZO L. REV. 331 (2003).

18. Harry G. Henn, *The Quest for International Copyright Protection*, 39 CORNELL L. Q. 43, 52 (1953).

19. Act of May 31, 1790, ch. 15, 1 Stat. 124, § 5.

20. Yu, *supra* note 17, at 341.

21. *See, e.g.*, R. KENT RASMUSSEN, MARK TWAIN A TO Z: THE ESSENTIAL REFERENCE TO HIS LIFE AND WRITINGS 54 (1995). Rasmussen noted:

> The absence of international copyright laws allowed Canadian publishers to prey on Mark Twain's early books. He was hurt badly in 1876, when the Toronto publisher Charles Belford issued *Tom Sawyer* before the American edition even appeared. To combat this problem, Mark Twain spent several weeks in Montreal in November–December 1881 with James R. Osgood to meet a residency requirement to protect his *The Prince and the Pauper* copyright.

Id.

22. Prior to 1891, some foreign authors circumvented America's refusal to honor copyrights of foreign authors by having an American citizen collaborate in the publishing process. Usually this would take the form of the American writing a short preface to the book and then registering the work with the U.S. Copyright Office under the collaborator's name. For example, Thomas Henry Huxley took this route to gain protection. *See, e.g.*, Philip V. Allingham, *Nineteenth-Century British and American Copyright Law*, VICTORIANWEB, Jan. 5, 2001, http://www.victorianweb.org/authors/dickens/pva/pva74.html (detailing the technical subterfuge and arduous machinations required of British authors to obtain American copyright protection both before and after 1891, respectively).

23. Chace Act, ch. 565, 26 Stat. 1106, 1110 (1891).

24. According to the Council on Foreign Relations' American Intellectual Property Rights Policy Study Group, the merely "nominal protection" of intellectual property rights and "indifference and resistance from American officials . . . to enforce copyrights for literary works" in the nineteenth century has given way in recent years to a regime of strong enforcement, with the United States "cast[ing] itself as the great proponent of intellectual rights worldwide . . . [by] tak[ing] the moral high ground in the battle against international piracy and counterfeiting, denouncing unfair practices abroad and claiming that strong rights can only help the economy in developing countries." CALLAN, *supra* note 10, at 1.

25. *See, e.g.*, James Boyle, *The Second Enclosure Movement and the Construction of the Public Domain*, 66 LAW & CONTEMP. PROBS. 33, 34–37, 40–41 (2003) (questioning the recent expansion of intellectual property monopolies by comparing it to the enclosure movement of the eighteenth century); Jessica Littman, *Creative Reading*, 70 LAW & CONTEMP. PROBS. 175, 180 (2007) (criticizing the prevailing position that any use of an existing work constitutes an infringement unless specifically exempted from liability by law); Robert P. Merges, *One Hundred Years of Solicitude: Intellectual Property Law, 1900–2000*, 88 CALIF. L. REV. 2187,

2191 (2000) (characterizing the history of intellectual property rights over the past one hundred years as a century of "solicitude" by corporate interests bent on maximizing monopoly-like protections for their intellectual properties); John Tehranian, *Et Tu, Fair Use? The Triumph of Natural-Law Copyright*, 38 U.C. DAVIS L. REV. 465, 466 (2005) (arguing "the fair use doctrine has actually enabled the expansion of the copyright monopoly well beyond its original bounds and has undermined the goals of the copyright system as envisioned by the Framers of the Constitution"); Rebecca Tushnet, *Copy This Essay: How the Fair Use Doctrine Harms Free Speech and How Copying Serves It*, 114 YALE L.J. 535 (2004) (criticizing existing copyright doctrine for failing to recognize adequately the public interest served through unauthorized non-transformative reproduction of copyrighted works); Pamela Samuelson, *The Copyright Grab*, WIRED.COM, Jan. 1996, http://www.wired.com/wired/archive/4.01/white. paper_pr.html (critiquing proposed expansions in copyright protection by the Clinton administration for their harm to the freedom and privacy of the general public).

26. *See, e.g.*, Shira Perlmutter, *Freeing Copyright from Formalities*, 13 CARDOZO ARTS & ENT. L.J. 565, 566, 568, 581 (2006). Perlmutter notes:

> Formalities have long been a hallmark of the American copyright system. . . . In the 1976 Act, Congress began the journey toward eliminating formalities from our copyright law . . . . The 1976 Copyright Act and adherence to the Berne Convention marked a sea change in U.S. copyright law—a profound shift in philosophy.

Id.; Malla Pollack, *Towards a Feminist Theory of the Public Domain, or Rejecting the Gendered Scope of United States Copyrightable and Patentable Subject Matter*, 12 WM. & MARY J. WOMEN & L. 603, 603–04 (2006) ("The Copyright Revision Act of 1976 moved the general line of protection from the point of publication to the point of fixation. In combination with the Berne Implementation Act, it eliminated most of the prior need for copyright formalities."); *see also* Pamela Brannon, *Reforming Copyright to Foster Innovation: Providing Access to Orphaned Works*, 14 J. INTELL. PROP. L. 145, 145, 158 (2006) ("Copyright protection prior to the 1976 Act was attended by a bevy of formalities. . . . The 1976 Copyright Act discarded most of these formalities, shifting to an 'opt-out' system that granted copyright protection upon the initial creation and fixation of a work."); Wendy J. Gordon, *Toward a Jurisprudence of Benefits: The Norms of Copyright and the Problem of Private Censorship*, 57 U. CHI. L. REV. 1009, 1010 (1990) ("One major reason for the increasing breadth of copyright scholarship is the 1976 Copyright Act, which simplified and rationalized the complexities and formalisms of prior law. . . ."); Matt Jackson, *The Digital Millennium Copyright Act of 1998: A Proposed Amendment to Accommodate Free Speech*, 5 COMM. L. & POL'Y 61, 71 (2000) ("Prior to the 1976 Copyright Act, authors had to comply with a laundry list of formalities in order to enjoy federal copyright protection.").

27. 17 U.S.C. § 102(a) (2006) ("Copyright protection subsists, in accordance with this title, in original works of authorship fixed in any tangible medium of expression, now known or later developed, from which they can be perceived, reproduced, or otherwise communicated, either directly or with the aid of a machine or device.").

28. 17 U.S.C. § 411(a) (2006) (requiring registration of a copyrighted work prior to the initiation of an infringement suit based thereon).

29. 2 MELVILLE B. NIMMER & DAVID NIMMER, NIMMER ON COPYRIGHT § 7.16[C][2] (2008). Nimmer states:" Under the 1909 Act . . . registration was only required . . . prior to the filing of an infringement action, and, in such an action, there might be a recovery (including, under

the 1909 Act, statutory damages and attorney's fees) with respect to infringing acts that occurred prior to, as well as after, registration." *Id.* (internal citations omitted).

30. Under the traditional American rule, parties bear the costs of their own representation, regardless of the outcome. By statute, however, prevailing plaintiffs in copyright infringement suits are eligible to receive their attorneys' fees—but only if the work was timely registered. Although the grant of fees lies squarely within the discretion of courts, prevailing plaintiffs often recover their fees. *See, e.g.*, Columbia Pictures TV v. Krypton Broad. of Birmingham, Inc., 106 F.3d 284, 296 (9th Cir. 1997) ("[A] plaintiff in a copyright action is generally awarded fees by virtue of prevailing in the action. . . .").

31. 4 NIMMER & NIMMER, *supra* note 29, § 17.01.

32. *See, e.g., id.* § 17.03 ("[U]nlike the United States copyright law, under virtually all foreign copyright laws . . . there are no administrative formalities that must be satisfied in order to create or to perfect a copyright.").

33. 2 NIMMER & NIMMER § 7.16[C][1].

34. 17 U.S.C. § 412(2) (2006).

35. *See infra* text accompanying notes 150–155.

36. AM. INTELL. PROP. LAW ASS'N, 2009 REPORT OF THE ECONOMIC SURVEY I-100 (2009).

37. *Id.* at I-101. When the amount at controversy exceeds $25 million, the mean cost of taking a case to trial is $1.292 million. *Id.*

38. Leslie Walker, *New Movement Hits Universities: Get Legal Music*, WASH. POST, Mar. 17, 2005, at E1 (noting the RIAA has filed "thousands of suits against people for sharing copyrighted material").

39. Johnson v. Jones, 149 F.3d 494, 506 (6th Cir. 1998); *accord* Derek Andrew, Inc. v. Poof Apparel Corp., 528 F.3d 696, 700–01 (9th Cir. 2008); Bouchat v. Bon-Ton Dep't Stores, Inc., 506 F.3d 315, 330 (4th Cir. 2007), *cert. denied*, 553 U.S. 1014 (2008); Troll Co. v. Uneeda Doll Co., 483 F.3d 150, 158 (2d Cir. 2007); Mason v. Montgomery Data, Inc., 967 F.2d 135, 142–44 (5th Cir. 1992).

40. *See Derek Andrew*, 528 F.3d at 701.

41. *See, e.g.*, Qualey v. Caring Ctr. of Slidell, 942 F. Supp. 1074, 1076 (E.D. La. 1996). The court noted:

> [B]ecause the defendants commenced the first alleged infringement (preparing derivative works) prior to registration and publication, plaintiff is barred from recovering statutory damages or attorneys fees not only for that specific act of infringement, but also for any subsequent infringements of the drawings commenced after registration (or within the three-month period between first publication and registration).

Id.; see also Mason, 967 F.2d at 144 (holding "a plaintiff may not recover an award of statutory damages and attorney's fees for infringements that commenced after registration if the same defendant commenced an infringement of the same work prior to registration").

42. Teevee Toons, Inc. v. Overture Records, 501 F. Supp. 2d 964, 966 (E.D. Mich. 2007).

43. *Derek Andrew*, 528 F.3d 696. The Ninth Circuit joined with the Second, Fourth, Fifth, and Sixth Circuits in barring recovery of statutory damages and fees when an infringement begins pre-registration and continues post-registration. *Id.* at 701.

44. *Id.* at 700–01.

45. 17 U.S.C. § 410(c) (2006) ("In any judicial proceedings the certificate of a registration made before or within five years after first publication of the work shall constitute prima facie evidence of the validity of the copyright and of the facts stated in the certificate.").

46. White v. Samsung Elecs. Am., Inc., 989 F.2d 1512, 1521 (9th Cir. 1993) (Kozinsky, J., dissenting).

47. Columbia Pictures Television v. Krypton Broad. of Birmingham, Inc., 106 F.3d 284, 296 (9th Cir. 1997) ("[A] plaintiff in a copyright action is generally awarded fees by virtue of prevailing in the action.").

48. 17 U.S.C. § 412 (2006). The statute states:

[N]o award of statutory damages or of attorney's fees . . . shall be made for . . . any infringement of copyright commenced after first publication of the work and before the effective date of its registration, unless such registration is made within three months after the first publication of the work.

49. Registration, even if untimely for purposes of section 412, is required for the plaintiff to have standing to bring an infringement suit. 17 U.S.C. § 411(b) (2006) ("[N]o action for infringement of the copyright in any United States work shall be instituted until preregistration or registration of the copyright claim has been made in accordance with this title.").

50. Charles Ossola, *Registration and Remedies: Recovery of Attorney's Fees and Statutory Damages under the Copyright Reform Act*, 13 CARDOZO ARTS & ENT. L.J. 559, 561 (1993).

51. *See, e.g.*, Torres-Negron v. J & N Records, LLC, 504 F.3d 151, 162 (1st Cir. 2007) (affirming judgment as a matter of law as to defendants on a copyright infringement claim on the grounds of improper registration as the songwriter's deposit of a reconstruction with his registration paperwork resulted in an incomplete application); Morris v. Bus. Concepts, Inc., 259 F.3d 65, 71 (2d Cir. 2001) (affirming grant of summary judgment to defendant for lack of subject matter jurisdiction on the grounds plaintiff had not properly registered articles appearing in a magazine as only the magazine itself had been registered); Raquel v. Educ. Mgmt. Corp., 196 F.3d 171, 180 (3d Cir. 1999) (dismissing a suit for lack of standing due to improper registration because the registrant had mischaracterized the work in question as audiovisual rather than musical in nature). *See also* Kodadek v. MTV Networks, Inc., 152 F.3d 1209, 1212 (9th Cir. 1998) (invalidating a copyright registration on the grounds the works deposited did not constitute bona fide copies of the original works). As Ossola points out:

If anyone is of the opinion that there are no such registration errors, he should sit through a deposition with a client when he is asked to justify his position on work made for hire in light of Reid factors, joint work in light of the recent case law, or what constitutes preexisting material for the purpose of derivative works. These are all questions that must be filled in on the application registration form, and they each provide fertile territory for attack in litigation.

Ossola, *supra* note 50, at 561.

52. Bucklew v. Hawkins, Ash, Baptie & Co., 329 F.3d 923, 931–32 (7th Cir. 2003) (dictum).

53. 4 NIMMER & NIMMER, *supra* note 29, § 14.02.

54. *Id.* Nimmer observes: "The Act provides that 'the copyright owner is entitled to recover the actual damages suffered by him or her as a result of the infringement. . . .' Yet neither its text nor the Committee Reports attempt to define the nature of those actual damages. Reference must therefore be made to both statutory and common law copyright case law." *Id.*; *see, e.g.*, Mackie v. Rieser, 296 F.3d 909, 917 (9th Cir. 2002) (noting "hurt feelings" cannot form the basis of damages awards under copyright law); Baker v. Urban Outfitters, Inc.,

254 F. Supp. 2d 346, 356–57 (S.D.N.Y. 2003) (providing an award to plaintiff based upon his personal feelings of moral debt is without basis).

55. *See* 17 U.S.C. § 504(b) (2006); Harper & Row Pub., Inc. v. Nation Enter., 471 U.S. 539, 567 (1985). The court noted:

> With respect to apportionment of profits flowing from a copyright infringement, this Court has held that an infringer who commingles infringing and noninfringing elements "must abide the consequences, unless he can make a separation of the profits so as to assure to the injured party all that justly belongs to him."

Id. (quoting Sheldon v. Metro-Goldwyn Pictures Corp., 309 U.S. 390, 406 (1940)).

56. *See, e.g.,* Buchwald v. Paramount Pictures Corp., No. 706083, 1992 WL 1462910, at *1–2 (Cal. Super. Ct. Mar. 16, 1992) (declaring Paramount's accounting methodology unconscionable when it showed the hit movie *Coming to America* had earned no net profits).

57. *See, e.g.,* Deltak, Inc. v. Advanced Sys., Inc., 767 F.2d 357 (7th Cir. 1985). Plaintiffs had not timely registered and therefore could not recover statutory damages. *Id.* at 359. Actual damages proved difficult to ascertain, as there was no provable out-of-pocket harm, such as lost sales, to the plaintiff. *Id.* at 360. Moreover, the court was "unable to determine what portion of the gross revenues were due to the infringement and what portion were due to their factors such as lawful marketing methods," thereby preventing any disgorgement recovery. *Id.* at 359. With what Nimmer dubs "triple circumstances (no out-of-pocket losses to plaintiff, no profits to defendant, no ability to recover statutory damages)" in play, the Seventh Circuit reversed an order denying plaintiffs any damages and allowed recovery of an implied license fee. *Id.* at 364. *See also* 4 NIMMER & NIMMER, *supra* note 29, § 14.02[B][1].

58. *Id.*; *see, e.g.,* Kleier Adver., Inc. v. Premier Pontiac, Inc., 921 F.2d 1036, 1040 (10th Cir. 1990); Roeslin v. Dist. of Columbia, 921 F. Supp. 793, 799–800 (D.D.C. 1995); Kleier Adver. Co. v. James Miller Chevrolet, Inc., 722 F. Supp. 1544, 1546 (N.D. Ill. 1989). *But see* Widenski v. Shapiro, Bernstein & Co., 147 F.2d 909, 911–12 (1st Cir. 1945). The court found the Copyright Act's provision for statutory damages serves as an absolute bar to the recovery of a reasonable license:

> [I]t seems to us highly significant that we have been referred to and have found no case applying the patent rule contended for by the defendant in a copyright case, and that the Supreme Court in the Sheldon case, supra, refused to sanction the closely analogous contention that damages in a copyright case ought to be the price at which the copyright proprietor had indicated his willingness to sell to the infringer.

Id. Cf. Childress v. Taylor, 798 F. Supp. 981, 990 (S.D.N.Y. 1992); Lundberg v. Welles, 93 F. Supp. 359 (S.D.N.Y. 1950). Arguably, older cases finding an absolute bar to the award of a reasonable licensing fee are distinguishable as they were decided under the 1909 Copyright Act. However, even modern cases under the 1976 Copyright Act have concluded the law bars recovery of a reasonable license fee when there are no lost sales or disgorgeable profits. In *Business Trends Analysts, Inc. v. Freedonia Group, Inc.,* 887 F.2d 399 (2d Cir. 1989), for example, the Second Circuit explicitly decline[d] to adopt *Deltak's* approach . . . . We see no room for such a speculative and artificial measure of damages under Section 504(b) . . . . It is surely true that where an infringer such as TFG sells the offending publication at a nominal price, and there is no evidence of lost sales of the infringed publication, a conventional profits test may seem inadequate. Nevertheless, we believe we must follow the statutory scheme.

Id. at 405.

59. *See* Barnet D. Wolf, *Selling Out*, COLUMBUS DISPATCH, Sept. 29, 2002, at 01E. On a related note, when U2 allowed "Vertigo" to be used in an iTunes commercial, the band took pains to explain to fans the use of the song was like a thirty-second music video and that Apple did not pay the band anything directly for use of the song in the advertisement. *See* Chris Ayres, *U2 Online Deal Hastens Last Spin for the CD*, THE TIMES (U.K), Oct. 30, 2004 ("Some fans feel cheated that the band is getting so corporate. Apple's latest iPod advertising campaign . . . features U2 performing their new single, Vertigo—in what could be construed as the band's first commercial endorsement."). However, the band's comments ignored the profit-sharing arrangement U2 enjoyed from sales of the special U2 iPod. *Id.* (noting the "unprecedented joint marketing and licensing deal" between U2 and Apple that was "by far the most lucrative [deal] signed by any rock band in history").

60. 17 U.S.C. § 502 (2006) (providing a court "may" grant injunctive relief "on such terms as it may deem reasonable to prevent or restrain infringement of a copyright"). Appellate courts have cautioned that preliminary injunctions, even in the intellectual property context, are considered to be "an extraordinary remedy involving the exercise of a very far-reaching power, which is to be applied 'only in [the] limited circumstances which clearly demand it.'" Direx Israel, Ltd. v. Breakthrough Med. Corp., 952 F.2d 802, 811 (4th Cir. 1991) (reversing a grant of preliminary injunction in a trade secret case).

61. 533 U.S. 483, 505 (2001) ("[I]t hardly follows from today's decision [finding infringement] that an injunction against [the infringing use] must issue."); *see also* 17 U.S.C. §502(a) (2006) (stating a court "may" enjoin infringement); Campbell v. Acuff-Rose Music, Inc., 510 U.S. 569, 578 n.10 (1994) (holding that goals of copyright law are "not always best served by automatically granting injunctive relief").

62. eBay Inc. v. MercExchange L.L.C., 547 U.S. 388 (2006).

63. In rejecting this general rule, *eBay* claimed true fealty to the traditional four-part balancing test historically used by courts of equity when contemplating injunctive relief. *Id.* at 392. As such, the Court actually characterizes an automatic-injunction rule as wayward and inconsistent with precedent. Nevertheless, the automatic-injunction rule dominated intellectual property jurisprudence in the twentieth century.

64. *eBay*, 547 U.S. at 392–93.

65. *See, e.g.*, MGM Studios, Inc. v. Grokster, Ltd., 518 F. Supp. 2d 1197, 1212 (C.D. Cal. 2007) ("[T]he longstanding rule that irreparable harm can be a presumed after a showing of likelihood of success for purposes of a copyright preliminary injunction motion may itself have to be reevaluated in light of *eBay*."); Allora, LLC v. Brownstone, Inc., No. 07-87, 2007 WL 1246448, at *5 (W.D.N.C. Apr. 27, 2007) (applying *eBay* to increase the burden on plaintiffs in requests for preliminary injunctions in copyright claims, thereby trumping older circuit court precedent); Canon, Inc. v. GCC Int'l Ltd., 450 F. Supp. 2d 243, 254 (S.D.N.Y. 2006) (drawing upon *eBay* to hold "the movant must demonstrate the likelihood of irreparable injury in the absence of a grant of the requested [preliminary] injunction"). *Cf.* Lorillard Tobacco Co. v. Engida, 213 Fed. Appx. 654 (10th Cir. 2007) (declining to address whether *eBay* changed the

standards for preliminary injunctions in intellectual property cases, but affirming a district court's decision to deny preliminary injunctive relief based on a balance of hardships).

66. *eBay*, 547 U.S. at 396–97 (Kennedy, J., concurring).

67. FED. R. CIV. P. 65(c).

68. *Id.*

69. *See* Lawrence v. St. Louis-San Francisco Ry., 278 U.S. 228, 233 (1929) (holding the recipient of a preliminary injunction assumes the risk of "being required to restore [the status quo ex ante] if it should be held that the . . . injunction was improvidently granted . . . and also the risk of having to compensate the [enjoined] . . . for any damages suffered by reason of the [injunction]").

70. As Nimmer argues, absent fraud, "a misstatement or clerical error in the registration application . . . shall neither invalidate the copyright nor render the registration certificate incapable of supporting an infringement action." 2 NIMMER & NIMMER, *supra* note 29, § 7.20; *see, e.g.*, Harris v. Emus Records Corp., 734 F.2d 1329, 1335 (9th Cir. 1984) ("Absent intent to defraud and prejudice, inaccuracies in copyright registrations do not bar actions for infringement."); Advisers, Inc. v. Wiesen-Hart, Inc., 238 F.2d 706, 708 (6th Cir. 1956) ("[I]nnocent misstatement . . . in the affidavit and certificate of registration, unaccompanied by fraud . . . does not invalidate copyright.").

71. 196 F.3d 171 (3d Cir. 1999).

72. *Id.* at 182 (Alito, J., dissenting).

73. Registration of Claims to Copyright, 65 Fed. Reg. 41,508, 41,509 (July 5, 2000).

74. *Id.*

75. *See, e.g.*, Tavory v. NTP, Inc., 297 Fed. App'x 986 (Fed. Cir. 2008) (affirming dismissal of copyright infringement claim on the grounds of improper registration because the programmer's deposit copy was not an original or bona fide copy); Torres-Negron v. J & N Records, LLC, 504 F.3d 151 (1st Cir. 2007) (affirming dismissal of copyright infringement claim on the grounds of improper registration because the songwriter's submission of a reconstruction with his registration application resulted in an incomplete application).

76. Kodadek v. MTV Networks, Inc., 152 F.3d 1209 (9th Cir. 1998) (invalidating a registration because of a mistake in the application in an infringement suit involving the Beavis and Butthead characters from MTV); Whimsicality, Inc. v. Rubie's Costume Co., 891 F.2d 452 (2d Cir. 1989) (invalidating registrations because of a mistake in the application in an infringement suit involving popular Halloween costumes).

77. THORVALD SOLBERG, LIBRARY OF CONGRESS, REPORT ON COPYRIGHT LEGISLATION 25 (1904).

78. Copyright, Designs and Patent Act, 1988, ch. 48, § 97(2) (U.K.) (allowing award of "additional" damages based on "flagrancy of the infringement" and "benefit accruing to the defendant by reason of the infringement").

79. Copyright, Designs and Patent Act, 1988, ch. 48, §§ 96(2), 103 (U.K.).

80. For statutory damages, *see, e.g.*, Copyright Act, R.S.C., ch. 42, § 34 (1985) (Can.), amended by 1997 S.C., ch. 24 (Can.) ("Where copyright has been infringed, the owner of the copyright is, subject to this Act, entitled to all remedies by way of injunction, damages, accounts, delivery up and otherwise that are or may be conferred by law for the infringement of a right."); Copyright Act, R.S.C., ch. 42, § 38.1(1) (1985) (Can.), amended by 1997 S.C., ch. 24 (Can.) ("Subject to this section, a copyright owner may elect, at any time before final judgment is rendered, to recover, instead of damages and profits referred to in subsection 35(1), an award of statutory damages for all infringements involved in the proceedings"). For attorneys' fees,

see Copyright Act, R.S.C., ch. 42, § 34(3) (1985) (Can.), amended by 1997 S.C., ch. 24 (Can.) (granting courts the discretion to grant full costs, including attorneys' fees, to a prevailing party).

81. Copyright Act, § 38.1(1).

82. 17 U.S.C. § 504(c)(2) (2006) ("In a case where the copyright owner sustains the burden of proving, and the court finds, that infringement was committed willfully, the court in its discretion may increase the award of statutory damages to a sum of not more than $150,000.").

83. Manitoba Inc. v. Parks, [2007] N.S.J. No. 128, 2007 NSCA 36 (Can.) (citing GEORGE S. TAKACH, COMPUTER LAW 122–23 (2nd ed. 2003)). The court stated:

> A court may award damages for copyright infringement even where the infringer made no profits. The Copyright Act also contains a statutory damages provision that permits a court to award monetary damages between $500 and $20,000. Punitive or exemplary damages for copyright infringement or trade secret misappropriation can also be awarded where the defendant's conduct is egregious and shows virtual contempt for the intellectual property rights of the plaintiff.

Id.; see also The Queen v. James Lorimer & Co., [1984] 1 F.C. 1065 (Can.) ("[I]t is well established that [exemplary damages] are, in appropriate circumstances, available . . . , [and there is] no reason why appropriate circumstances should be different in the case of copyright infringement than in the case of any other civil invasion of another's rights."); Osmont v. Petit Journal Inc., [1934] 73 Que. S.C. 465, 473 (Can.) (providing for availability of exemplary damages to punish copyright infringement as a species of theft).

84. Council Directive 2004/48, art. 13, § 1, 2004 O.J. (L 157) 78 (EC).

85. Intellectual Property (Enforcement, etc.) Regulations, 2006, S.I. 1028, art. 3, ¶¶ 1, 2 (U.K.).

86. *Id.* at ¶ 2.

87. Bürgerliches Gesetzbuch [BGB] [Civil Code] Sept. 9, 1965, BCB II 27 at 1273, § 97(2), as amended by the Law of July 16, 1998 (F.R.G.).

88. Groller v. Wolofsky, [1934], 72 Que. S.C. 419 (Can.). For a more extensive discussion on damages available, see *Chaplin v. Hicks*, [1911] 2 K.B. 786.

89. Derek Andrew, Inc. v. Poof Apparel Corp., 528 F.3d 696, 700 (9th Cir. 2008); *see also* Johnson v. Jones, 149 F.3d 494, 505 (6th Cir. 1998). The court noted that

> [i]n addition to giving copyright owners incentive to register, [section] 412 also provides potential infringers with an incentive to check the federal register. If [section] 412 succeeds in encouraging copyright owners to register and in encouraging potential infringers to check registration, then it will have reduced both the search costs imposed on potential infringers and the enforcement costs borne by copyright owners.

Id.

90. 2 NIMMER & NIMMER, *supra* note 29, § 7.16[A][2][b].

91. Copyright Act of 1909 §§ 13–14 (codified as amended at 17 U.S.C. 11, 61 Stat. 652 (1947)) (repealed by Copyright Act of 1976, Pub. L. No. 94-553, 90 Stat. 2541).

92. 306 U.S. 30 (1939), *reh'g denied*, 306 U.S. 668 (1939).

93. *See, e.g.*, Samet & Wells, Inc. v. Shalom Toy Co., No. 74-C-695, 1975 U.S. Dist. LEXIS 13683, at *20 (E.D.N.Y. Feb. 24, 1975) ("[T]he delay in filing the copyright notice may prevent plaintiff

from complaining of any [infringing] titles which were sold [prior to filing of registration].");
Kontes Glass Co. v. Lab Glass, Inc., 250 F. Supp. 193 (D.N.J. 1966), *aff'd*, 373 F.2d 319 (3d Cir.
1967) (stating delay in registration may create a defense of laches).

94. 2 NIMMER & NIMMER, *supra* note 29, § 7.14[A][1] (describing how failure to observe
proper notice requirements regarding a work used to lead to its dedication to the public
domain); *see* Neimark v. Ronai & Ronai, LLP, 500 F. Supp. 2d 338, 341 (S.D.N.Y. 2007) (noting
"works published without a copyright notice prior to the enactment of the Berne Convention
on March 1, 1989 are injected into the public domain and thus lose any copyright protection to
which they might otherwise have been entitled").

95. One notable exception is works authored by citizens of countries that have not signed
the Berne convention or that do not have copyright laws.

96. However, available remedies are profoundly affected by registration status. This affects
the viability of many potential lawsuits.

97. U.S. COPYRIGHT OFFICE, CIRCULAR 23, THE COPYRIGHT CARD CATALOG AND THE
ONLINE FILES OF THE COPYRIGHT OFFICE 1 (2009), *available at* http://www.copyright.gov/
circs/circ23.pdf.

98. U.S. COPYRIGHT OFFICE, CIRCULAR 22, HOW TO INVESTIGATE THE COPYRIGHT STATUS
OF A WORK 1 (2009), *available at* http://www.copyright.gov/circs/circ22.pdf [hereinafter
CIRCULAR 22].

99. 2 NIMMER & NIMMER, *supra* note 29, § 7.16[B][1][a][i]. Nimmer observes that

> [17 U.S.C. § 411(a)] provides that "[t]he effective date of a copyright registration is the
> day on which an application, deposit, and fee, which are later determined by the
> Register of Copyrights or by a court of competent jurisdiction to be acceptable for
> registration, have all been received in the Copyright Office." The legislative history
> explains that "[w]here the three necessary elements [of application, deposit and
> fee] are received at different times, the date of receipt of the last of them is
> controlling. . . ."

Id.

100. CIRCULAR 22, *supra* note 98, at 4 ("Since searches are ordinarily limited to registrations
that have already been cataloged, a search report may not cover recent registrations for which
catalog records are not yet available.").

101. X17 is one of Hollywood's leading celebrity and news photography agencies.

102. *Muhammad Ali Knocks Out Sonny Liston* (photograph) (1965); *Muhammad Ali Taunting
Sonny Liston* (photograph) (1965).

103. Alfred Eisenstaedt, *V-J Day in Times Square* (photograph) (1945).

104. Joe Rosenthal, *Raising the Flag on Iwo Jima* (photograph) (1945).

105. Apollo 17 Crew, *The Blue Marble* (photograph) (1972). Because the image is likely
considered a government work, it is in the public domain. 17 U.S.C. § 105 (2006) ("Copyright
protection under this title is not available for any work of the United States Government.").

106. Alberto Korda, *El Guerrillero Heroico* (photograph) (1960).

107. Sarah Levy, *A Copyright Revolution: Protecting the Famous Photograph of Che Guevara*,
13 L. & BUS. REV. AM. 687, 693 (2007). Levy notes:

> The newspaper likely did not request that Korda photograph Guevara specifically, as
> evidenced by the fact that the newspaper did not even use the photo in its article
> about the funeral the following day. Korda recalled that the newspaper did keep the

photo on file, however, and used it in a subsequent publication alongside an announcement that Guevara would be speaking at a public event.

Id. It should be noted that others claim publication did not occur until later. *See id.* ("[O]ther sources claim the photo remained unpublished in Korda's studio for the next seven years, leaving Korda's possession for the first time in 1967 when an Italian publisher named Giangiacomo Feltrinelli requested a copy of the image.").

108. Copyright Law, Gaceta Oficial de la República de Cuba, No. 49, art. 47, 30 de diciembre de 1977 (Cuba), *translated in* 1 COPYRIGHT LAWS & TREATIES OF THE WORLD (U.N. Educ., Scientific & Cultural Org. et al. eds., 2000). Decree Law no. 156, September 28, 1994 extended the copyright term for photographs to twenty-five years from date of first publication. However, Korda's work would have already fallen into the public domain by 1971. Moreover, even if Decree Law No. 156 resurrected protection for works already in the public domain, the copyright would have expired in 1986.

109. *See, e.g.,* Golan v. Gonzales, 501 F.3d 1179, 1197 (10th Cir. 2007) (finding the URAA does not violate the Copyright Clause, but remanding to the district court for First Amendment review).

110. *But see* Levy, *supra* note 107 (concluding the work may still be protected).

111. *Cf.* Hearn v. Meyer, 664 F. Supp. 832 (S.D.N.Y. 1987) (suggesting that more than minimal creativity is required to copyright modifications to a work in the public domain). *But cf.* Feist Publ'ns v. Rural Tel. Serv. Co., Inc., 499 U.S. 340 (1991) (holding that, generally, only minimal creativity is required for copyrightability).

112. *See* 17 U.S.C. § 408(a) (2006) ("[T]he owner of copyright or *of any exclusive right in the work may obtain registration. . . .*") (emphasis added); 37 C.F.R. § 202.3(c)(1) (2009) ("An application for copyright registration may be submitted by any author or other copyright claimant of a work, or the owner of any exclusive right in a work, or the duly authorized agent of any such author, other claimant, or owner.").

113. *See* Huthwaite, Inc. v. Sunrise Assisted Living, Inc., 261 F. Supp. 2d 502, 510 (E.D. Va. 2003) (noting it is not necessary "the party bringing the infringement must have itself registered the claim"); Tang v. Hwang, 799 F. Supp. 499, 503–05 (E.D. Pa. 1992) (noting "there is no requirement under the statute that the only person who may bring an action is the person who applies for the copyright registration" and that the law merely provides "there must be registration of the copyright"); 3 NIMMER & NIMMER, *supra* note 29, § 12.02[B] (stating "the plaintiff in court obviously need not be the same party who initially registered the subject work").

114. 3 NIMMER & NIMMER, *supra* note 29, § 10.02. Nimmer explains:

> An exclusive license, even if it is "limited in time or place of effect," is equated with an assignment, and each is considered to be a "transfer" of copyright ownership. Nonexclusive licenses, however, do not constitute "transfers," and some residue of the impact of indivisibility with respect to licenses under the 1909 Act remains under the current Act *vis-a-vis* nonexclusive licenses.

Id. (internal citations omitted); David C. Tolley, Note, *Regulatory Priorities Governing Stem Cell Research in California: Relaxing Revenue Sharing & Safeguarding Access Plans*, 23 BERKELEY TECH. L.J. 219, 240 (2008) ("The distinction between an exclusive and a non-exclusive license is not easy to draw in practice. As one treatise author points out, 'commercial practice yields a wide variety of differing transactional frameworks . . . making drawing a simple distinction between exclusive and nonexclusive licenses difficult.'") (quoting Raymond Nimmer & Jeff Dodd, Modern Licensing Law § 5:1 (2007)).

115. Circular 22, *supra* note 98, at 3.

116. Abend v. MCA, 863 F.2d 1465, 1469 (9th Cir. 1988).

117. *See, e.g.,* Kay Berry, Inc. v. Taylor Gifts, Inc., 421 F.3d 199, 204–05 (3d Cir. 2005) (finding a garden sculpture included in a copyrighted catalog of sculptures was an individually recognizable element of that single work, and thus was entitled to the benefits of the catalog's copyright registration, regardless of whether it was "related" to other sculptures in catalog); Warren v. Fox Family Worldwide, Inc., 171 F. Supp. 2d 1057, 1065 (C.D. Cal. 2001) (finding a copyright registration of a motion picture or television show serves to register the musical compositions contained on the soundtrack of the film or show); Greenwich Film Prods., S.A. v. DRG Records, Inc., 833 F. Supp. 248, 250 (S.D.N.Y. 1993) (musical compositions in motion picture were registered with copyright office by virtue of registration of motion picture in which they were contained, and musical compositions did not have to be separately registered).

118. The registrations were part of a suit by X17, Inc. against Mario Lavandeira, aka Perez Hilton, a celebrity gossip blogger accused of infringing X17's copyrighted photographs en masse. *See* X17 v. Lavandeira, 563 F. Supp. 2d 1102 (C.D. Cal. 2007).

119. X17, Inc., VA0001390186, registered December 1, 2006.

120. X17, Inc., VA0001390193, registered December 1, 2006.

121. Berne Convention Implementation Act of 1988, Pub. L. No. 100-568, 102 Stat. 2853 (codified as amended in scattered sections of 17 U.S.C.).

122. 134 Cong. Rec. H3079-02 (daily ed. May 10, 1988) (statement of Rep. Kastenmeier).

123. Ralph Oman, *The Impact of the Berne Convention on U.S. Copyright*, Patent, Copyrights, Trademarks, and Literary Property Course Handbook Series, Practising Law Institute, PLI Order No. G4-3981, 455 PLI/Pat 233, 255 (Oct. 1996).

124. William Belanger, *U.S. Compliance with the Berne Convention*, 3 Geo. Mason Indep. L. Rev. 373, 393 (1995).

125. *Final Report of the Ad Hoc Working Group on U.S. Adherence to the Berne Convention, reprinted in* 10 Colum.-VLA J.L. & Arts 513 (1986).

126. 4 Nimmer & Nimmer, *supra* note 29, § 17.01(B).

127. U.S. Copyright Office, http://www.copyright.gov/history/bios/oman.pdf. Oman's bio states:

> In 1982, Mr. Oman became Chief Counsel of the newly revived Subcommittee on Patents, Copyrights, and Trademarks, and in 1985 he scheduled the first Senate hearing in 50 years on U.S. adherence to the Berne Convention for the Protection of Literary and Artistic Works. From the Chief Counsel position, he was appointed Register of Copyrights on September 23, 1985. As Register, Mr. Oman helped move the United States into the Berne Convention in 1989.

Id.

128. Berne Convention for the Protection of Literary and Artistic Works art. 5(2), Sept. 9, 1886, as last revised at Paris, July 24, 1971, 828 U.N.T.S. 221, S. Treaty Doc. No. 99-27.

129. *Id.* at art. 9(1).

130. Marbury v. Madison, 5 U.S. 137, 163 (1803). The court stated:

> The very essence of civil liberty certainly consists in the right of every individual to claim the protection of the laws, whenever he receives an injury. One of the first duties of government is to afford that protection. . . . The government of the United States has been emphatically termed a government of laws, and not of men. It will certainly cease to deserve this high appellation, if the laws furnish no remedy for the violation of a vested legal right.

Id.

131. Although she does not necessarily argue the registration requirement explicitly violates the requirements of Berne, Shira Perlmutter has flagged its philosophical incompatibility with Berne. *See* Shira Perlmutter, *Freeing Copyright from Formalities*, 13 CARDOZO ARTS & ENT. L.J. 565, 565–66, 575–76 (1995).

132. WIPO Copyright Treaty art. 1(1), Dec. 20, 1996, 36 I.L.M. 65, S. TREATY DOC. NO. 105-17 ("This Treaty is a special agreement within the meaning of Article 20 of the Berne Convention for the Protection of Literary and Artistic Works, as regards Contracting Parties that are countries of the Union established by that Convention.").

133. *Id.* at art. 14(2).

134. Of course, this is only true as long as these works remain under copyright protection.

135. *Cf.* Chris Williams, *Big Fine Could Be Big Trouble in Music Downloading Case*, Associated Press Newswire, June 19, 2009. The article noted that Tom Sydnor, director of the Progress & Freedom Foundation's Center for the Study of Digital Property, defended the verdict, arguing "[l]legally acquiring a license to give copies of a song to potentially millions of Kazaa users might well have cost $80,000 per song." *Id.*

136. *See* BMW of N. Am. v. Gore, 517 U.S. 559, 581 (1996) (concluding the relevant ratio for determining punitive damages as compared to compensatory damages is "not more than 10 to 1"); *see also* State Farm Mut. Auto. Ins. Co. v. Campbell, 538 U.S. 408, 425 (2003) ("Our jurisprudence and the principles it has now established demonstrate . . . few awards exceeding a single-digit ratio between punitive and compensatory damages, to a significant degree, will satisfy due process.").

137. *See, e.g.*, NIMMER & NIMMER, *supra* note 29, § 13.01 (reflecting that state of mind is not a relevant element in making a prima facie case of copyright infringement).

138. Copyright Reform Act of 1993, H.R. 897, 103d Cong. (1993). Senator Dennis DeConcini introduced a related bill in the Senate. Copyright Reform Act of 1993, S. 373, 103d Cong. (1993). On November 17, 1993, Hughes's bill received a favorable report from the Subcommittee on Intellectual Property and Judicial Administration of the House Committee. *See* John B. Koegel, *Bamboozlement: The Repeal of Copyright Registration Incentives*, 13 CARDOZO ARTS & ENT. L.J. 529, 529 n.1 (1995); Copyright Reform Act of 1993, H.R Rep. 103–388 (1993).

139. H.R. 4307, 103d Cong. (1994).

140. Perlmutter, *supra* note 131, at 572.

141. *Copyright Reform Act of 1993: Hearing on S. 373 Before the Subcomm. on Patents, Copyrights and Trademarks of the S. Comm. On the Judiciary*, 103d Cong. (1993) [hereinafter *Hearings*] (witness list).

142. *Id.* Poet and novelist Erica Jong, a member of the Authors Guild, testified in support of the legislation, but she appeared only in her individual capacity because her opinion was not shared by the organization. *Id.* (statement of Erica Jong) ("I emphasize that I am here as an individual author and not in any official capacity.").

143. Association of American Publishers, http://www.publishers.org/(last visited Feb. 13, 2010). According to its "Membership" page, approximately 260 publishers belong to the AAP.

144. Association of American University Publishers, http://aaupnet.org/membership/directory.html (last visited Feb. 21, 2010).

145. *Hearings, supra* note 141 (statement of Scott Turow) ("appearing . . . in [sic] behalf of The Author's Guild, Inc.").

146. There are currently over eight thousand authors in the Authors Guild. The Authors Guild, History, http://www.authorsguild.org/about/history.html (last visited Feb. 13, 2010).

147. The Authors Guild, *Membership Eligibility*, https://www.authorsguild.org/join/eligibility.html (last visited Feb. 13, 2010).

148. *See, e.g.*, PRESUMED INNOCENT (Warner Bros. Pictures 1990) (theatrical film version of Turow's novel of the same name); *The Burden of Proof* (1992) (television miniseries version of Turow's novel of the same name); *Reversible Errors* (2004) (television miniseries version of Turow's novel of the same name).

149. *Hearings, supra* note 141 (statement of Scott Turow).

150. Deltak, Inc. v. Advanced Sys., Inc., 574 F. Supp. 400 (N.D. Ill. 1983).

151. *Id.* at 402.

152. *Id.* at 411.

153. *Id.* at 403–04, 411–12.

154. *Id.* at 412. Ultimately, on appeal the Seventh Circuit carved out a relatively novel exception by allowing recovery of a reasonable license fee in such situations. The court therefore remanded the case for recalculation of damages. However, in other circuits, such as the Second, the possibility of such recovery has been clearly disavowed, regardless of the harsh and seemingly inequitable consequences. *See* Business Trends Analysts, Inc. v. Freedonia Group, Inc., 887 F.2d 399, 406 (2d Cir. 1989).

155. *Id.* at 406 (citing 3 NIMMER & NIMMER, *supra* note 29, § 14.02[A]).

156. *Hearings, supra* note 141 (statements of the American Association of Publishers and the American Association of University Presses).

157. *See, e.g.*, Princeton Univ. Press v. Michigan Document Servs., Inc., 99 F.3d 1381, 1400 (6th Cir. 1996); Basic Books, Inc. v. Kinko's Graphics Corp., 758 F. Supp. 1522, 1532 (S.D.N.Y. 1991) (holding that, although the particular coursepacks at issue were copied for educational purposes, this did not qualify as fair use because, inter alia, they were made for profit).

158. 17 U.S.C. § 107 (2006). In spite of this language, courts have still managed to find a plethora of instances where use of a copyrighted work for teaching, research, or scholarship constitutes infringement. *See, e.g.*, Princeton Univ. Press, 99 F.3d at 1391; Am. Geophysical Union v. Texaco, 37 F.3d 881, 899 (2d Cir. 1994); Television Digest, Inc. v. U.S. Tel. Ass'n, 841 F. Supp. 5, 11 (D.D.C. 1993); *Basic Books*, 758 F. Supp. at 1547.

159. Founded in 1978 by a group of publishers and authors, the CCC is a clearinghouse for the licensing of "millions of books, journals, newspapers, websites, ebooks, images, blogs and more." Copyright Clearance Center, About Us, http://copyright.com/viewPage.do?pageCode=au1-n (last visited Nov. 25, 2009).

160. *See, e.g.*, the copyright insert for STEVE NEALE, GENRE AND HOLLYWOOD (2000).

161. Jason Mazzone, *Copyfraud*, 81 N.Y.U. L. Rev. 1026, 1028 (2006).

162. *See* Ossola, *supra* note 50, at 560 (1995). Ossola states:

Photographers present special problems, given the tremendous volume of works created, but these problems are not unique to them. With thousands of images created each year, it is literally impossible for anybody, even the most successful photographers, to register those images in the Copyright Office. As a result, even the most successful photographers consistently fail to register their works.

Id. In their analysis of copyright registrations and renewals from 1910 through 2000, William Landes and Richard Posner determined that even small fee increases can result in precipitous declines in registrations and renewals. WILLIAM M. LANDES & RICHARD POSNER, THE ECONOMIC STRUCTURE OF INTELLECTUAL PROPERTY LAW 245 (2003).

163. 17 U.S.C. § 408 (2006) (providing for group registration of certain copyrighted works).

164. *See, e.g.,* Willa Paskin, *WHO KILLED THE MOVIE STAR?: Hollywood's A-list Idols Are Losing Their Movie-Selling Mojo*, RADAR MAG. (July/Aug. 2008).

165. *See* Andrew McWhirter, *Film: Fameless Faces—Hidden Art of Screenwriting Revealed*, TRIBUNE MAG., Jan. 19, 2009, *available at* http://www.tribunemagazine.co.uk/2009/-01/19/film-fameless-faces-%E2%80%93%C2%Aohidden-art-of-screenwriting-revealed/.

166. Edmund Wilson, *The Boys in the Back Room, in* CLASSICS AND COMMERCIALS: A LITERARY CHRONICLE OF THE FORTIES 19, 56 (1950).

167. *Id.*

168. HUBERT BUTLER, INDEPENDENT SPIRIT: ESSAYS 271, 272 (2000).

169. Writers Guild of America, West, Registry, http://www.wga.org/subpage_-register.aspx?id=1183 (last visited Sept. 29, 2009).

170. WGA West: Registry, http://www.wgawregistry.org/ (last visited Sept 29, 2009).

171. WGA West Registry, Frequently Asked Questions, Does Registration Take the Place of Copyright?, http://www.wgawregistry.org/webrss/regfaqs.html#quest14 (last visited Sept. 29, 2009).

172. *Id.*

173. The copyright protection a treatment or story outline receives may be thin, depending on the nature of the content and considerations such as the idea/expression dichotomy and the scènes à faire doctrine.

174. Online WGAW Registration costs $10 for WGA members in good standing and $20 for the general public. Online registration of a copyright with the Copyright Office currently costs $35.

175. K.J. Greene, *Copyright, Culture & Black Music: A Legacy of Unequal Protection*, 21 HASTINGS COMM. & ENT. L.J. 339, 358–59 (1999).

176. *Id.* at 343.

177. *Id.* at 356–57.

178. *See* SIVA VAIDHYANATHAN, COPYRIGHTS AND COPYWRONGS: THE RISE OF INTELLECTUAL PROPERTY AND HOW IT THREATENS CREATIVITY 117–48 (2001) (tracing the appropriation of blues by rock' n' roll artists over time); K.J. Greene, *Intellectual Property at the Intersection of Race and Gender: Lady Sings the Blues*, 16 AM. U. J. GENDER, SOC. POL'Y & L. 365, 371–74 (2008); K. J. Greene, *"Copynorms," Black Cultural Production, and the Debate Over African-American Reparations*, 25 CARDOZO ARTS & ENT. L.J. 1179, 1193 (2008) ("The fleecing of Black artists was the basis of the success of the American music industry."). One example where rights were reasserted several decades later occurred when the Estate of Willie Dixon successfully went after Led Zeppelin for the group's uncredited, unauthorized, and uncompensated lifting of "You Need Love" for its song "Whole Lotta Love." *See* Keith Aoki, *Distributive Justice and Intellectual Property: Distributive and Syncretic Motives in Intellectual Property Law*, 40 U.C. DAVIS L. REV. 717, 763 (2007).

179. 17 U.S.C. § 102(a)(7) (2006) (placing sound recordings within the subject matter of copyright protection); 1 NIMMER & NIMMER, *supra* note 29, § 2.10 (noting copyright protection was extended to sound recordings fixed on or after Feb. 15, 1972).

180. General Revision of Copyright Act of Feb. 3, 1831, ch. 16, § 1, 4 Stat. 436.

181. Aoki, *supra* note 178, at 760.

182. *See, e.g.*, Peter Jaszi, *Contemporary Copyright and Collective Creativity*, in THE CONSTRUCTION OF AUTHORSHIP: TEXTUAL APPROPRIATION IN LAW AND LITERATURE 29 (Martha Woodmansee & Peter Jaszi eds., 1994); Olufunmilayo B. Arewa, *From J.C. Bach to Hip Hop: Musical Borrowing, Copyright and Cultural Context*, 84 N.C. L. REV. 547, 550–51 (2006) ("Copyright legal structures and the classical music canon have thus relied on a common vision of musical authorship that embeds Romantic author assumptions. Such assumptions are based on a vision of musical production as autonomous, independent and in some cases even reflecting genius.").

183. 17 U.S.C. § 412 (2006). The section states:

In any action under this title, other than an action brought for a violation of the rights of the author under section 106A(a), an action for infringement of the copyright of a work that has been preregistered under section 408(f) before the commencement of the infringement and that has an effective date of registration not later than the earlier of 3 months after the first publication of the work or 1 month after the copyright owner has learned of the infringement, or an action instituted under section 411(b), *no award of statutory damages or of attorney's fees*, as provided by sections 504 and 505, shall be made for—

(1) any infringement of copyright in an unpublished work commenced before the effective date of its registration; or

(2) any infringement of copyright commenced after first publication of the work and before the effective date of its registration, unless such registration is made within three months after the first publication of the work.

Id. (emphasis added).

184. *See, e.g.*, Pamela Samuelson, *Preliminary Thoughts on a Copyright Reform Project*, 2007 UTAH L. REV. 551 (making the case for preliminary consideration of a holistic reform of copyright law).

185. *See* John Tehranian, *Whither Copyright? Transformative Use, Free Speech, and an Intermediate Liability Proposal*, 2005 B.Y.U. L. REV. 1201 (2005).

186. *See* Pamela Samuelson & Tara Wheatland, *Statutory Damages in Copyright Law: A Remedy in Need of Reform*, 51 WM & MARY L. REV. 439 (2009) (arguing the present statutory damages scheme is both inconsistent with congressional intent and in violation of the Supreme Court's due process jurisprudence regarding punitive damages awards).

187. *See, e.g.*, Mazzone, *supra* note 161 (arguing Congress should amend the Copyright Act to create a cause of action against overreaching claims of copyrightability by purported rightsholders).

188. Prevailing parties can, at the court's discretion, receive attorneys' fees. 17 U.S.C. § 505 (2006). However, despite the absence of any statutory language distinguishing between prevailing plaintiffs and defendants, courts have historically applied a bifurcated analysis on the fees question, and continue to do so despite the Supreme Court's dictate that they take an evenhanded approach. We shall explore this subject further in Chapter 5.

CHAPTER 5

1. Declan McCullagh, *Wal-Mart Backs Away from DMCA Claim*, CNET News, Dec. 5, 2002, *available at* http://news.cnet.com/2100-1023-976296.html.

2. *Wal-Mart Now Going After Search Engines for Linking to Sites with Black Friday Ads*, http://www.techdirt.com/articles/20081113/1511542826.shtml.

3. *Id.*

4. *See, e.g.*, Feist Publ'ns v. Rural Telephone Serv., 499 U.S. 340 (1991).

5. *See, e.g.*, Kregos v. Associated Press, 3 F.3d 656 (2d Cir. 1993).

6. Gabriel J. Daly, *Coop Discourages Notetaking in Bookstore*, Sept. 19, 2007, http://www.thecrimson.com/article.aspx?ref=519564.

7. John G. Palfrey, Jr., Wendy M. Seltzer, & Angela Kang, *Has Sense Flown the Coop*, HARVARD CRIMSON, Sept. 26, 2007, http://www.thecrimson.com/article.aspx?ref=519661.

8. Daly, *supra* note 6.

9. Jason Mazzone, *Copyfraud*, 81 N.Y.U. L. REV. 1026 (2006).

10. *Id.* at 1028.

11. *Id.*

12. Sam Bayard, *Copyright Misuse and Cease-and-Desist Letters*, Oct. 11, 2007, http://www.citmedialaw.org/copyright-misuse-and-cease-and-desist-letters.

13. *Id.*

14. *Id.*

15. *See, e.g.*, Major League Baseball, MLB.com, Terms of Use Agreement, http://mlb.mlb.com/mlb/official_info/about_mlb_com/terms_of_use.jsp. ("Except for Submitted Content (defined below), the MLBAM Properties are either owned by or licensed to MLBAM. The applicable owners and licensors retain all rights to the MLBAM Properties, including, but not limited to all copyright, trademark and other proprietary rights, however denominated. Except for downloading one copy of the MLBAM Properties on any single computer for your personal, non-commercial home use, you must not reproduce, prepare derivative works based upon, distribute, perform or display the MLBAM Properties without first obtaining the written permission of MLBAM or otherwise as expressly set forth in the terms and conditions of the MLBAM Properties. The MLBAM Properties must not be used in any unauthorized manner."); *see also* MLB.com, MLB Productions Frequently Asked Questions, http://mlb.mlb.com/mlb/video/mlb_productions/feature.jsp?content=faq (last visited Sept. 29, 2009).

16. *See* National Football League, NFL.com website Terms and Conditions, http://www.nfl.com/help/terms (last visited Sept. 29, 2009).

17. *See, e.g.*, BIGGER STRONGER FASTER* (Magnolia Pictures 2008) (showing images of, among others, Barry Bonds and Mark McGwire in a discussion about steroids).

18. *See, e.g.*, Random House, Inc., Copyright & Permissions, http://www.randomhouse.com/about/permissions.html ("Written permission is required from the publisher if you wish to reproduce any of our material. . . ."); *see also* Mazzone, *supra* note 9.

19. *See* 17 U.S.C. § 111 (allowing cable operators to retransmit both local and distant over-the-air television and radio broadcasts), § 119 (allowing satellite carriers to retransmit distant over-the-air television broadcasts for private viewing) and § 122 (allowing satellite carriers to retransmit local over-the-air television broadcasts for private and commercial viewing).

20. 17 U.S.C. §§ 111, 122 (subject to a minimum basic royalty).

21. 17 U.S.C. § 204 (dictating a "transfer of copyright ownership" is not valid unless it is in writing) and 17 U.S.C. § 101 (defining a "transfer of copyright ownership" as including

"an assignment, mortgage, exclusive license, or other conveyance, alienation, or hypothecation of a copyright or of any of the exclusive rights comprised in a copyright").

22. *See, e.g.*, Johnson v. Jones, 149 F.3d 494, 500 (7th Cir. 1998); Lulirama Ltd., Inc. v. Axcess Broadcast Servs., Inc., 238 F.3d 872, 879 (5th Cir. 1997).

23. *See* Abbey Klaassen, *Fantasy Sports Generate Booming New Online Ad Market*, ADVERTISING AGE, Aug. 8, 2006, http://adage.com/digital/article.php?article_id=110891.

24. *See* C.B.C. Distrib. & Mktg., Inc. v. Major League Baseball Advanced Media, L.P., 443 F. Supp. 2d 1077, 1107 (E.D. Mo. 2006).

25. *Id.* at 1086, 1107 (finding "facts themselves are not copyrightable because '[t]he *sine qua non* of copyright is originality'" and holding "undisputed facts establish that the players do not have a right of publicity in their names and playing records as used in CBC's fantasy games and that CBC has not violated the players' claimed right of publicity").

26. C.B.C. Distrib. & Mktg. v. Major League Baseball Advanced Media, L.P., 505 F.3d 818, 823 (8th Cir. 2007) (concluding "that it would be strange law that a person would not have a First Amendment right to use information that is available to everyone").

27. Major League Baseball Advanced Media v. C.B.C. Distrib. & Mktg., Inc. 128 S. Ct. 2872 (2008).

28. 17 U.S.C. § 512 (2006).

29. Letter from Wendy Seltzer to DMCA Complaints, YouTube, Inc. (Feb. 14, 2007), *available at* http://wendy.seltzer.org/media/DMCA-counter-notification.pdf.

30. *See* Letter from NFL to YouTube (dated Feb. 13, 2007), *available at* http://wendy.seltzer. org/media/NFLAntipiracy03_takedown_2007.02.13.txt.

31. 17 U.S.C. § 512(f)(1).

32. 391 F.3d 1000 (9th Cir. 2004).

33. *Id.* at 1004–05.

34. Order Granting Defendants' Motion to Dismiss with Leave to Amend As to Claims 1 and 2 and Without Leave to Amend As to Claim 3, Lenz v. Universal Music. Corp., 5:07-cv-03783-JF (Apr. 8, 2008), at 5.

35. Lenz v. Universal Music Corp., 572 F. Supp. 2d 1150, 1154 (N.D. Cal. 2008) ("Whether fair use qualifies as a use 'authorized by law' in connection with a takedown notice pursuant to the DMCA appears to be an issue of first impression. Though it has been discussed in several other actions, no published case actually has adjudicated the merits of the issue.").

36. *Id.* at 1154 (citing 17 U.S.C. § 512(c)(3)(A)(v)).

37. 572 F. Supp. 2d at 1155.

38. 17 U.S.C. § 512(f)(2).

39. Lenz v. Universal Music Corp., No. C 07-3783 JF, 2010 WL 702466, at *10, (N.D. Cal. Feb. 25, 2010).

40. *Id.*

41. *Id.*

42. Frank Music Corp. v. Metro-Goldwyn-Mayer Inc., 886 F.2d 1545, 1556 (1989), *cert. denied*, 494 U.S. 1017 (1989) ("Plaintiffs in copyright actions may be awarded attorney's fees simply by virtue of prevailing in the action: no other precondition need be met, although the fee awarded must be reasonable.").

43. *See, e.g.*, Warner Bros. Inc. v. Dae Rim Trading, Inc., 877 F.2d 1120 (2d Cir. 1989) (stating "[a] heavier burden [is] imposed on defendants who seek fees"); Olson v. Nat'l Broad. Co., Inc., 855 F.2d 1446, 1454 (9th Cir. 1988) (declining to adopt an evenhanded approach to awarding fees). *But see* Lieb v. Topstone Indus., Inc., 788 F.2d 151, 156 (3d Cir. 1986)

(adopting an evenhanded approach in the Third Circuit to the grant of attorneys' fees under the Copyright Act).

44. Reader's Digest Ass'n, Inc. v. Conservative Digest Ass'n, Inc., 821 F.2d 800, 809 (D.C. Cir. 1987).

45. 510 U.S. 517, 534 (1994).

46. *Id.* at 534.

47. *Id.* at 527.

48. *Id.* at 534 (noting "there is no precise rule or formula for making these determinations," but instead equitable discretion should be exercised "in light of the considerations we have identified") (quoting Hensley v. Eckerhard, 461 U.S. 424, 436–37 (1983)).

49. 510 U.S. at 535 n.19 (citing Lieb v. Topstone Indus., Inc., 788 F.2d 151, 156 (3d Cir. 1986)).

50. Columbia Pictures Television v. Krypton Broad. of Birmingham, Inc., 106 F.3d 284, 296 (9th Cir. 1997), *rev'd on other grounds sub nom.* Feltner v. Columbia Pictures Television, 523 U.S. 340 (1997).

51. 106 F. 3d at 296. The Ninth Circuit ultimately reversed the fees award of the lower court because the lower court had not provided any basis for it. However, in so doing, the court appeared far more concerned about its ability to ascertain the reasonableness of the award, not the fact of the award itself. As the court wrote, "This Circuit has a 'long-standing insistence upon a proper explanation of any fee award' by a district court. . . . The district court, rather than providing a reasoned explanation of its fee award, simply included the entire amount requested in the final judgment. Thus, without expressing any opinion on whether or not the fees claimed were reasonable, we must vacate the district court's fee award and remand the matter so that the district court may provide a reasoned explanation supporting the amount of fees awarded." *Id.* at 296 (citations omitted).

52. *Id.* at 290.

53. 4-14 MELVILLE B. NIMMER & DAVID NIMMER, NIMMER ON COPYRIGHT § 14.10[D][3][b] (2008).

54. 317 F.3d 385 (4th Cir. 2003).

55. *Id.* at 398.

56. No. 00 Civ. 5827, 2003 U.S. Dist. LEXIS 16940 (E.D.N.Y. Sept. 1, 2003).

57. *Id.* at **20–21.

58. 960 F.2d 301 (2d Cir. 1992).

59. *Id.* at 309.

60. As the Second Circuit noted in remanding the case to the district court, "given Koons' willful and egregious behavior, we think Rogers may be a good candidate for enhanced statutory damages pursuant to 17 U.S.C. § 504(c)(2)." 960 F. 2d at 313.

61. 396 F. Supp. 2d 476 (S.D.N.Y. 2005).

62. Blanch v. Koons, 485 F. Supp. 2d 516, 517 (S.D.N.Y. 2007).

63. 485 F. Supp. 2d at 518.

64. NIMMER & NIMMER, *supra* note 53, §14.10[D][3][b].

65. 485 F. Supp. 2d at 518.

66. *Id.*

67. CAIR, *National Radio Host Goes on Anti-Muslim Tirade,* Nov. 11, 2007, http://www.cair.com/ArticleDetails.aspx?mid1=777&&ArticleID=23608&&name=n&&currPage=3.

68. Savage v. Council on American-Islamic Relations Inc., 87 U.S.P.Q.2d (BNA) 1730 (N.D. Cal. 2008).

69. Savage v. Council on American-Islamic Relations Inc., No. C 07-06076 SI, 2009 U.S. Dist. LEXIS 4926, at **2-*3 (N.D. Cal. Jan. 26, 2009).

70. *Id.*

71. *Id.* ·

72. *Brave New Films Sues Michael Savage over YouTube Takedown*, L.A. TIMES, Oct. 10, 2008, *available at* http://latimesblogs.latimes.com/webscout/2008/10/brave-new-films.html.

73. TorresNegron v. J & N Records, LLC, 504 F.3d 151, 164–65 (1st Cir. 2007) (finding a defendant who obtains a dismissal for lack of subject matter jurisdiction cannot receive fees under section 505 of the Copyright Act as that party has not prevailed on the merits); McCormick v. Amir Constr., Inc., 2008 WL 4534266, at **1–2 (C.D. Cal. Oct. 6, 2008) (declining to award attorneys' fees under section 505 despite invalid claim of copyright ownership by plaintiff because of lack of subject matter jurisdiction to do so, but ultimately granting fees under Fed. R. App. P. 38 for the appellate portion of the suit). *Cf.* Cook v. Peter Kiewit Sons Co., 775 F.2d 1030, 1035 (9th Cir. 1985) (finding a district court lacks the ability to opine on the merits of a claim after deciding it lacks subject matter jurisdiction over the claim); W.G. v. Senatore, 18 F.3d 60 (2d Cir. 1994) (finding a court lacks jurisdiction to award attorneys' fees based on a claim if it lacks subject matter jurisdiction over that claim).

74. Of course, if a court lacks jurisdiction to grant fees after dismissing a case for lack of subject matter jurisdiction, one could similarly argue a court also lacks the ability to impose Rule 11 sanctions on similar grounds.

75. 17 U.S.C. § 403.

76. *See* 35 U.S.C. § 292(a) (2000) ("Whoever marks upon, or affixes to, or uses in advertising in connection with any unpatented article, the word 'patent' or any word or number importing that the same is patented for the purpose of deceiving the public; or Whoever marks upon, or affixes to, or uses in advertising in connection with any article, the words 'patent applied for,' 'patent pending,' or any word importing that an application for patent has been made, when no application for patent has been made, or if made, is not pending, for the purpose of deceiving the public—Shall be fined not more than $500 for every such offense.").

77. 1802 Amendment to the Copyright Act of 1790, enacted April 29, 1802, codified as section 11 in the Copyright Act of 1831.

78. Personal, N.Y. TIMES, Dec. 23, 1857. Ironically, the reproduction of the column from the newspaper in 1857, which is provided by *The New York Times* on its website at http://query. nytimes.com/gst/abstract.html?res=9F0DEFD8173CEE34BC4B51DFB467838C649FDE, contains the following language: "Published. December 23, 1857. Copyright © The New York Times." If section 11 of the 1831 Copyright Act were still in effect, *The New York Times* would have violated it with this notification.

79. 175 F. 875 (C.C.S.D.N.Y. 1910), *aff'd* 183, F. 107 (2d Cir.).

80. 175 F. at 876.

81. Buck v. Jewell-Lasalle Realty Co., 283 U.S. 191, 198 (1931).

82. However, contributory infringement—a form of secondary liability—does require knowledge.

83. The selection of actual damages or statutory damages remains entirely with an eligible plaintiff. *See* 17 U.S.C. § 504(c)(1) ("the copyright owner may elect, at any time before final judgment is rendered, to recover, instead of actual damages and profits, an award of statutory damages"). Also, the reduction in innocent infringement awards appears to apply only to statutory damages awards. *See* 17 U.S.C. § 504(c)(2) ("In a case where the infringer sustains the

burden of proving, and the court finds, that such infringer was not aware and had no reason to believe that his or her acts constituted an infringement of copyright, the court in its discretion may reduce the award of statutory damages to a sum of not less than $200.").

84. Bright Tunes Music Corp. v. Harrisongs Music, Ltd., 420 F. Supp. 177 (1976).

85. *Id.* at 180–81.

86. ABKCO Music, Inc. v. Harrisongs Music, Ltd., 508 F. Supp. 798 (S.D.N.Y. 1981), *aff'd,* 722 F.2d 988, 993 (2d Cir. 1983).

87. R. Anthony Reese, *Innocent Infringement in U.S. Copyright Law: A History,* 30 COLUM. J.L. & ARTS 133 (2007).

88. In fact, some observers have argued the harsh consequences of copyright liability combined with the occasional difficulty in distinguishing between infringing and legitimate content has stifled digital distribution. For example, Gaia Bernstein has drawn on this point to at least partly explain the relatively slow growth of digital music files as a share of music sales when compared to the rapid diffusion and adoption of CDs when they were introduced in the 1980s. Gaia Bernstein, *In the Shadow of Innovation,* 31 CARDOZO L. REV. 2257 (2010), *available at* http://papers.ssrn.com/sol3/papers.cfm?abstract_id=1395779.

89. *See* Declaration of Michael Robertson in Opposition to EMI's Motion to Dismiss and Request for Reconsideration of the Denial of Its Motion to Stay Discovery, *available at* http://beckermanlegal.com/pdf/?file=/Lawyer_Copyright_Internet_Law/capitol_mp3tunes_081230 OppositionRobertsonDeclaration.pdf.

90. Of course, although EMI might have the right to control when and where its products are given away for free, the issue in the case was whether they misrepresented this in their DMCA takedown notifications, which are signed under penalty of perjury.

91. Ned Snow, *Copytraps,* 84 INDIANA L.J. 285 (2009).

92. 438 U.S. 265 (1978).

93. *Id.* at 317–18.

94. *Id.* at 407.

95. McGeorge Bundy, *The Issue Before the Court: Who Gets Ahead in America,* ATLANTIC MONTHLY 54 (Nov. 1977).

96. Linda Greenhouse, *A Tale of Two Justices,* 11 GREEN BAG 2d 37, 40–41 (2008).

97. LINDA GREENHOUSE, BECOMING JUSTICE BLACKMUN 133 (2005).

98. Parents Involved in Cmty. Sch. v. Seattle Sch. Dist. No. 1, 551 U.S. 701, 748 (2007).

99. Parents Involved in Cmty. Sch. v. Seattle Sch. Dist., No. 1, 426 F.3d 1162, 1222 (9th Cir. 2005) (Bea, J., dissenting).

100. Parents Involved in Cmty. Sch. v. Seattle Sch. Dist. No. 1, 551 U.S. 701, 862 (2007) (Breyer, J., dissenting).

101. 17 U.S.C. § 504(c)(2).

102. Of course, this is only true as long as these works remain under copyright protection.

103. *See* BMW of N. Am. v. Gore, 517 U.S. 559, 581 (1996) (finding "that the relevant ratio" for determining punitive damages as compared to compensatory damages is "not more than 10 to 1."). *See also* State Farm Mut. Auto. Ins. Co. v. Campbell, 538 U.S. 408, 425 (2003) (holding "[o]ur jurisprudence and the principles it has now established demonstrate . . . few damages awards exceeding a single digit ratio between punitive and compensatory damages, to significant degree, will satisfy due process").

104. *See, e.g.,* Zomba Enters., Inc. v. Panorama Records, Inc., 491 F.3d 574, 586–88 (6th Cir. 2007) (rejecting both due process and Eighth Amendment challenges to an award of statutory damages that was forty-four times greater than the actual damages suffered); Louis Vuitton

Malletier, S.A. v. Akanoc Solutions, Inc., Order Granting in Part and Denying in Part Defendants' Post-Trial Motions, at 22–25, No. C07-03952 JW (N.D. Cal. Mar. 19, 2010) (rejecting due process challenge to infringement award of $10,800,000 in statutory damages).

105. 92 F. Supp. 2d 349 (S.D.N.Y. 2000).

106. Feltner v. Columbia Pictures Television, Inc., 523 U.S. 340, 355 (1998).

107. *See* 17 U.S.C. § 504(c).

108. NIMMER & NIMMER, *supra* note 53, § 14.04.

109. Columbia Pictures Television, Inc. v. Krypton Broad. of Birmingham, Inc., 259 F.3d 1186, 1195 (9th Cir. 2001), *cert. denied*, 534 U.S. 1127 (2002).

110. *Id.*

111. Defendant's Motion and Memorandum for New Trial or Remittitur, Sony BMG Entm't. v. Tenenbaum, 1:07-cv-11446-NG (D. Mass. Jan. 4, 2010).

112. *Id.* at 13.

113. TMZ Staff, *"Love Guru" Costs Dumbass 6 Months of Freedom*, http://www.tmz.com/2009/06/19/love-guru-costs-dumbass-6-months-of-freedom/(June 19, 2009).

114. *See* Anthony McCartney, *Blogger Arrested over Leak of Guns N' Roses Songs*, ASSOCIATED PRESS, Aug. 28, 2008; Daniel Kreps, *"Chinese Democracy" Leaker Arrested on Suspicion of Violating Federal Copyright Law*, ROLLING STONE MAGAZINE ONLINE BLOG, Aug. 27, 2008, http://www.rollingstone.com/rockdaily/index.php/2008/08/27/chinese-democracy-leaker-arrested-on-suspicion-of-violating-federal-copyright-law/.

115. *See* David Kravets, *Feds Demand Prison for Guns N' Roses Uploader*, http://blog.wired.com/27bstroke6/2009/03/feds-demand-6-m.html (Mar. 13, 2009).

116. *See* http://www.rollingstone.com/rockdaily/index.php/2008/09/02/did-guns-n-roses-leaker-know-he-broke-the-law-kevin-cogill-asks-for-financial-aid/.

117. Various criminal activities are discussed in Slash's autobiography. *See* SAUL HUDSON (DBA SLASH) & ANTHONY BOZZA, SLASH (2008) (selling with the tagline "It seems excessive but that doesn't mean it didn't happen").

118. Jon Baumgarten & Peter Jaszi, *Why Section 412 Should Be Retained, reprinted in* ACCORD REPORT, H.R. Rep . No. 388, 103d Cong., 1st Sess. 12–13 (1993), at A85–A91; Peter Jaszi, *Section 412, reprinted in* ACCORD REPORT, H.R. Rep . No. 388, 103d Cong., 1st Sess. 12–13 (1993), at A92–A93; John B. Koegel, *Bamboozlement: The Repeal of Copyright Registration Incentives*, 13 CARDOZO ARTS & ENT. L.J. 529 (1995).

119. John Tehranian, *Infringement Nation*, 2007 UTAH L. REV. 537 (2007).

120. *See infra.*

121. *Cf.* Shira Perlumutter, *Freeing Copyright from Formalities*, 13 CARDOZO ARTS & ENT. L.J. 565, 586–87 (1995).

122. 537 U.S. 186, 221 (2003). However, the Court did suggest the D.C. Circuit spoke too broadly when it stated copyright cases are categorically immune from First Amendment challenges. *See id.*

123. 471 U.S. 539, 560 (1985); *see also* New Era Publ'ns Int'l, ApS v. Henry Holt & Co., 873 F.2d 576, 584 (2d Cir. 1989) (holding "the fair use doctrine encompasses all claims of first amendment in the copyright field").

124. 74 F. Supp. 2d 1, 3 (D.D.C. 1999) (emphasis added).

125. 537 U.S. 186, 221 (2003) (emphasis added).

126. *Id.*

127. BENJAMIN KAPLAN, AN UNHURRIED VIEW OF COPYRIGHT 2 (1966).

128. Jessica Litman, *Copyright as Myth*, 53 U. PITT. L. REV. 235, 243–44 (1991).

129. 107 U.S.C. § 107(1) (2000).

130. Campbell v. Acuff-Rose Music, Inc., 510 U.S. 569, 576 (1994).

131. Pierre N. Leval, *Toward a Fair Use Standard*, 103 HARV. L. REV. 1105, 1116 (1990).

132. The *Campbell* Court, citing Leval's work, emphasized the importance of transformative use in the copyright infringement calculus and the need to determine whether "the new work merely 'supersede[s] the objects' of the original creation, or instead adds something new, with a further purpose or different character, altering the first with new expression, meaning, or message." 510 U.S. at 579 (internal citations omitted).

133. *Compare Campbell*, 510 U.S. 569 (finding fair use in 2 Live Crew's parody of Roy Orbison's song "Pretty Woman") *with* Rogers v. Koons, 960 F.2d 301 (2d Cir. 1992) (finding no fair use in Jeff Koons's satirical appropriation of Art Rogers's *Puppies* photograph). As Naomi Voegtli argues, under the fair use test, appropriationist works are unlikely to survive a fair use defense:

> First, the purpose of the use is often commercial; second, appropriative works generally do not fall within a category of works for which the courts have traditionally granted fair use . . . ; third, appropriative works often take a substantial portion of the original and/or a portion of the original that is considered most valuable; and fourth, many appropriative works appeal to a different audience, and thus have little effect on the market of the original. . . . [Courts often] presume[] a negative economic effect based on the commercial nature of defendant's appropriative work.

Naomi Abe Voegtli, *Rethinking Derivative Rights*, 63 BROOK. L. REV. 1213, 1227–28 (1997).

134. *Campbell*, 510 U.S. at 580–81.

135. *See* Leval, *supra* note 131, at 1105–06.

136. The idea/expression dichotomy bears heavily on the second factor of the fair use test, which judges the nature of the copyrighted work, granting greater fair use rights to factual (idea-based) materials and lesser fair use rights to fanciful (expression-based) materials. *See* 17 U.S.C. § 107(2) (2000).

137. Nichols v. Universal Pictures Corp., 45 F.2d 119, 121 (2d Cir. 1930).

138. "The factors contained in Section 107 are merely by way of example, and are not an exhaustive enumeration." 4 MELVILLE B. NIMMER & DAVID NIMMER, NIMMER ON COPYRIGHT § 13.05[A] (2005). *See also* Castle Rock Entm't, Inc. v. Carol Publ'g Group, Inc., 150 F.3d 132, 141 (2d Cir. 1998) (noting "the four listed statutory factors in § 107 guide but do not control [a court's] fair use analysis").

139. One exception, perhaps, is the fourth factor (market harm), which the Supreme Court has mysteriously deemed the most important factor in the balancing test. *See* Stewart v. Abend, 495 U.S. 207, 238 (1990).

140. *See, e.g.*, BRUCE P. KELLER & JEFFREY P. CUNARD, COPYRIGHT LAW: A PRACTITIONER'S GUIDE § 8.2 (noting the "exact contours [of the fair use doctrine] are difficult to define precisely").

141. Rebecca Tushnet, *Copyright as a Model for Free Speech Law: What Copyright Has in Common with Anti-Pornography Laws, Campaign Finance Reform, and Telecommunications Regulation*, 42 B.C. L. REV. 1, 24 (2000). Despite the explicit text of the 1976 Copyright Act, which states "the fair use of a copyrighted work, . . . for purposes such as . . . teaching (including multiple copies for classroom use), scholarship, or research, is not an infringement of copyright," 17 U.S.C. § 107, the courts have still managed to find a plethora of instances

where use of a copyrighted work for teaching, research, or scholarship constitutes infringement. *See, e.g.*, Princeton Univ. Press v. Michigan Document Servs., 99 F.3d 1381 (6th Cir. 1996); Am. Geophysical Union v. Texaco, 37 F.3d 881 (2d Cir. 1994); Duffy v. Penguin Books, 4 F. Supp. 2d 268 (S.D.N.Y. 1998); Television Digest, Inc. v. U.S. Tel. Ass'n, 841 F. Supp. 5 (D.D.C. 1993); Basic Books, Inc. v. Kinko's Graphics Corp., 758 F. Supp. 1522 (S.D.N.Y. 1991).

142. *See* Tushnet, *supra* note 141, at 24.

143. *See, e.g.*, United States v. Carolene Prods. Co., 304 U.S. 144, 152 n.4 (1938) (noting the application of heightened scrutiny to government action implicating First Amendment rights).

144. *See, e.g.*, Rosemary J. Coombe, *Objects of Property and Subjects of Politics: Intellectual Property Laws and Democratic Dialogue*, 69 TEX. L. REV. 1853, 1867–68 (1991); Jessica Litman, *Reforming Information Law in Copyright's Image*, 22 U. DAYTON L. REV. 587, 612–13 (1997); Tushnet, *supra* note 141, at 24.

145. Coombe, *supra* note 144, at 1868 ("Faced with the threat of legal action, most local parodists, political activists, and satirical bootleggers will cease their activities.").

146. 17 U.S.C. § 504(c)(2) (2000).

147. For a small (but emblematic) example, see Fred S. McChesney, *Just Let Me Read Some of That Rock'n Roll Music*, 1 GREEN BAG 2d 149 (1998) (describing the reluctance of publishers to allow the quotation of music lyrics, no matter how short, in academic books for fear of legal action).

148. *See* Campbell v. Acuff-Rose Music, Inc., 510 U.S. 569, 590 (1994).

149. *See, e.g.*, A & M Records, Inc. v. Napster, Inc., 239 F.3d 1004, 1014 n.3 (9th Cir. 2001) (resting the burden of proof with respect to a fair use claim in a preliminary injunction hearing on the defendant); Video Pipeline, Inc. v. Buena Vista Home Entm't, 192 F. Supp. 2d 321, 335 (D.N.J. 2002); Hofheinz v. AMC Prods., Inc. 147 F. Supp. 2d 127, 137 (E.D.N.Y. 2001); Columbia Pictures Indus., Inc. v. Miramax Films Corp., 11 F. Supp. 2d 1179, 1189 (C.D. Cal. 1998).

150. *See, e.g.*, Near v. Minnesota, 283 U.S. 697 (1931) (deeming prior restraints invalid in all but the most extreme circumstances).

151. *Campbell*, 510 U.S. at 579. The definition of what constitutes a transformative work is, of course, subject to great debate. As I argue, however, this is an issue in which the courts should more vigorously engage themselves as it goes to the heart of the utilitarian rationale for copyright protection. *See infra* Part IV.C.2.a. For the purposes of the intermediate liability proposal, I draw upon the definition adopted by the Supreme Court in *Campbell*. *See infra* note 154 and accompanying text.

152. *See* U.S. CONST. art I, § 8, cl. 8 (empowering Congress to "promote the Progress of Science and useful Arts, by securing for limited Times to Authors and Inventors the exclusive Right to their respective Writings and Discoveries").

153. *See* Sony v. Universal, 464 U.S. 417 (1985) (deeming fair use time shifting—the use of a VCR for the purposes of recording a television program for later viewing).

154. *Campbell*, 510 U.S. at 579; *see also* Leval, *supra* note 131, at 1111 (defining transformative use as one that "adds value to the original—if the quoted matter is used as raw material, transformed in the creation of new information, new aesthetics, new insights and understandings").

155. I am indebted to a conversation with Pamela Samuelson for this aspect of the proposal.

156. *See* 17 U.S.C. § 1201(a)(1)(B)–(E) (2000); Exemption to Prohibition on Circumvention of Copyright Protection Systems for Access Control Technologies, 67 Fed. Reg. 63,578-01 (Oct. 15, 2002); Exemption to Prohibition on Circumvention of Copyright Protection Systems for Access Control Technologies, 65 Fed. Reg. 64,556, 64,574 (Oct. 27, 2000).

157. Of course, subject to deference to the Copyright Office, federal courts would have the right to review a determination of transformative use.

158. As I argue later, it is anticipated most copyright users and copyright owners will enter into arrangements much more nuanced than this default option. *See infra.* On a related note, therefore, most enforcement will fall in private hands with the option of litigation should the parties breach their contractual profit-sharing arrangements.

159. *See* Ronald H. Coase, *The Problem of Social Cost*, 3 J.L. & ECON. 1 (1960).

160. *Id.*

161. *Id.*

162. "[T]he goal of copyright, to promote science and the arts, is generally furthered by the creation of transformative works." Campbell v. Acuff-Rose Music, Inc., 510 U.S. 569, 579 (1994).

163. *See* THEODOR H. NELSON, LITERARY MACHINES (87.1 ed. 1987); *see also* Pamela Samuelson & Robert Glushko, *Intellectual Property Rights for Digital Library and Hypertext Publishing Systems*, 6 HARV. J.L. & TECH. 237, 247–55 (1993).

164. Samuelson & Glushko, *supra* note 163, at 249.

165. 17 U.S.C. §§ 101, 201(a).

166. Rebecca Tushnet, *Copy This Essay: How the Fair Use Doctrine Harms Free Speech and How Copying Serves It*, 114 YALE L.J. 535, 568–72 (2004); Lloyd L. Weinreb, *Fair's Fair: A Comment on the Fair Use Doctrine*, 103 HARV. L. REV. 1137, 1143 (1990).

167. Tushnet, *supra* note 166, at 568–72 (arguing pure copying can advance First Amendment interests in self-expression, persuasion, and affirmation). Many of her examples, however, are arguably transformative and not pure copying, such as cover versions of songs or plays and original juxtapositions of copyrighted works. *See id.*

168. *Id.* at 553.

169. *See* Robert P. Merges, *One Hundred Years of Solicitude: Intellectual Property Law, 1900–2000*, 88 CAL. L. REV. 2187, 2191 (2000).

170. *See* John Tehranian, *The High Court in Cyberspace: A Preview of* MGM Studios v. Grokster, UTAH B.J. 28 (Mar/Apr. 2005).

171. Testimony of Jack Valenti, President, Motion Picture Association of America, Inc., Hearing on Home Recording of Copyrighted Works, H.R. 4783, H.R. 4794, H.R. 4808, H.R. 5250, H.R. 5488 and H.R. 5705, House of Representatives Committee on the Judiciary, Subcommittee on Courts, Civil Liberties, and the Administration of Justice, April 12, 1982.

172. *Id.*

173. Campbell v. Acuff-Rose Music, Inc., 510 U.S. 569, 579 (1994).

174. Ty, Inc. v. Publ'ns Int'l, Ltd., 81 F. Supp. 2d 899 (N.D. Ill. 2000).

175. Matthew D. Bunker, *Eroding Fair Use: The "Transformative" Use Doctrine After* Campbell, 7 COMM. L. & POL'Y 1, 11 (2002).

176. 17 U.S.C. § 106(2) (2000).

177. As noted earlier in the book, Congress overturned the *Stowe* decision by statute in 1870, explicitly adding the right to translate one's work to the list of exclusive rights guaranteed to a copyright owner. *See* Copyright Act of 1870, ch. 230, § 86, 16 Stat. 198, 212 (1870) (current version at 17 U.S.C. ch. 1 (2000)). In the meantime, the protection afforded to abridgement and commentary has shrunk markedly over the past century, particularly in recent years. *See, e.g.*, Twin Peaks Prods., Inc. v. Publ'ns Int'l, Ltd., 996 F.2d 1366, 1370 (2d Cir. 1993) (finding defendants' book about the television program *Twin Peaks* infringed copyrights in teleplays for series); *cf.* Castle Rock Entm't v. Carol Publ'g Group, Inc., 955 F. Supp. 260, 268

(S.D.N.Y. 1997) (holding the *Seinfeld Aptitude Test*, a trivia book on all things Seinfeld, constituted an unauthorized derivative work that infringed Castle Rock's copyright in the *Seinfeld* television program).

178. 17 U.S.C. § 101 (emphasis added).

179. Oren Bracha, *The Ideology of Authorship Revisited* (2005) (unpublished manuscript, on file with author).

180. *Id.* As discussed earlier, such "inferior" works included translations and abridgements. *See supra* Part II.A.

181. Naomi Abe Voegtli, *Rethinking Derivative Rights*, 63 BROOK. L. REV. 1213, 1267 (1997).

182. *See, e.g.*, Laura G. Lape, *Transforming Fair Use: The Productive Use Factor in Fair Use Doctrine*, 58 ALB. L. REV. 677, 724 (1995) (arguing even the meager renewed emphasis on productive use hailed by the *Campbell* Court "stands in the way of sensible application of fair use and should be abandoned as a doctrinal dead-end").

183. For example, Laura Lape argues:

> Disadvantages of the productive use doctrine include: (1) courts are unclear as to what productive use is; (2) productive use doctrine focuses on productivity as an end in itself; (3) the productive use factor distracts attention from the central consideration of the first factor of section 107, the social utility of the use; (4) to the extent that productive use is equated with non-superseding use, productive use doctrine permits the fourth factor of section 107 to be counted twice, thus canceling out the impact of the first factor; and (5) productive use doctrine encourages courts to evaluate the quality of any work produced by the defendant.

Id. at 724.

184. Bleistein v. Donaldson Lithographing Co., 188 U.S. 239, 251 (1903).

185. Comedy III Prods. Inc. v. Gary Saderup, Inc., 21 P.3d 797, 809 (Cal. 2001). The court later added, "Although the distinction between protected and unprotected expression will sometimes be subtle, it is no more so than other distinctions triers of fact are called on to make in First Amendment jurisprudence." *Id.* at 811; *see, e.g.*, Miller v. California, 413 U.S. 15, 24, 93 (1973) (requiring determination, in the context of a work alleged to be obscene, of "whether the work, taken as a whole, lacks serious literary, artistic, political, or scientific value").

186. *See* Campbell v. Acuff-Rose Music, Inc., 510 U.S. 569, 579 (1994).

187. *Id.* (citation omitted).

188. Conversation with Jay Daugherty, Southern California Intellectual Property Scholars Forum, University of California at Irvine, Irvine, California, May 13, 2010.

189. This is, admittedly, one negative by-product of the proposal endorsed here. However, such a concern is less pressing in an American context than European context, where the copyright regime gives more recognition to the moral rights of authors. Given the utilitarian slant of American copyright law (in both theory and origin), such concerns become deflated when weighed against the vital First Amendment interests at stake and the proposal's ability to advance the creation and dissemination of creative works.

190. Samuelson & Glushko, *supra* note 163, at 257.

191. 17 U.S.C. § 115 (2000).

192. Register of Copyrights, Marybeth Peters, has recently advocated the repeal of the section 115 compulsory license, but that position appears to be a function of recent

technological developments in the online digital transmission of music and not a response to the general merits of the compulsory license in the pre-digital era or the arguments being made here. *See Music Licensing Reform: Hearing Before the Subcomm. on Courts, the Internet, and Intellectual Property of the H. Comm. on the Judiciary*, 109th Cong. 2 (2005) (statement of Marybeth Peters, Register of Copyrights).

193. 17 U.S.C. § 115(a).

194. *Id.* § 115(b).

195. *Id.* § 115(c).

196. *Id.* § 115(a)(2).

197. H.R. DOC. NO. 90-83, at 66 (1967), *quoted in* LAWRENCE LESSIG, FREE CULTURE 58 (2004).

198. *Copyright Term, Film Labeling, and Film Preservation Legislation: Hearings on H.R. 989, H.R. 1248, and H.R. 1734 Before the Subcomm. on Courts and Intellectual Property of the H. Comm. on the Judiciary*, 104th Cong. 55 (1995) (statement of Jack Valenti, President and CEO, Motion Picture Association of America) (quoted in Tyler Ochoa, *Origins and Meanings of the Public Domain*, 28 U. DAYTON L. REV. 215, 256 (2002)).

199. *See* http://www.jibjab.com/162.html (last visited November 8, 2005).

200. *See* Electronic Frontier Foundation, *Music Publisher Settles Copyright Skirmish over Guthrie Classic*, Aug. 24, 2004, *available at* http://www.eff.org/news/archives/2004_08.php.

201. For a discussion of recoding, see Justin Hughes, *"Recoding" Intellectual Property and Overlooking Audience Interests*, 77 TEX. L. REV. 923 (1999).

202. *Id.*

203. WILLIAM M. LANDES & RICHARD POSNER, THE ECONOMIC STRUCTURE OF INTELLECTUAL PROPERTY LAW 486–88 (2003)(noting the value consumers may derive from uniformity in cultural icons).

204. *Id.* at 958.

205. "That people need some stability in the meaning of cultural objects does not mean that laws are needed to ensure that stability. Many cultural objects retain stable meanings even when they are unprotected. Examples might be the Statue of Liberty, the *Mona Lisa*, Mount Rushmore, and the Eiffel Tower." *Id.* at 961.

206. Mark A. Lemley, *Ex Ante Versus Ex Post Justifications for Intellectual Property*, 71 U. CHI. L. REV. 129, 145 (2004).

207. Pierre N. Leval, *Copyright in the Twenty-First Century:* Campbell v. Acuff-Rose: *Justice Souter's Rescue of Fair Use*, 13 CARDOZO ARTS & ENT. L.J. 19, 22–23 (1994).

208. Comedy III Prods., Inc. v. Saderup, 21 P.3d 797, 808 (Cal. 2001).

CONCLUSION

1. JOHN FISKE, UNDERSTANDING POPULAR CULTURE 19 (1989).

2. PIERRE BOURDIEU & JEAN-CLAUDE PASSERON, REPRODUCTION IN EDUCATION, SOCIETY, AND CULTURE (Richard Nice trans., Sage Publishing 1977).

3. *Id.* at 56 (referring to a diploma as a "juridically sanctioned validation of the results of inculcation").

4. LAWRENCE LESSIG, FREE CULTURE: THE NATURE AND FUTURE OF CREATIVITY (2005).

5. By and large, works by foreign authors did not enjoy copyright protection in the United States from 1790 through 1891. *See* Seth M. Goldstein, *Hitchcock's "Rear Window" and International Copyright Law: An Examination of* Stewart v. Abend & *Its Effect on International Copyright Renewal and Exploitation*, 14 CARDOZO J. INT'L & COMP. L. 247, 258 (2006).

6. Niels B. Schaumann, *Copyright Protection in the Cable Television Industry: Satellite Retransmission and the Passive Carrier Exemption*, 51 FORDHAM L. REV. 637, 637–40 (1983). Without this exception, cable television would have had a much harder time gaining its foothold in the American living room. Imagine how cable would have fared without unauthorized retransmission of network signals: cable companies could have offered consumers a panoply of untested alternatives—a crazy 24/7 news channel, a wacky station that played only music videos all day long, a network devoted to B movies—but it would have come without regular network programming. And, of course, the cable stations would have been hard-pressed to obtain licenses for retransmission from the major networks as the networks had no interest in fueling their own demise by making the transition to cable all the more palatable. The networks wanted cable to come at a cost: you either received the networks or you received the cable stations. When cable provides cable stations plus crystal-clear feeds of network channels, the temptation of subscribing to cable becomes all the greater, if not irresistible.

7. SCOTT EYMAN, LION OF HOLLYWOOD: THE LIFE AND LEGEND OF LOUIS B. MAYER 53 (2005).

8. Peter Edidin, *La-La Land: The Origins*, N.Y. TIMES, Aug. 21, 2005 (noting "Los Angeles's distance from New York was also comforting to independent film producers, making it easier for them to avoid being harassed or sued by the Motion Picture Patents Company, aka the Trust, which Thomas Edison helped create in 1909").

9. In 1909, Edison and nine other patentees formed the Motion Picture Patents Company (MPPC) to pool their intellectual property rights and effectively control nearly all motion picture technology. The MPCC rigorously enforced its patent rights against independent movie producers, bringing infringement claims against any producer not using properly licensed equipment. Alexandra Gil, *Breaking the Studios: Antitrust and the Motion Picture Industry*, 3 N.Y.U. J. L. & LIBERTY 83, 91–92 (2008).

10. LESSIG, *supra* note 4, at 22–23 (2004) (noting "the catalog of Disney work drawing upon the work of others is astonishing when set together: Snow White (1937), Fantasia (1940), Pinocchio (1940), Dumbo (1941), Bambi (1942), Song of the South (1946), Cinderella (1950), Alice in Wonderland (1951), Robin Hood (1952), Peter Pan (1953), Lady and the Tramp (1955), Mulan (1998), Sleeping Beauty (1959), 101 Dalmatians (1961), The Sword in the Stone (1963), and The Jungle Book (1967)").

11. *See, e.g.*, Leslie Espinoza & Angela Harris, *Afterword: Embracing the Tar-Baby—Latcrit Theory and the Sticky Mess of Race*, 85 CAL. L. REV. 1585, 1598–99 (1997) (noting "[i]n the 1950's, many white artists became superstars either by re-recording black music for white audiences, like Pat Boone, or by drawing more indirectly on African-American musical traditions, like Elvis Presley. Indeed, the phenomenon called "rock 'n' roll," now associated primarily with white artists and white audiences, emerged from the African-American blues tradition").

12. Robert P. Latham, Jeremy T. Brown, & Carl C. Butzer, *Legal Implications of User Generated Content: YouTube, MySpace, Facebook*, *available at* http://images.jw.com/com/publications/892.pdf.

13. *See, e.g.*, Viacom Intl, Inc. v. YouTube, Inc., No. 06-02103 (S.D.N.Y.).

14. *See* Ed Henry, *Obama to Order Guantanamo Bay Prison Closed*, CNN.COM, Jan. 12, 2009, *available at* http://www.cnn.com/2009/POLITICS/01/12/obama.gitmo/.

15. *See Performers Angry Their Music Used in Guantanamo Interrogations*, REUTERS, Oct. 22, 2009, *available at* http://blogs.reuters.com/frontrow/2009/10/22/performers-angry-their-music-used-in-guantanamo-interrogations/.

16. Cahal Milmo, *Pop Stars Demand Details of Guantanamo Music "Torture,"* THE INDEPENDENT WORLD, Oct. 22, 2009, *available at* http://www.independent.co.uk/news/world/

americas/pop-stars-demand-details-of-guantanamo-music-torture-1807255.html ("Campaigners say there is evidence that music played repeatedly at ear-splitting levels was used to 'humiliate, terrify, punish, disorient and deprive detainees of sleep' as part of efforts to break detainees during interrogation. Former inmates at Guantanamo have previously testified that songs from AC/DC, Britney Spears, the Bee Gees and Sesame Street were played as part of a psychological onslaught.").

17. Martyn McLaughlin, *Rock Legends Want to Silence Guantanamo's Torture Tunes*, THE SCOTSMAN, Dec. 10, 2008, *available at* http://news.scotsman.com/topstories/Rock-legends-want—to.4782083.jp.

18. *Panama No Place to Run*, TIME MAGAZINE, Jan. 8, 1990.

19. Roberto Suro, *After Noriega: Vatican Is Blaming U.S. for Impasse on Noriega's Fate*, N.Y. TIMES, Dec. 30, 1989.

20. *Tripped Up By Lies*, TIME MAGAZINE, Oct. 11, 1993.

21. *Nick Davies, Lost in America*, THE GUARDIAN, Jan. 14, 1994.

22. Clive Stafford Smith, *Welcome to "the Disco,"* THE GUARDIAN, June 19, 2008, *available at* http://www.guardian.co.uk/world/2008/jun/19/usa.guantanamo.

23. Quoted in Lane DeGregory, *Iraq 'n' Roll*, ST. PETERSBURG TIMES, Nov. 21, 2004, *available at* http://www.stpetersburgtimes.com/2004/11/21/Floridian/Iraq__n__roll.shtml.

24. Trent Reznor, *Regarding NIN Music Used at Guantanamo Bay for Torture*, NIN.COM, Dec. 11, 2008, http://forum.nin.com/bb/read.php?9,302470.

25. *Id.*

26. *Trent Reznor Speaks Out Against RIAA*, Sept. 17, 2007, http://virtualvote.net/content/trent_reznor_speaks_out_against_riaa.

27. *See* Stafford Smith, *supra* note 22.

28. Phanesh Koneru, *The Right "To Authorize" in U.S. Copyright Law: Questions of Contributory Infringement and Extraterritoriality*, 37 IDEA 87, 89 (1996) ("The Copyright Act is presumed to have no extraterritorial application, which means that infringement occurring outside the United States is not actionable under the Act.").

29. *Boumediene v. Bush*, 553 U.S. 723, 128 S. Ct. 2229, 2236 (2008) ("the Government's view is that the Constitution has no effect there, at least as to noncitizens, because the United States disclaimed formal sovereignty in its 1903 lease with Cuba").

30. *Id.* at 2236–37.

31. *See* Borge Varmer, *Copyright in Territories and Possessions of the United States*, Copyright Office Study No. 34 (noting how the U.S. Virgin Island and Puerto Rico, among other territories, have such enabling acts).

32. Title 3, Chapter 18, § 391 of the Panama Canal Code (approved June 19, 1934).

33. As Nimmer writes: "[I]f, and to the extent, a part of an 'act' of infringement occurs within the United States, then, although such act is completed in a foreign jurisdiction, those parties who contributed to the act within the United States may be rendered liable under American copyright law." 4-17 MELVILLE NIMMER & DAVID NIMMER, NIMMER ON COPYRIGHT § 17.02 (2008) (citing Subafilms, Ltd. v. MGM-Pathe Commc'ns. Co., 24 F.3d 1088, 1094 n.9 (9th Cir. 1994) (en banc); P&D Int'l v. Halsey Pub. Co., 672 F. Supp. 1429 (S.D. Fla. 1987); Palmer v. Braun, 376 F.3d 1254, 1258 (11th Cir. 2004) (per curiam); De Bardossy v. Puski, 763 F. Supp. 1239, 1243 & n.7 (S.D.N.Y. 1991); Ahbez v. Edwin H. Morris & Co., 548 F. Supp. 664 (S.D.N.Y. 1982); G. Ricordi & Co. v. Columbia Graphophone Co., 270 F. 822 (S.D.N.Y. 1920); Famous Music Corp. v. Seeco Records, Inc., 201 F. Supp. 560 (S.D.N.Y. 1961); ABKCO Music, Inc. v. Harrisongs

Music, Ltd., 508 F. Supp. 798 (S.D.N.Y. 1981), *aff'd in part, modified in part*, 722 F.2d 988 (2d Cir. 1983), *later opinion*, 944 F.2d 971 (2d Cir. 1991)).

34. Cuban Copyright Act Dec. 14, 28, 1977 (as amended in 1994), *available at* http://web.archive.org/web/20060406140949/http://www.cerlalc.org/dar/leyes_reglamentos/cuba.htm.

35. *See, e.g.*, Hamdi v. Rumsfeld, 542 U.S. 507 (2004) (holding, inter alia, that detainees who are American citizens are entitled to challenge their detention before an impartial federal judge).

36. U.S. CONST. amend. XI.

37. Hans v. Louisiana, 134 U.S. 1 (1890).

38. Alden v. Maine, 527 U.S. 706 (1999).

39. 28 U.S.C. § 1338(a).

40. 17 U.S.C. § 501.

41. Atascadero State Hospital v. Scanlon, 473 U.S. 234 (1985); Seminole Tribe of Florida v. Florida, 517 U.S. 44, 55 (1996).

42. 17 U.S.C. § 511(a); Copyright Remedy Clarification Act, 104 Stat. 2749, 2750 (1990) (dictating "[a]ny State, any instrumentality of a State, and any officer or employee of a State or instrumentality of a State . . . shall not be immune, under the Eleventh Amendment . . . from suit in Federal Court . . . for a violation of any of the exclusive rights of a copyright owner").

43. 15 U.S.C. § 1122 (added 1992), Trademark Remedy Clarification Act, 106 Stat. 3567, 3568 (1992).

44. 15 U.S.C. § 1114(1) (added 1992).

45. Fitzpatrick v. Bitzer, 427 U.S. 445, 456 (1976); Florida Prepaid v. College Savings Bank, 527 U.S. 627, 637 (1999).

46. City of Boerne v. Flores, 521 U.S. 507 (1997).

47. *Florida Prepaid*, 527 U.S. at 639 ("We thus held that for Congress to invoke § 5, it must identify conduct transgressing the Fourteenth Amendment's substantive provisions, and must tailor its legislative scheme to remedying or preventing such conduct.")

48. College Savings Bank v. Florida Prepaid Postsecondary Education Expense Board, 527 U.S. 666 (1999) (striking down the TRCA as unconstitutional); Florida Prepaid v. College Savings Bank, 527 U.S. 627, 637 (1999) (striking down the PPRCA as unconstitutional).

49. *See., e.g.*, Chavez v. Arte Publico Press, 204 F.3d 601, 608 (5th Cir. 2000); Romero v. Cal. DOT, 2009 U.S. Dist. LEXIS 23193 (C.D. Cal. Mar. 12, 2009); Mktg. Information Masters, Inc. v. Bd. of Trustees of the Cal. State Univ. Sys., 552 F. Supp. 2d 1088, 1094 (S.D. Cal. 2008).

50. Review of *Love*, ENTM'T WEEKLY, Nov. 17, 2006, *available at* http://www.ew.com/ew/article/0,1560886,00.html.

51. *Id.*

52. Cory Doctorow, *EW Picks Grey Album for Best of 2004*, BOINGBOING.NET, Dec. 28, 2004, http://boingboing.net/2004/12/28/ew-picks-grey-album-.html.

53. As scholar Jonathan Zittrain observed, "As a matter of pure legal doctrine, the Grey Tuesday protest is breaking the law, end of story. But copyright law was written with a particular form of industry in mind. The flourishing of information technology gives amateurs and homerecording artists powerful tools to build and share interesting, transformative, and socially valuable art drawn from pieces of popular cultures. There's no place to plug such an important cultural sea change into the current legal regime." Quoted in MATTHEW RIMMER, DIGITAL COPYRIGHT AND CONSUMER REVOLUTION 134 (2007).

54. *See* 17 U.S.C. § 506 (providing for criminal penalties for certain forms of willful copyright infringement).

55. *See* Noah Shachtman, *Copyright Enters a Gray Area*, WIRED, Feb. 14, 2004, *available at* http://www.wired.com/entertainment/music/news/2004/02/62276.

56. Max Weber, *Class, Status, and Party, in* ESSAYS IN ECONOMIC SOCIOLOGY 93 (Richard Swedberg, ed. 1999).

57. LAWRENCE LEVINE, HIGHBROW/LOWBROW: THE EMERGENCE OF CULTURAL HIERARCHY IN AMERICA 230 (1988).

58. Works created after January 1, 1978, enjoy copyright protection for the lifetime of the last surviving author plus seventy years. 17 U.S.C. § 302(a) & (b). Of course, musical compositions by The Beatles were written before January 1, 1978. As a result, they are protected under American law for ninety-five years from their date of creation. 17 U.S.C. § 304(a).

59. *See, e.g.*, Grand Upright Music, Ltd. v. Warner Bros. Records, Inc., 780 F. Supp. 182, 183 (S.D.N.Y. 1991) ("Thou shalt not steal"); Bridgeport Music, Inc. v. Dimension Films, 383 F.3d 390, 398 (6th Cir. 2004) ("Get a license or do not sample").

60. 17 U.S.C. § 504(c)(2) ("In a case where the copyright owner sustains the burden of proving, and the court finds, that infringement was committed willfully, the court in its discretion may increase the award of statutory damages to a sum of not more than $150,000.").

61. 17 U.S.C. § 505 (providing a court may "award a reasonable attorney's fee to the prevailing party" in an infringement suit).

62. $150,000 per act of infringement multiplied by 130 acts of infringement. *See* 17 U.S.C. § 504.

63. Of course, this is only true so long as these works remain under copyright protection.

64. 17 U.S.C. § 408.

65. 17 U.S.C. § 504(c).

66. 17 U.S.C. § 505.

67. 17 U.S.C. § 506.

68. Actors, directors, and writers. One could also add producers to this list.

69. The Writer's Guild Registry does not "bestow any statutory protections." *See* WGA West Registry, Registration Details *available at* http://www.wgawregistry.org/webrss/regdetails.html.

70. Business Trends Analysts, Inc. v. Freedonia Group, Inc., 887 F.2d 399, 406 (2nd Cir. 1989) (citing 3 NIMMER & NIMMER, *supra* note 33, § 14.02[A] at 14-14).

71. Bleistein v. Donaldson Lithographing Co., 188 U.S. 239 (1903).

72. As Holmes argued, "That these pictures had their worth and their success is sufficiently shown by the desire to reproduce them without regard to the plaintiffs' rights." *Id.*

73. *Id.* at 251.

74. Robert A. Gorman, *Copyright Courts and Aesthetic Judgments: Abuse or Necessity?*, 25 COLUM. J.L. & ARTS 1 (2001).

75. Gracen v. Bradford Exch., 698 F.2d 300, 304 (7th Cir. 1983).

76. Alfred C. Yen, *Copyright Opinions and Aesthetic Theory*, 71 S. CAL. L. REV. 247, 266–97 (1998).

77. U.S. CONST., art. I, § 8, cl. 8.

78. Gorman, *supra* note 74.

79. Joseph P. Liu, *Copyright Law's Theory of the Consumer*, 44 B.C. L. REV. 397, 415–20 (2003) ("Whether 'productive' or 'transformative' use guides the first fair use factor, either inquiry threatens to trap courts and litigants into making the kinds of aesthetic judgments that the copyright system expressly disclaims.").

80. *Id.*

81. Yen, *supra* note 76, at 248–49.

82. Suntrust Bank v. Houghton Mifflin Co., 136 F. Supp. 2d 1357 (N.D. Ga. 2001).

83. *Id.* at 1363.

84. *Id.* at 1378.

85. *Id.* at 1374. The court found commercial use: " *The Wind Done Gone* is unquestionably a fictional work that has an overarching economic purpose . . . . [T]he commercial purpose of *The Wind Done Gone* weighs strongly in favor of the plaintiff on the first factor."

86. *Id.* at 1382.

87. *Id.*

88. WILLIAM SHATNER & DAVID FISHER, UP TILL NOW 287 (2008) ("Well. Kirk may have been dead in the movies, but there was no reason he had to be dead in the publishing industry. I sold my treatment to Simon & Schuster and *Star Trek: The Return* became a best-selling novel.").

89. ROSS SHEPARD KRAEMER, WILLIAM CASSIDY, & SUSAN L. SCHWARTZ, RELIGIONS OF STAR TREK 161 (2003).

90. Suntrust Bank v. Houghton Mifflin Co., 268 F.3d 1257, 1283 (11th Cir. 2001) (citing Fisher v. Dees, 794 F.2d 432, 438 (9th Cir. 1986)).

91. *Id.* (citing Leibovitz v. Paramount Pictures Corp., 137 F.3d 109, 115 n.3 (S.D.N.Y. 1998)).

92. 268 F. 3d at 1282.

93. *Id.*

94. *Id.* at 1259.

95. Concluded the concurrence: "The law grants copyright holders a powerful monopoly in their expressive works. It should not also afford them windfall damages for the publication of the sorts of works that they themselves would never publish, or worse, grant them a power of indirect censorship." *Id.* at 1283.

96. The Eleventh Circuit's decision is also significant in another light. What the district court saw as property—an interest in the preservation and consecration of something over which Mitchell Estate was said to possess dominion—the appeal court saw as speech. This is an aesthetic judgment as to the nature of a copyrighted work: whether it is simply a piece of private property, outside of the scope of the First Amendment, or whether it constitutes a form of speech, subject to First Amendment protection.

97. Salinger v. Colting, 641 F. Supp. 2d 250 (S.D.N.Y. 2009).

98. Salinger v. Colting, 607 F.3d 68 (2d. Cir. 2010).

99. *Salinger*, 641 F. Supp. 2d at 268.

100. Quoted in *Suntrust Bank*, 136 F.Supp.2d at 1369.

101. *See* Andrew Albanese, *Temporary Restraining Order Issued in Salinger Case*, PUBLISHER'S WEEKLY (June 17, 2009) (announcing the "ruling is the first time that the Second Circuit has explicitly ruled that a single character from a single literary work is copyrightable"). Although Holden Caulfield appeared in only one book, his character did appear in two published short stories. *See* J.D. Salinger, *I'm Crazy*, COLLIERS MAGAZINE (Dec. 22, 1945); J.D. Salinger, *Slight Rebellion Off Madison*, THE NEW YORKER (Dec. 21, 1946). His family appeared

in at least one other. *See* J.D. Salinger, *Last Lady of the Last Furlough*, SATURDAY EVENING Post (July 15, 1944).

102. *Salinger*, 641 F. Supp. at 268.

103. Borrowing terminology from John Fiske, Sonia Katyal refers to "semiotic disobedience" as the act of "alter[ing] existing intellectual property by interrupting, appropriating, and then replacing the passage of information from creator to consumer." But, by making certain symbols immune from remix or alteration, "propertization offers a subsidy to particular types of expression over others." Sonia K. Katyal, *Semiotic Disobedience*, 84 WASH. U. L. REV. 489, 493–96 (2007).

Table of Cases

Index

Note: Page numbers followed by "*f*" denote figures.